"By far the most complete book to date, and undoubtedly the most balanced and best researched, drawing on numerous interviews . . . A gripping account."

— *The Philadelphia Inquirer*

"A captivating reconstruction of Plath's childhood, marriage and career. *Rough Magic* is strongest in filling in the details of a life and death many of us are familiar with. It also poignantly explores the contrast between Plath's numerous if piecemeal publications and the wholehearted embrace of Hughes' work."

— *Detroit Free Press*

"A full-bodied biography . . . the best so far."

— *Kirkus Reviews*

"Alexander's opening chapter, recreating the high-risk ferment of the writer, is galvanizing; his book's concluding paragraph is bold and damning. He gives evidence of a vitality in Plath that was as intense as any death wish, and makes her passing and her poetry exceedingly poignant."

— *Newsday*

"In many ways an exciting and satisfying book."

— *Mademoiselle*

"This book deserves many readers—and should cause many of those readers to seek out Plath's

"This well-written account con figures in Plath's life and giv elsewhere."

— *San Francisco Chronicle*

PENGUIN BOOKS

ROUGH MAGIC

Paul Alexander is the editor of *Ariel Ascending*, a collection of essays about the life and work of Sylvia Plath. A former reporter for the Houston bureau of *Time* magazine, he has published articles in *M inc.* and *The New York Times Magazine*. He has taught at the University of Houston and at Hofstra University. He lives in New York City.

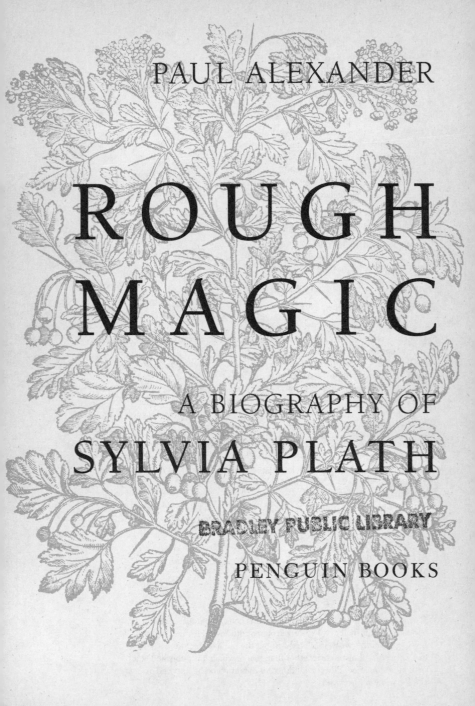

PAUL ALEXANDER

ROUGH MAGIC

A BIOGRAPHY OF

SYLVIA PLATH

PENGUIN BOOKS

PENGUIN BOOKS
Published by the Penguin Group
Viking Penguin, a division of Penguin Books USA Inc.,
375 Hudson Street, New York, New York 10014, U.S.A.
Penguin Books Ltd, 27 Wrights Lane,
London W8 5TZ, England
Penguin Books Australia Ltd, Ringwood,
Victoria, Australia
Penguin Books Canada Ltd, 10 Alcorn Avenue, Suite 300,
Toronto, Ontario, Canada M4V 3B2
Penguin Books (N.Z.) Ltd, 182–190 Wairau Road,
Auckland 10, New Zealand

Penguin Books Ltd, Registered Offices:
Harmondsworth, Middlesex, England

First published in the United States of America by
Viking Penguin, a division of Penguin Books USA Inc., 1991
Published in Penguin Books 1992

10 9 8 7 6 5 4 3 2 1

Grateful acknowledgment is made to the following for permission to
reprint copyrighted material:
    Robin Morgan for an excerpt from "Arraignment." Copyright © 1972
by Robin Morgan. Reprinted with permission.
    Clarissa Roche for excerpts from her essay appearing in *Sylvia Plath:
The Woman and the Work* edited by Edward Butscher, Dufour Editions.
    Ruth Barnhouse, Edward Cohen, Wilbury Crockett, and Janet Wagner
Rafferty for their respective letters or portions therefrom.

THE LIBRARY OF CONGRESS HAS CATALOGUED THE HARDCOVER AS FOLLOWS:
Alexander, Paul, 1955–
Rough magic : a biography of Sylvia Plath / Paul Alexander.
p. cm.
ISBN 0-670-81812-7 (hc.)
ISBN 0 14 01.0281 7 (pbk.)
1. Plath, Sylvia — Biography.   2. Poets, American — 20th century —
Biography.   I. Title.
PS3566.L27Z5637   1991
811'.54 — dc20   91–50155

Printed in the United States of America
Set in New Caledonia
Designed by Francesca Belanger

For Garnette, Lauren, Annie;
for Lucretia, Dallas, Lisa;
for my sister and my mother;
and for Amanda Vaill

But this rough magic
I here abjure, and, when I have requir'd
Some heavenly music, which even now I do,
To work mine end upon their senses that
This airy charm is for, I'll break my staff,
Bury it certain fathoms in the earth,
And deeper than did ever plummet sound
I'll drown my book.

—WILLIAM SHAKESPEARE,
The Tempest, Act V, Scene i

Author's Note

I am deeply grateful to Frances Kiernan who read a copy of this book in manuscript form. Her insights and suggestions were invaluable. I would also like to thank Martin Garbus and Maura Wogan, at Frankfurt, Garbus, Klein, and Selz; James Stein, my agent at the William Morris Agency; Carlynne Abrams; Margaret Tufts; Dona Munker; Glen Hartley and Lynn Chu; Victoria Black-Lewis; and Alexander F. Schilt, who, years ago, at the University of Houston, saw to it that I got a research grant that allowed me to do my first biographical work on Plath. For their friendship and hospitality, I would like to thank Tom and Elizabeth McBride.

I am happy to be a member of the Biography Seminar at New York University, where a session was devoted to my work on Plath as I was writing this book. At Viking Penguin, I would like to thank Christine Pevitt, Kathryn Court, Paul Slovak, Lydia Weaver, Kate Griggs, Scott Edward Anderson, Natasha Reichle, Francesca Belanger, Terry Zaroff, and Michael Kaye. Finally, I want to acknowledge my profound debt to Amanda Vaill, my editor, who, with intelligence, wit, and understanding, supported me through a book that was not easy to write. Without her, this book would not exist.

—P. A.

Contents

ROUGH MAGIC

Preface

I first read the poetry of Sylvia Plath in 1974, when I was a sophomore in college. At once, I was struck by each poem's arresting emotion, by the sheer power of its language. Over and over that semester, I read the poems I admired most—"Morning Song," "Blackberrying," "Elm," "Edge"—and was taken into a world so vividly realized that I was moved to anger, sympathy, awe. My connection with Plath did not result from any psychological identification. I was not then, nor have I ever been, suicidal. I am not a woman. My father did not die when I was eight years old. I simply fell in love with the beauty of the language of her poems. It was my admiration for Plath's work that, years later, made me want to edit *Ariel Ascending*, an anthology of essays about her life and writings that appeared in 1985. And it was during my research for that book that I became taken with the idea of doing Plath's biography.

Before I began the writing of this book, I read in full the two major Plath archives, those housed at Smith College and those at Indiana University—and gathered information from many other university and community libraries that maintain smaller Plath holdings. I conducted some three hundred individual interviews with people who knew Plath, a number of whom had never before spoken openly about her. Though I have quoted from these interviews, I have been sparing in my use of Plath's own words—the words that made me want to write her biography. The reason is both complex and simple.

Because Plath died without leaving a will, Ted Hughes, the husband from whom she was estranged at the time of her death in 1963, inherited the copyright to her entire literary canon, both published and unpublished work. In time, he appointed his sister, Olwyn Hughes, as the agent for Plath's estate. To many friends of Plath, this decision seemed odd. Comments made by Olwyn such as those quoted in a London newspaper article— "You liked her," she had written to Clarissa Roche, "I think she was pretty straight poison. God preserve me from mixed-up kids"—suggest that through the years, on the subject of Plath, Olwyn Hughes has had an ax to grind. At the very least, one can surmise that Ted and Olwyn Hughes, the parties who control Plath's copyright, are anything but disinterested bystanders.

Historically, when an author has submitted a manuscript to the Plath estate for permission to quote, the Hugheses have asked the author for changes in substance as well as quotation in exchange for that permission. I decided early on that I would not subject myself to the constraints of the estate, and so I did not quote from unpublished sources, although much information in my biography is gleaned from such sources. I also determined that I would not quote so extensively from published material that I would have to seek permission from the estate.

I was, however, careful not to exclude Ted Hughes's participation in this book. In September 1988, on one of my three research trips to England, I wrote to Hughes, whom I had met on previous occasions in Boston and New York City, to request a formal interview. "I would like to ask if you would agree to meet with me," I wrote, pointing out that I would soon be in North Tawton where he still lives in Court Green, the house he and Plath bought in the early nineteen-sixties. "The conversation could either be on or off the record—your decision—but I would like at least to see you while I am in England, if for no other reason than to discuss with you the image of Plath I am now forming." My answer came a few days later. "I don't suppose you will be surprised to hear that I have no interest, I'm afraid, in anything to do with biographical or critical writings about SP, beyond making some effort to protect myself from the legal consequences," Hughes wrote. "And I hope it doesn't sound too strange if I say that my home is the one place that I can keep reasonably clear of the agitations and foolishness of the public Plath debates, and that I wish to keep it so. . . . Otherwise, I wish your research well."

I answered Hughes in early October. "I can't say that I'm altogether shocked by your statement that you have no interest in anything to do with biographical writings about Sylvia Plath," I said. (In fact, in the nearly thirty years following her death, he has *never* given an interview on her.) "However, I was hoping that you might be willing to talk with me on some level so that I would be able to detail more accurately situations in which you were involved—to set the record straight, I suppose you could say." In my letter I included a temporary address in London at which he could reach me, should he change his mind. I never heard from him again.

The Blue Hour

The landscape surrounding the country house in Devon lay dead, silent—typical for this hour of the early morning. To the side of the house, the dark yard gave way to a shadowy block of bare ground, the location of the summer flower and vegetable gardens, while past the gardens skeletal shapes of trees, blacker still, rose up to break the sky's fragile horizon. The main source of light, except for a scattering of stars, was a low moon that illuminated a clump of cherry trees growing on a knoll beside the house. In this darkness, all lines of demarcation faded; the whole scene appeared blurred, out of focus. Similarly, the morning's stillness filled the interior of the house. In one upstairs bedroom, two small children, a girl not yet three and an infant boy ten months old, slept peacefully in their beds. Down the hall, in a room converted into a study, a young woman, the house's only other inhabitant, hunched at her desk. Her frame was thin—for several months, she had been steadily losing weight—and her face was chalky and pale. Her long brown fall of hair hung down tangled and unkempt. Absorbed in her task, she perched on the edge of her chair as she studied the marked-up papers strewn on the desktop before her. Occasionally, she would glance out the window to catch sight of the predawn landscape—the stark moon or the bare trees or the hazy figures of tombstones rising up from the cemetery that lay between the country house and the twelfth-century stone church next door. She did not indulge this impulse often, however, for she had to proceed with her work—the reason, after all, she had awakened at four o'clock in the morning.

Not that this was anything new. She had been rising at the same hour for several weeks' running, because once her children rose, around eight, she had to stop writing and devote her full attention both to their care and to myriad household duties. What was more, these days, she felt an even greater responsibility towards her children, now that she and her husband were separated. Her infant son had been—and remained—oblivious to recent upsetting developments, but her baby girl, who sensed the tension around her, had become chronically fretful. Meanwhile, the young woman, who would be known one day to wide audiences although at the moment she was considered merely a promising young poet, fought off a fear of abandonment, which she had first encountered in the wake of the untimely death of her father when she was eight years old, and struggled to cope as best she could. She did this, at least in part, at least to her own thinking, through the very act of writing.

Today, Tuesday, October 16, 1962, Sylvia Plath worked on a poem that, by the end of her writing session, she would title "Medusa." She labored on the poem in the same manner she had on any recent piece. With a keenly focused tunnel vision, she pored—urgently, exhaustingly—over each line, each word. The poem was evolving surprisingly slowly, through no fault of its own, but because, for the better part of a week now, Plath had suffered from a cold, a sinus infection, and a low-grade fever that alternated with chills. Most people in her physical condition would have shunned work for sleep. Not Plath. Left alone to face the demands of maintaining a country house and its grounds, of supervising the hired help (she employed, part-time, a nanny and a cleaning woman), and of caring for her children, Plath had found that the hours between four and eight in the morning were her only quiet time. So, even though she was sick, she forced herself to get out of bed to write. And in the weeks she had followed this schedule, she had experienced breathtaking results—almost a poem a day, some of them the best she had ever produced.

Her method was simple. Each morning, she settled into a chair at her desk in her study and there, on the back of a rough draft of *The*

Bell Jar—her novel, soon to be published under a pseudonym in England—or on unused Smith College stationery shipped to her from America by a friend, she sketched out, first in longhand and then on a manual typewriter, draft upon draft of a poem, until she brought it into a state she considered final. In the four hours of writing she managed each morning, she took a poem through numerous rewrites, occasionally as many as ten. But when a poem was done, it was done; she rarely went back to a poem a second day. Working in this fashion, Plath had completed—just over the last seventeen days—eleven poems, among them "Daddy," "A Birthday Present," "The Applicant," and a series of five poems about beekeeping that she had grouped under the title "Bees."

While she drafted "Medusa," Plath began to think about these recent poems. She was convinced that she had now forged the ultimate break-through, evidence of her ability to write on an entirely new level. "I am a genius of a writer; I have it in me," she told her mother in a letter later that day. "I am writing the best poems of my life; they will make my name." Despite this tone of self-assurance, Plath could never have imagined the extent to which her prediction would fulfill itself. She simply could not have foreseen the days when, in the shadow of her death, her first posthumous poetry collection would be read in massive numbers by a devoted audience who would cast her in the role of feminist martyr; when *The Bell Jar,* upon being released in America under Plath's own name, would become *the* commercial sen-sation of 1971, occupying *The New York Times'* best-seller list for six solid months; or when the publication of her subsequent posthumous volumes of poetry and prose would be heralded as major literary events. In October 1962, though she sensed that her latest poems were ex-ceptional, she knew only that she could not avoid writing them. No matter what, Plath had to rise each morning and brave the "still, blue, almost eternal hour"—the phrase she used to describe that singular blend of darkness and silence that emerges as dawn approaches in Devon.

After she finished "Medusa," Plath realized how little its strategy re-sembled that of her other October poems. Unlike "Bees," in which apparent autobiography is really calculated melodrama, or "Daddy" and "The Applicant," in which apparent autobiography is really black farce, "Medusa" relies for success on its artful construction: an imagined narrator, placed in the throes of an invented situation, responds in direct and emotional language. The repulsive monster Medusa, the feared Gorgon whose stare can turn a mortal into stone, attacks the poem's unnamed "I"—this is the invented situation. The narrator, under siege, is horrified, but all the "I" can do is recoil from the monster's advances. Ironically, these actions are unlike those of the original Greek myth's hero, a superhuman who slays Medusa by hacking off her head with a sword. To Plath, such acts of valor are impossible. Indeed, in Plath's re-creation of the myth, the central figure ultimately plays the part of victim.

At no stage in her career did Plath engage in writing strict autobiography. Yet the strained voice of "Medusa"'s narrator echoed the pain Plath felt as she wrote the poem. Physically ill and emotionally wrung-out, she had reached her metaphorical edge. Most probably, her current crisis had begun in London two and a half years earlier, on April 1, 1960, when she gave birth to her first child, a daughter. Under the limited medical supervision of a midwife, Plath delivered her baby at home without the help of anesthesia or painkilling medication. In the months following the birth, Plath flung herself into the prepublication frenzy surrounding the appearance in England of her first book, *The Colossus and Other Poems*. But her enthusiasm soured noticeably when, in October 1960, at the time of the book's release, and in the months to follow, the British press ignored *The Colossus*. All told, only a few reviews appeared, the collective tone of which was decidedly cool. "One might criticise the rather baffling obliqueness of some of Miss Plath's work," Thomas Blackburn commented in December in *The New Statesman*, voicing a pervasive skeptical attitude among reviewers towards the book, "[along with the discovery] that her imagery tends to get out of hand, so that the poem becomes not a single experience but a series of intriguing 'literary gems.'" Plath had given a good portion of her adult life to the writing of this book. That the end product would go all but unnoticed became devastating to her. "Since I got no prize or any American publisher, [William

Heinemann hasn't] bothered to advertise [*The Colossus*], so I probably won't make a penny on it," she wrote in a letter near the end of 1960, adding, with a deadpan candor that doesn't quite disguise her grave disappointment, "Well, it's a nice gift book."

If the year 1960 was hard on Plath, the next eighteen months were worse. After she endured a miscarriage and an appendectomy—in February and March 1961, respectively—she devoted much of the rest of the year to finishing *The Bell Jar*. Also, in the fall she moved, with her husband and daughter, from London to a spacious but dilapidated manor house hours by train south of the city, in Devon's North Tawton, where, only days into the new year, on January 17, 1962, she gave birth to her second child, a son. (In the space of thirty months, Plath had sustained three separate pregnancies, two to full term.) The most damaging blow to her psyche came in July 1962, on the afternoon when she accidentally discovered that her husband of six years, the man whom she had revered as the center of her universe, her "Adam," was having an affair. Betrayed and insulted, Plath forced him, through her open displays of anger, to live away from their house for much of August. In early September, the couple went on a vacation to Ireland without the children. This last-ditch effort to save the marriage did not work. Following four days of a proposed week-long holiday, Plath was deserted—her word—by her husband, who returned to London—and his mistress. By October, Plath's marriage had all but ended. Her husband collected his belongings, Plath began searching for a suitable flat in London into which she and the children could move, and the couple agreed to pursue a legal separation. So, as she worked on "Medusa" that morning in October 1962, Plath easily identified with the role of victim. In her mind, justified or not, she felt she had come to embody the very meaning of the word.

Later in the day, "Medusa" completed and the children awake, Plath went about her regular schedule. She fed and tended the children, performed minor outdoor chores, and trudged through a list of household duties. At some point in the afternoon, she became extremely uneasy. To calm her nerves, she wrote the letter to her mother, who still lived in Wellesley, Massachusetts, the quaint, stylish Boston suburb where Plath spent most of her girlhood. Though almost all of the nearly one thousand letters she had written her mother over the past decade projected optimism and joy, Plath could feign neither emotion this afternoon. She simply could no longer hold back her despair, which she normally vented more privately, in her journal. "I can go nowhere with the children"—her mother had suggested she travel to Wellesley—"and I am ill, and it would be psychologically the worst thing to see you now or to go home," she wrote, soon becoming more self-indulgent. Craving the company of family, she longed for someone to assist her while she endured the "daily assault of practical nastiness," to stand by her if the ordeal of a divorce weighed her down. She dreamed of the security of home, she said, but could not imagine giving up her safe harbor—England. So she made a request. Could either Dorothy, an aunt, or Margaret, the new sister-in-law whom she had never even met, spare her six weeks and come to England? Desperate, Plath offered to pay for room, board, and travel expenses for either one of them—money she did not have but would find. Plath's cry for help, so totally out of character for her, would alert her mother to the acute mental distress of which it was a symptom. Yet Plath remained unaware of, or perhaps unconcerned about, the serious worry her letter might provoke. As soon as she had finished it, she mailed it.

That night, Plath prepared supper, bathed the children, put them to bed. Finally, she became consumed by an intense feeling of lone-liness. To counteract this, she wrote her mother a second letter. In it, Plath begged for Margaret to come right away, then continued, "Do I sound mad? Taking or wanting to take Warren's wife?" If she did sound mad, she had cause. She felt sick and exhausted, she admitted, sometimes even a "bit delirious." But all would be well by spring, she speculated, when the weather would be better, she and the children would be healthier, and friends and relatives would arrive for visits. If only she had someone to help her through her present dilemma. If only she had Margaret for six weeks . . . Plath closed the letter by offering love to them all, her family.

(The day Plath's mother received these letters, she wired a friend in Devon with instructions to hire her daughter a full-time housekeeper immediately—a stopgap solution, Plath's mother hoped, to Sylvia's problems. "Salary paid here," the telegram said.)

With the second letter ready to be mailed, Plath went to bed. At four the next morning, she awoke and, although still sick, drafted another poem, "The Jailer." A tense psychological monologue spoken by a prisoner about her captor, the poem chills with its biting honesty and unrelenting hopelessness.

Not quite four months later, on February 11, 1963, Sylvia Plath— plagued by flu, a sinus infection, and a depression caused in large part by the events of the summer and fall of 1962 and also by a new romance that ended before it really began—succeeded at an act she had attempted on at least one prior occasion: she killed herself. In the years following her death, the poems she had written each morning at the blue hour in October 1962 *would* make her name. They would earn for her in death the recognition, fame, and honor she had wanted so badly while she was alive.

Otto and Aurelia

1

On the last day of the spring semester that year—1930—a handsome German professor stood before his class of a dozen students, his figure rugged against the blackboard behind him. The semester had been a good one—not a surprise, since the professor, who taught both German and biology, had become a virtual legend on campus. Yearbook citations bore witness. From 1926: "We interviewed him. 'What is your greatest interest?' He smiled. 'Bees,' he answered. 'Yes,' we persisted, 'but what is your—your ambition?' He smiled. 'Bees,' he said. 'We mean,' we patiently explained, 'what is your passion—that of which you dream?' He smiled—opened his mouth. . . . But we fled, remembering Hamlet pointing to his head, and saying to Polonius, 'B-z-z.' " From 1927: "Once there was a sturdy youngster with round eyes who sat in a school room on warm June days with a German reader propped up before him and gazed beyond it straight out the window at a bee sailing round the clover tops. His schoolmates called him *Bienen-König*. Even today the Herr professor breaks into a German declension with talk of locusts and wild honey." Yet this folklore paled, compared with the "rat" episode, which year after year he perpetrated on his students. To demonstrate man's illogic, the professor would skin a dead rat, slice meat from its bones, sauté the meat in a pan, and, as his students gazed on in horror, proceed to eat the fried meat piece by piece. "Rat meat might be thought of as disgusting and inedible," he would declare, munching heartily, "but it is really no different from rabbit meat, which people have eaten as a delicacy for centuries."

Today, while he lectured, he occasionally glanced at a young woman who had attracted his attention all year. Though he had been careful to keep his dealings with her strictly professional, he believed he had somehow come to know her well. She was enamored of the romantic, yet bound to the real world by an overpowering sense of the practical. She held herself with dignity—her face, round and bold as a full moon, personified her forthright nature—yet she was shrouded by timidity. She could be foolish and enjoy herself, he saw, but did not lose sight of the fact that foolishness, like everything else in life, has its place. Some days he wondered if she could read his thoughts, for lately he had been powerfully drawn to her even though, at forty-five, he was nearly twice her age.

During the year, Aurelia Schober *had* noticed her professor, Otto Plath. How could she not? Tall and slender, he struck an imposing image in front of his class. His piercing blue eyes and delicate lips were complemented by vivid red cheeks. He kept his shock of chestnut-brown hair cut short and combed neat, in accordance with the day's fashion. Aurelia was not alone in her interest in Plath. Many of his young women students adored him. At German Club picnics some students' main activity was flirting with Professor Plath. "Oh, Mr. Plath, what kind of bug is this?" a coed would coo as she dangled an insect before him. To which Plath would respond by giving the insect's Latin name. But even if Aurelia had secret designs on Plath, what could she do? At this time in America, a young woman did not initiate a relationship with a man, especially one old enough to be her father.

So, after class, Aurelia tried to forget Plath as she headed across the campus on which she had spent so much of her life over the past six years. In the fall of 1924, when she had entered Boston University as a freshman, her father vehemently protested her earning a degree in a field filled with financial uncertainty. Instead of signing up for a curriculum featuring English and German, her first choices, she selected Vocational Studies as her major. Nevertheless, as if the degree plan *were* of her choosing, Aurelia maintained an excellent academic record in undergraduate school while holding down odd jobs to supplement the partial scholarships the school had awarded her. She also participated in such extracurricular activities as the English Club, the Writers' Club, the Student Government Board, the German Club (for which she served as both vice-president and president), and *Sivad,* her college's junior yearbook, on which she served as editor-in-chief. "The German Club nearly lost its sensational 'young man,' when *Sivad* won an efficient editor-in-chief," the staff members wrote under her picture that year, "but Aurelia played both roles admirably. The staff will never forget those board meetings, those would-be 'scoldings,' and those cherished words of approval and praise." Eclipsing even her high-school performance—she graduated as the second-highest-ranking student in her class, and therefore salutator, from Winthrop High School in 1924—Aurelia graduated as the top-ranking student, and therefore valedictorian, for the class of 1928 at BU's College of Practical Arts and Letters.

Her bachelor's degree in hand, Aurelia Schober pursued English and German after all, by accepting a job teaching those subjects at Melrose High School. But she had barely started her year of teaching when she decided to go for a master's degree. Enrolling in BU's College of Liberal Arts in the fall of 1929, she signed up for Otto Plath's Middle High German and asked him to serve as both her academic adviser and her thesis reader. During the year, their relationship never became personal, so, when she stopped by Plath's office on the day after the spring term ended to thank him for his help, she was shocked to be told that a colleague of Plath's, Joseph Haskell, and his wife, Josephine, had invited Plath to bring a friend to an end-of-the-year weekend celebration at their country home—and she, *Aurelia,* was the friend he would like to take along. For a moment, Aurelia did not know what to say. Finally, she answered. Of course, she would be happy to join him, she said; it could be fun.

At the Haskells', Otto explained to Aurelia that, though he had been infatuated with her throughout much of the year, William Marshall Warren, dean of liberal arts, had implored him not to show his feelings until she had completed her degree. Beyond being attracted to her physically, Otto also admired her intelligence. He believed that her thesis, *The Paracelsus of History and Literature,* a study of the controversial Swiss physician Paracelsus, whom many consider the father of modern chemistry, ranked among the best he had read recently. As the weekend progressed and Otto began to feel comfortable with Aurelia, he made an even more dramatic confession. Though "single," Otto remained legally married to a woman he had not seen in thirteen years, a woman he would have to divorce should he ever wish to remarry. Despite his frankness, Otto mentioned neither his wife's name, Lydia Clara Bartz, nor her whereabouts, Wisconsin. Besides revealing his marriage to her, Otto did not discuss Lydia Bartz at all.

By the end of the weekend Aurelia had become fascinated enough with Plath so that when he suggested they remain in touch she agreed. Over the summer, as Plath taught summer school in Boston and Schober worked as a business manager at a camp for underprivileged children in Pine Bush, New York, they engaged in a correspondence during which Otto sketched in the story of his life.

On April 13, 1885, in the village of Grabow, Germany, he was born Otto Emil Platt, the first of six children of Theodore, an energetic blacksmith, and Ernestine (née Kottke), a deeply melancholic woman who as she aged appeared to be progressively weighed down by the care of her children, and by an ulcer on her leg that would never fully heal. In the summer of 1900, Otto, realizing that blacksmithing was falling out of demand as Germany reformed land ownership and industrialized its economy, set out on his own version of the immigrant's journey. On September 8, after traveling by carriage and by train to Hamburg, he boarded the S.S. *Auguste Victoria* and endured the week-long voyage across the Atlantic to New York City. He was accompanied by a friend, Louis Schultz, and intended to head for Fall Creek, Wisconsin, to join his grandparents, who had immigrated there the year he was born. Otto stood on the deck of the ship that inched its laborious way into the harbor of New York and stared dreamily at the buildings of Manhattan towering up in the middle distance—beacons, he hoped, to a new future.

Taken with the city, Otto remained in Manhattan, living with an uncle in whose food-and-liquor store he clerked, and altering his name from "Platt" to "Plath." He audited English classes at a grammar school until, after one year, he could read, write, and speak English flawlessly. A year after that, ready to tackle his next step—a formal education— he solicited financial support from his grandfather John, who agreed to underwrite his education *if* Otto would enter seminary, become a minister, and devote his life to the family religion, the Lutheran church. Eventually, Otto agreed. In the fall of 1903, he traveled to Watertown, Wisconsin, to enroll in the preparatory school affiliated with North- western College. Completing his junior, middle, and senior years while living with his grandparents in Fall Creek, he entered Northwestern College in the fall of 1906 and selected classical languages as his major. He graduated in 1910, distinguished by an all-A-and-B performance, and then began the Wisconsin Lutheran Seminary in Wauwatosa that fall. Just weeks into the term, though, Otto became disenchanted with the right-wing synod's conservatism. When he told his grandfather about his misgivings, Otto was stunned by his reaction. Should Otto drop out, John warned, the repercussions would be considerable. Otto finally decided to withdraw anyway, and, as promised, John's vengeance was severe. He excommunicated Otto from the family, a punishment he symbolized by striking—literally, with a pencil—Otto's name from the Plath Bible.

Devastated but relieved, Otto moved to Seattle, where, while teach- ing German at the University Heights School, he studied the language at the University of Washington. Plath was to spend the next two decades crisscrossing the country, studying and teaching German and biology, the latter of which he acquired a passion for at Northwestern after reading Darwin. In those years, he earned a master of arts (Uni- versity of Washington, 1912), a master of science (Harvard University, 1925), and a doctorate of science (Harvard, 1928). He also held grad- uate and faculty posts in German and biology at Columbia, M.I.T., Johns Hopkins, and the universities of Washington and California (Berkeley). On November 5, 1918, his father died at the age of sixty- eight, of an abscess on his lung, in Harney, Oregon, where he had lived as a farmer following his initial immigration to North Dakota.

Plath found a home at Boston University in 1922. During the twen- ties, he advanced from instructor of German to instructor of German and biology to professor of biology. Over the years, he also engaged in research in various biological fields, including the crossbreeding patterns of finches, the lives of fly larvae that suck the blood of nesting birds, and the habits of bumblebees. He published his findings in such journals as *Psyche, The American Naturalist, Biological Bulletin,* and *The Bulletin of the Brooklyn Entomological Society.*

So, by the fall of 1929, the semester Aurelia re-entered Boston University to become his student, Plath was well on his way towards establishing a national reputation in his field. Not that he had achieved this professional plateau without suffering. Because of the transient nature of his employment, and because of the endless hours he spent working in laboratories or libraries, all Plath had to show for his private life over the past twenty years was a marriage to Lydia Bartz, whom he had met at Northwestern through his friend (her brother) Rupert Bartz, which lasted only months.

During the summer of 1930, Aurelia answered each of Otto's letters, in the process chronicling her own family history. In 1894, not far from Grabow, Germany, a fourteen-year-old boy, Franz Schober, left his birthplace of Bad Aussee, Austria, and traveled through the Alps to northern Italy to settle in a village near Venice. Two years later, he moved to Paris; two years after that, London. One afternoon, at the London hotel where he worked as a waiter, Franz, unwavering in his self-confidence, boasted to fellow employee Joseph Grunwald, as he looked at a photograph of his sixteen-year-old sister, Aurelia, "Someday I'll marry the girl." By 1902, the odds of this happening seemed small, since Aurelia lived in Vienna and Franz had sailed from England to Boston to take up residence in a boarding house owned by Joseph, who had immigrated somewhat earlier than he had. If by 1904 Franz, who Americanized his first name to Francis (nicknamed Frank) at the same time Joseph changed his last to Greenwood, felt any doubts about his last move, they were dispelled on the afternoon he answered the boarding-house door to discover the girl in the photograph—Aurelia. He had known she was sailing to America, but here she was—even more beautiful than he had imagined.

As the romance immediately started to grow between Aurelia and Frank, Aurelia's father voiced objections, but these only strengthened their commitment to each other. Finally, on July 3, 1905, the day Aurelia turned eighteen—the minimum age in Massachusetts at which one could marry without parental consent—she and Frank filed for a marriage certificate. On July 10, once the required one-week grace period had elapsed, Frank Schober married Aurelia Greenwood in a civil ceremony. Not a year later, on April 26, 1906, Aurelia gave birth to a daughter, whom they decided to name after them both, Aurelia Frances.

The Schobers rented a two-story house at 33 Peter Polly Road in the Boston suburb of Jamaica Plain, then soon afterwards purchased a house in Winthrop Center, a village northeast of Boston on the Winthrop Peninsula. But within a year they had relocated a third—and final—time, buying a rambling beach house on the southeastern-most tip of the peninsula, Point Shirley. And here, at 892 Shirley Street, on a road that literally dead-ended into water, the Schobers raised a family that grew to include a son and another daughter (Frank Junior and Dorothy, respectively five and thirteen years younger than Aurelia). Behind the house lay the Atlantic Ocean. Out front, beyond a row of houses lining the other side of the two-lane road, Boston Harbor's water rose and fell peacefully. Directly to the south of the peninsula was Deer Island, home of a state prison. It would be in this location that the younger Aurelia spent most of her girlhood—an exotic world that instilled in her a lifelong love of the ocean.

Becoming citizens as soon as they were eligible, Frank and Aurelia proceeded to assimilate themselves into the mainstream in America; they even bucked the trend of most immigrants of the day and voted Republican. In the 1910s, swept up by the day's booming financial climate, Frank began working as an accountant for the Dorothy Muriel Company, often supplementing his salary with wise stock-market investments. (In the twenties, he lost substantial sums through errant market speculations, after which Aurelia assumed control of the family's money.) Yet regardless of how they embraced the American system, the Schobers did not shun their German ancestry; they spoke the language at home until their children entered grammar school. As a result, at the beginning of World War I, which broke out when Aurelia was eight years old, the Schobers became open targets for anti-German attacks in Winthrop, a predominantly Irish-Italian community. Usually this harassment took the form of verbal assaults, although once a student shoved Aurelia to the ground from the door of the school bus while the driver and her fellow students turned their heads the other way.

Chauvinism notwithstanding, Aurelia had an almost idyllic youth on Point Shirley. An excellent student, she spent the summers enjoying the beach and reading—tirelessly. By her senior year in high school, she knew much of Scott, Dickens, Thackeray, Eliot, Hardy, Galsworthy, Cooper, Hawthorne, Melville, and Henry James. Though she loved the Brontës and Jane Austen, her favorite writer was not a novelist but a poet, Emily Dickinson. Soon Aurelia decided to become a writer. After all, she had so much to write *about*. Life near the ocean brought with it picnics in rowboats a mile out to sea, beachcombing at midnight, and floods that washed up such treasures as mussel shells, tea sets, and (on one occasion) a dead shark. But in the face of her father's strong disapproval she did not pursue her impulse to write as diligently as she might have.

Drawn closer together by the letters they had exchanged that summer, Otto and Aurelia began dating when Aurelia returned to Boston in September to assume the Brookline High School faculty post she had been offered. Almost immediately, weekend hiking trips, afternoon strolls through the Arnold Arboretum, and nights at the theatre launched the couple into a serious romance. Before long, they openly discussed marriage. Finally, just after Christmas 1931, they left Boston by car and, chaperoned by Aurelia's mother, drove cross-country to Carson City, Nevada, where on Monday, January 4, 1932, Otto filed for and received a divorce from Lydia Bartz, the woman he had not seen in over a decade. Later that same day, Otto Plath and Aurelia Schober, each of whom swore in writing to be a current resident of Reno, Nevada, were married in a civil ceremony in Carson City, at Ormsby County's courthouse.

Following a honeymoon in Nevada, the Plaths, still accompanied by Aurelia's mother, drove back to Boston to begin their married life. Aurelia moved into Otto's apartment, a six-room first-floor rental in a house at 24 Prince Street in Jamaica Plain. Before she could resume her teaching job at Brookline High, Otto insisted that she resign, which she did even though she was a successful teacher and a probable future chairman of the German Department. Otto wanted Aurelia to become a full-time housewife, and he wished to start a family as soon as possible. In fact, they would become parents much sooner than even Otto had hoped: only weeks into the marriage Aurelia became pregnant. In anticipation of the event, Aurelia readied a nursery, bought baby clothes, and began to read about the various philosophies of child-rearing. Finally, on Thursday, October 27, 1932—three weeks early, the Plaths retorted to smiling friends who had been keeping track of the months—Aurelia checked in to Memorial Hospital on Stoughton Street in Boston and at ten after two in the afternoon gave birth to an eight-pound-three-ounce baby girl. The attending physicians, Drs. J. J. Abrams and Edwin Smith, reported that the infant appeared healthy, content, alert. And when the new parents examined the list of names they had assembled, they determined—for no other reason than because they liked the sound of the name—that she would be Sylvia, Sylvia Plath.

2

Disregarding the day's popular parenting trends, which had mothers feeding their babies according to strict timetables, coddling them sparingly, and ignoring them if they cried, Aurelia followed her own instincts and fed Sylvia on demand, rocked her frequently, and picked her up when she was fretful. Aurelia strengthened her convictions about child-rearing by studying experts who deviated from accepted trends, such as Friedrich Froebel, whose *Educating Man* she read at Otto's suggestion, and Maria Montessori.

Sylvia proved to be an easy baby who slept well and nursed about every four hours, and her physical and emotional development, documented during regular pediatric checkups, seemed to attest to the success of Aurelia's approach. She gained weight steadily, jumping from ten to sixteen pounds between the ages of six months and one year;

shot up in height at a rate expected for a happy baby, increasing from twenty-two to twenty-nine inches in her initial eighteen months; and acquired ambulatory skills on schedule, crawling first, creeping alone at ten months, and toddling soon afterwards. Indeed, in Sylvia's infancy, only one distinguishing personality trait emerged, but this—a trait so odd that while diligently chronicling her daughter's growth in a baby book chockful of observations, dates, and numbers—Aurelia recorded in labored detail. At the age of six or eight weeks, Sylvia began, with purpose and determination, to try to speak. First a vowel, then a consonant, Sylvia gurgled syllable after syllable, bits and pieces of sound she clearly longed to shape into words.

Early in her marriage, even though she was preoccupied by her pregnancy with and subsequent care for Sylvia, Aurelia also carved out time to assist Otto in rewriting his dissertation, which bore the academic title *Bumblebees: Their Life History, Habits, and Economic Importance, with a Detailed Account of the New England Species,* into a general-interest volume that a trade publisher could acquire. Because Otto was not particularly adept at writing, Aurelia did the job, though revising a scientific treatise was significantly different from creating the books she had hoped one day to write on her own—novels based on the lives of her parents. Once Aurelia had completed the revision, Otto checked the text for factual accuracy. Pleased with the document, the Plaths showed it to publishers, ultimately selling it to the Macmillan Company. When the book appeared in 1934, under the more commercial title *Bumblebees and Their Ways,* Plath had added a foreword written by Harvard's William Morton Wheeler, his friend and teacher, as he described him in the book's dedication. In his own introduction, Plath tried to humanize the book's subject matter by tracing the genesis of his curiosity about bumblebees:

> The foundations of this book were laid during my early boyhood in Central Europe, after my interest had been aroused by the discovery that bumblebees make delicious honey. Having repeatedly observed the activities of a neighboring bee-keeper, I thought it might be possible to transfer bumblebee colonies to artificial domiciles, and thus have honey available at all times. This idea was carried out a few weeks later, and during that and the two following summers

about twenty-five bumblebee colonies belonging to six European species were placed in cigar-boxes and transferred to the family garden. The method employed in "transplanting" these colonies was rather crude, and so it happened that I was sometimes severely punished by the more vindictive species.

For her work on the book, Aurelia received nothing approaching co-author credit, but instead a brief routine nod in the acknowledgments that mentioned how she had "aided [her husband] greatly in editing the manuscript and in proofreading." Consequently, critics and readers of *Bumblebees and Their Ways* lavished praise on Otto alone for producing an entertaining book on a subject that in lesser hands could have been dull. In May 1934, for example, *Booklist* ran a representative notice touting the book as "a real contribution" to "the literature of the subject." The volume received equally favorable notices when it appeared in Europe, Japan, and Australia. In time, *Bumblebees and Their Ways* would become, in the estimation of both lay and scientific audiences, nothing short of a landmark study in the field of entomology, a watershed for future biologists.

As the Plaths were finishing *Bumblebees and Their Ways*, Carl Murchison, chairman of the department of psychology at Clark University, approached Otto about writing an essay for *A Handbook of Social Psychology*, an anthology he was assembling for the university's press. Always anxious to advance his career, Plath agreed. To begin his essay, "Insect Societies," Plath selected his background material—a cache of some seventy books. But faced with actually gleaning information from those books, Otto turned to Aurelia, who, although absorbed in mothering Sylvia, set aside enough hours to read and take notes on this mound of texts. From her notes Aurelia produced a rough draft, after which Otto wrote a second; finally, Aurelia edited and polished the manuscript. The article completed, Otto submitted "Insect Societies" to Murchison, who happily included it in his anthology, printed by Clark in 1935.

While they produced "Insect Societies" and basked in the excellent reviews for *Bumblebees*, the Plaths learned a different sort of good news: Aurelia was pregnant once again. As winter turned to spring and the baby's due date approached, Aurelia worried how Sylvia, almost two and a half, would respond to a new infant. To prepare her for the birth, Aurelia made the baby real for Sylvia by taking her shopping for baby clothes and by allowing her to press her ear to Aurelia's stomach to hear the baby kick. In early April, Aurelia arranged for her parents to baby-sit Sylvia. When she took her to Point Shirley later in the month, Aurelia stayed on several nights until Sylvia felt comfortable with her new surroundings. Still, Sylvia cried on the day Aurelia left. On April 27, 1935, Aurelia traveled back across the harbor into Boston, checked into Jamaica Plain's Faulkner Hospital, and, after going into labor, gave birth—again three weeks early—to a boy, whom she and Otto named Warren Joseph.

By now Otto and Aurelia had been married for three years and four months. In that time, Otto had maintained a demanding teaching schedule, Aurelia had given birth to two babies, and together they had ushered into print a book and a major academic article. They had *not*, however, built any semblance of a social life. Always outgoing, Aurelia lamented this void, whereas Otto, fiercely career-oriented, content to be alone, and set in his antisocial ways, preferred work. This difference created a tension that had surfaced early in the marriage. But when Aurelia brought up her displeasure with this life of all work and no play, she was startled to learn that Otto cared for no one's feelings except his own. Throughout their whirlwind courtship, Aurelia— apparently—had overlooked this aspect of Otto's personality. And when, after their marriage, she called his attention to this ugly streak, she realized that he would never change himself for anybody. His nature, as headstrong as his grandfather's, reinforced by all those years of bachelorhood, had rendered Otto intractable. "By the end of my first year of marriage," Aurelia Plath would one day write, "I realized that if I wanted a peaceful home—and I did—I would simply have to become more submissive, although it was not my nature to be so." One of the few couples with whom the Plaths did associate was their neighbors George and Helen Hennessy, parents of a daughter, also named Helen. The two mothers often strolled their babies together—

Warren in one carriage pushed by Sylvia, Helen, who would grow up to publish literary criticism under the name Vendler, in the other.

As Aurelia embraced harmony, Otto gloried in his role of *der Herr des Hauses* and controlled almost every aspect of his family's home life, from plotting their long-term financial security to paying monthly bills. Otto even handled the grocery shopping, stopping by Faneuil Hall in downtown Boston on his way to and from school to buy meats and vegetables on the days they were cheapest. (North End vendors usually reduced their prices on Fridays and Saturdays, rather than risk goods' getting ruined over the weekend.) In addition, Otto expected Aurelia to behave within boundaries that he had carefully prescribed for her. If she did not, she made him angry. In this way too, he seemed to be his grandfather's grandson. So, if Aurelia dared to invite guests over to supper, the event took on subversive, clandestine overtones, as though it were as exotic as the secret rendezvous of spies. The meal had to occur on the night of the week Otto taught, and had to be finished before he returned home. During the many months the couple worked on "Insect Societies," Aurelia had to draw a plan of the arrangement of the books, notes, and manuscripts he kept stacked on the dining-room table so that, once she and her guests had finished supper, each item could be returned to its appropriate spot. Of course, early in her marriage, more than Aurelia's social life suffered. With each page she wrote for her husband and each diaper she changed, Aurelia lost her drive to try to write fiction. Her dream of novel-writing, destroyed initially by her father and now by Otto, would just have to wait.

In the spring of 1936, Otto and Aurelia thought about moving, both because they needed more room and because they wanted to buy a home. But before they started house-hunting, summer arrived and it became so hot that Aurelia decided she and the children would escape the heat at her parents' house on Point Shirley. Previously, in the summers of 1932 and 1933, the Schobers had rented their house to vacationers, but this year they stayed there themselves. Since Otto remained in Jamaica Plain to commute to his summer-school classes, Aurelia, always the good wife, came back from Winthrop to Jamaica Plain each week to prepare food, wash clothes, and spend time with her husband. By the end of the summer, Aurelia, whose love of the ocean had been rekindled, convinced Otto to look at houses in Winthrop. Luckily, one of the first they saw—a spacious seven-room, two-story brown stucco located at 92 Johnson Avenue, only three miles from the Schobers'—was perfect, and its owners, the Rohes, were anxious to sell. Agreeing on a price of ten thousand dollars, of which one thousand would be paid down, the Plaths and the Rohes concluded a deal with such haste that, by the fall of 1936, all legal and financial transactions had been completed and the Plaths had moved into their new home.

In the mid-thirties, Boston and its suburbs, like the rest of the country, still reeled from the 1929 stock-market crash and the ensuing Great Depression. So, each morning, as he left Winthrop to go by train, ferry, and subway to Boston's Copley Square, Otto felt grateful for his job. After several weeks, Aurelia had settled in enough to devote much of her attention to Sylvia and Warren again. In particular, she continued an ambitious program of reading books aloud to her children. Beginning with nursery rhymes, fairy tales, and poems in *Sun Under the Silver Umbrella,* Aurelia had progressed in time to A. A. Milne, J. R. R. Tolkien, Robert Louis Stevenson, Dr. Seuss, and Kipling's *Just So Stories.* Of what she had read so far, Sylvia and Warren's favorites included *The Wind in the Willows, Heidi, Mrs. Wiggs of the Cabbage Patch,* Byrd's *Christmas Carol,* and Lamb's *Tales from Shakespeare.*

In the spring of 1937, the William Freemans moved in next door to the Plaths. The husbands became acquaintances, but Aurelia and Marion Freeman struck up a close friendship. Both housewives and mothers (Marion had two children—David, six months older than Sylvia, and Ruth, eighteen months older than Warren), they were approximately the same age as well. Soon the Plath and the Freeman children were spending countless hours together in one house or the other. Until summer arrived, that is; then, their mothers with them, the children passed the hot, muggy months playing on the beach. Sylvia learned to swim one day in the early part of the season, when she waded far out into the water, fell into the over-the-head deep, and suddenly started swimming. Later that summer, Aurelia and Marion began to wonder if for the fall they should enroll David and Sylvia, both of whom would be underage, at the Sunshine School, a private elementary school in the neighborhood. Since David would be five, and Sylvia only four, Marion's decision was easier than Aurelia's. Finally, because the Sunshine School's first grade met just half a day and because Sylvia seemed ready (thanks to Aurelia's reading program, Sylvia could already read simple stories), Aurelia decided to go ahead.

Each morning beginning in September, Sylvia awoke, dressed, ate breakfast, and walked to the nearby Sunshine School. Dismissed at noon, she came home and, over lunch, exuberantly talked about the morning's activities with her mother and Warren. Within weeks, as Sylvia performed well, the school staff, specifically Headmistress Hope Cusiter, were congratulating Aurelia on making a wise decision. By the end of the year, Aurelia decided Sylvia was ready for public school. In the fall of 1938, Sylvia entered the Annie F. Warren Grammar School, Winthrop's public elementary school, which required her to follow a much different schedule. First, the second grade met for both morning and afternoon sessions; second, since the school was farther from her home, Sylvia's walk to and from school became considerably longer. Even so, her performance did not falter: Sylvia went on to earn excellent grades as well as high recommendations from her teacher.

Historically, the most memorable event in the lives of the Plaths in the fall of 1938 was not Sylvia's change of school but an act of nature. On September 21, beginning at five o'clock in the morning, a major hurricane tore through the Boston area, unleashing its force particularly hard on Winthrop, since it is the city's easternmost suburb. After a restless night, Sylvia and Warren hid with Aurelia downstairs in Otto's study while, for three frantic hours, they listened to the hurricane roar overhead. Later, the storm having passed, the Plaths emerged from 92 Johnson Avenue to discover boats tossed about the shore, cottages afloat in the harbor, and telephone poles snapped in two like toothpicks. As evidenced by a poem and an essay she would write many years afterwards, this sight—the result of a world suddenly turned on itself—would stick with Sylvia for the rest of her life.

Compared with its start, the remainder of Sylvia's second-grade year passed unmomentously. Earning a string of A's marred by only a sprinkling of B's, Sylvia advanced to the third grade, where her performance was also judged excellent. And so it was that, by the fall of 1940, when she entered the fourth grade at E. B. Newton, Winthrop's premiddle school, Sylvia seemingly demonstrated the growth patterns of any bright, motivated youngster. She filled her school days with studying, her summers with outings on the beach, while her mother and maternal grandparents provided her with love and support. In fact, only a profound curiosity in and susceptibility to various art forms distinguished her from her peers. Once, as Aurelia read aloud a poem by Matthew Arnold that contained the lines "Where the sea snakes coil and twine, / Dry their mail and bask in the brine, / Where great whales come sailing by, / Sail and sail, with unshut eye, / Round the world forever and aye," Sylvia, listening in silence, became visibly shaken by the poem's music and rhythm. Yet Sylvia aspired to *create* art as well. One night, while Aurelia and her children stood on the beach and gazed up at a new moon, Sylvia began composing a poem on the spot that in tone and rhythm echoed Arnold's.

Sylvia had been writing poetry well before that night on the beach. By age five she was finishing whole poems, short but crafted. Of her early attempts, the first one that she recopied in final form, dated, and saved was "Thoughts," an unrhymed couplet celebrating Christmas, written in 1937.

Through faithful practice, Sylvia was producing poems, as of the fall of 1940, at a consistent pace. She considered several—"Snow," "My Mother and I," "Perils of Dew"—successful enough to recopy, date, and save, as she had "Thoughts." Until now her poems had been innocent distillations of daily life. Soon this habit would change. An emerging tragedy had captured her attention. It had started subtly, not long after Warren's birth. As time passed, it manifested itself more obviously. It concerned her father's health—how he felt, acted. And to Sylvia, who observed the tragedy with an uninformed yet knowing perception, the ordeal, which culminated in November 1940, came to represent all that was not happy in her happy childhood.

3

In the summer of 1935, Aurelia became worried about her husband's health. Signs of incipient illness—a slight weight loss, a hacking cough, an uncharacteristically low threshold for anger—became detectable to her. A year later, family and friends could remark upon the weight loss; and his anger, now triggered by inconsequential events, threw him into frightening fits of rage. As of the fall of 1937, Otto had deteriorated to the point that, upon returning home from school, he collapsed on the living-room sofa from sheer exhaustion. His daily regimen of lecturing and paper-grading, a routine on which he had thrived for two decades, had become prohibitive, rendering him so feeble he could barely struggle through a week. Around this time, Sylvia and Warren's spirited playing—and sometimes the children's mere presence—became a strain on Otto. Because of this, Aurelia implemented an upstairs-downstairs policy in the house, whereby if Otto was home the children remained upstairs, Otto down. At night, then, Sylvia and Warren amused themselves upstairs in their playroom as Otto worked or rested downstairs, usually in the living room or in his study. Later, after the children ate supper at their miniature table and chairs in their playroom, and after she and Otto had eaten their own, separate supper downstairs, Aurelia allowed Sylvia and Warren to come downstairs and spend thirty minutes with their father. These occasions, the only time during the day that the entire family assembled, had a theatrical quality. With Otto as their audience, the children became performers. Warren would sing a song or recite a poem he had written. Sylvia would list the scientific names of insects or recite her own poem. When the children completed their brief revue, Otto hugged each affectionately—otherwise, he seldom touched his children—and Aurelia quickly put them to bed.

Over the years, Aurelia had begged Otto to see a doctor about his health. He had never gone to a doctor in his life, Otto retorted, and under no condition would he start now. Why? Aurelia wanted to know. Finally, Otto told her. After he had recently watched a colleague die from lung cancer, Otto had concluded that he had similar symptoms.

If he was going to die from lung cancer, Otto wanted the death to be as swift as possible. In the late thirties, because the medical community knew next to nothing about the disease—not its cause, or its pathology, much less its cure—a diagnosis of cancer spelled a sure death, which surgery, the current prescribed "treatment," only delayed. Also, cancer was veiled in mystery; patients and their families often met with ridicule from a public who feared it might "catch" the disease. So, to avoid subjecting himself and his family to humiliation, but mostly to avoid prolonging his life needlessly, Otto refused medical attention. "I know what my ailment is," Otto would explain, "and I'm not going to submit myself to any butchering."

Throughout 1938 and 1939, Otto's health continued to fail. During those years, Warren suffered two separate attacks of bronchial pneumonia, and also developed an asthmatic condition complicated by allergies. With Warren and Otto occasionally sick at the same time, 92 Johnson Avenue resembled a hospital more than a home, Aurelia a nurse more than a homemaker. To ease her workload, Aurelia periodically arranged for Sylvia, who had bouts of sinusitis but was healthy compared with her brother and father, to live with the Schobers. From Point Shirley, Sylvia communicated with her mother daily, not only by telephone but also, because Aurelia could not emphasize enough the importance of the written word, by mail. This practice established a habit of letter-writing in which the two would engage for years to come. With Sylvia gone, Aurelia could devote her undivided attention to caring for Otto and Warren, a job that took its toll. Aurelia was rarely able to sleep through the night.

The year 1940 brought no reprieves. Month after month, Otto became afflicted by new symptoms: insomnia, a persistent thirst, and leg cramps so harsh that when they struck he bent double, grabbed his calves, and cried out in pain. Sylvia and Warren were horrified by these episodes, the sight of which etched lasting impressions on their imaginations. Then, one morning in August, while he dressed for school, Otto stubbed his left foot's little toe on the base of a bureau in his bedroom. No catastrophe—a common enough mishap. Even though his toe throbbed, he proceeded to school to teach his classes. But during the day, Otto noticed something odd. Instead of improving, his foot hurt *more*. On returning home late that afternoon, he took off his sock and shoe only to discover—to his bewilderment—that his toes had turned a purplish black while red streaks of infection climbed up his shin. Otto was perplexed: a minor accident should not have created such a serious injury, and, what was more, a grossly infected foot was *not* a sign of lung cancer. Dumfounded, Otto acquiesced and allowed Aurelia to call a doctor. Their family physician, Dr. Abrams, conducted a physical examination, took blood and urine samples, and left, promising to telephone his results right away. When he did, his diagnosis shocked Aurelia. According to Abrams, Otto suffered not from cancer but from a debilitating—though quite treatable—form of diabetes mellitus. How many years had he had it? Aurelia asked. As many as ten, Abrams guessed. And *that* was the problem. Otto had avoided medical help for so long that the disease might now be fatal. Finally, Abrams's diagnosis explained so much. An insatiable sweet tooth (Otto's had first surfaced during his German boyhood), flushed cheeks, an unquenchable thirst—all were textbook warning signs of diabetes. In addition, Aurelia remembered Otto's descriptions of his mother's poor health. Because the open wound on her leg and her spells of melancholia could be indications of diabetes, Aurelia decided that Otto might easily have inherited the disease from her. Had Otto sought treatment—as late as 1938 or 1939, Abrams said—he could have maintained a relatively normal life by modifying his diet and taking insulin injections. Since Otto's condition had now become life-threatening, Abrams saw few available options.

As Otto undertook a crash program to save his life, which included a radically altered diet and massive doses of insulin, he contracted pneumonia. After a two-week stay in Winthrop Hospital, he was released, but at home he remained under the supervision of a practical nurse who, because Otto's condition was so grim, worked every day except Wednesday. Of course, the nurse proved a huge expense, the more so since Otto had refused through the years to take out health insurance. But Aurelia had no choice in the matter; Otto was now too sick for her to care for him by herself. In early October, on one of the nurse's Wednesdays off, Otto felt well enough for Aurelia—at his suggestion—to take the children to the beach for some fresh air. Aurelia did not like the idea of Otto being in the house alone. Giving in to his protests, she finally placed medicine and a glass of water by his bedside, gathered the children, and left the house. On the beach, Aurelia could not relax; she kept worrying about Otto. Eventually, her anxiety turned to panic, so she had a friend watch Sylvia and Warren while she went to check on him. Walking to the house, she was visited by a strange feeling of impending doom. The instant she opened the front door, her fears became justified. There before her, sprawled on the stairs, lay Otto, immobile and unconscious, seemingly dead. Terrified, Aurelia rushed to his side and violently shook his shoulders and slapped his cheeks, trying to revive him. Slowly he regained consciousness, although his eyes remained unfocused and his speech was an incoherent mumble. Somehow Aurelia managed, with Otto's meager help, to hoist him to his feet. Then, as she guided him, they stumbled up the rest of the stairs and down the hallway into his bedroom. Lying in bed, Otto frequently became incoherent as he tried to talk. When he *was* lucid, he reconstructed the events that had led to his collapse. Feeling a momentary burst of energy and a powerful urge to see his flower garden, Otto had gotten out of bed and gone down the stairs, through the house, and out into the backyard. In the crisp afternoon air, he pored over his flowers until he became weary. Returning inside, he was climbing the stairs to go to his bedroom when he suddenly became light-headed and passed out. Sitting on the edge of the bed, Aurelia stared blankly at Otto. His face was crimson, his mouth bone-dry; his eyes darted from side to side. Aurelia resolved to bear up and be strong for Otto and for the children.

That night, thrashing in bed, Otto sweated profusely. Aurelia kept having to change his wringing-wet pajamas and bed linen. By morning, because Otto's condition had not improved, Aurelia rushed him to Winthrop Hospital, where staff doctors called in Dr. Harvey Loder, one of Boston's foremost diabetes specialists. Examining Otto, Loder determined that the restricted blood flow characteristic of diabetes had made Otto's left leg gangrenous. His recommendation: amputate the leg. Since Otto's condition warranted emergency treatment, Loder checked him into New England Deaconess Hospital in Boston, and there, on October 12, 1940, performed an above-the-knee amputation.

Afterwards, Loder, encouraged by Otto's response, told Aurelia that her husband could have a normal future once he learned to walk with a prosthesis. In the days following the operation, Loder's optimism waned as Otto underwent a series of reversals. In agony, Otto himself soon suspected that he might never recover.

Before long, Otto's health was declining at such a rapid pace that Aurelia could chart his demise by simply watching him: the nurses did not need to report his vital signs. On the night of November 5, as Aurelia sat beside his bed, Otto seemed to resign himself to his fate. "I don't mind the thought of death at all," he whispered in a strained voice, pausing as he looked up at her from his bed, "but I would like to see how the children grow up."

Shaken, Aurelia could barely keep herself from breaking down. Surely Otto was not going to die. At fifty-five, he was too young. Aurelia decided to go home and compose herself so that she could be of comfort to him the next morning. She had reached Winthrop and was unlocking the door when the telephone began to ring. Dashing to the telephone, Aurelia clutched the receiver in her hand and then listened to the doctor's voice on the other end of the line. An embolus, dislodged from somewhere in his bloodstream, had struck Otto's lung, killing him instantly. He had probably not even been conscious of his own dying. The next day, a hospital doctor, a Dr. Holmes, would sign a statement that read: "I hereby certify that I attended deceased from 10/7/40 to 11/5/40. I last saw him alive on 11/5/40, death is said to have occurred on the date stated above, at 9:35 PM. Immediate cause of death [is] diabetes mellitus [and] broncho pneaumonia [sic] due to gangrene left foot."

Since the children were already upstairs asleep, Aurelia decided to wait until morning to break the news to them. When she told Sylvia, who had been sitting up in bed reading a book, Sylvia blurted out, "I'll never speak to God again," and pulled her blanket over her head.

Because she believed the children were not old enough to witness an event as traumatic as the funeral of their father, Aurelia arranged for Marion Freeman to baby-sit. At three o'clock on the afternoon of November 9, Aurelia, supported by her parents, attended her husband's funeral, which was held at First Methodist Church in Winthrop under the direction of Reverend Harry Belmont Hill. After the services, interment took place in the newest—and third—section of Winthrop's nondenominational Town Cemetery. With Hill reciting final prayers and Howard S. Reynolds serving as undertaker, Otto was buried in Grave Number 1123 on the cemetery's Azalea Path.

Wellesley

1

Following Otto's death, Aurelia and the Schobers were forced to make sweeping changes in their lives. Within a week of their father's funeral, both Sylvia and Warren became ill. Each contracted measles; Sylvia also came down with sinusitis, Warren with pneumonia. Nursing her children, Aurelia realized that she would somehow have to overcome her own sorrow so that she could provide her children with the parental love—and financial support—they needed. The former did not worry her—in many ways, Otto had been a phantom parent—but the latter did. Otto had left Aurelia strapped for money. Throughout their nearly decade-long marriage, the Plaths had amassed little savings besides Otto's modest university retirement account, for they had used the majority of Otto's salary to meet monthly bills. Also, Otto's life-insurance coverage amounted to a mere five thousand dollars, from which doctor, hospital, and funeral expenses had to be paid. Settling the bills, Aurelia realized a cash sum, counting insurance, savings, and Otto's retirement, of about two thousand dollars. To make matters worse, Otto's salary (naturally) stopped at the end of the fall term. During his illness, a colleague, Irving Johnson, and a graduate student, Carl Ludwig, had conducted Otto's classes without remuneration; but now that source of income had stopped. Luckily, Braintree High School offered Aurelia a job for the spring term. To teach three German and two Spanish units on a full-time temporary basis, she would be paid twenty-five dollars per week.

Not long after Otto's death, the Dorothy Muriel Company laid off Frank Schober because of management restructuring. At Christmastime that year, Aurelia and her parents tried to make the holidays as festive as possible for Sylvia and Warren, but Otto's death cast a shadow over the season. Two recurrent topics—Aurelia's Braintree job and Frank's premature retirement—led them to discuss the practicality of alternative living arrangements. With Frank unemployed and Aurelia in need of help around the house, the Plaths and the Schobers decided to merge their households. The Schobers rented out their Point Shirley home and moved into 92 Johnson Avenue. Grammy—the children's name for their grandmother—assumed the lion's share of domestic duties. She bought groceries, cooked meals, cleaned house, minded Sylvia and Warren, even chauffeured the family in the Schobers' secondhand Plymouth. (Otto and Aurelia had never owned a car.) Because she had no household responsibilities, Aurelia could devote all of her energies at home to class preparation and, more important, to her children.

Since Braintree's position was temporary and involved a commute, Aurelia accepted a permanent job for the coming fall at Winthrop Junior High School, a position that involved teaching ninth grade and overseeing a substantial part of the school's accounting services. She carefully weighed the job's pros and cons before accepting it, for Otto's protracted illness had taken its toll and had left Aurelia with a duodenal stomach ulcer. The year at Winthrop, if her accounting duties proved as stressful as she thought they might, could make things worse. But Aurelia had to provide for her children, so she took the job.

At the end of the spring term, the high point of which was Aurelia's sister Dorothy's wedding to Joseph Benotti on April 19—the reception was at 92 Johnson Avenue—Sylvia eagerly awaited summer. After she had a tonsillectomy (Warren had one too), she sunbathed on Winthrop's sandy white beaches, combed "the flats" at low tide in search of seashells, sailed with her Uncle Frank in a boat he had built himself, and, once recovered from her operation, swam in the harbor with her grandfather. One other activity engaged her imagination as well. For more hours than usual, Sylvia would sit in her room and study the airplanes landing and taking off at Logan, Boston's municipal airport, located across the harbor from Winthrop and in full view from Sylvia's bedroom window. "I marveled at the moving beacons on the runway and watched, until it grew completely dark, the flashing red and green lights that rose and set in the sky like shooting stars," comments a narrator of a short story Plath would one day write. "The airport was my Mecca, my Jerusalem. All night I dreamed of flying."

But mostly Sylvia worked at something that was slowly becoming a compulsion—writing. To Sylvia, the single most important day of the summer of 1941, August 11, was the date on which the Boston *Herald* published one of her poems in its children's section, "The Good Sport Page"—the first time the byline "Sylvia Plath" appeared in print. Introduced by a brief explanatory note—"I have written a short poem about what I see and hear on hot summer nights"—the poem, entitled simply "Poem," was a childlike effort about crickets and fireflies. Submitting creative material to periodicals is not a regular activity of most eight-year-olds; it is telling, then, that, even at such a young age, Sylvia wanted to see her work in print badly enough to submit it for publication.

In the fall, Sylvia enrolled in the fifth grade, Warren the second, while Aurelia, who over the summer had tutored remedial English and Spanish, began her sixteen-hundred-dollar-a-year teaching position at Winthrop Junior High. But as the term progressed, world events, not school, dominated their minds. Since 1938, when Germany had annexed Austria, Americans of German heritage, like both the Plaths and the Schobers, had felt the sting of anti-German sentiment. Now, in Europe, Adolf Hitler's Third Reich bombed London—one more step in its aspirations towards world domination. In the Pacific, Japan, a wealthy and powerful country, tested its own military muscle. On December 7, 1941, international events were further personalized for Americans when the Japanese attacked Pearl Harbor. The next day, a banner headline in the Boston *Herald* read, JAPS OPEN WAR ON U.S. / BOMB HAWAII, KILL 350. That afternoon, President Roosevelt requested and received from Congress a formal declaration of war against Japan. All across the country, Americans huddled around radios to hear breaking news reports. The Plaths and the Schobers were no different. Years later, Plath would write a short story inspired by events that occurred during this disturbing time. "I remember sitting by the radio with Mother and Uncle Frank feeling a queer foreboding in the air," says the narrator. "Their voices were low and serious . . . and Mother kept saying over and over about Daddy: '. . . I'm only glad Otto didn't live to see it come to this.' "

On December 11, Congress passed and Roosevelt signed a proclamation of war against Germany and Italy, Japan's Axis partners. Afterwards, Congress expanded the draft age to include all men between eighteen and sixty-four, making some forty-one million available for military enlistment. Eventually, during Sylvia's fifth grade, Frank Junior would be drafted. For the Plaths, as for others, the war had become a painful reality. The December 16 *Herald* article JAP ATTACK UNITES ALL BOSTON BEHIND WAR TO MOP UP AXIS exemplified Americans' growing concerns, although in the end it did not predict history. "When college students pass up their suppers to talk about it," the article began, "when truckdrivers hang around the garage to hash it over, when the Italians blast Mussolini, the Germans run down Hitler and the Irish talk about patching things up with Britain, you somehow get the idea that a unified Boston is in there pitching for the United States to win this war and win it quick."

As Otto's death had last year, World War II darkened moods in the Plath-Schober household during Christmastime 1941. That spring semester, while the war raged on, Aurelia taught and the children studied. In June, both Sylvia and Warren having graduated with high marks, the Plaths anticipated a quiet summer—and, they hoped, the end of the war. On June 27, 1942, Frank, bound for military duty, married Louise Bowman in a ceremony in which Sylvia served as flower girl, Warren ring-bearer. In this discouraging season, Aurelia met with an unexpected personal triumph when the secretary department in Boston University's College of Practical Arts and Letters, which that fall would offer a new degree program in medical-secretary procedures, invited her to develop and then oversee the program. Because the stress from handling Winthrop Junior High's monies had aggravated her stomach ulcer, and because she wanted to enter the more comfortable field of university teaching, Aurelia accepted BU's job offer, which brought with it an annual salary of eighteen hundred dollars. By the fall, Aurelia had assembled the new degree plan and was prepared to teach her first students.

In late summer, Aurelia had begun to consider moving out of Winthrop. The ocean exacerbated the children's chronic respiratory and sinus infections and Aurelia's arthritis, now in its early stages. From Winthrop, Boston University was no easy commute. Most important, Aurelia did not want her children to grow up in Winthrop's working-class community. Consequently, she scouted several inland Boston neighborhoods and, as she did, rediscovered Wellesley, some fifteen miles west of the city. Examining the town closely, Aurelia saw that real-estate taxes were surprisingly low; the town's demographics, which ranged from middle to upper-middle class, would guarantee Sylvia and Warren a suitable environment; and as a resident Sylvia would be eligible for an all-expense-paid town scholarship to Wellesley College, a Seven Sisters school. When she looked at possible houses to buy, Aurelia fell in love with 26 Elmwood Road, a two-story Cape Cod built on a wooded half-acre corner lot. And so, by Sylvia's tenth birthday, October 27, 1942, Aurelia had sold 92 Johnson Avenue—at a loss, since real-estate prices had slipped—and purchased 26 Elmwood Road. In the coming months, Sylvia would miss many elements of her old life, particularly the Freemans, but none more than the one most evident to Winthrop residents—the ocean. "And this is how it stiffens, my vision of that seaside childhood," Plath would later write. "My father died, we moved inland. Whereupon those nine first years of my life sealed themselves off like a ship in a bottle—beautiful, inaccessible, obsolete, a fine, white flying myth." It was as if the nearly four years she had lived in Jamaica Plain before moving to Winthrop had never existed.

2

The Charles River, curving in on itself as it flows eastwards to Boston and the Atlantic beyond, winds around Wellesley's borders, but the town has many other bodies of water as well: Morse's Pond, Longfellow

Pond, Lake Waban, and brooks like Fuller and Rosemary. Still, it is trees, in particular elms and maples, that define Wellesley's character. They are, in fact, everywhere, lining the narrow two-lane streets, shading front and back yards, composing the forest that establishes the town's northern border. In the summer, Wellesley is awash with green; in autumn, oranges, yellows, reds. The leaves were well into their changing by October 1942, the month the Plaths and the Schobers moved to Wellesley. On the surface, the town, dominated as it was by these trees, projected a picture of charm and hominess. What there was of the town, that is: with only fourteen thousand residents, Wellesley was relatively small. Enclaves of houses, most built in the last four decades, were connected by lanes that bore such archetypal New England names as Brook Street, Green Street, and Elmwood Road. Downtown consisted of several plate-glass-window-fronted stores that lined the main street; a number of churches, among them the Unitarian; a combination town hall–library housed in a huge granite-and-red-sandstone building designed in the French château style; and customary small-town establishments like a post office, a police station, and a firehouse. Perhaps the town's most elegant section was the Wellesley College campus, the wooded grounds dominated not by the stately buildings which created an unmistakable Ivy League aura but by the long sloping hill that overlooked Lake Waban. The town's newest civic structure, completed in 1938, was the Gamaliel Bradford High School, a contemporary red-brick building that boasted a gymnasium, an auditorium, a cafeteria, corridor upon corridor of classrooms, plus metal and wood shops. Connecting Wellesley with Boston were the Worcester Turnpike, the Boston and Albany Railroad, and a modern trolley system—all needed, since many of the town's inhabitants—like Aurelia—worked in Boston.

In many ways, the staid, peaceful façade created by the town was misleading. The Great Depression had ravaged Wellesley throughout the thirties. The town's upper-crust white-collar workers, left unemployed by the failure of countless financial institutions, signed on as menial laborers while their wives took in sewing and knitting. Then, in 1938, the worst hurricane in recent memory had struck. And just as the final stages of the town's long-term rebuilding program neared an end, the harshest blow of all—World War II. A local historian describes Wellesley in late 1942:

> Gas rationing so tight you could scarcely motor beyond the town's borders. Shortages of rubber so you couldn't patch your tires to go anywhere safely, even if you had the gasoline by virtue of a B or C ration book. Town canning kitchens, local knitting circles, endless work on surgical dressing. A town with no young men. Lists of casualties that were the center of daily conversation. The thrill of managing to wangle a rare stick of butter or occasional bit of sugar. Daily life without them, without meat. Horsemeat, soybeans, oleo you had to mix with food coloring to make it acceptable at table. Anxious nights glued to the H. V. Kaltenborn broadcasts of war news. Living rooms with maps spread out so people could trace the action and guess at the locations of their sons' units. A sober dedication to service; long hours of volunteer work, and raising money for refugees. Collecting every bit of metal for the scrap iron collection, including old car bodies that youngsters retrieved from the woods on their carts. Rolling balls of tin foil salvaged from cigarette packages. Victory gardens and war stamps books, filled in by bringing coins to school. A citizens' auxiliary police force, and air raid wardens. Drills. Headlights half blacked out with paint and shades on street lights. Fears, after reports of submarine sightings along the New England coast.

Around the time the Plaths and the Schobers relocated, Frank Senior secured a new job. Because his vision had become impaired by a degenerative eye disease, and because he remembered fondly the years he had supported himself in Europe as a waiter, he applied to become Brookline Country Club's maître d'hôtel, a position with numerous advantages—a good salary and perks—but one significant drawback —a requirement that the maître d' reside at the club during the week and visit home only on weekends. In Winthrop, with Grammy in charge days, Aurelia home nights, and Grampy—the children's name for Frank—present whenever he was not working, Sylvia and Warren had enjoyed a more traditionally European upbringing, as multiple generations harmoniously lived under the same roof. Once they moved to Wellesley and Frank began his Brookline job, the Plath-Schober household turned into a matriarchy—not an altogether positive development, in Aurelia Plath's eyes.

Appreciably smaller than 92 Johnson Avenue, 26 Elmwood Road contained, downstairs, one bedroom, one bath, a living room, a dining room, a kitchen, and a screened-in sitting room that connected the house to a single-car garage. Upstairs consisted of two bedrooms and a second bath. The Schobers took the first-floor bedroom, and Warren required a bedroom of his own (he and Sylvia were too old to share a room), so Sylvia was relegated to the third bedroom, which she had to share with her mother. For a young girl approaching her teenage years, these living arrangements could have been better. Yet Sylvia faced far greater strains. The move to Wellesley itself represented a source of anxiety. She had to worry about making friends, adjusting to a different school, and learning her way around unfamiliar places. But this seemed nothing compared with the pain she still felt over the death of her father. The tragic loss of a parent can crack the foundations of any child's personality. To Sylvia, her father's death proved even more troubling because he could have prevented it merely by getting medical help. In a real way, Otto had willed himself to die, had committed, as Sylvia would later confide to friends, a kind of suicide. Therefore, when Sylvia thought about her father's death, she became more confused, not less. How could her father, an international expert in the field of biology, so misdiagnose his own case?

To ground her daughter in this time of uncertainty, Aurelia decided to enroll Sylvia at Wellesley's Marshall Perrin Elementary School not in the sixth grade, which she had started in Winthrop, but in the fifth. Holding Sylvia back a year, which would allow her to study familiar subjects, might help her navigate this period of transition in her life. It would also narrow the two-year age gap between Sylvia and her fellow students, a result of Sylvia's having started the first grade at age four. Aurelia now feared that if the gap persisted Sylvia might grow up physically, emotionally, and socially out of step with her peers. The move to Wellesley provided the perfect chance to carve one year off that difference. So, in Wellesley, Sylvia, thanks to a lightened academic workload, had time to pursue such extracurricular activities as piano,

Girl Scouts, and reading, and to establish neighborhood friendships. One of note was with Betsy Powley, a cute ten-year-old who lived nearby on Parker Road.

Aurelia also made several friends in Wellesley. One woman to whom she would become especially close was Mildred Norton, the wife of a colleague of Otto's. Since the friendship brought their families together, the Norton boys—Dick, Perry, and David—were soon visiting with the Plath children either at 26 Elmwood Road or at the Nortons' home in Wellesley Fells, a Wellesley subdivision. The families saw each other regularly at the Unitarian church, after Aurelia, who had been raised Catholic but wanted a more open religion, converted to Unitarianism. Before long, the Plaths and the Nortons had become so intimate that Sylvia and Warren referred to Mildred Norton as Aunt Mildred, just as the Norton boys called Aurelia Aunt.

In February 1943, Aurelia suffered an acute gastric hemorrhage, for which she was hospitalized for three weeks; she then convalesced a fourth week at Dorothy's home before resuming a regular routine. Sylvia and Warren endured the crisis well; their grades never slipped. But, by June, both children longed for a vacation. This summer, their first inland, would be considerably different. To amuse herself without the help of the ocean, Sylvia drew pictures, read books, wrote—and sunbathed, an obsession she had her whole life. And because trees dominate Wellesley's landscape just as water does Winthrop's, Sylvia took to climbing a backyard apple tree in whose branches, thick with the scent of blossoms or, later in the season, apples themselves, she would sit for hours as she read and wrote. Sylvia's playtime with Betsy also involved foliage. "I'll never forget what she and I did that first summer we were friends," remembers Powley. "Behind my house, the land sloped off down into a valley. It was all thick woods, and there was a little brook on either side of the valley. The woods were full of ferns. What we did was, we went down and built a hut in the woods. We'd frame it up with little saplings; then we would weave ferns into the sapling to build an igloolike fern hut. In the rear part of the hut we had a secret room where we could hide. The hut was gorgeous, as huts go. We played in it a lot that summer—two girls happy and innocent, seemingly without a care in the world."

Seemingly, for early in the summer Aurelia's ulcer had hemorrhaged again. In July, while Aurelia recovered, Sylvia attended Girl Scout camp in New Hampshire. Occasionally, she showed in her postcards home the dread she felt over her mother's health: she included deceptively short passages that asked how she felt or expressed her concern because she did not write regularly. After camp, Sylvia returned to Wellesley for August—and more sunning, writing, and playing in the fern hut with Betsy. In September, she entered sixth grade, and in this year her achievements remained high. That spring semester alone, she read so many books that on May 3 she earned an honor certificate from the state Division of Public Libraries' Department of Education. One month later, the school awarded her a similar certificate.

Sylvia did not devote *all* of her time to academic pursuits. Like any eleven-year-old, she livened many of her nights by listening to the radio, especially "The Jack Benny Show" and "The Lone Ranger." One highlight of the late winter of 1944 occurred when Aunt Dorothy treated Sylvia and Warren to *Lassie Come Home,* starring Roddy McDowall and Elizabeth Taylor. But mostly Sylvia drew, wrote, and read. True to form, when the spring semester ended on June 16 (she received her string of A's and B's), Sylvia celebrated the arrival of summer by reading—in two days—*Gone with the Wind,* a book she had now read three times.

That summer, following a month of Girl Scout camp, Sylvia passed August relaxing in Wellesley. In early September, she started the seventh grade at Alice L. Phillips Junior High. Now, approaching adolescence, Sylvia became concerned about her popularity. After adjusting to Phillips in the fall, she made a concerted effort to develop her social life in the spring. Although she did quit Girl Scouts, she served as vice-president for her guidance (homeroom) class, for that same class managed Defense Stamps (stamps sold to support the American effort in the war), and joined the girls' basketball team. In addition, she attended various social functions, often escorted by boys. Outside school, she found time to draw, study music, read, and write. In 1944, she wrote the story "The Thrilling Journey of a Penny" and mapped out a novel to be narrated by a girl named Nancy; in the fall, she finished several poems, among them "In the Corner of My Garden" and "A Wish upon a Star." By spring, Sylvia was writing poetry at an astonishing rate and a surprising level of sophistication. She had also become adamant about saving her poems, copying them into one of three books—a scrapbook, a diary, or a document she called *Life Poem Book*. She continued to publish, now in the junior-high newspaper, *The Phillipian*, which printed not only her poems but her drawings.

On January 20, 1945, Aurelia took Sylvia and Warren into Boston to see the Colonial Theatre's production of *The Tempest*, the children's first play. After reading both Lamb's version and Shakespeare's original, Sylvia and Warren eagerly awaited the show, which did not disappoint them. "They were completely transported to the magic land of Prospero," Aurelia wrote in a note to herself at the time, "and Sylvia, in particular, will remember the enchantment that was continued on the train ride home. Everything conspired together to make this a celestial occasion—even the snowstorm that had been predicted to strike blizzard-force this day withheld itself. The sun shone instead on the piles of snow already heaped everywhere; the children were well, and their spirits ready and eager for transport, ready to receive 'such stuff as dreams are made of.'" Sylvia would also remember, specifically, certain speeches, characters, and lines from the play for years to come. That night, as she sat spellbound in the audience, she saw onstage for the first time the airy spirit Ariel, released from more than a decade of captivity in a tree by his liberator, Prospero. She marveled at the supernatural workings of Prospero, who, finally seeing the error of his ways, decides to give up "this rough magic." And she heard a poem whose subject rang chillingly true for her. About the death of a father, "Ariel's Song" reads:

> Full Fathom Five thy father lies;
>   Of his bones are coral made;
> Those are pearls that were his eyes:
>   Nothing of him that doth fade
> But doth suffer a sea-change
> Into something rich and strange.
> Sea-nymphs hourly ring his knell.

3

In the spring of 1945, while sitting for a portrait on April 12, President Franklin D. Roosevelt collapsed and died. Hearing the news on the radio, Sylvia wrote in her diary, at the top of that day's page, "Roosevelt Dies." Then, only days after Harry Truman assumed the presidency, a series of startling Allied victories forced Germany and Italy to surrender on May 7. As Sylvia listened to the car horns and firecrackers, it sounded as if all of Wellesley would erupt in celebration. Now, there was only the war in the South Pacific. Still, to Sylvia, the arrival of June meant not just the end of another academic year but the prospect that her Uncle Frank might come home. For her scholastic achievement— her final report card contained seven A's and a B in music—Sylvia received an honor certificate for reading; commendation cards for "her unusual creative work in English," for "her outstanding quality of oral and written work, for her careful application to daily work, and for her helpfulness in class discussion," and for her "excellence in taking care of war stamps sales"; and the seventh grade's Wellesley Award.

On July 1, the Powleys drove Sylvia and Betsy to Camp Helen Storrow in Buzzards Bay, Massachusetts. At Storrow, where she was overseen by, as she called them, the "Ash" Trio—Dash, the camp leader; Flash, her assistant; and Splash, the person in charge of water sports—Sylvia pursued such time-honored camp activities as hiking, picnicking, and swimming. Judging from her letters home, the activity she enjoyed most was eating. At one lunch alone, she consumed six plates of chicken-and-vegetable casserole, five cups of punch, and a scoop of ice cream. If the family was running low on ration points when she came home, she wrote to her mother after describing a meal, they could slaughter her and eat her for pork.

Once she returned to Wellesley on July 15, Sylvia entertained herself for a week, practicing the piano. Her favorite pieces included Beethoven's "Moonlight Sonata," Paderewsky's "Minute," Deeme's "Tarentelle," and Bohrom's "The Murmuring Brook." On the 23rd, the Plaths traveled to Oxford, Maine—by train to Portland, by bus from there—to visit Sylvia's friend Margot Loungway's family at their summer home. They stayed until August 8, during which time the children worked on the farm and Sylvia wrote poems about shooting stars and northern lights. On a layover in Portland on the train ride home, Aurelia picked up a newspaper in which Sylvia read the initial reports about the bombing of Hiroshima. One cold statistic—60 percent of the city lay in ruins—struck her hardest. Two days later, Sylvia read accounts of the chaotic state of affairs the bombing had produced in Japan. The descriptions of the destruction of Hiroshima and (subsequently) Nagasaki sounded as horrific as new tales coming from Europe—reports about German concentration camps and the execution of Jews. By the 14th, peace in the Pacific appeared near. Throughout the day, which Sylvia passed by reading *Separate Star,* radio reports depicted Japan hovering on the verge of surrender. At seven o'clock, during supper, came official word from Washington: Hirohito had forwarded to Truman a note that read, "We surrender unconditionally."

In this time of optimism, Sylvia entered the eighth grade at Phillips on September 6, 1945. Six days later, her homeroom elected her its president. For Sylvia's birthday, Ruth Freeman arrived for a spend-the-night party. In the spring term, Sylvia maintained a heavy reading schedule of novels like *The Scarlet Pimpernel, Twenty Thousand Leagues Under the Sea,* and *Pride and Prejudice.* Also in the spring term, Sylvia—now thirteen and a full-fledged teenager—developed a keen interest in boys. In February 1946, she and Perry Norton attended a Unitarian church dance and a Girl Scouts' Valentine's Day party at which they played spin-the-bottle, much to Perry's disgust. Then, in April, Dick Mills, a friend, took Sylvia to a small dance party at Donnie Russell's. In the Russells' basement playroom, four teenage couples ate cookies, drank Coca-Colas, and danced to music playing on the phonograph. For Sylvia, the evening's climax occurred at the moment she settled down on the sofa next to Dick Cunningham—another friend—and he slipped his arm around her shoulder, a move that prompted Dick Mills to rush over and ask for a dance. The next day, visiting Ruth in Winthrop, Sylvia met an old friend, Wayne Sterling, who made such an impression on her that she dreamed about him for nights.

In July, after earning all A's for the year, Sylvia went back to Camp Helen Storrow, this summer with Betsy and Ruth. There the girls swam, took arts-and-crafts classes, and put on a minstrel show in which, even though she had a teenager's squawky voice, Sylvia performed as guest star—Frank Sinatra—because she had, according to the other campers, who unanimously chose her, the "perfect" build. Though she may have found Storrow's cuisine awful, Sylvia ate heartily anyway, normally overindulging herself like a glutton. One day at lunch, she finished two bowls of vegetable soup, one slice of bread, two portions of raisin-and-carrot salad, two portions of potatoes and cabbage, a slice of cake, and seven cups of milk.

At Storrow, Sylvia was frugal. In all four weeks of camp, she spent only three dollars, most of it on crafts, stamps, and writing supplies. Indeed, one of the memorable episodes of the summer involved money. On July 17, Sylvia's unit hiked two miles to a blueberry farm whose owner paid the girls ten cents for each quart they could pick. Taking off only for lunch and a brief rest period, the girls picked berries from the fruit-laden bushes all day. Sylvia and Ruth worked in tandem and picked twenty quarts, which netted one dollar for each of them. Sylvia felt anxious about earning extra money to help pay for camp—or so she wrote to her mother that night in a letter she signed "Sylvia," a break from her recent practice of employing the nicknames "Sivvy" and "Siv." The day had been, according to Sylvia, her best yet at camp.

Following Storrow, which concluded on July 27, Ruth and Sylvia visited each other—first in Wellesley, then in Winthrop. When she was not discussing her newest fascination—boys—Sylvia thought about her true love—writing. In August, she sifted through a sheaf of poems she had written over the past nine years and decided to select, order chronologically, and copy by hand in a composition notebook those she considered to be her best. Illustrating many poems with crayon or ink drawings, she called her anthology *Poems by Sylvia Plath.* After she read *A Tale of Two Cities, Oliver Twist,* and *David Copperfield* in early September, she started the ninth grade. Coming home on the first day, September 16, 1946, Sylvia found her mother and brother chatting with a stranger—a cute, athletically trim, expressive boy about Warren's age. He introduced himself—his name was Philip McCurdy—and Sylvia became intrigued. On that day and over the next several weeks, Philip told her much about his young life.

Philip had grown up in a household consisting of his grandmother, his mother, and two older sisters. He believed his father had died by falling from a ladder while painting the house. But in sixth grade, he examined his permanent-record card and learned that his sister was actually his mother. Confronting his family, Philip was told that, as she worked as a waitress at the Belmont Hotel in Bermuda in the summer of 1934, his mother/"sister" had become pregnant. She had moved with her mother from their home in Brookline to West Roxbury, and it was there that she gave birth to her baby—Philip. Afterwards, the three of them returned to Brookline, where Philip's grandmother claimed the baby as her own. Life remained fairly normal until Philip discovered the truth. The man who had fallen to his death while painting—this episode did occur—was actually his grandfather. Philip's father was still very much alive, although through the years he had maintained no contact with Philip's family. To make matters even more complicated, Philip's mother had married soon after Philip's discovery. At present, his mother, his stepfather, and Philip all lived together in a house in Wellesley, on Durant Street, having moved there just days before school started. In a manner of speaking, Philip had *three* fathers—a stepfather, a "ghost" father (his real father, whom he had never met), and a "dead" father (the man who fell from the ladder). Sylvia became fascinated. As she struggled with her own father's death, a subject about which she spoke to Philip but never freely, Philip's story reassured Sylvia. Here was someone with a father situation more complicated than hers.

Soon Sylvia and Philip became close friends. Often, after school, they went on hikes or long bike rides. On clear nights, they would sneak out, climb up to the top of Honeywell Hill, and, lying on their backs on the damp ground, study the constellations. Before long, they were asking obvious questions. Were they "brother" and "sister"? Boyfriend and girlfriend? Simply soul mates? And, in the end, did it matter?

Except for the arrival of Philip, the fall of 1946 resembled any other autumn. Outside of school, Sylvia wrote and saw boys; principal among them was Wayne Sterling, her Winthrop friend, whom she described in her diary as (oddly enough) extremely boring. The spring term, her last in junior high, began on a low note. On January 17, 1947, she lost in her attempt to become class secretary. Five days later, a boy defeated her for first place in a spelling bee; she was appeased somewhat since, as she wrote in her diary, she believed it was always better for a boy to be ahead of a girl. After this, the semester turned around. At a series of assembly dances, she was as popular as any girl there. The semester's most eventful dance, however, was March 7's, an event to which she was escorted by Wayne Sterling.

Before the dance, Sylvia and Wayne, who took the bus over from Winthrop to spend the night at the Plaths', listened to "The Anniversary Song." Following supper, Wayne put on his tuxedo, Sylvia her black dress, and they went to the school. In the dim light of the gymnasium, Wayne and Sylvia danced for hours. Later, at home, Warren rose to join them for a snack and a chat which lasted until bedtime. The next morning, when Sylvia came down for breakfast, Wayne would hardly speak to her—much to her surprise. After breakfast, Sylvia confronted him and forced him to reveal that, before he and Warren had gone to sleep in Warren's room, Warren had shown him Sylvia's diary. The section in which Sylvia described him as being boring had hurt him badly. Deeply concerned, Sylvia tried to explain the affront: she often wrote passages in her diary that she did not mean moments later, she said. Regardless of Sylvia's efforts, the damage was done. Their day, which included walks to Wellesley College and to Morse's Pond, remained tense. As Wayne boarded the late-afternoon bus for Winthrop, Sylvia concluded that she would never hear from him again. So, when he called at seven-forty-five to apologize for reading her most private thoughts, Sylvia felt relieved. All's well that ends well—this is what she wrote in her diary for that day.

On April 13, Sylvia started a correspondence with Hans-Joachim Neupert, a Ruckersdorf, Germany, teenager who would become her pen pal. In her first letter, she revealed that she hoped to grow up to become a foreign correspondent, a journalist, a writer, or an artist. To this end, she continued to read and write, besides maintaining a demanding academic schedule that once again culminated with excellent grades. At final assembly, she won a fifth and a sixth school letter; a school pendant and a commendation card for being the only student in the school's history to earn enough credits to win a sixth letter; a copy of Robert Penn Warren's *Understanding Poetry* for being a "special student"; an achievement certificate for winning first place in a national art contest sponsored by the Carnegie Institute; and commendation cards for punctuality and for earning all A's and B's during her three years of junior-high school. On June 17, her last day of school, seventy-five friends autographed her yearbook.

Hoping for a change this summer, Sylvia attended—alone—the Vineyard Sailing Camp, but its activities ended up duplicating those of other camps. On the Vineyard, she seemed truly to enjoy only one function—eating. She consumed such enormous meals that, at five feet eight inches in height, she might have been expected to weigh more than 119 pounds. On July 10, after just two weeks, Sylvia went home to Wellesley, where she would remain for the rest of the summer.

4

On September 8, 1947, the first day of classes at Gamaliel Bradford High School, Wilbury Crockett, compact in build, soft-spoken, bespectacled, stood before his students in Room 216 and, using his trademark grammar-perfect sentences, listed the demands he expected of them for the coming academic year. In sophomore English, students would cover American literature—Melville, Hawthorne, Faulkner, and so on. British literature would come junior year; world, senior. This year, students would read forty-five major works—novels, long poems, plays. There would be no tests. Instead, each student would write four five-thousand-word essays that, standing before class, he would read and defend. In short, since Crockett considered it his duty to prepare students for college (in fact, many former students matriculated at Ivy League schools), he would run his course like a college seminar. Among the thirty or so students who had gathered at the U-shaped table to listen to Crockett's opening lecture was Sylvia. She had never heard a teacher speak with such inspiration about literature. Because of this, she looked forward to the year—indeed, the next three, for Crockett taught all advanced English at Bradford. Yet not every student did; many considered Crockett too demanding. These shied away from (or were awed by) the "Crocketteers," the students who admired Crockett's challenging, probing brand of instruction so much that they revered him almost like a guru.

On September 9, when he walked into Room 216 to see that after his opening-day lecture a good third of the class had transferred to a less demanding section, Crockett said with a smile, "It seems we've had quite a desertion." Along with the other remaining students, Sylvia laughed at Crockett's joke. The last thing she would do, she thought, was transfer out of *this* class. For all of her academic career, she had been waiting for a teacher who, through his wit and intelligence, could push her to live up to her abilities. Now she had found him. She took other interesting courses, which were a part of the college-preparatory curriculum track for which she had signed up at Bradford—Latin, math, French, art, orchestra, gym—but she truly savored only one class, English. To Sylvia, Crockett was, as Sylvia would describe him, "the teacher of a lifetime."

From the start, Crockett rewarded her enthusiasm. One day near the beginning of the term, he made students read aloud paraphrases they had written the night before. When the last paper was read, he asked which one the students thought was the best. "Sylvia's," John Pollard said immediately. "I decidedly think so," Crockett added. Indeed, Crockett encouraged Sylvia so much that during the initial week of school she wrote her first poem since May. Later, in early October, she handed in four new poems. After he read the group aloud, Crockett told the class that he believed Sylvia had a natural lyrical gift. Also, "I Thought That I Could Not Be Hurt," one of his two favorites ("Alone and Alive" was the other), displayed a quality rare to a poem written by a fourteen-year-old—a deeply felt sense of anguish. Based on an actual episode in which Grammy accidentally blurred one of Sylvia's pastel still-lifes when she tossed an apron on a table, the poem's meaning hinges on the pivotal lines in which the narrator responds to the mundane occurrence—the blurring of a pastel—by revealing that it left her in a "dull and aching void." The use of these words seems hardly fitting yet represents an early window into Plath's potentially extreme emotional states. The narrator's solipsism notwithstanding, the poem impressed Crockett with its technical skill and strong, if peculiar, sentiments. Sylvia was thrilled over Crockett's comments, the only inspiration she needed to write even more poems.

In the fall, while she studied diligently, Sylvia also developed a social life. In junior high, as she passed through that awkward physical stage and became interested in boys, she had placed importance on being accepted by her contemporaries. Now, in high school, she tried even harder to fit in. She attended Saturday football games; joined the staff of *The Bradford,* the newspaper for which she wrote feature articles; and participated in basketball and orchestra. Early in the year, she had waited for the school's two sororities, Sugar 'n' Spice and Sub-Deb, to extend membership invitations. When Sub-Deb asked her to pledge, Sylvia accepted and submitted herself to an initiation week that required her to serve as slave to a Big Sister, embarrass herself publicly when a sister told her to (by hanging from a tree limb or insulting a stranger), and refrain from washing or combing her hair and from wearing makeup. (Later, offended by the condescending manner with which members treated nonmembers, Sylvia resigned the sorority.)

As the fall progressed, Sylvia attended other social functions. In early November, dressed in a peach gown and accompanied by her friend Prissy Steele, Sylvia went to her first high-school formal, an occasion on which she danced with numerous boys. Three weeks later, wearing a velvet dress and joined this time by Perry Norton, Sylvia took in another formal. Again she danced with many boys, although the high spot of the evening took place as Sylvia, Perry, and another couple stole a picture of a football player, which had been positioned among the decorations on a table, so that they could give it to him at school on Monday morning. After this, Sylvia and Perry danced the last dance together. Then, his arm clutched firmly around her, Perry walked her home.

That spring term, Sylvia attended assembly dances, had a crush on Tom Duggan, and went to her first junior prom, to which her friend

John Pollard was her escort even though she preferred Perry Norton. Also, she fostered new friendships with girls her own age, among them Patricia O'Neil and Louise Geisey. Meanwhile, she continued to chalk up academic and creative successes. R. H. White presented her with a certificate of merit to mark the inclusion of her artwork in a student exhibition at Carnegie Institute. She finished more poems, many of which Crockett admired. In particular, in March, she wrote "Youth's Appeal for Peace," her most ambitious effort yet. The poem's first section, "The Storm Clouds Gather," paints a picture of a desert—its loneliness is defined by a solitary plant—on which a storm forms in the distance. The second, "The Approach of the Horsemen," depicts four horsemen riding across the desert as bombs explode and a wind echoes four words—war, famine, sickness, death. The third, "The Appeal," documents the plant's plea for the horsemen to turn back so that the youth of the world will have a chance to mature, a plea with which the horsemen comply. Its statement marred by a naïve idealism, the poem does represent another step in her evolution as a serious, if still somewhat innocent, poet.

On July 1, 1948, after she received for her sophomore year all A's save for a B in orchestra, Sylvia returned to the Vineyard Sailing Camp, joined this summer by Betsy Powley and Ruth Freeman. Once they had unpacked by flashlight on their first night there, "The Three Musketeers," as they called themselves, spent the following days swimming, sailing, and visiting with friends. A week into her stay, Sylvia concluded that she had become too old for camp. She would return next year only as a counselor, she decided, although even that idea did not excite her. Next summer she would concentrate on art and writing.

In early September, Sylvia started her junior year, perhaps *the* most academically challenging in high school. Taking English, Latin, French, American history, math, and art, she performed effectively in the fall term; she also worked hard in the spring. In March, the month when she won an achievement key in the Scholastic Art Awards Competition from R. H. White, she and Jeanne Woods, speaking on behalf of the members of English 31, composed a letter to Columbia University's Irwin Edman. In that month's issue of *The Atlantic Monthly*, Edman had published "A Reasonable Life in a Mad World," an article in which he suggested that modern man should rely on his own ability to reason logically in order to further society. Distressed by the idea, the Crocketteers contended that in order to live fully—and not just survive—man also should embrace the universe's spiritual element and celebrate "the inner compulsion of every man to seek beyond himself for guidance." If we accept divinity and grow spiritually, Plath and Woods wrote, then and only then will we understand the nature of human life. ("Your letter states very well some of the traditional beliefs about the nature of the universe," Edman later replied in a curt note, "but these beliefs have often been questioned, and I must ask you to wait until you get to college to hear them discussed more thoroughly.") Finally, near the end of the term, *The Bradford* selected next year's co-editors—Plath and Frank Irish. In 'BRADFORD' ANNOUNCES INCOMING EDITORS, an article that ran in June, the staff predicted that, because of her "exceptional ability as a writer" and because she had "not only . . . a keen critical eye, but also the noteworthy reputation of sticking to a task until it is done—a quality that will stand her in good stead in next year's work," Plath would be "an exceedingly able editor." In June, Plath also received a year-end report card of straight A's plus such additional accolades as an honorable mention in *The Atlantic Monthly*'s annual student-poetry contest, a distinction she had now earned two years' running.

Too old to go to camp, even, she decided, as a counselor, Sylvia remained in Wellesley during the summer of 1949. For employment, she baby-sat for neighborhood families, earning about seventy-five dollars in spending money. In her free time, she worked on poems and stories, several of which she submitted to magazines. She saw her friends—Philip McCurdy, Pat O'Neil, Louise Geisey. But mostly she filled her summer by dating a dozen different boys. In fact, during this summer Sylvia experienced her true sexual awakening, which in the late forties could only spell confusion. Over the past couple of years, as she felt attracted to boys, she became anxious. If she was drawn to a boy physically, she dared not act on her desires for fear of being labeled "easy." On the other hand, society's standards allowed—one might even argue, encouraged—boys to "have intercourse," as she called it. Confronted with this hypocritical double standard, Sylvia did not know what *she* should do. Though emotionally mature and sexually curious, she would never permit herself to move beyond kissing and hugging. Nonconsummative clitoral experimentation was so exotic as to be foreign. Having intercourse was out of the question. Not that Sylvia did not *want* to; the subject seemed to hover in the back of her mind all the time. During the past year, she had written about sex in her journal, once meditating on her own virginity. In one particular passage, she described how she longed to be dominated by a man, for only then, she said, did she feel *she* could be dominant.

Sylvia would spend the summer of 1949 struggling with issues of sexuality. At the local tennis courts in early June, when Bob Reidemann, a friend, introduced her to Denison University student John Hodges, she and Hodges played tennis for hours. Hodges's tendency to yell at her for missing a ball did not seem to bother her; the next day, when she bumped into Hodges again at the courts, she engaged in a conversation that resulted in their dating the rest of the month. The breakup of their brief courtship started with Sylvia's trip to Portsmouth, New Hampshire, for a week-long Unitarian conference in late June. While staying at the Oceanic Hotel, with a friend named Ginny, Sylvia dated several boys; two were a bellhop from Wellesley to whom Ginny had introduced her and a boy from Kentucky with whom she spent an afternoon lunching, strolling the beach, and watching basketball on television. On July 6, after she had returned to Wellesley, and was ready to play the field, Sylvia went with Paul Hezlett to the King Philip, a club in Wrentham. A pleasant sprawling one-story building approached by a manicured driveway, the club featured, out back overlooking a lake, a polished-stone terrace on which Sylvia and Paul danced. The evening's denouement occurred as the couple bumped into Bruce Elwell and Rod Leavell, both with dates. After the three couples had retired to the bar, and Bruce, by speaking French, convinced the waitress to serve him a Tom Collins—at eighteen, Bruce was well below the state's legal drinking age of twenty-one—Sylvia vowed to herself that she would go out with him eventually.

Which she did, two days later—Bruce took her to the stock-car races—and then for the rest of the summer. Of all the boys she had dated so far, Bruce was the most worldly. At a party at Rod's in mid-

July, he offered Sylvia a sip of his bourbon and ginger ale, her first taste of alcohol. Afterwards, outside on Rod's terrace, as they lay on a lounge chair and looked up into the black sky, Sylvia and Bruce kissed until Sylvia felt tempted to go further, although she did not. Ten days later, on yet another date with Bruce, she was tempted again. While they sat in their seats at the stock-car races, the brightly painted cars barreling around the speedway below them, Sylvia said cryptically to Bruce that she hoped to see a thrilling wreck, whereupon, in the second turn, a car spun out of control and crashed over the guard rail and high-wire fence into the crowd. Ambulances arrived to take away the injured—seven all together. Following this, Bruce drove Sylvia home; with the crash only miles behind them, they necked wildly in his car. Again Sylvia thought about the—now—familiar question: how far should she go? Even if she wanted to explore her sexual emotions to the fullest, she knew that she should not. Only days before, her relationship with John Hodges had ended because, according to Hodges, Sylvia had "forced" the issue.

It had been a dreary, rainy day. After John called on her in the morning, they drove around that afternoon until they stopped at Fell's Playground. Once Sylvia had told him about the playground's history, John said, "I've run out of conversation." She agreed and they suddenly embraced. Her face buried in his shoulder, Sylvia said that she thought he was nice. Then John whispered, "I think you're wonderful," and kissed her. Later, dropping her off at home, John implied that Sylvia had staged the whole scene just to trick him into kissing her. His accusation made Sylvia admit, to herself but not to him: this morning she had decided she did want to kiss him—*today*. And now she had. Perhaps subconsciously she *had* staged the scene. At what price, though—the risk of John's breaking up with her because she was easy? Frustrated, Sylvia went on a date that night with Paul Hezlett (they saw the Ann Blythe movie *Red Canyon* in Boston) but could hardly kiss him good night. Days later, on that night in Bruce's car, Sylvia did not make another mistake. They went only "so far," and then at *his* instigation.

In August, Sylvia dated several boys besides Bruce. One was John

Hall, whom she met through a friend. In the month they spent together—he returned to Williams College in mid-September—they played tennis, scaled Dean's Tower, went to the nightclub Totem Pole, and cruised in John's car. The day Sylvia would remember all winter was August 30. That morning, Sylvia and John drove to John's friend Hoka's house in West Falmouth. In the afternoon, Sylvia went swimming with John and Hoka, remarked on John's body (she considered it perfect), and then later, with John alone, drove into town. Here they ran into friends of John's, one of whom, a girl, purred to him, "Oh, you big, handsome brute!" Hearing the comment, Sylvia shot back, "Isn't he, though?" She felt pleased, as she told her diary, that he belonged to her. The next evening, Sylvia and John cuddled in the front seat of his car at the drive-in in Dedham. As the movie flickered before them on the screen, they discussed various subjects. At one point, even though they had known each other only a matter of days, they actually touched on marriage.

Then summer ended. Over the last year Sylvia had dated some twenty boys. None compared to John Hall, who believed, he told Sylvia, that "love is more than just a physical attraction" (he knew a couple who "had intercourse" almost weekly—"like a couple of dogs") and that a tender kiss, the kind they shared, "doesn't mean passion or emotion— just love." So, when she began her senior year, in September 1949, the same month Warren started Exeter on scholarship and she finally had a bedroom of her own, Sylvia struggled to force John from her thoughts. With college approaching, she had to commit herself to this year's classes: world literature, college biology, United States history, French III, advanced art (painting), and gym.

Soon after school started, Sylvia began considering the colleges to which she would apply. Naturally, she would approach Wellesley College, since she seemed to be a shoo-in for a town scholarship. Also, Sylvia had decided to try Smith College, one of the premier women's colleges in America. In her letter of application, dated November 7, 1949, Plath stated that she wanted to attend Smith because the school provided an excellent faculty, generous offerings in art and English, and a large number of scholarships. However, she did not mention one underlying reason that Smith appealed to her: its location in Northampton, Massachusetts, one hundred miles—and a lengthy train ride—from Wellesley. If she hoped to mature as a person, she had to cut the apron strings, she believed—a conclusion with which Aurelia agreed.

In her letter of application, Plath stressed her achievements and prizes; her membership in organizations such as the Unitarian church's Young People's Association, the high-school yearbook staff, the girls' basketball team, and the World Federalist Organization; and her commitment to a study of world literature. To exemplify her reading habits, she provided a selected bibliography of works she had finished recently. It included Plato's *Republic*, Aeschylus's *Agamemnon*, Ruskin's *Sesame and Lilies*, Emerson's essays, A. E. Housman's *A Shropshire Lad*, Eliot's *The Waste Land*, Sherwood Anderson's *Winesburg, Ohio*, Thomas Mann's *Buddenbrooks* and *Doctor Faustus*, Hardy's *Return of the Native*, Wharton's *Ethan Frome*, Undset's *Kristen Lavransdatter*, Huxley's *Point Counter Point*, Willa Cather's *My Ántonia* and *Death Comes for the Archbishop*, and Sinclair Lewis's *Main Street* and *Arrowsmith*. Along with her letter, Plath submitted a standard application form. She also requested for Smith the results of her Scholastic Achievement Test. On it, she had scored respectably—700 in the verbal and 567 in math, for a total of 1,267—if not as well as IQ tests, which consistently categorized her as a genius.

To support her application, Plath lined up references from Wilbury Crockett, Mrs. Duane Aldrich (a neighbor), and Bradford Principal Samuel Graves. In his letter, which he did not write until February 1950, Graves wrote:

> Sylvia is a superior candidate for college. She has a keen, analytical, well-disciplined mind and her intellectual interests and power reflect a superior family background as well as her own high standards of academic achievement. In English and in Art she has shown creative ability; in science, mathematics, and language, her capacity for thoroughness is clearly evident; in history her work shows outstanding analytical ability and grasp of principles. . . . She is [someone] who contributes greatly to the morale of a group and uses her talents in serving the group—as editor of the school's newspaper, poster committee and decorating committee, yearbook art staff, and the or-

chestra. In school, in her home, and in her church, she has shown to a marked degree the ability to direct her own work. Following her father's death and her mother's becoming a college instructor, Sylvia has carried many home responsibilities and has taken care of children whenever she could be spared from her own home duties. . . . She will gain much from college and no one could be more eager for a college education. May college mean some "fun" for her as well as intellectual accomplishments.

That fall of 1949, besides studying, Sylvia maintained an active social life, the center of which remained John Hall—at least until Thanksgiving. Before Thanksgiving, all seemed well. On October 28, the day after her seventeenth birthday, Sylvia took the train to Williamstown for a college weekend, her first. John had carefully planned their activities, which included a Friday-night pep rally, the "big" game on Saturday (which Williams lost to Union, 14–6), and a house party following the game. Back home, Sylvia remembered the weekend with pleasure, but, for reasons she could not easily identify, she sensed she did not love John. So, when two boys asked her for dates over the long Thanksgiving weekend, she accepted, even though she knew that John would be in Wellesley. Out of courtesy, Sylvia wrote him about the dates. John's arrival at 26 Elmwood Road for supper on his first night home, an evening they had scheduled well in advance of her letter, was not without tension. After supper, Sylvia finally broke the news to him: though she admired him as a person, she did not love him, and never would. Because of this, she believed that they should break up. John left Sylvia's house, the tears in his eyes belying the smile plastered on his face. Later, she wrote in her journal that, not hearing his car drive off, she cracked the front door open and spotted John sitting in the car slouched over the steering wheel, crying. Peeking out, she could hear his hoarse, throaty sobs. Slamming the door, she rushed upstairs to her bedroom. The next day, Thanksgiving, after she attended a football game with him, she made it clear to John that she meant what she had said about their breaking up. Again they said good-bye, now for the last time.

During the fall, Plath produced a steady stream of poems, completing, among others, "Adolescence," "Lonely Song," "Question,"

"White Phlox," "Gone Is the River," "The Farewell," and "City Streets." Over the last two years she had submitted her work to various magazines. In eight separate batches, she mailed at least thirty poems to *Seventeen.* To *Ladies' Home Journal,* she tried one batch; to *The Atlantic Monthly,* the poem "The Invalid." And to *Mademoiselle* she had sent the story "East Wind." None was accepted. Yet Plath was not deterred. As she anticipated 1950, she planned to mail her work to other publications. And she *did.* In the weeks following Christmas, she submitted four poems to *The Christian Science Monitor* and several stories and poems to *Seventeen.* Again, none was accepted.

Early in the spring term, her final in high school, Plath and Perry Norton composed for Crockett's English class "A Youth's Plea for World Peace," an essay in which the authors argue against President Truman's recent directive to the Atomic Energy Commission to develop the hydrogen bomb further. Once Plath and Norton summarized the president's logic (if the United States remained ahead of the Soviet Union in atomic capability, "there would be no danger of destruction . . . because a nation such as ours which follows humanitarian principles would never be the aggressor or use the bomb to kill anyone," they wrote), they confronted the political issue. "Already we have succeeded in killing and crippling a good part of humanity, and destruction, unfortunately, is always mutual. Is it any wonder, then, that some of us young people feel rebellious when we watch the futile armaments race begin again? How much experience do we need to realize that war solves no problems, but creates them instead?" Government should "see beyond the present dilemma of nationalism" to the potential for world peace, Plath and Norton concluded. "For those of us who deplore the systematic slaughter legalized by war, the hydrogen bomb alone is not the answer."

At Crockett's suggestion, Plath and Norton submitted their essay to *The Christian Science Monitor,* which bought it for five dollars and ran it on March 16, 1950. On that same day, Plath received more good news. After holding her story "And Summer Will Not Come Again" for months, Margot Macdonald finally accepted it for *Seventeen.* Macdonald ended her letter, which stated that Plath would be paid fifteen dollars for the story, by requesting from her a snapshot and a brief biography. Around this time, Plath also tried out for the senior play, J. M. Barrie's *The Admirable Crichton*—"a fantasy in four acts" that would be directed at Bradford by Crockett. To her surprise, Sylvia won a major part, Lady Agatha Lasenby, and received third billing, behind Frank Irish's Ernest Woolley and Richard McKnown's Crichton. On the evening of April 14, the senior class performed the play to a small but enthusiastic audience in the school's auditorium.

During the spring, as she worked hard—one major project involved writing a thirty-page paper on Thomas Mann (whose work, she wrote, stirred in her feelings of patriotism)—Sylvia became tired of social activities. Early in the semester, she had complained to her pen pal Hans Neupert about the meaningless parties at which she saw the same blank faces with fake smiles. Still, in February, she went to Winter Carnival at the University of New Hampshire; she attended a formal on Friday, and, on Saturday, an afternoon ski exhibition, an early dinner, and the "Stardust" dance.

As the term progressed, the major unanswered question was her college plans. Though Wellesley College offered her a town scholarship, Plath had decided that of the two schools she preferred Smith. (She applied to only two schools.) But to go to Smith she would need substantial financial aid since her mother's annual salary, just under $3,700, was not enough for her to cover Smith's yearly cost of $1,600 ($850 for tuition, $750 for room and board). On May 10, 1950, Ruth W. Crawford, director of admissions, wrote to Plath to accept her at Smith. That same day, her request for residency in a "self-help" dormitory, in which a girl worked for one hour a day to reduce her yearly room-and-board fee by $250, was turned down. Despite this setback, she heard much better news from Mary Mensel, director of scholarships and student aid: Plath had won an $850 scholarship. Eight days later, Wellesley's Smith Club, a private organization composed of Smith alumnae, granted her a scholarship of $450. Because this left only $300, a sum Aurelia could handle (though barely), Sylvia went to her high-school graduation, on June 7, in the school's Alumni Hall, happy in the knowledge that she would be going to Smith. After a program that consisted of opening remarks by Mr. Graves; a speech, "The Best Things in Life Are Free," given by Senior Class President William

Moore, Jr.; a keynote address by Brown University Vice-President Bruce M. Bigelow; the singing of the class song, for which Plath had written words, Robert Blakesley music; and a benediction given by Reverend Robert Blakesley, Plath received her diploma. Of the 158 graduates, Plath was first in her class. She was also one of only twenty-three members of the National Honor Society. For the year, she had earned all A's except a B in gym. In her yearbook, she was pictured in two groups, the National Honor Society and the staff of *The Bradford*. Under her senior portrait appeared this character sketch:

> Warm smile . . . Energetic worker . . . Coeditor of Bradford . . . Bumble Boogie piano special . . . Clever with chalk and paints . . . Weekends at Williams . . . Those fully packed sandwiches . . . Basketball and tennis player . . . Future writer . . . Those rejection slips from Seventeen . . . Oh, for a licence.

5

Until the summer of 1950, Sylvia had never held a "real" job. She had baby-sat and sold a handful of poems and stories, but she had generated little more than a trickle of money, nothing like the amount she now needed. After all, for her first semester at Smith, she would have to buy clothes, books, and miscellaneous materials, the cost of which was separate from and above the basic tuition bill, which her scholarships did not fully cover and her mother could barely pay. As a result, that June, Sylvia sought high-paying employment. She passed over summer jobs available to teenagers—a store clerk, say, or a movie-theatre usherette—and applied for and acquired a position that could not have been more out of the ordinary: a field hand on a truck farm in nearby Natick. On June 10, just days after graduation, Sylvia started her twenty-five-dollar-a-week, six-day-per-week job. She got up each morning at six, dressed in her work clothes—faded blue jeans and a cotton shirt —before she rushed downstairs to eat a hearty breakfast and ride her bicycle five miles to the farm. Along the way, she passed through the

Wellesley College campus, where she sometimes stopped to smell the scent of pine needles or notice a squirrel scurry up a tree. On the farm, under the watch of foreman Cyrus Jeness, Sylvia put in an eight-hour workday harvesting beans and radishes, weeding corn, or setting out strawberry runners. On her breaks, she often manned the stand at which customers bought the freshly picked produce. Finally, at the end of her shift, she pedaled back home and then, exhausted and famished, devoured supper, soaked in a hot bath, and fell into bed by nine. The moment she drifted off to sleep—or so it seemed—the alarm rang, and she started her whole routine again.

Appropriately named, Lookout Farm, located on a hilltop, over-looked mound upon mound of rolling green fields. Sylvia loved to stand in the field and stare into the huge blue sky. She also liked to "study" her fellow workers, most of whom were minorities, displaced persons, and college-age teenagers who, like Sylvia, needed money. Out of this group, one boy, Ilo Pill, a tanned, muscular blond who had recently immigrated from Estonia, caught Sylvia's eye. From the start Ilo made a point of trying to talk with her. As they worked in the field, the sun beating down so hot that their clothes stayed soaked with sweat, they discussed subjects as varied as the relative merits of Renaissance painters—in his thick German accent, Ilo, a fledgling artist, mostly talked about Raphael and Michelangelo—and the latest hit single by Frank Sinatra, America's reigning heartthrob. In time, Ilo demonstrated his fondness for Sylvia by giving her a pen-and-ink sketch of the farm he had drawn himself.

Unlike the majority of Lookout Farm's employees, Ilo lived on the premises. Into a cramped room constructed in the barn loft he had stuffed his belongings, which included a huge collection of art supplies. One rainy afternoon well into the summer, Sylvia saw his room first-hand: they had both finished their duties for the day, when Ilo invited her up to look at the drawing of a co-worker he had just completed. However, it was not long after they had climbed the wooden stairs to the barn loft, and he closed the door behind them, that Sylvia learned Ilo's real motive. Once Sylvia had looked at the picture, Ilo suddenly pressed close to her and, forcefully embracing her, crushed her body into his. Then, in the tiny room whose air was thick with the stench

of hay and farm animals, Ilo French-kissed her. Startled, Sylvia struggled free from his grasp. Why did he do that? she demanded. But Ilo
offered her, instead of an explanation, a glass of water. Sylvia bolted
from the room, leaving Ilo standing by himself.

She might have escaped Ilo—she would have nothing else to do
with him that summer—but she could not avoid the larger issue of
sex. "And Summer Will Not Come Again," the story *Seventeen* published in August, deals with a young woman's bittersweet romance.
Appearing in the magazine's "It's All Yours" section and accompanied
by a postage-stamp-size reproduction of Plath's senior portrait and a
contributor's note that ended by revealing that "[j]azz makes [Sylvia]
melt inside, Debussy and Chopin suit her dreamier moods," the story
addressed the issue of unrequited teenage love. One rainy afternoon
in late August, Celia, the story's narrator, reflects back on the summer's
events, which led to her being hurt by "a freckle-faced boy named
Bruce," her former boyfriend. "[T]all, with knife-sharp eyes that can
see right into you and tell what you're thinking," Bruce was, as it turned
out, unfaithful. Meeting at the tennis courts, Celia, sixteen, and Bruce,
nineteen, set out on an innocent romance: they enjoyed canoe rides
on a lake at night, lots of tennis, and dates to an ice-cream parlor. They
would have continued their involvement, Celia states, had she not
accidentally bumped into Bruce and "an adorable blonde girl" walking
out of the ice-cream parlor one afternoon. The next day, when Bruce
tried to make up, Celia angrily rebuffed him, saying their relationship
was over. "All right, Celia," Bruce said. "I won't bother you any more.
I hadn't figured you were like this. My mistake." Alone, Celia found
comfort in a Sara Teasdale poem. "With my own will I turned the
summer from me," the poem's speaker says. "And summer will not
come to me again."

Sylvia identified with Celia. In her diary she revealed that the inspiration for Bruce was John Hodges, who had told her he loved her
and then proceeded to date a cute, blond-haired girl. Readers also
responded favorably to the story. One was Eddie Cohen, a twenty-
one-year-old Chicago college student and English major. In a fan
letter—Plath's first—written in early August, he said with studied
shame that he sometimes nabbed his "kid sister" 's copy of *Seventeen*

to "keep up on my short story technique." After this, he discussed Plath's story in positive but guarded language. "Why it should have so captivated me, I don't fully know. In part, though, it was because I felt that there was a thought behind the story which was expressed rather more subtly than the usual *Seventeen* hit-'em-with-a-brick technique, and also because it seemed that the author (or authoress, as it developed) had an insight into people which was a little above average." In the end, he asked Plath to tell him "a bit more about yourself, or even let me read some more of your writing," adding finally, "I will spend a good deal of time the next few weeks in peering anxiously into the mailbox, so please don't let me down."

Flattered, Sylvia responded on August 6. She confessed her skepticism about his letter; then she proceeded, using a chatty pen-pal prose style, to paint a thumbnail sketch of her life. She lived in a six-room suburban house; her father was dead and her mother taught; she had a younger brother; she planned to enter college next month; and she wanted to be a writer so badly that she had endured the humiliation of receiving fifty rejection slips from an assortment of magazines before a single piece of her creative writing had been accepted. "And Summer Will Not Come Again" had been that first acceptance. When she finished describing herself, Sylvia felt a rush of doubt. What if Eddie was not dealing with her honestly and his letter was a fake? (Unlike Eddie, she considered "And Summer Will Not Come Again" typical *Seventeen* "drivel"—nothing more.) Giving in to her fears, she posed to Eddie an improbable—but to her mind possible—scenario: because he had a bet with Ernest Hemingway on his ability to trick young women writers, maybe Eddie was setting her up to make fun of her in his next letter. Anyway, how on earth had he gotten her home address? (Eddie had mailed his letter to 26 Elmwood Road, not *Seventeen*.) And at what college *was* he an English major? Her walls of defense in place, Sylvia sent the letter.

On August 8, Eddie wrote back. About her address: he had found it in a Boston telephone directory in Marshall Field & Co., that "venerable Chicago institution." About his schooling: after two years on scholarship at the University of Chicago, he now went to Roosevelt College, a school that "owes its fame to the fact that it is a little too liberal for some tastes." About himself: dark-brown-haired and blue-eyed, he was "an even six feet, on the rare occasions when I stand up straight, and have 155 pounds scattered pretty evenly over the frame, not muscle-bound to be sure, but not anemic, either"; preferred informal dress (normally he wore a T-shirt and jeans or a "slightly soiled" sport shirt and slacks); considered himself "unconventional," "semi-bohemian," and a "cynical idealist" although he had been born on affluent Lake Shore Drive ("I've had my share of convertibles and sport coats, dances and socials"); and aspired to be a writer or an artist. "And as for you," he concluded, "I rather like what I know of you so far. . . . So let us have more."

In his letter Eddie did not mention the real circumstances under which he first read "And Summer Will Not Come Again." Strolling through Marshall Field one day, he felt an overpowering force draw him to the magazine rack—and *Seventeen* magazine. Compelled, he scanned the table of contents, ran across Sylvia's name, and read the story straight through as he stood in the middle of the store. Afterwards, he walked over to the section of telephone directories, found the Boston book, and looked up her address. It was almost as if some greater spirit had guided him to Sylvia's story—and to Sylvia—but he could not tell her this. It simply sounded too far-fetched.

It did not matter. On August 11, the day *The Christian Science Monitor* printed in its Youth Section "Bitter Strawberries," her first poem to appear in a national publication, Sylvia answered Eddie's letter. Once she had described her physical appearance—five feet eight, slim, her hair streaked blond by the sun, she was so deeply tanned that women stopped her on the beach to ask what suntan oil she used— Sylvia said, in terms of her personality, she was unconventional, sarcastic, and skeptical. As for religion, she considered herself an atheist by theory, a Unitarian by practice. Next she set out her overriding problem with boyfriends. When they looked at her, they believed that she was not intelligent. Sensing she could trust Eddie, Sylvia finally delved into her family and told him that she was more like her mother than she had been like her father, a college professor and author of a book on bumblebees who was now dead.

Over the next two weeks, Eddie wrote Sylvia four letters—three from Chicago and one from Mexico City, where he went on vacation. In those letters he continued to reveal himself. Although he wanted to go into psychiatry as a profession, since "the workings of people's minds [are] the most fascinating subject which I have yet encountered," he did not have the industry to attend medical school for six years. "[G]enerally labeled [an] atheist," he was really an agnostic. He had once been engaged to a young woman named Bobbe, but had broken things off. And, most surprising to Sylvia, he found himself "in the ridiculous and embarrassing position of being infatuated with a girl I never even met"—Sylvia! "Right now that 1500 miles [the distance from Chicago to Boston], like all chaperones, is becoming rather annoying," Eddie wrote, "and if you don't stop building yourself up to me, you are liable to wake up some morning and find me sitting in a tent on your front lawn." Sylvia answered each letter. Now, as she would in the future, she opened up to Eddie. Maybe he saw the fifteen-hundred-mile chaperone as an obstacle to be overcome; on the contrary, Sylvia regarded it as a buffer that allowed her to reveal herself to Eddie without risking any physical—or romantic—involvement.

That August, Sylvia continued to submit poems and stories to magazines, and at mid-month, *Seventeen* bought "Ode to a Bitten Plum." She constantly ran errands, now that Smith was only weeks away. She also dated throughout the month. Of those dates, one Saturday night would stand out in her mind. After Emile, a temporary boyfriend, picked her up for a double date with Warren (a friend) and Warren's girlfriend, they all drove to Ten Acres, a local dance club. Unable to buck her all-American-virgin persona, Sylvia ordered ginger ales while her three friends drank beer. Following a long chat, Emile took Sylvia out onto the dance floor, where, their talk having broken the ice, they embraced affectionately as they danced. Soon, in an open display of sexuality, Emile rubbed his body so forcibly into Sylvia's that she felt his erect penis against her stomach. Aroused, Sylvia pressed her breasts hard against his chest. Before the dance ended, Emile buried his face in her hair and whispered hoarsely, "Don't look at me." Why? she asked. "I've come out of a swimming pool, hot and wet."

Later, at Warren's, after a drive during which they necked in the back seat of the car, Emile and Sylvia slow-danced in the faint light of

the living room to music drifting from a phonograph. Still later, in the
dark kitchen, Emile kissed her again. "You don't give a damn about
me, except physically," Sylvia said, and Emile responded by kissing
her even more forcefully. Finally, Emile drove her home. Upstairs in
bed, Sylvia thought about the night. She hated Emile for the very
injustice she had accused him of—not caring about her "except
physically"—yet she also felt a strong sexual attraction towards him.
This was, in fact, her predicament. She wanted to act on her sexual
urges but could not because she was afraid she would be labeled "fast"
and lose the respect of the very boys she hoped to date.

On September 1, after ten weeks, Sylvia quit her Lookout Farm job.
In sum, she regarded the experience with pleasure. From the white-
collar, cerebral household in which she lived, she had ventured out
into a world where she worked with her hands in the dirt beside people
who were often less fortunate than she. In addition, she adored, as she
had in those summers when she played on Winthrop's beaches, being
outside. Early in September, Sylvia reflected on her weeks at Lookout
Farm in an essay entitled "Rewards of a New England Summer," which
The Christian Science Monitor ran on the 12th. In a move that would
become habit throughout her life, Sylvia took recent personal events
and, because she wanted both the money and the prestige that resulted
from publication, used them as the basis for a piece of creative work.
As she would also do in the future, she manipulated those events to
achieve a desired result. Even though the Lookout Farm job represented long days of sweaty work in the hot sun and a near-disastrous,
sexually suggestive encounter with Ilo, Sylvia painted a sweetly senti-
mental picture in "Rewards of a New England Summer." Near the
conclusion of the essay, she wrote:

And then, suddenly, it was the end of August—my last day of work.
I could hardly believe I wouldn't be biking up to the farm any more.
All the days of my ten weeks there had flowed together, melted into
each other so that only one solid impression remained, a blend of
blue skies, sunlight, and green fields.

Full Fathom Five

1

By way of Elm Street, a visitor arrived at Smith College from North-ampton, a quaint, claustrophobic town that boasted three hotels, a bus station, a train depot, a police station, a movie theatre, several retail stores and restaurants, and a variety of small businesses that catered to Smith clientele—The Quill Bookstore, The Hampshire Bookshop, The Coffee Shop (an English Department hangout), and two competing pizzerias, Joe's and Rahar's. Encircling the business district were residential neighborhoods in which the town's year-round citizens lived. But, for all practical purposes, Northampton existed because of Smith College. Scenically, the campus, large if not sprawling, emanated grace and beauty. A central cluster of buildings comprised of a library, a gymnasium, and classroom and administration buildings—all red-brick three- and four-story structures that had been built after the turn of the century—was surrounded by the school's "houses." With names like Haven, Northrop, and Chapin, these multistory brick buildings, in which between fifty and seventy-five girls lived, contributed to a pervasive pastoral gentility, which Smith's most famous landmark, Paradise Pond, seemed best to personify.

Founded in 1871 when Sophia Smith, an area resident, bequeathed a trust fund of four hundred thousand dollars with "the design to furnish for my own sex means and facilities for education equal to those which are afforded now in our colleges for men," Smith had become, by 1950, one of the country's premier undergraduate institutions. In keeping with its socially conservative tradition, the school demanded that each of its twenty-four hundred students conform to steadfast regulations. "We were lemmings unto the sea," remembers Judy Ettlinger, a Smith student in the early fifties; "we were a generation that did not question."

At that time no one stopped to question Smith's requirement that every incoming freshman pass a hygiene test (failure meant a course in hygiene), undergo a swimming test by swimming two lengths of an indoor pool (failure meant swimming lessons), and submit to "posture pictures," nude photographs, both front and side angles, taken by members of the physical-education department to determine whether there was proper alignment (failure meant a posture-training course). Obediently, each Smith student attended mandatory Wednesday chapel; checked in and out when leaving campus on weekends; met curfews of ten o'clock on school nights, twelve on Fridays, and one on Saturdays; and wore appropriate attire to supper, which, being formal, was served on linen tablecloths. Certainly no one questioned the college's requirement that each student adhere to strict social and academic honor systems.

On Mountain Day, students noted the arrival of fall by scouting the countryside to admire the leaves' changing colors. On Rally Day, originally a commemoration of George Washington's birthday but later broadened to become a celebration of Smith itself, seniors wore their graduation robes for the first time. In the auditorium seniors, dressed in black robes, sat in a single group surrounded by underclassmen, all of whom wore white. One could not help remarking the stunning sight—a knot of black engulfed by an ocean of white. And, on Graduation Day, seniors rolled hoops down a sloping green lawn. The young woman who rolled her hoop most expertly, and reached the finish line first, won "the prize," which was, according to campus folklore, the promise that she would marry before any other senior. That a "Smithie," as she was nicknamed, had put in four years at one of the country's top colleges did not mean she was not also expected to marry, have a family, and run a home. "At Smith, you were attempting to do some good work to fill in the time before you got married," remembers Gloria Steinem, another student from the early fifties. "Your only real life-changing mechanism was marriage, and then after that you assumed your husband's existence. At the time, this was the way life was."

The subject of young men—and courtship culminating in marriage—often dominated a Smith student's mind. "In the fifties we were girls, not women," declares Polly Longsworth, another contemporary of Plath's at Smith. "We came from middle- and (mostly) upper-middle-class homes, and had had rather sheltered upbringings. We were interested in boys, academics, and athletics, probably in that order. Sexual experimentation tended to be somewhat limited, largely because we came from 'nice' families and because fear of pregnancy (and especially the accompanying social humiliation) was strongly operative. Inevitably, there was more going on than most would own to— the inherent quest for a mate was part of the four years at college, and 'going steady' the prized norm. Few, however, were casual or promiscuous about sex." Rules governing dating were not that different from those at other Northeastern colleges. Usually, a boy from an Ivy League college invited a Smith student on a date. (Smithies favored boys from Harvard and Yale.) If the boy and girl did not already know each other (many had attended prep school together), a third party often put the two in contact; blind dating played a major role in the social life of many students. Once asked, a Smithie traveled by bus or by train to the boy's school, where she stayed near campus in a bed-and-breakfast. On their date, the boy took her to campus events like football or basketball games and the affiliated parties. Naturally, a girl could invite a boy to Smith—proms and dances were logical occasions for dates—at which time the sequence of events was reversed. And of course sex, in the form of sexual intercourse, remained relatively taboo. Should a couple have sex—only after dating for some time—they did *not* discuss it with others. One place a couple would *never* have sex was a Smith house, for rules prohibited boys from going above the house's first floor. If a girl did take a boy upstairs, she was supposed to shout, "Man on the floor!"—so that all girls within earshot would be properly forewarned.

Sylvia Plath first traveled down Elm Street as a Smithie on September 24, 1950. In her early days on campus, as she settled into the room she had been assigned in Haven House, she met the house's other forty-seven girls, one of whom, Ann Davidow, became a friend immediately. Some girls knew of Plath, having seen her byline in magazines. But even from the start, Sylvia allotted little time for socializing. Once she had passed her posture, hygiene, and swimming tests, she signed up for a standard courseload of English, Introduction to French Literature, Botany, Art, European History, and Physical Education. At Smith, as at any other academically challenging school, scholarship students were expected to uphold an overall B average; fee-paying students, on the other hand, needed only to maintain passing grades to stay enrolled. If a scholarship student failed to sustain "a satisfactory grade of work," the college's letter of scholarship notification stated, she would lose her financial aid. For Plath, this was all the catalyst she needed to make her work hard from the start. While she studied, she squeezed out a few hours here and there to write letters. Besides her mother, to whom she corresponded regularly, she wrote to Eddie. Recently, Sylvia had accused him of sending her a "nonplatonic" letter. Eddie had replied: "What it is, is a reflection of the warmth I felt on realizing that females of your caliber actually do exist. After the experience with B., which is only a few months old, I had a rather bad taste in my mouth about women. . . . If I do get East sometime, I'll look you up . . . but as for a random letter ending up in a Big Romance—even *Seventeen*'s editors couldn't swallow that whole, I'm afraid." Days later, after mailing her a bracelet he had bought in Mexico, Eddie sent her a one-thousand-word discourse on sex. Finally, in response to a letter in which she implored him not to "stop talking to me," he wrote:

It amazes me how much you have been able to get under my skin. . . . At first . . . I liked your sense of humor, primarily. Then one or two things made me conscious of the possibility that you were also rather mature and perceptive. . . . And you flatter me nicely, which no male can resist . . . and yet at the same time you are no "Yesgirl". . . . You ask me not to stop writing. Don't worry about that. Control of the matter passed out of my hands some time back.

In early October, Sylvia countered Eddie's obvious overtures with her own variety of flirtation. She hoped he would find the right girl, she wrote to him, and added that *she* would not be married after college since she did not want to be dismissed so easily. Answering her, Eddie pushed for a commitment. "I cannot get it out of my head that you are saying something that you did not put into writing, perhaps because you can't get your fingers around it yourself. Yet it is there, I am sure." He then asked about her boyfriends from last summer and suggested he might materialize in Northampton in the spring.

By October, Eddie's trip had become of secondary importance to Sylvia. While she did date sparingly—she went on a blind date with an Amherst College boy; two weeks later she double-dated with Ann—Sylvia devoted most of her time to schoolwork. English, French, Botany, and Art all challenged her, but she believed she might actually fail European History. Many did, she wrote to her mother; her class contained more than a few sophomores and juniors. To stay ahead, she had to work constantly. Work brought fatigue; fatigue, homesickness. As of mid-October, not a month into the academic year, Sylvia was already dreaming of a single day of peace and quiet at home. Her exhaustion brought on a minor depression, which caused her to see life as chaotic, civilization as barbarian. Late in October, her depression lightened somewhat. She celebrated her birthday by opening the presents from her mother (a Vigella maroon blouse, a bureau scarf, socks). She also met with Mary Mensel, who told her who her scholarship's sponsor was—Olive Higgins Prouty. Best known for *Now, Voyager,* a novel that had been made into a movie starring Bette Davis, and *Stella Dallas,* a novel that had been adapted into both a Barbara Stanwyck movie and a popular radio serial, Prouty had written some of the best-selling books of her day. Sylvia could hardly wait to take Mensel up on her suggestion that she write Prouty a letter to thank her for her scholarship.

In November, *Seventeen* published Plath's "Ode to a Bitten Plum," a short, Keats-inspired poem in which the narrator, contemplating a plum, decides its seed represents more abstract concepts like time and eternity. Though encouraged by the publication, she had become so busy with her studies that she had all but stopped writing. Walking through College Hall one afternoon, she was amused to find "Ode to a Bitten Plum" posted on the bulletin board reserved for Smith students in the news. It made her think of herself as a writer even if she wasn't writing. One person who read the poem was Eddie Cohen. Because she had "tried to make too much out of the subject," he felt "somewhat disappointed" by it. After revealing this in one of his November letters, Eddie then made a startling leap of logic. "Maybe two writers could never get along together anyhow," he said. "They are apt to commit double homicide over each other's criticisms of their work." Since he feared he had offended her, Eddie ended his letter by saying, "At any rate, in recognition of the factors involved, the least (and most) I can do is blow a kiss into the warm west wind and hope that it finds you."

In November, Sylvia fought her depression, which had not been cured by the diversions of late October. Over Thanksgiving weekend, she went to Wellesley for four days, at which time she visited with her mother, her grandparents, and Warren, home from Exeter. But when she returned to Smith she became homesick—and even more depressed. Determined to meet her social obligations despite her depression, Sylvia wrote Olive Higgins Prouty—a beautiful lyrical letter—near the end of the month. She recounted her thrill over being accepted into Smith on scholarship—"I went about the house for days in sort of a trance . . . saying, 'Yes, I'm going to Smith' "—and confessed to being inward-looking, which she probed through drawing and writing poetry. Then Sylvia listed her influences, who included Edna St. Vincent Millay, Sinclair Lewis, Stephen Vincent Benét, and Virginia Woolf. And though she hoped for a career in writing, that remained in the future; now there was Smith. "I wonder . . . if I have revealed even a small part of my love for Smith. There are so many little details that are so wonderful—the lights of the houses against the night sky, the chapel bells on Sunday afternoon, the glimpse of Paradise from my window. . . ." Concluding, Sylvia addressed Prouty directly. "I just want you to understand that you are responsible, in a sense, for the formation of an individual, and I am fortunate enough to be that person."

A week after she mailed the letter, Sylvia received Prouty's reply. "I have read your letter with great interest and am much impressed by it," Prouty wrote. "I am having it typed with several carbons as I want others to read it. I think there is no doubt that you possess a gift for creative writing. Your descriptions of your first impressions of college . . . brought a blur of tears to my eyes as I read your letter aloud to my husband. He, too, was moved by it." Then Prouty invited Sylvia to her home in Brookline for tea during the upcoming Christmas holidays. Excited by the invitation, Sylvia could hardly wait for the two weeks to pass before Christmas break. It did, though, and on her first day back in Wellesley she dressed in her only wool suit and set out on the short trip to Brookline.

2

On that cold, beautiful December afternoon, Sylvia Plath got off the bus and walked with purpose up the curving driveway to 393 Walnut, a handsome two-story mansion. At the door she checked her watch—five o'clock, on time—just before she rang the bell. After a moment, a maid answered and ushered her through a foyer into a huge oblong living room which spanned the house's entire width. The maid told her that Mrs. Prouty would soon appear, then left. As Plath stared into the fire crackling noisily in the fireplace, a voice behind her cried, "Why, you must be Sylvia." She turned to see a well-dressed, pleasant-looking woman motion for her to sit on the sofa. Joining her there, Olive Higgins Prouty, whose face radiated warmth and kindness, chatted in a quiet voice while she served Sylvia tea and cucumber sandwiches. In time, Prouty and Sylvia touched on a subject dear to them both—writing. Sylvia wanted to write, she said, on grand topics—traveling in exotic locales, shooting tigers, scaling volcanoes. But she hadn't *done* any of these things. "Wait a minute," Prouty said. "Is there any time in your life you've had a problem, a real conflict which seemed terribly important to you at that moment?" Yes, Sylvia said, and told her how in high school she had been both attracted to and repulsed by her sorority, which treated badly girls who were not admitted—the reason Sylvia had resigned from the Sub-Debs. "Seems to me there's a story there," Prouty said. "An interesting one too. Take life! Think of the material you have!"

Before long, it was six o'clock—time for Sylvia to go. "You'll be coming to visit me again," Prouty said, on their way to the door. Outside, as she walked down the street towards the bus stop, Sylvia thought about the implications of Prouty's words. An author had to search no farther than the world around her—her family, her friends, herself—for characters about whom to write. Although Sylvia may not have been fully aware of it at the moment, although she may never have adequately documented its importance in the future, Prouty's comment sank deep into her consciousness.

During the next week, Sylvia celebrated Christmas and New Year's at home in Wellesley. On Christmas Eve, she wrote her pen pal, Hans, a political letter in which she contended that the atom bomb would never purge the world of evil and, besides, that democracy would be worthless in a post-nuclear age. In January, she returned to Smith to study for and then write her final exams. Sylvia's first-semester marks—English, B+; Physical Education, B−; Art, A; Botany, A; French, A−; and European History, A− (this in the course she had expected to fail)—indicated that in college she would continue her superior academic performance.

Upon her return to Northampton, Sylvia learned that, while home for the holidays in Chicago, Ann Davidow had withdrawn. Though saddened, Sylvia was not surprised, for she knew that at school Ann had been racked with anxieties. One day in December, Sylvia could not forget, Ann had appeared so wildly and unnaturally happy that Sylvia forced her to discuss her problem. "I can never do it, never," Ann had said, referring to her inability to succeed at Smith. Then she confessed that she had been hoarding sleeping pills and razor blades in case she decided to commit suicide. Apparently, Sylvia now saw in January, Ann had gone home, figured Smith wasn't worth it, and dropped out. Soon Sylvia wrote Eddie to suggest that he contact Ann. "I must remember to look up . . . Ann . . . ," Eddie replied, "provided that she has not already placed her head in an oven, or something like that. . . . Anyone with suicidal tendencies should fit neatly into the

group of neurotics and semi-psychotics with whom I surround myself."
In truth, if Eddie had contacted Ann, he would have done so only to
learn more about Sylvia. "Let us face it, Eddie boy, you are still interested in the gal [Sylvia] for far more than the purpose of writing
exercises," he had told her in a recent letter. "Now, if the onlookers
will pardon the splattered ink, a man will demonstrate how to hang
himself with a typewriter ribbon."

In January, *Seventeen* wrote Plath that "Den of Lions," her story
based on her failed "love affair" with Emile, had placed third in its
fiction contest. Besides earning one hundred dollars, the story would
be published in May. Later in January, Plath enjoyed a (for her) different sort of publication. On the 23rd, the Peoria, Illinois, *Star* ran
"Teen Triumphs"—the first biographical piece about Plath to appear
in print. "Sylvia Plath, 17, really works at writing," the article stated.
"To get atmosphere for a story about a farm she took a job as a
farmhand. Now she's working on a sea story [for which she'll get a job
on a boat]. . . . A national magazine has published two of her brain-
children, the real test of being a writer." Sylvia had discovered the
clipping on the same College Hall bulletin board on which "Bitter
Strawberries" had been posted. Her reaction was, how *did* the Peoria
Star learn about her in the first place?

To save fifty dollars on housing for the spring term, Sylvia moved
to a second-floor room in Haven in which she shared bunk beds with
Marcia Brown, a bright and energetic girl from New Jersey. In the
absence of Ann Davidow, Sylvia struck up a friendship with Marcia
that the two girls cemented in early February on a weekend trip with
Marcia's mother to visit a woman known affectionately as "Aunt." At
this time, as she continued the two-semester courses she had started
in the fall, Sylvia made an effort to have a social life. In early January,
she dated Bob Humphrey. Then, on the 30th, Dick Norton, the cute,
intelligent Wellesley friend with whom she had had little contact since
leaving for Smith, wrote from Yale to invite her to the school's annual
Swimming Carnival in mid-February. On the 17th, she boarded a morning train down to New Haven, but it rained so hard that day that she
and Dick had to hole up in his room and amuse themselves by discussing
such subjects as science, sociology, and mental illness. The next day,

which was sunny and clear, the two of them took in several Carnival events, becoming so caught up in what they were doing that Sylvia missed the last train that would have put her in Northampton ahead of curfew. Because she was late, Sylvia had to appear before the Judicial Board, which required her, as punishment, to be in her room by nine o'clock each night for a week.

Three weeks later, Sylvia again took the train to New Haven, this time to go to the Yale junior prom with Dick. All in all, she enjoyed herself immensely. Dick did too, and during the following weekend, while at Smith to escort another girl to Smith's sophomore prom, he wrote Sylvia a note to accompany a photograph taken of her on their prom date. At the end of the note, he said that if he missed "seeing [her] (briefly), here is a sigh of disappointment." The tone rang all too clearly. Like several other boys now, Dick had become infatuated with Sylvia. Of course, one of those other boys was Eddie, who in his letters in March had revealed his emotions. "Regardless of how much I may seem to have neglected you at times," he wrote on the 19th, "or what the situation with Rita"—his new girlfriend—"may have been, the passing months have only served to strengthen my determination not to commit myself to anything permanent, like marriage, until such time as I have a chance to actually see you. As a matter of fact, I have a lingering suspicion that much of the reason for my being unable to wholly give myself to Rita has been my unconfirmed idea of what might possibly exist in points east."

His chance to meet Sylvia in person came on the first day of her spring break. As Sylvia packed her suitcase upstairs in her room at Haven an hour before she and a friend were supposed to ride home together, someone yelled from downstairs, "Oh, Syl, there's a boy to see you." When Sylvia rushed down the stairs to the living room, she was startled to discover, as she would later describe him, an odd boy with dark-colored hair. "This is the third dimension," the boy said, and then it occurred to her: this was *Eddie Cohen*. "I've come to drive you home," he said, puffing his pipe. Stunned, Sylvia finally agreed to allow Eddie to pack her suitcases in his car. On their way to Wellesley, Eddie revealed that he had driven some thirty hours straight from Chicago to Northampton, enduring bad weather much of the way, just to drive her home. But this confession did not achieve the effect on Sylvia that Eddie had wanted, for their three-hour journey turned into one long, painful ordeal. Sylvia could not accept that this strange-looking boy was the same one to whom she had spilled out her most intimate secrets in her letters. Also, Eddie, who Sylvia thought would be strong-minded and articulate, was actually nervous and bashful. And in a gesture that seemed too calculated to lend him an air of intellectuality, he even smoked a pipe.

A stop at a restaurant did not help. They got back in the car only to resume their trip—and more strained, awkward talk. By the time they reached Wellesley, Sylvia was nearing her breaking point. Immediately after Eddie had parked the car and they had walked to the front door of 26 Elmwood Road, she thanked him for driving her home, introduced him to her mother, who had come to the door, and dashed upstairs. Confused and insulted, Eddie left Wellesley for New York, where he spent the night with a friend before heading back to Chicago. Only later did Aurelia discover *which* Eddie this was, and when she did she felt embarrassed over Sylvia's rudeness. On the other hand, Sylvia did not. She had neither invited Eddie east nor, when he tried to invite himself, encouraged him to come. He had therefore acted of his own volition, which meant that he was taking a risk by driving to Northampton to meet her unannounced. She felt no obligation to do anything other than respond to him honestly. And she had. If others—her mother, for example—interpreted her behavior as cruel, that was their problem, not hers. If she *had* invited (or even encouraged) him to visit her and subsequently acted rudely, then she would feel badly. But she had not.

To herself, Sylvia had to admit *why* she had not wanted Eddie to visit her. Frankly, she did not wish to have a relationship with him. But why not? Was he not handsome enough? Was he too neurotic? Did his future as a breadwinner appear too uncertain? Probably she could have adjusted to many shortcomings, but the one he seemed most to display was the one quality in a man she could not accept: because he was not a "challenge" for her, she did not see him as her equal.

Vacation did contain some pleasant experiences for Sylvia. Traveling to New Jersey, she visited Marcia, with whom she went into Manhattan, a city Sylvia had never seen before. Enthralled, she became the typical tourist—window-shopping on Fifth Avenue, dining at the Automat, sightseeing at the Empire State Building. She and Marcia even saw *Darkness at Noon*, starring Claude Rains.

Back at Smith, Sylvia suffered the fallout from Eddie's trip. After writing her one letter in which he revealed that "my return trip from New York ended up (predictably?) in a head-on collision somewhere in Ohio," another in which he stated that "[y]our mother was quite right—you were incredibly rude," and a third in which he began to relinquish his anger somewhat although he would not apologize for being "sarcastic, [and] at times outright insulting," Eddie finally could not help himself. "This much . . . I would like to make clear—whatever you may have done . . . I like you none the less for it. If anything, I perhaps think more of you; by behaving in a manner something less than perfect, you have become considerably less of a goddess and considerably more of a human being in my eyes. . . . I am sharply aware now of just how solid and wholesome certain aspects of our relationship are. For which I can only say again . . . thanks . . . for being you." Like other boys who had fallen and would fall in love with Sylvia, Eddie worked out a way in his mind to ignore, even justify, any of her personality faults.

For the most part, Sylvia ignored Eddie's angry letters, not only because she assumed no responsibility for his coming to Northampton but because she was overwhelmed with schoolwork. She could barely eke out time to date Dick, with whom she enjoyed anything but an even-tempered relationship. In mid-April, while Dick visited Northampton for the weekend, Sylvia became, according to Dick, "very queer and lightheaded" on Saturday night and did something, which remains unclear, that disturbed him greatly. The following morning, he telephoned her from his room and told her coolly that he would not see her before dinner. Then, after dinner, he left—early—for New Haven. Days later, they had made up enough for Dick to write a—for him—typical letter to Sylvia.

At the end of April, Dick returned to Northampton for a date that went more smoothly. "From a very me-ish point of view," he later wrote in language that revealed his odd personality, "our get-together . . . was extraordinarily pleasant. . . . I cannot so much say: thank you for your hospitality to me, as say: the visit was mutually stimulating and you were a dear to plan it so for us." Then, on May 11, on her way to New Jersey, Marcia dropped Sylvia off in New Haven. Over the weekend Sylvia and Dick sunbathed, read Hemingway, and went to the theatre one night to see Thornton Wilder's *The Skin of Our Teeth*.

While she dated Dick, Sylvia tried to deal with society's double standard about sex. She longed for a male "organism" to understand her, she told her journal, but had concluded that most American men regarded a woman as a "sex machine with rounded breasts and a convenient opening in the vagina." She had decided, what was more, that being a young woman meant that she had to "pour my energies through the direction and force of my mate"—a prospect that led her to question whether she even wanted to marry. On the subject of men, she could not help wondering if her father's death had produced in her a "craving for male company." It would be ironic if it had, since she did *not* wish to be treated like a "sex machine," especially if she could not treat men the same way in return.

Interpersonal relationships is one issue addressed in "Den of Lions," Plath's story that appeared in *Seventeen* in May. Of all the letters she received from friends and family who had read the story, Eddie's disturbed her most. "You are good, Syl—mighty good. You have the eyes and ears of a great writer. Personally, though, I wonder whether you have the heart of one." Sylvia liked much better letters from Dick and Nancy Rule, a fan in Nashville, Tennessee. "May I be the first to tell you that you can expect wonderful things of Sylvia Plath," Rule told *Seventeen*'s editors. "The marvelous figures of speech in her story . . . prove that she can, and should, develop into a well-known writer. Although her story shows some immaturity, in the sense of being 'too-flowery,' her well-applied imagination makes up for it!"

Because she and Sylvia had begun to wonder how they would earn money over the summer, Marcia registered in Smith's Vocational Office for possible employment. In the office's job listings, Sylvia ran across an advertisement for two friends to baby-sit for two families who lived in houses near each other in Swampscott, Massachusetts. When the girls applied for the jobs, each of which paid twenty-five dollars for a six-day week, the woman in the Vocational Office hired them on the spot. Her summer plans in place, Sylvia devoted all of her energies to finishing the semester, but she worked so hard on classes and extra-curricular activities (Studio Club and Freshman Prom Decoration Committee were two she had signed up for in the spring) that she came down with a severe cold and landed in the infirmary. A life pattern had begun to emerge. During periods of intense stress, Sylvia's body weakened so badly that she became physically ill, which then brought on a depression. Soon she had recovered enough to check out of the infirmary and finish the term, for which she earned the following grades: English, B+; French, A; Botany, A; Art, A; European History, A−; and Physical Education, C. She could accept the low mark in Physical Education (in school she had never really excelled in organized sports), but the B+ in English bothered her. Granted, the course had been hard; but what did it indicate if, among all her academic courses, she made lowest in the subject in which she had now decided to major?

For two weeks in Wellesley, Sylvia relaxed; she played tennis with Philip, chatted with Mr. Crockett on the telephone, and dated Dick. At one point, a letter from Eddie arrived. "I do question whether you have often, or ever, cast off those restraints which mean the difference between living and living right up to the ultimate," he declared. "Anyone with any sensitivity can have a good share of those moments which one calls living. But tearing down those last restraints entails something of a gamble, for there is always an element of risk involved, a chance to get smacked in the teeth as well as gain the ultimate. . . . Why this sudden deluge of words? It arises from one line in your last letter— 'I won't say I'm in love. I don't believe in the word.' " Naturally, Sylvia had been referring to Dick, though she did not name him. On June 18, Sylvia escaped (to a degree) her ambivalent feelings about Dick: she reported for her mother's-helper job at the home of Dr. and Mrs. Frederick Mayo at 144 Beach Bluff Avenue in Swampscott. On that first day, Mrs. Mayo told Sylvia that she would be responsible for the care of the Mayo children—Freddy, six; Pinny, four; and Joey (a girl), two. Sylvia would oversee their daily schedules, fix some of their meals, and launder their clothes. The job description did not sound too demanding, so Sylvia felt hopeful as, following her meeting with Mrs. Mayo, she went upstairs to unpack. Once she had arranged her clothes in the bureau in her bedroom, which seemed to her as big as the whole first floor of 26 Elmwood Road, Sylvia stared out the room's windows at the Atlantic, which, as it stretched out before her, intrigued her with its color and beauty. Later, when she ventured outside the eleven-room house, Sylvia discovered a vegetable garden, a fruit orchard, and a huge backyard featuring a children's playhouse—all of this atop a wooded hill that gradually descended to the ocean. Sylvia also learned that only a short walk away, in Marblehead Harbor, the Mayos' yacht *Mistral* was anchored alongside a sixty-foot yacht owned by the Blodgetts, the family for whom Marcia would be working when she arrived from Long Island on July 5.

Sylvia realized immediately that her duties for the Mayos were going to be more demanding than they had sounded. This was a typical day: rise at seven; cook the children's breakfast (eggs, bacon, and toast); wash dishes, make beds, launder clothes while the children play indoors; oversee the children as they play in the neighborhood or on nearby Prescott Beach; fix a hot lunch; rest when the children nap; in the afternoon, oversee more outside playing; then, following supper, which she did not have to cook, bathe the children and put them to bed. Finally, after working almost nonstop for thirteen hours, Sylvia had an uninterrupted hour or two alone in her bedroom. Throughout July, she kept this grueling pace. On her weekly day off, or during the evenings when the Mayos took care of the children themselves and she could steal an extra hour of free time, she strolled the beach or swam in the ocean. After her arrival at the Blodgetts' in July, Marcia dropped by regularly. During that month, Sylvia also saw Dick, who was waiting tables close by at the Latham Inn.

In August, Sylvia's schedule did not change appreciably. She minded the Mayo children during the day, a task that became easier as she began to feel more a part of the household; visited after work with Marcia, who was dating John Hodges, Sylvia's old boyfriend; and, when she had time, read. As of August 8, she was deep into J. D. Salinger's recently published *The Catcher in the Rye*, a book that left such a lasting impression on her that years later, as she wrote a novel of her own—*The Bell Jar*—she turned to it as a model. But perhaps August's most memorable date was the 20th, which she spent with Dick. On that date, they had to cancel their picnic because of a thunderstorm, so they visited a friend instead. They ate most of the picnic, which Sylvia had prepared, while sitting in Dick's car. Despite the rain, they were entertained by their conversation (one topic was Dick's recent acceptance into Harvard Medical School for the fall), and Dick invited Sylvia to the Cape following her baby-sitting job. Later that night, back at the Mayos', Sylvia felt restless and anxious. Deciding that the ocean, which appeared angry and gray, was too alluring to pass up, Sylvia slipped into her bathing suit, left the house, and tiptoed across the dewy yard and down the hill to the shore. As she waded out into "her" ocean and started to swim, the water warm from the morning's rain, she occasionally glanced up the hill to the Mayos' enormous house, its lights bright against the darkness.

On September 3, her job at the Mayos' finished, Sylvia returned to Wellesley. Throughout the month, until she left for Smith, she often visited Dick, joining him and his family for the four-day trip to the Cape they had planned. But spending time with Dick only further perplexed her. She loved him—or so she thought, despite her statement that she didn't believe in love—and he loved her, yet something about their relationship disturbed her. She decided she had to discuss her predicament with someone, so she chose, in a perverse move, Eddie. She and her boyfriend loved each other, Sylvia confessed to Eddie in a letter—*that* was the problem. Eddie answered by asking, *what* problem? If a problem did exist, he believed it resulted from the guilt she felt since she really *didn't* love her boyfriend. "If I seem a bit harsh at times, it is only because it seems to me that there are certain inconsistencies in your thinking and behavior, and that unless you come into sharper contact with reality and resolve these problems, it will become more and more difficult for you to reconcile the life you lead and the life you want to lead. And the reconciliation of these two, after all, is what makes for happiness."

Despite Eddie's warnings, Sylvia continued to date Dick. While in Wellesley at the end of September, a stay during which she attended a Smith Club of Wellesley tea and ate supper with Mr. Crockett, she and Dick found themselves one night in a field, a starry sky spread out above them. In this romantic setting they engaged each other in a "truth talk." He wished she were three years older, Dick said, but he wanted to marry her anyway. Or someone "like" her. If the wording of Dick's statement did not escape Sylvia, it did not necessarily offend her either. In a way, his sentiments merely reflected the thinking of a certain class which evaluates a person first according to type, then according to individual traits.

3

Soon after Sylvia returned to Smith for her sophomore year, she and Marcia, with whom she still roomed at Haven, were invited to Maureen Buckley's coming-out party. One of ten children—her older brother William had just published the controversial book *God and Man at Yale*—Maureen had grown up at The Elms, the Buckley estate in Sharon, Connecticut. On Saturday, October 6, 1951, Sylvia, Marcia, and a dozen or so other Haven girls—Maureen invited the whole house—were driven in cars supplied by the Buckleys to The Elms. After resting and freshening up in the afternoon at Stone House, guest living quarters near the main residence, Sylvia and Marcia were taken by limousine to the Sharon Inn to join the other girls for supper. When they came back to the Buckley estate, Sylvia and Marcia lay down for an hour in "their mansion"—Sylvia's phrase. Getting up, they dressed and proceeded to the gala ball, which took place on the lawn behind the main house. From two bars, waiters filtered through the crowd to serve drinks. Balloons decorated tables covered with white linen. A band performed on a platform that had been constructed especially for the occasion. At nine-thirty, once all guests had been announced and received, the dancing began. Sylvia chose a number of partners, among them boys named Eric and Carl, two who did not impress her;

Plato Skouras, the son of the head of production at Twentieth Century–Fox; and Constantine. Sidamon-Eristoff, a Princeton senior who so captivated her that she eventually left the party with him for a night drive that did not end until he dropped her off at Stone House late in the morning. The next day, following a one o'clock brunch with the Buckleys, Sylvia and four more girls rode back to Haven in a black Cadillac. First thing, Sylvia sat down in her room and typed a long letter home in which she detailed the weekend's fairy-tale-like events. "To have had you see me!" Sylvia said to her mother. "I am sure you would have cried for joy." Then and later, Sylvia and Aurelia openly acknowledged that Aurelia lived vicariously through Sylvia's experiences. Growing up as she had, Aurelia had not enjoyed luxuries like a Smith education and invitations to the coming-out parties of the daughters of wealthy families.

The Saturday night after the Buckley party, Dick, now at Harvard Medical School, and his friend Ken Warren double-dated Sylvia and her friend Carol Pierson in Northampton. They had supper at the Yankee Peddler, then drinks at Joe's. That night, one topic of conversation between Sylvia and Dick concerned her recently completed story "The Perfect Set-up"—the one about baby-sitters, as she referred to it—which she hoped would fare better at magazines—she had written it for *Seventeen*—than her latest batch of poems, which *The Saturday Review of Literature* had turned down. Back at Harvard, Dick wrote Sylvia: "You were your own incomparable self, sweet and generous, understanding and thoughtful. Knowing you is a warm and reassuring and exciting experience." All of Dick's letters of late had not been so enthusiastic. In a recent one, he rhapsodized about how lovable and kind Sylvia was only to turn the page and draw a detailed diagram of the muscles of the human back. This zaniness, which put Sylvia off, was merely one reason why she had second thoughts about marrying Dick. He felt attracted to beautiful women, Sylvia wrote in her journal, and considered a wife a "physical possession." And, as if those two black marks did not offend her enough, she also concluded that she was really not in love with him.

Immediately after Dick's visit, Sylvia overworked herself, keeping up with her demanding courses—Nineteenth and Twentieth Century Literature, Introduction to Politics, Writing, Visual Expression, Introduction to Religion, and Physical Education—and contracted a case of sinusitis that became so bad she checked into the infirmary. "Sinusitis plunges me in manic depression," she wrote at this time; however, the quicker she hit bottom the quicker she started to rebound. No doubt part of her depression, which was not so serious as past or future depressions, more an extreme example of adolescent-schoolgirl funk, stemmed from her confusing situation with Dick. As she had previously, Sylvia asked Eddie for advice. Referring to him as "Allan," Sylvia described her boyfriend as handsome, brilliant, personable, athletic. But she feared marrying him, because—*this* was the reason she posed to Eddie—she doubted she could ever live up to his set of standards. Eddie replied to her letter quickly. "Doesn't it sound just the slightest bit like a rationalization? What sounds extremely more probable to me is that Allan does not come up to your standards." Then Eddie changed subjects, imploring her to "[t]ry not to panic too much" if he revealed that he planned to "call for the East" during Christmas vacation. "I don't much care for a repetition of our last encounter," he added, "but if you would like to give it another try, let me know and we'll see if we can't get into contact somehow."

After her infirmary stay, Sylvia took a written exam in religion; had lunch with a woman from *Mademoiselle* who was interviewing girls for College Board, a nationwide network of students who served as quasi-correspondents for the magazine; read a fan letter from Hong Kong for "Den of Lions"; and went to Wellesley for her nineteenth birthday. Again at Smith, in a letter in which she thanked her mother for her birthday gifts and cake, Sylvia discussed, as would-be boyfriends, Eddie Cohen; Ed Nelson, a University of Massachusetts student whom she knew from Bradford High; and Constantine, her "date" from the Buckley party, who had recently invited her to Princeton for the weekend. (Although she wanted to go, the weekend had conflicted with schoolwork.) But her greatest source of anxiety was three upcoming writtens. To convey her state of mind, she drew on the bottom of the last page of her letter a tombstone on which she had inscribed: "Life was a hell of a lot of fun while it lasted."

In November, to make extra money besides the modest amount she earned from selling her creative work for publication, Sylvia began to report for Press Board, a pool of paid student journalists who provided area newspapers with coverage of events at Smith. Then, over Thanksgiving weekend, in Wellesley, Sylvia and Dick argued so badly that upon her return to Northampton Sylvia wrote Eddie that she and "Allan" had broken up for good. In December, as she sank into another severe depression, Sylvia struggled with her feelings about Dick. Her private life became more confused when a friend named Eric, whom Sylvia barely knew, wrote to tell her that he was falling in love with her. Sylvia decided that he had done so because of intimate conversations they had had (in one he admitted to having had sex with a prostitute). But Sylvia did not love Eric. She wanted only to take Constantine up on his latest offer—to go with him to New York. Yet, despite Eric's overtures, her fantasies about dating Constantine, and her contention that she had broken up with Dick at Thanksgiving, Sylvia spent much of her Christmas vacation, including both Christmas Day and New Year's Eve night, with Dick. This did not help her depression, since dating Dick aroused such conflicting emotions. Sylvia became even more confused on the day when she joined him at Boston Lying-In Hospital to witness the birth of a baby, and Dick, who had implied he was innocent about sexual matters, told her that he had lost his virginity. The revelation disgusted her, Sylvia wrote to Ann Davidow. It also infuriated her: Sylvia was jealous of men, she continued in her letter to Ann, because they did not have to worry about society stigmatizing them if they had sex indiscriminately, something for which women suffered ridicule. How could society tell boys to act on their sexual urges at the same time it denounced women for doing the same?

After January finals brought her her customary good grades—English, A; Government, A; Writing, A; Religion, A–; Art, B; and Physical Education, B—Sylvia worked on Press Board, anticipated her spring classes (which were essentially continuations of the fall's), and, though she really did not want to, dated Dick. "Why is your face and form wildly attracting rather than merely pretty?" Dick wrote her following a weekend together in Wellesley in early February 1952. "Is it an inner radiance, a glow, a deep pleasure in existing and moving and creating and accomplishing? . . . I do think we are an unusual pair of humans." While Dick viewed Sylvia as "an unusual human" full of "inner radiance," Eddie perceived an entirely different person. Her general unhappiness had prompted Eddie to write her a pointed letter in which he advised her to see a psychiatrist. She did not do so, even though, as of February, her depression now caused her to question her ability to write. After a *Seventeen* rejection made her feel untalented, a lecture by the Hampshire Bookshop president about publishing bolstered her confidence enough so that, in composing a letter of application for an Elks Scholarship, she looked forward to preparing for creative work. But once she mailed off the Elks application, she again concluded that she had lost her talent—a fear that would plague her repeatedly in the future.

Because she believed much of her apprehension grew out of her confusion about boys and sex, Sylvia wrote Eddie that she believed she suffered from schizophrenia, penis envy, and an inferiority complex. She also fought a powerful sex drive, she told him. Eddie responded with a demand that she "[f]orget this stuff." Her unhappiness did not result from "schizophrenia, inferiority or the lack of a male sex organ"; she was depressed because she was dating a young man she did not love. "You are further disturbed because you are frank enough to admit to yourself that you have a physical drive towards sex," Eddie said. "The fact that you have no satisfactory outlet for this stems from the fact that society is maladjusted to the welfare of the individual, and not because there is anything wrong with you." As for the inconsistent quality of her writing, about which she had also written him, he suggested she read Hemingway's *The Sun Also Rises* and *Across the River and Into the Trees*, "just to see how much variation there can be in quality, even in the best of us." Eddie concluded this letter—never missing the opportunity—by saying that, "if the physical barrier between us were removed, I should be quite headily and overwhelmingly in love with you. As I yet may well be some day."

March began on an up note—*Seventeen* announced that her "The Perfect Set-up" had won honorable mention in its annual fiction contest—but afterwards Sylvia became bogged down in her regular grind of coursework and extracurricular activities. Besides volunteering to teach children's art classes at Northampton's People's Institute, she served on Haven's House Committee and the Sophomore Prom Entertainment Committee, which she chaired. She also dealt with Eddie's requests to see her. "I really feel that a second try wouldn't turn out badly at all," Eddie wrote in a letter in March. "And spring vacation cometh." He even admitted he had almost bought her a round-trip airplane ticket to Chicago but did not because he was afraid she would turn him down. The month's strangest episode, though, happened at mid-month, during a trip from Wellesley to Northampton. On the bus, Sylvia sat beside a young man who, covered up by his raincoat, slept for the first hour of the trip. Following a brief stopover the bus made at the Flying Yankee Diner, Sylvia arrived back at her seat to find the young man awake and eager to talk. Which they did, all the way to Northampton. In their conversation, Sylvia learned that the young man—his name was Bill—was completing a doctorate in entomology at M.I.T. Later, in Northampton, where they stopped in a coffee shop to chat some more, Sylvia had said, "You know, my dad wrote a book on bumblebees once." Bill's reply thoroughly surprised Sylvia: "Not *Bumblebees and Their Ways*." Still later, after Bill carried her suitcases to campus and told her good night, Sylvia realized that she could never see him again even if in some small way she had fallen in love with him.

Around this time, Sylvia had another odd encounter. Finally agreeing to see Eddie again, Sylvia hosted him and a friend briefly in Wellesley on her spring vacation. Unlike their first meeting, this visit proceeded in a comparatively normal fashion. "One night we went into Boston," Cohen remembers, "and wandered around the city until we dropped in on a jazz club. Terrible jazz. But Sylvia was or pretended to be enjoying this bad jazz greatly. It was on this night that I saw that she was *all mask*. After the jazz club we went and sat on the Commons for three or four hours. As we talked, it became increasingly clear to me that she was posing a lot. She was not at all like she was in her letters. There was no spontaneity. She seemed incapable of an impulsive remark." Previously, Eddie had not been able to discern this "posing"; now that he had, he was turned off by it. The next day, Eddie and his friend drove to New York and left Sylvia behind, although at one point she had planned to travel there on her break. Following this trip, they continued to correspond regularly and at length, but Eddie no longer considered Sylvia a potential romantic interest.

Spring break over, Plath focused on her literary life. In April, she finished "Sunday at the Mintons'," a story that she had drafted during vacation and which now, almost on a whim, she entered in *Mademoiselle*'s fiction contest. She also heard several guest speakers—Robert Frost, Ogden Nash, Joseph McCarthy—and wrote at least one poem, "Go Get the Goodly Squab." When not studying or writing, she pursued outside activities like Press Board. By reporting for the Springfield *Daily News*, she netted ten dollars a month. Apart from writing articles, she received several honors. She was chosen secretary of Honor Board; inducted into the Society of Alpha Phi Kappa, an honorary arts society, and the Sophomore Push Committee, a group of girls who were "special" to her class; and invited to join the editorial board of *The Smith Review*, the school's literary magazine. On May 1, The Belmont, a resort hotel in West Harwick-by-the-Sea, Massachusetts, offered her a seven-day-a-week waitressing job for the summer, a position she now needed, even more desperately than when she had applied for it, because she had been turned down for an Elks. And at present, though their relationship seemed as precarious as ever, Sylvia still dated Dick. In her journal she revealed that she believed Dick suffered a mother complex from which he tried to break himself through his rebellion, which took the form of—or at least this was the way Sylvia saw Dick's recent confession about losing his virginity—"seducing a waitress, a Vassar girl." If Dick's confession troubled her, a larger question lingered in her mind. Could she alter her "attitude and subordinate *gladly*" to Dick's life? In short, could she devote herself to wifehood if it meant neglecting her art? "Thousands of women would!" Sylvia wrote in her journal, unsure of whether *she* could.

Following finals, which brought her more good grades, Sylvia rested a few days in Wellesley before assuming her waitressing job at The Belmont in early June. At once, management told her that, since she had no previous experience, she could not work the main dining room, where tips and salary could have earned her five hundred dollars for the season. Instead, she would wait Side Hall, the employee dining room, in which she could make about half as much. Plath had begun to feel resentment over their decision—she had passed up a job at The Pines to work at The Belmont—when, on the 11th, she received a telegram forwarded to her by her mother. Tearing open the envelope, Sylvia read:

DEAR MISS PLATH: CONGRATULATIONS ON WINNING MADEMOISELLE'S COLLEGE FICTION CONTEST. COULD YOU AIRMAIL US PHOTOGRAPH AND BIOGRAPHICAL MATERIAL IMMEDIATELY? LETTER FOLLOWS.

She could hardly believe it: "Sunday at the Mintons'" had won one of *Mademoiselle*'s two five-hundred-dollar first prizes in its fiction contest.

Now that she did not have to worry about money, Sylvia relaxed somewhat. At mid-month, she dated a bellhop named Lloyd, who took her out for a cheeseburger and beers. She attended a birthday party where she met a boy named Clark, a first-year Harvard law student. Nursing a Tom Collins, she ate coconut cake; then she and Clark went to the employee dormitory. As they sat outside on a bench, Clark rested his head in Sylvia's lap while she read to him poems by T. S. Eliot. The next morning, Clark forgotten, Sylvia set out on a twelve-mile bicycle ride with Perry and Dick to Long Pond.

Near the end of June, a Mr. Driscoll, Sylvia's Belmont supervisor, offered her the chance to earn an extra thirty dollars a month by putting out the linen after the dining rooms had closed. Figuring up the time required to perform this task—thirty hours weekly—Sylvia refused, which angered Driscoll, especially since Sylvia had complained about having to work Side Hall. Within days, the point was moot. Sylvia came down with sinusitis, no doubt because of her nonstop nightlife, which started at ten-thirty and lasted until dawn. On orders of the hotel doctor, she prepared to go home to recuperate. Philip McCurdy had been coming to play tennis with her at The Belmont, so on the day he arrived, instead of playing tennis, Sylvia drove back to Wellesley with him. Along the way, when both went to pat Philip's dog at the same time, their hands touched. Perhaps she *could* become interested in Philip, Sylvia wrote about the event in her journal.

After lingering for days in a blur of penicillin, Sylvia felt better by July 4, the date on which The Belmont called to ask if she planned to come back to her job. Since she was still sick, she'd have to give it up, Aurelia said—at Sylvia's urging. The following day, more good literary news arrived—a letter from Harold Strauss, editor-in-chief of Alfred A. Knopf, who had just read proofs of "Sunday at the Mintons'," forwarded to him by *Mademoiselle*'s managing editor, Cyrilly Abels. Strauss was so impressed by the story that he urged Sylvia to consider writing a novel for Knopf. Flattered, she wrote back to say that she would keep his offer in mind. Days later, Sylvia felt well enough that, when an ad in *The Christian Science Monitor* for a mother's helper caught her eye, she responded. Her potential employer, Margaret (Mrs. Michael) Cantor, offered to interview Sylvia for the twenty-five-dollar-a-week job, which entailed sitting for two small children and acting as a companion to an older teenage daughter. When they met, Mrs. Cantor offered Sylvia the job without hesitation. On July 19, Sylvia arrived for work at the Cantors' home at 276 Dorset Road in Chatham, Massachusetts. Unlike the Mayos, the Cantors went out of their way to include Sylvia as part of the family. From the start, they let her drive their two Chevrolets; encouraged her to take the children—Joan, Sue, and Bill—on outings, such as the weekly town concert; and gave her plenty of time off. In all, Plath worked at the Cantors' for six weeks, during which the most memorable event was the publication of "Sunday at the Mintons'" in the August *Mademoiselle*. Plath first saw the issue on the 2nd, when Grammy and Grampy, having driven to the Cantors' to visit Sylvia on her day off, brought a copy to her.

A longish, cleanly written story, "Sunday at the Mintons'" focuses on an elderly brother and sister, Henry and Elizabeth Minton. A daydreamer, Elizabeth is exasperated with Henry, whose mind is so practical that he can actually plot out on a mental map the direction in which he is moving as he travels. At the story's climax, which finds the couple taking a stroll on a boardwalk, fantasy and reality merge when Elizabeth in her imagination "kills" Henry who has descended from the boardwalk onto rocks to retrieve a brooch she dropped. Dreaming, Elizabeth pictures Henry struck by an unusually large wave that drags him out into the ocean. But the last lines of the story firmly root it in the real: " 'Come along home, Elizabeth,' Henry said. 'It's getting late.' " And Elizabeth answers: " 'I'm coming.' "

While she wrote the story in March, Plath had based Henry and Elizabeth on Dick and herself. Indeed, once the story appeared in print, she was concerned that Dick would decipher her characterizations and become angry. Could Dick discern "his dismembered self"? she asked her mother in a letter. If he did, he did—this was what she decided—for all creative pieces have a "germ of reality," regardless of how "fantastic" they are. Aurelia did not comment on the underlying reason that, as she structured "Sunday at the Mintons'," Sylvia felt compelled to have Elizabeth (Sylvia) "kill" Henry (Dick). Nor did Sylvia.

Unlike her previous two summer jobs at the Mayos' and at The Belmont, Sylvia did not want to leave the Cantors, which she did on August 31. The sentiment was mutual. "Sylvia is an exceptionally fine girl," Margaret Cantor wrote to Smith's Vocational Office. "Her manners and deportment are beautiful. Her consistently sunny disposition and her ability to express herself in . . . vivid language make her a most interesting and welcomed person." Her work behind her, Sylvia tried to rest. Early in September, Sylvia, Warren, and her mother vacationed on the Cape; then, back in Wellesley, she sunned, wrote, saw Philip, and visited Mr. Crockett. During one afternoon talk with Crockett, Sylvia suddenly realized that, after she graduated from Smith, she wanted to go to Oxford or Cambridge. She also dated Dick in September. He had pressed her to marry him during much of the summer, but she had resisted, *now* because she did not want to marry into the Norton family (she never said why) and because she considered herself and Dick too similar. Blissful and free—these were the words Sylvia used to describe the way she felt when she decided (once again) that she would not marry Dick.

4

On September 23, 1952, Dick drove Sylvia back to Smith for the fall term of her junior year, for which her roster of classes included Howard Patch's Medieval Literature, R. G. Davis's Style and Form, Kenneth Sherk's World of Atoms, plus Honors hours. In her first days on campus, Sylvia heard about "Sunday at the Mintons' " from a number of people—friends who loved it; Olive Higgins Prouty, who detailed its many virtues in a letter; Mary Ellen Chase, the novelist and Smith professor, who sent a note from Maine—she was on leave—to convey her congratulations; and Allen T. Klots, of Dodd, Mead, who wrote to inquire if Plath would like to submit to him a longer project, such as a novel. While assuming her new role of star writer—recently she had also published a poem, "White Phlox," in *The Christian Science Monitor*—Sylvia adjusted to a new private life as well. In the spring her application to Lawrence, a "self-help" house, had been accepted. To meet her house obligations that fall in Lawrence, Sylvia—star writer or not—had to wait tables at lunch, log in one hour of watch per week, and perform various weekend duties. Since Marcia had moved off campus to live with her mother, who had relocated to Northampton, Sylvia had a new roommate too—a brilliant, scientifically inclined girl named Mary.

Within days of the beginning of the semester, her workload so overwhelmed Sylvia that, in an act that indicated just how little she understood her own substantial intellectual abilities, she described herself as "pitifully stupid," "inadequate and scared." This negative view of herself foreshadowed a more ominous development. As the term progressed, Sylvia would gradually slip into one of her worst depressions yet. Her perception that she was inadequate, which caused her to be fearful, only forced her to descend more deeply into her darkening emotional state.

Presently, Sylvia wrote Eddie—the first time since early summer—to ask him to return the many letters she had sent him over the last two years. (She did not tell him so, but she wanted the letters to write a short story based on them.) "I was a little taken aback at receiving your chummy little mash note this morning," Eddie answered, not fooled by Sylvia's pleasant prose, "for I had long ago given up searching the mailbox on the theory that you had either married Allan, gotten a psychiatrist, or put me on your Shit List for one reason or another. . . . [Or] can it be that suddenly falling into fame and fortune has made you too good to associate casually with everyday, run-of-the-mill college journalists?" Eddie refused to promise to return the letters.

Meanwhile, Plath was contemplating other literary ambitions. In September, she applied for *Mademoiselle*'s College Board, the first step in an arduous process that could end with her winning a prize of which only now, following her success with "Sunday at the Mintons'," she dreamed—a guest editorship at the magazine for the coming summer. According to contest rules, a young woman applied to join College Board by writing a fifteen-hundred-word criticism of the magazine's latest August college issue, starting with an overview of the whole thing and then zeroing in on the section that most appealed to her. If a girl was chosen to the board (and about 750 out of the two thousand who applied would be), she became eligible to pursue the twenty guest-editor slots. To do *that*, she wrote three assignments during the academic year. One prize of fifty dollars and nine prizes of ten dollars were given for each assignment, which created a pool of thirty from which the *Mademoiselle* staff would choose the guest editors. Winners were paid a salary "plus expenses (room, travel, and most meals)"—so read a contest advertisement—to live in New York City and work at the magazine for the month of June. Hopeful, Sylvia initiated her application soon after the fall term began. In October, she received definite encouragement when *Seventeen* published "The Perfect Set-up" and awarded another of her stories, "Initiation," the two-hundred-dollar second prize in its fiction contest.

Still, because of Press Board deadlines, *Smith Review* commitments, and classes that were proving to be unusually difficult, Sylvia felt emotionally exhausted. During October, developments in Dick's life made her feel even worse. On the 3rd, he told her that he had possibly contracted tuberculosis, a disease that then afflicted many medical students. Fearing that Dick's left lung's upper lobe had become infected, doctors took chest X rays, the results of which would be known soon. (Sylvia too had an X ray; it came out negative.) Three days later, Dick informed Sylvia that he did not have the disease. Regardless, a weird energy defined their visit on the weekend of the 10th. After that weekend, Dick described Sylvia as having "lovely-long-blonde-cleanly-fresh hair, merry brown eyes, and a rather saucy and quite red mouth"—language that did not reflect the uncertainty in their relationship. As the month wore on, Dick's problems continued. Hospitalized on the 22nd for a reassessment, he learned that he *did* have active tuberculosis. The treatment, his doctors said, would be highly disruptive to his life, since tuberculosis, untreatable with medication at that time, would require him to be committed to a sanitarium for one to three years.

In early November, Dick began his convalescence in Ray Brook, a sanitarium in Saranac, New York. Sylvia's reaction to this hospitalization can only be described as bizarre. "Sick with envy," she wrote in her journal, because after reading a letter from Dick she imagined him "lying up there, rested, fed, taken care of, free to explore books and thoughts at any whim." The catalyst for this decidedly abnormal sentiment was Sylvia's further descent into a depression that had actually prompted thoughts of suicide. She felt in her head a "numb, paralyzing cavern, a pit of hell, a mimicking nothingness," she wrote. "I want to kill myself . . . to crawl back abjectly into the womb." Clearly out of control, she summed up her mental state. "Time, experience: the colossal wave . . . drowning, drowning." On the 14th, in Marcia's off-campus bedroom, she broke down, weeping helplessly. It felt good to "let go, let the tight mask fall off," she confessed of the episode. And as she had talked to herself, the "stone of inertia [rolled] away from the tomb."

At mid-month, looking for a scapegoat, Sylvia concluded that her instability resulted from the hatred she felt for her physical-science class. The course was a waste of time, she thought, and the hours she spent studying for it were torture. On the 19th, two days after she had had tea in Alumni House with *Mademoiselle*'s Marybeth Little, who was traveling to campuses to get to know girls who, like Sylvia, had been accepted for College Board, Sylvia wrote her mother an alarming

letter in which she confessed to considering suicide. And why? Because
of this dreadful science course! she said. Should she see the school
psychiatrist? Would the college possibly allow her to drop the year-
long science class at Christmas? "I am driven inward, feeling hollow,"
she said, so ill that a stay in the infirmary would not "cure the sickness in me." Instead, she looked forward to Thanksgiving holidays, for
then she hoped that visits with her family and the Cantors would cheer
her up. As it happened, the visits—a traditional dinner at home on
Thanksgiving Day, a trip to the Cantors' the next afternoon—*did* help.
But when she went back to Smith on the 30th, she was by no means
well. To complicate matters, upon her arrival she discovered an angry
letter from Eddie, who answered her recent proposal that they collab-
orate on a story by saying, "The two letters I have received from you
since June indicate that I have ceased to be, as I once was, a real
person . . . and have become instead, as have so many others of the
males you have told me about, material for one of your future books,
and a byproduct of your life."

Had it not been for her physical illness and emotional distress—the
source of which she still identified as her science course—how she
hated jargon like erg, joules, valences, watts, coulombs, and amperes—
December might at times have been an upbeat month. *Seventeen*
published her poem "Twelfth Night," which prompted from Olive
Higgins Prouty praise and an invitation to tea over Christmas break.
Mary Ellen Chase presented her with a copy of her *Recipe for a Magic
Childhood* in which she had inscribed, "For Sylvia Plath with admiration and confidence." And the Fall 1952 *Smith Review* reprinted
"Sunday at the Mintons'." Professionally, the month's only setback was
a *New Yorker* rejection. It was, in fact, her second from the magazine.
(The first, refusing a single poem, contained the anonymously written,
although—to Plath—encouraging, note, "Please try us again," a request that had prompted Sylvia to write her mother a letter in which
she fantasized that one day she might actually publish a poem in *The
New Yorker.* "Well, nothing like being ambitious.")

Also in December, Sylvia struck out on a new romance. During
Thanksgiving break, at a supper at the Nortons', she had met a friend
of Perry's from Yale, a slender, good-looking boy named Myron Lotz.

Sylvia had made an effort to get to know him. The son of impoverished Austro-Hungarian immigrants, Myron, nicknamed Mike, was so brilliant—first in his class at Yale—that he was on a three-year undergraduate track to Yale Medical School, and so athletic—one only had to glance at his body to see this—that during the summer he pitched for the Detroit Tigers' farm team. (Over the past summer, he had earned the impressive sum of ten thousand dollars by playing baseball.) After the supper, Sylvia offered and Mike accepted an invitation to the Lawrence House Dance. On the afternoon of the night of the dance, Mike arrived early, and in the course of taking a long walk to get to know each other he and Sylvia ended up straying all the way into Northampton. Passing the mental hospital located in the town, they stopped to stare at the building, whereupon, in the quiet hush of twilight, they could hear the patients' wolfish screams echoing from inside. "Ooooooo," one patient wailed. The voices stayed with Sylvia. Back at Lawrence, she could still hear them clearly in her mind as she held Mike close to her, dancing.

Despite her promising early encounters with Mike, Sylvia's boyfriend throughout December remained, at least superficially, Dick. In several letters at the beginning of the month, he detailed his current writing and reading habits, which had become extensive since he had nothing but free time. He considered some influential literary figures to be—and Plath appeared to concur—Eliot, Faulkner, Hemingway, Pound, Ford Madox Ford, and Gertrude Stein. At the moment, he was reading D. H. Lawrence's *Women in Love,* about which he commented to Sylvia that "Lawrence certainly writes in your style" and that he was "amused at the way the men sit around naked most of the time and admire themselves." Also, he had just completed writing a longish Hemingwayesque boys' adventure story which, after he sent it home for comment—"favorable"—he submitted to *Boys' Life.* Previously, he had suggested that Sylvia travel to Ray Brook during Christmas break. There was a ski slope located near the sanitarium—"for, uh, amateurs," he pointed out. And, he added, Mount Pisgah stood only four miles away.

Early in the month, Plath began suffering from insomnia, which weakened her body and caused her to develop a sore throat. Fed up with her physical and emotional problems, she relented on December 15 and saw the school psychiatrist. Afterwards, she checked into the infirmary, where she remained until Christmas break. At home, between the 20th and Christmas Day, Sylvia had tea at Mrs. Prouty's, dated John Hodges, ate supper with the Nortons twice, spent an afternoon at the Cantors', and hiked with Philip. Following Christmas, she decided to take Dick up on his offer of a skiing trip. The Nortons drove her to Ray Brook and visited with Dick briefly; Sylvia stayed on for a week, lodging with the Nortons' friends the Lynns. On the 27th, even though she had never skied before, Sylvia borrowed skis and, with Dick—a rank amateur—as her instructor, hit the slopes of Pisgah. That day, all went well. But the next day she took a spill—she slammed, cartwheeling, into a snowbank—and injured her left leg. Though not in pain, she played it safe and had her leg X rayed on the 29th. The X ray revealed that she had fractured her fibula, a break that would require her entire leg to be placed in a cast. Wiring her mother, Sylvia downplayed the episode, even joking that she guessed her leg would be "tricky to manipulate while Charlestoning." On the 30th, fractured fibula and all, Sylvia left Saranac.

When a friend inquired about their romance, Dick, who naturally felt saddened by Sylvia's departure, had responded, or so he wrote to Sylvia, "I-was-fond-of-Sylvia-but-don't-know-how-she-feels." Finally, he was beginning to sense the ambivalence that Sylvia had felt for months. In fact, after wavering so long, when the issue of marriage came up in conversation on her first day in Saranac, Sylvia made up her mind once and for all. She simply could not spend the rest of her life with Dick: this is what she told herself, if not Dick. In the future, she would interpret her broken leg as a symbol for her final "break" with Dick. Actually, the Saranac trip did spell the end to their relationship. They were never close again.

When she returned to Smith, Sylvia realized how difficult life was going to be with her leg in a cast. Merely to get across campus was an ordeal, especially given the snow that covered the ground. She just could not make some trips on foot, which meant that she had to hire a taxi—an added expense. (Sylvia approached Miss Mensel and learned that such emergency expenses could be deferred by a Smith fund out of which Mensel presented her with a twenty-dollar bill on the spot.) Also, Sylvia could only bathe by lowering herself into the tub sideways, and she had great difficulty moving from floor to floor in Lawrence. Despite all this, she reported that she remained cheery about her circumstances. She was, in fact, extremely upset. Over Christmas, bad with a broken leg, she had written Eddie to complain about "Allan," her science course, and her new roommate, Mary, whom she regarded as horribly inarticulate. Eddie's no-holds-barred reply was dated January 2, 1953. Concerning "Allan," he did not waver. "You may recall that on our last night together, I spent several hours trying to convince you that the relationship between you and Allan was vicious, biting and competitive, and would end, if pursued as far as marriage, in unhappiness if not violence." Eddie was just as honest when he wrote about Mary. "Is there any chance you dislike her so much because she is such an apt portrayal of everything you have most feared being yourself?" As for the science course, her hysterical reaction to it was a metaphor for a larger mental instability. Her "behavior and state of mind" caused him to be "vitally and deeply concerned." Fearing she was approaching "the ultimate breaking point," he begged her to seek medical help. "Syl, honey, I think you've moved much too close over these past few months, and, if my words and judgement mean anything at all to you, let me implore you to get yourself into some sort of psycho-therapy as soon as possible."

Around Christmas, Sylvia had presented the Administrative Board with a petition requesting that she be allowed to audit her science course in the spring term. In late January the board, much to her delight, approved her request. She felt ecstatic, she wrote her mother, adding that, instead of anguishing through her "hated" science class, she could take Milton for credit. As for science, she would only have to sit in on the classes: there would be no reading, studying, or tests. With this issue settled, Sylvia looked forward to her other courses. Besides Milton, she would sign up for Elizabeth Drew's Modern Poetry, Davis's Creative Writing, and Honors hours. On the day she began her classes, Eddie wrote "to nag you on the subject of a psychiatrist." Jokingly, he threatened to fly east and "seize you by your pretty hair and drag you, caveman style, into the office of the nearest available witch-doctor." That same day, Dick related his own literary news. *Boys' Life* had rejected his story, but *The New England Journal of Medicine* had accepted his biographical sketch of William Carlos Williams, whose *Paterson* Dick had recently read and admired. (When Dick had mailed him a copy of the sketch, Williams, a general practitioner, responded favorably.) Dick also attached to his letter something else he had just written—a "review," as he called it, entitled "Individualism and Sylvia Plath: An Analysis and Synthesis," which discussed "Den of Lions," "Sunday at the Mintons'," "The Perfect Set-up," "Dialogue," "Initiation" (which appeared in the January *Seventeen*), and a selection of Plath's religion papers. Interestingly, Sylvia never told Eddie about the "review," which Eddie would surely have attributed to Dick's unconscious desire to compete with her. Then, on January 31, Mike arrived in Northampton for the weekend; he and Sylvia had ginger ales at Rahar's on Saturday night and dinner and supper at Lawrence on Sunday. As Mike revealed details of his life to Sylvia, she realized that his youth had been much more austere than she had thought. Growing up among minorities in underprivileged neighborhoods, he had little chance of ending up at Yale. But here he was.

In February, after finals, Plath received her grades. In her "hated" science course, which she was sure she was going to fail, she earned an A −. With the pressure of the semester weighing down on her, she had obviously lost all ability to perceive her own talent accurately. She also did well in her other two classes, making an A − in Creative Writing and the only A in a class of ten students in Medieval Literature. Encouraged by these grades, Sylvia tried to resolve her relationship with Dick. In February, she wrote him four letters in which she strongly hinted that their involvement had disintegrated into a friendship. On the 25th, she spelled out her feelings to her mother. She could not marry Dick, she said, because she needed a man who was, physically, a "colossus," who, mentally, would not be "jealous of my creativity in other fields than children." For his part, Dick finally deduced Sylvia's feelings, not only from her letters but from her actions. When he asked her to join him at the Middlebury Carnival, which took place on February 20, she refused. When he invited her to visit him during her spring vacation, she would not commit herself. This could not have happened at a worse time for Dick: in early February, he learned that his condition had not improved sufficiently for him to re-enroll in medical school for the fall.

As Dick faded from the picture, Sylvia dated other boys. Besides Mike, who was so taken with her that he had written that he could "think much more clearly while away from [her] biological magnetism," and whom Sylvia described as a "hercules" with a photographic memory, she was seriously attracted to one other boy. An Amherst College senior, an English major enchanted by Joyce, a graduate of Choate, and a resident of Wellesley (where he and Sylvia had never met), Gordon Lameyer had been told by his mother about an adorable, intelligent blonde—Sylvia—who had addressed the Smith Club of Wellesley back in the fall. Lately, Gordon had telephoned Sylvia to ask for a date on February 7, the day after her leg was to be re-X-rayed. (The bone had not mended.) That night, when Gordon arrived at Lawrence, Sylvia clunked down the stairs, her leg still in a cast. Even on crutches, she was as captivating as Gordon's mother had said. Peering from the steps, Sylvia saw a vision of her own: tall, slim, handsome, Gordon was all one could hope for in a blind date. Because of her cast, they kept the evening simple; following supper in Gordon's fraternity, they went up to his room to listen to music and to read Joyce aloud. Later, once Gordon had dropped Sylvia off at Lawrence, she suspected she would be seeing more of him, although she felt concerned by what she perceived as Gordon's jealousy over her literary success.

Subconsciously, Sylvia was haunted by thoughts of boys—and sex. For years now, she had fought her sexual urges, sometimes with success, sometimes not. Lately, the urges had become clouded by an air of violence. In one recent journal entry, she recorded a telling fantasy, that of being taken to a mountain cabin to be "raped in a huge lust like a cave woman, fighting, screaming, biting in a ferocious ecstasy of orgasm." It would be years before she would meet a man who satisfied this dream.

Dates—no matter with whom—came easier after February 19, the day Dr. Chrisman cut the cast off her leg. Although the fibula wasn't totally healed, which caused her to stumble and feel acute pain when she walked, and although the sight of her yellow, shriveled leg horrified her, Sylvia was excited to have the cast off. On the 23rd, she wrote to her mother that she could now put all of her weight on the leg without its hurting at all. This was fortuitous, because so much was happening in her life, both professionally and socially, that she needed nothing to hold her back. For her guest editorship application, she was submitting manuscripts to *Mademoiselle*. In late January, she had mailed in a cartoon spread and an article about health; in early February, a short story (not part of the requirement, but it would help her chances if the magazine accepted it, she hoped); and in late February, her recent theme, "The Ideal Summer," and an essay about a Harvard Medical School dance. In its March issue, *Seventeen* published her poem "Sonnet: The Suitcases Are Packed Again," which prompted the college newspaper to run an article about Plath and the poem. It had been written, the paper said, "when she was returning home for summer vacation [in 1951]." Then, on March 5, she headed by train to New Haven for a long weekend with Mike. On Friday, they toured Yale's baseball facilities and ate a rare-roast-beef supper at Silliman. That night, they went to the Yale junior prom and danced, along with the other five hundred couples, to the Tommy Dorsey band until the early hours of the morning. On Saturday, they drove along the Connecticut shore; on Sunday, Sylvia had lunch with Perry, who, during their whole meal, never mentioned Dick.

In March, Sylvia continued to drift out of Dick's life. In particular, Sylvia's dates with other boys threatened him. Instead of confronting her directly, he made an unusual move: he wrote to Aurelia. In his letter, Dick expressed his concern about the future of his and Sylvia's relationship and wondered if Aurelia believed they would marry. To his cordial but inquisitive letter, Aurelia responded immediately. "When Sivvy came home from the Cape this summer, she did say to me very positively that she was, *at present,* 'not at all matrimonially minded'. To the query—why then did she go out with you so much—came the answer—because she enjoyed being with you more than with any other person. . . . 'I probably won't be married for a long long long while yet,' [Sylvia continued]. 'I have a lot of growing up to do still.' "

Closing her letter to Dick, Aurelia wrote: "I only hope with all my heart that no hurt comes to you through . . . any of us. In my affections you have a place very close to that of my two who come first."

Meanwhile, Sylvia had become busy with her career. *The New Yorker* rejected two villanelles, but an editor, who told her to "Try Us Again," had penciled in changes on the poems. *Seventeen* bought "Sonnet: To a Dissembling Spring." She received a manuscript back from *The Atlantic Monthly*. And *Mademoiselle* returned her short story—a bad omen, she decided, for her guest-editorship application. By the end of March, Plath considered herself a failure; she even signed one letter to her mother "Your rejected daughter." Yet, despite her feelings of defeat, Plath remained a mainstay of the invitation-only teas Mary Ellen Chase had at her home on Paradise Road. During these teas, Plath talked to Ruth Mortimer, an English Honors student now writing a senior thesis on Dostoevsky with the working title *The Design of the Dream in "Crime and Punishment."* (It would be the first Smith thesis devoted wholly to a Russian author.) They also discussed Plath's thesis, in which she planned to write about Joyce.

April was an even more important month in Plath's literary life. *Seventeen* published her poem "Carnival Nocturne." On the 10th, she attended a reading given by W. H. Auden at Sage Hall. One of England's most respected poets, Auden was serving as a visiting Neilson Professor at Smith for the spring term. Obviously consumed by his thoughts—or perhaps transported into his own world by the alcohol he was rumored to abuse—Auden had often been sighted strolling about campus in his bedroom slippers. Thin, big-headed, gray-haired, he was perfect, according to Plath—not just because of his writerly appearance but because of his poetry. During the reading, Plath sat enthralled; in Auden she had discovered her "God." Afterwards, as she walked back to Lawrence with Gordon, whom she had run into at the reading, she referred to Auden as an angel. Days passed, seven of which she spent sick in the infirmary, before, on the 24th, Russell Lynes of *Harper's* purchased, for one hundred dollars, three poems— "Doomsday" and "To Eva Descending the Stair," the villanelles *The New Yorker* had rejected, and "Go Get the Goodly Squab." Three days later, *The Smith Review* appointed Plath editor-in-chief for the coming

year. That same day, she enjoyed Auden's visit to Chase's Modern
Poetry. In Chase's living room, while he spoke about a number of
subjects, he theorized that Caliban is the "natural bestial projection,"
Ariel the "creative imagination." Finally, at the end of the month, the
telegram for which Plath had been hoping arrived. Signed Marybeth
Little, it read:

HAPPY TO ANNOUNCE YOU HAVE WON A MADEMOISELLE
1953 GUEST EDITORSHIP. YOU MUST BE AVAILABLE
FROM JUNE 1 THROUGH JUNE 26. PLEASE WIRE
COLLECT IMMEDIATELY WHETHER OR NOT YOU ACCEPT
AND IF YOU WANT HOTEL RESERVATIONS. GIVE MEANS
AND COST OF TRANSPORTATION BETWEEN HERE AND
HOME IN SEPARATE WIRE IF NECESSARY.

The accolades continued in May. Plath's Press Board articles appeared regularly; *The Smith Review* printed three villanelles, the two
Harper's had bought and "Mad Girl's Love Song"; and Olive Prouty
wrote to congratulate her on her successes and to invite her, Warren,
and Aurelia to tea. The month's only source of frustration came from
boyfriends. Beginning on May 1, Ray Wunderlich, a Columbia Medical
School student whom she had met at The Belmont, treated her to a
trip to Manhattan. She may have expected Ray to try to seduce her
(she jokingly wrote to Warren that she was afraid he might), but nothing
of a sexual nature occurred. On Friday, after they had supper at La
Petite Maison and saw *The Crucible,* they went to Delmonico's and
stayed until five in the morning. On Saturday afternoon, they attended
Carmen—Plath's first opera; later, they ate supper at the Gloucester
House before seeing Tennessee Williams's *Camino Real,* which Plath
described as surreal and shocking. Perhaps because of this trip, Sylvia
became disillusioned with Mike, whom she visited on the weekend of
May 9 at Yale. She now considered him emotionally insecure and overly
concerned about his own problems, never anyone else's. Yet the most
disturbing news of the month involved Dick, who was operated on for
tuberculosis. (A twenty-stitch scar would be left under his left shoulder
blade.) Though she felt concern for Dick, she became angry at his

mother who was not happy over Sylvia's refusal to accept a summer waitressing job that had been lined up for her in a town near Ray Brook. The purpose of the job was clear: if she were close to Dick, she could see him regularly. But how could she turn down a *Mademoiselle* guest editorship? To pass up Manhattan for a waitressing job near Saranac was nothing short of absurd.

Sylvia's only real worry centered on money. The $150 *Mademoiselle* paid for one month's work would be a fraction of what she needed to earn over the summer. Also, if, as planned, she attended Harvard Summer School beginning in July—she wanted to take Frank O'Connor's fiction-writing class—she would have no time for a lucrative summer job. So, she decided she would just have to supplement her *Mademoiselle* salary by selling her own writing—one of the stories she hoped to write in O'Connor's class, an article about her New York experience, or the ten-thousand-word pulp piece, "I Lied for Love," that she had cranked out in April in hopes of selling it to *True Story*.

May was hectic for Plath, in part because *Mademoiselle* required her to start two assignments early. One was an article about five young poets—George Steiner, William Burford, Alastair Reid, Anthony Hecht, and Richard Wilbur, the last of whom she had met through his mother-in-law, Edna Ward, a friend of Aurelia's. The other was a profile of Elizabeth Bowen, whom she interviewed on the 26th at the home of May Sarton at 14 Wright Street in Cambridge. Back at Smith, Plath prepared for her final exams, which she had to take early to get to New York by June 1. When the exams were done, she had earned her usual excellent grades: Modern Poetry, A; Creative Writing, A; and Milton, B+. (At present, Plath ranked first in her class.) Also, the college awarded her two prestigious prizes for poetry, the Elizabeth Babcock Poetry Prize and the Ethel Olin Corbin Prize. On the 29th, the day the *Daily Hampshire Gazette* ran the article "Smith Correspondent for Gazette Honored," which detailed Plath's upcoming stint at *Mademoiselle*, Sylvia returned home for two days to pack and to write her piece on Bowen. Finally, on May 31, she boarded the train for Manhattan, where she was to spend twenty-six days that would change her life forever.

5

In the aftermath of World War II, New York City was booming. Business had never been better, and when the United Nations decided to locate its headquarters on the East River, the city could claim to be the most influential in the world. Day and night Manhattan never stopped moving. Trains rattled below street level and along elevated tracks one story or more above ground. At rush hour, yellow cabs, cars, and buses crowded the streets and avenues, some still boasting trolley tracks or cobblestone paving. And everywhere you turned you saw row upon row of skyscrapers, new steel-and-glass boxes rising up amid the pre-war stone buildings. Not only did New York attract a constant flow of tourists, but by the early fifties it had became a mecca for artists and intellectuals. Writers and academics settled on the Upper West Side, because of its low rents and proximity to Columbia University. Sculptors and painters congregated in Greenwich Village; a group of abstract expressionists led by Jackson Pollock, Willem de Kooning, and Barnett Newman emerged to capture world attention and be acclaimed as the New York School. George Balanchine choreographed dances. Joe DiMaggio played for the Yankees. In 1953, the city replaced existing mayor Vincent Impellittei with Robert F. Wagner, Jr. The former had taken over for William O'Dwyer, who, implicated in several city government scandals, had been quickly appointed by the President as ambassador to Mexico. But this was not the only political scandal that demanded the attention of New Yorkers in the early fifties. A second one proved considerably more sensational. International in scope, it involved spying, Russia, and a married couple named Rosenberg.

Victorian, stately, ornate, the Barbizon Hotel for Women, where *Mademoiselle* put up its guest editors, stood on the corner of Lexington Avenue and Sixty-third Street, in the middle of Manhattan's Upper East Side. A fixture of the neighborhood since 1927, through the years the hotel had been a favorite of young women attending Seven Sisters schools. Stepping from the taxi she had caught at the train station,

Sylvia headed for the hotel. After she checked in, she rode the elevator to the thirteenth floor and walked down the hall to the group of small, single rooms reserved for seventeen of the guest editors. (Three had arranged private lodgings.) In her room, which contained a bed, bureau, and chairs but no bath, since the girls shared one at the end of the hall, Sylvia took in her view of the Third Avenue elevated train, the tops of buildings, rooftop gardens, and a slice of the East River. Later, once she had unpacked, Sylvia mingled with the other girls, most of whom had now arrived. The other guest editors were: Janet Wagner from Knox College; Laurie Totten, Syracuse University; Candy Bolster, Bryn Mawr; Carol LeVarn, Sweet Briar; Betty-Jo Boyle, Allegheny College; Anne Burnside, University of Maryland; Neva Nelson, San Jose State University; Anne Shawber, Northwestern University; Laurie Glazer, University of Michigan; Malinda Edgington, Miami University; Eileen McLaughlin, Pratt Institute; Dinny Lain, Stephens College; Gloria Kirshner, Barnard College; Ruth L. Abramson, University of Pennsylvania; Grace Macleod, University of Oklahoma; Margaret Affleck, Brigham Young University; Nedra Anderwert, Washington University; Madelyn Mathers, University of Washington; and Del Schmidt, Skidmore College. These young women, students in some of the country's better schools, were bright, ambitious, highly motivated. They reflected Sylvia's own talents and motivations in many ways. But over the next four weeks one difference would emerge. In coming to know her fellow guest editors, Sylvia learned that they did not feel the same pressure to excel intellectually as she did. Though smart, they had been encouraged by their schools and families, at least more than she had, to express their emotions.

One timely topic of conversation among the young women was, of course, the impending execution of Julius and Ethel Rosenberg. In a front-page trial that had ended in March 1951, the Rosenbergs, accused of spying for the Soviet Union, had been found guilty and sentenced to die in the electric chair. Because their appeals had been denied and President Eisenhower had refused all pleas for clemency, the executions were scheduled for this June. Excited to be in Manhattan yet strangely anxious about the Rosenbergs' imminent death, Sylvia slept restlessly her first night at the Barbizon. Early the next morning, she ate breakfast (the hotel coffee shop became a favorite haunt of the girls) and walked the handful of blocks to 575 Madison Avenue, the address of *Mademoiselle*'s offices. Upstairs, on the sixth floor, Sylvia and the other guest editors, most of whom wore hats and gloves to accessorize their "business" dresses, gathered in the conference room for a meeting that convened at nine o'clock.

Following Marybeth Little's opening remarks, Editor-in-Chief Betsy Talbot Blackwell took over. A diminutive, pretty woman who was "so tightly corseted that she had difficulty walking in her little heels," as her copyeditor Sally Jenks remembers, Blackwell addressed the group, her trademark cigarette-smoker's voice crackling. Speaking only briefly, she stressed that the girls should put "health before genius." Then she introduced the other editors, two of whom were legendary. Fiction Editor Margarita G. Smith, the sister of Carson McCullers, headed a department known for publishing the first work of such authors as Ilona Karmet, William Goyen, and Truman Capote. More notorious than Smith was Managing Editor Cyrilly Abels. Immaculately groomed and seriously intellectual, Abels enjoyed close friendships with literary giants like Katherine Anne Porter and Dylan Thomas. On the job, she demanded that her staff meet every deadline even while they aspired for perfection. But just as memorable as her personality was her physical appearance. "She was something of a paradox," Jenks recalls. "She had a lovely figure. A great sense of style when it came to dressing. But an ugly face. A face that I would prefer not to look at directly too long. Watery blue eyes and a pursed mouth. She wore blue, almost invariably, because it brought out the blue in her eyes. It transformed an ugly face, by my standards, into something not quite so difficult to look at."

After Blackwell, other editors spoke quickly. The meeting broke up at ten, and each girl proceeded to a conference with the editor to whom she had been assigned to work. For Sylvia, this meant reporting to Cyrilly Abels: even though she had requested guest fiction, Plath had been appointed guest managing editor. A former winner of the magazine's fiction contest and a published short-story writer, Plath would have been natural for guest fiction, as would have Guest Health and Beauty Editor Dinny Lain, who was interested in writing prose and who would subsequently publish both fiction and nonfiction as Diane

Johnson. That first morning, Sylvia immediately met with unpleasant news when Abels told her that her "Poets on Campus" would have to be rewritten in a style more appropriate to *Mademoiselle*. Once she had spent the rest of the morning beginning that rewrite, Sylvia had lunch alone with Blackwell and Abels at the Drake Room—an honor afforded her because of her guest-managing-editor status. In the afternoon, Sylvia left her rewriting long enough to be photographed. Holding a freshly cut red rose, she sat on a divan. As he had each of the other guest editors, the photographer posed her. "You always look as if you are going to cry when you are laughing," he said at one point, and Sylvia broke into tears. "I too was on the verge of crying," remembers Neva Nelson, another guest editor. "The photographer was very concerned with himself, explaining that he was a delicate creature and used to only the best equipment and top models and was working under terrible conditions."

Monday's pace set the tone for the week. When she was not working in the office, she attended a fashion show at the Hotel Roosevelt and a tour of Richard Hudnut's Fifth Avenue salon. But for the most part, Sylvia, whose typing-table desk sat next to Abels's regular-size one, remained at 575 Madison to finish her "Poets on Campus" revision, write "MLLE's Last Word," read manuscripts, and type rejection letters. She felt a certain amount of satisfaction—and no doubt learned a lesson about the inner workings of the publishing industry—on the day she typed out and signed a rejection letter turning down work by a member of the staff of *The New Yorker*.

Her second week was just as busy. On separate occasions, she met Paul Engle, editor of that year's O. Henry short-story collection and founder of The Writers' Workshop at the University of Iowa, and Vance Bourjaily, a first-novelist who had just edited the premier issue of the literary magazine *Discovery*. One night, she attended a formal dance in the Saint Regis Hotel's Terrace Room, where in the frigid ballroom—the hotel had turned the air-conditioning system up too high—she remarked how the tablecloths, chairs, and decorations were all colored pink, how the city lights glowed brightly beyond the windows, and how the music never ceased, since two bands alternated, one band descending into the stage floor as the other ascended and picked up with the same song. The week's most memorable night began when, on their way to the New York City Ballet, the taxi in which Sylvia and three other guest editors were riding became stuck in traffic. As they sat there in the heat, a tall, pleasant-looking man approached the car and said, "Too many pretty girls for one taxi. I'm Art Ford, the disc jockey. Come in for a talk." While Ford paid their fare, the girls piled out to join him for a drink. In the bar, Ford talked Carol LeVarn and Sylvia into meeting him after his radio show, which ended at three in the morning.

At the ballet, Sylvia watched George Balanchine's *Metamorphoses* and *Scotch Symphony*, Lew Christensen's *Con Amore*, and Jerome Robbins's *Fanfare*. Afterwards, she and a friend barhopped Third Avenue. Then she and Carol met Art Ford, who showed them Greenwich Village. The next morning, with almost no sleep, Sylvia dragged herself into the office for a full day of work.

Over the past two weeks, the pace she had been keeping, and the unsettling nature of the events themselves (the evening with Art Ford had contained its share of sexual energy) had started to affect Sylvia. Neva Nelson heard her complain about how she hated the drudgery and the "ugly details" of her job, and Polly Weaver, a full-time *Mademoiselle* editor, stopped in Abels's office one afternoon to find Sylvia crying because she had to work late. The next two weeks, though, would be even more disturbing.

Because she did not have the money for the train fare to Andover, Sylvia missed Warren's Exeter graduation exercises, which took place on the weekend of the 13th. Instead, she wrote her mother that her thoughts were with her and with Warren, who had received a full scholarship to Harvard for the fall. Sylvia stayed in New York and mailed in late her writing sample—"Sunday at the Mintons' "—in support of her application to O'Connor's Harvard Summer School class.

Her third week in New York was the most eventful—and traumatic. On Monday, the guest editors toured *Living* magazine; Tuesday, the offices of the advertising agency Batton, Barton, Durstine, and Osborn, where they were treated to a luncheon featuring crabmeat salad. That night, Sylvia dated Gary Kaminloff, a Wellesley friend now employed as a simultaneous interpreter at the United Nations. Back in her hotel room, she awoke nauseated in the middle of the night. Sure she was going to throw up, Sylvia rushed to the bathroom, only to find it full of other guest editors who were also sick. The crabmeat salad, they soon determined, was tainted and gave them all ptomaine poisoning. The next day, few girls made it to work. Later in the week, most felt well enough to tour the United Nations and the magazines *Vanity Fair* and *Charm*, go to the premiere of the Jane Wyman–Ray Milland movie *Let's Do It Again*, and visit John Fredericks Hats.

On June 19, a Friday, the Rosenbergs were executed as scheduled. "The morning of the executions, Sylvia met me in the Barbizon coffee shop looking very down," Janet Wagner, a guest editor who had become a friend of Sylvia's, would one day write.

> She refused breakfast and argued about the appropriateness of the impending executions with one of the other girls. Suddenly she turned to me in disgust and asked how I could eat when the Rosenbergs were about to be fried just like the eggs on my plate. I immediately lost my appetite. Sylvia got up in a huff without eating at all, and I followed her out. Then the strangest thing happened. It was a very hot, humid day so we decided to go underground through the cool subway to work. Along the way, Sylvia kept asking me the time. Finally, at exactly nine o'clock, she looked at me in horror and said, "Now it's happening," meaning the Rosenberg execution. She stopped and held out her arms to me and there were, raising up on her arms from her wrists to her elbows, little bumps. Soon, they sort of bled together like welts from burns. Obviously, Sylvia was experiencing burns all over her arms in empathy for the Rosenbergs who were—she believed—being electrocuted at that moment. I was mortified yet, deep down, impressed with the eerie strangeness of it all. It somehow connected in my mind with the Stigmata of Christ that sometimes happens to very religious people. We continued on to the office in silence. Neither of us ever brought the subject up again, but it stuck vividly in my mind forever.

(In fact, Sylvia mistook the hour of the Rosenberg execution, which did not take place until evening.)

There had been other instances of Sylvia's occasional weird behavior.

The most telling had been what came to be known to some of the guest editors as "the Dylan Thomas episode." That summer, Abels was negotiating with Thomas for the rights to his drama *Under Milkwood*. On the day Abels had lunch with Thomas unexpectedly, Guest Fiction Editor Candy Bolster accompanied Abels, because Sylvia was out of the office. When Sylvia found out, she fumed. For the next two days, she became obsessed with Thomas. She hung out in his favorite tavern and lurked in the hall by his hotel-room door. She never saw him, and eventually she gave up, but her distress seemed grossly exaggerated.

On the weekend after the Rosenberg execution, the guest editors went to a New York Yankees–Detroit Tigers baseball game at Yankee Stadium in the Bronx. Also, on Saturday night, Sylvia and Janet attended, along with some of the other guest editors, a dance at the tennis club in Forest Hills, Queens. The climax of the evening occurred when a Peruvian United Nations delegate, with whom Sylvia had become friendly at the party, made a sexual advance to her. Fortunately, Sylvia and Janet were escorted back to Manhattan by Sylvia's date, which the magazine had provided.

On Monday, Sylvia plunged herself into her last week in New York. She toured the New York *Herald Tribune* and Macy's, went to George Bernard Shaw's *Misalliance* at the Barrymore Theatre, and stopped by a farewell cocktail party at Mrs. Blackwell's Fifth Avenue apartment. On Sylvia's last day of work, Cyrilly Abels took her to lunch as a token of her appreciation. Since the August issue had been put "to bed," Plath, the issue's major contributor, could see the result of her month of work. Besides her interview with Bowen and "Poets on Campus," she had contributed "MLLE's Last Word," blurbs under pictures, and her poem "Mad Girl's Love Song." Also, she appeared in photographs—a group shot taken in Central Park and the portrait of her sitting on a divan holding a rose. Finally, her career was discussed in "Jobography," and her handwriting was analyzed by expert Harry O. Teltscher. "Sylvia will succeed in artistic fields," Teltscher wrote. "She has a sense of form and beauty and an intense enjoyment in her work." But because the magazine would not list each girl's weaknesses, the following was not printed: Sylvia must "[o]vercome superficiality, stilted behavior, rigidity of outlook."

To celebrate her last Friday night in New York, Sylvia went on a date with Ray Wunderlich, her friend from Columbia Medical School. The date, which included a ride on the Staten Island Ferry, progressed without incident, but Sylvia's last encounter with Janet Wagner was another matter. "Sylvia came in my room [at the very end of the month] and asked if she could have a dress to travel home in because she had thrown all hers off the roof of the hotel," Wagner later wrote about an episode that Aurelia Plath would deny happened. "At the time I dismissed this as one of Sylvia's fictions, said to attract attention. I offered her my old green print dirndl skirt and the white peasant blouse with the eyelet ruffles on the sleeves." In return, Sylvia gave her her bathrobe, which she insisted Janet accept even though Janet did not want to.

By mid-afternoon on Saturday, Sylvia had checked out of the Barbizon and was on her way to Wellesley by train. It had been an exhausting month. During her final week, she wrote her mother that at home she wanted to sleep, play tennis, and go sunbathing, for, though she had been excited by her month at *Mademoiselle,* she had also become severely depressed. Because of this, she hoped her mother would meet her at the station when her train—"my coffin"—arrived. More than fatigue was plaguing Sylvia; she suffered from extreme disillusionment as well. The world had "split open . . . like a watermelon," she wrote from New York, the city's "guts" spilling out before her "gaping eyes." She had been stunned by the callousness and promiscuity present in the city. When she discussed her feelings with fellow guest editors—and she did specifically with Laurie Totten, a Wellesley resident whose outlook on life coincided with hers—she realized just how disappointing the *Mademoiselle* experience had been. And, in an act of transference, she came to see herself as having disappointed others, especially those whom she regarded as her sponsors. Near the end of June, Sylvia wrote Wilbury Crockett a note in which she apologized at length for letting him down, much to Crockett's puzzlement. Like so many other clues from the summer of 1953, her note to Crockett showed that Sylvia was descending into a dangerously unhappy mental state, the true severity of which no one in her life at that time fully identified.

6

In Wellesley, as she got off the train, Sylvia saw a welcome sight—her mother and Grammy waiting on the station platform. Tired and haggard, Sylvia hugged the two women, who were both glad to see her. Then the three of them loaded Sylvia's baggage into the car. On their way home, they talked casually until Aurelia said to Sylvia, as if offering an aside, "By the way, Frank O'Connor's class"—at Harvard Summer School—"is filled; you'll have to wait for next summer before you register for it again." Nervously, Aurelia glanced in the rearview mirror to see Sylvia's reaction. Her mother may have chosen her words, tone, and occasion carefully, but Sylvia deduced the obvious: the class was not full, O'Connor had *rejected* her. All at once, seized by an overwhelming sense of panic, Sylvia could feel her face drain white and a knot of sickness form in her stomach. To any other student, the failure to be admitted to a writing workshop might have been a disappointment. For Sylvia, whose work as a writer and an intellectual had come to define her to herself, whose ambitions had been encouraged not just by the adoration of her mother, the respect of her friends, and the special treatment of the entire Smith faculty but by successes with publication practically unprecedented for a person her age, the effect was alarming. It was as if a major portion of the structure of her life, which she had worked so hard to construct, had suddenly eroded.

Over the rest of the weekend and the coming week, Sylvia tried to unwind from her year of studying, writing, and working capped by her singular month in New York—*and* to accept O'Connor's rejection. She went on a picnic with Marcia Brown in Cambridge, on the banks of the Charles River; dated Gordon Lameyer, who was home awaiting his enlistment in the navy's Officer Candidate School—one afternoon they read aloud Joyce's *Finnegans Wake*—but mostly she debated with herself whether, now that she could not take O'Connor's class, she should even *go* to Harvard Summer School, which began on July 6. (On the partial scholarship Harvard had granted her, she could have chosen from many other subjects.) As she wrote an entry in her journal that she titled "Letter to an Over-grown, Over-protected, Scared,

Spoiled Baby," she weighed the pros and cons. Finally, she concluded: "I AM NOT GOING TO HARVARD SUMMER SCHOOL." Instead, she would remain in Wellesley, study shorthand with her mother, and write on her own, even though she felt terrified by the latter since she feared she might fail.

During that first week home, however, Sylvia found she could not focus her attention, could not—and this disturbed her most—write. In the backyard, while she sunbathed on a lounge chair, she could not concentrate enough on a book to comprehend the meaning of its sentences. She just stared at the pages. One particular book she could not read was *Ulysses*, which she needed to finish, because she still intended to write her senior thesis on Joyce. Often, Sylvia wandered about the house in a daze. Finally, she confided in her mother that she had lost her imagination and that she had let down those people who had championed her most, although she did not reveal one thought forming in her mind: *she wanted to die*.

During her second week home, Sylvia continued her visits with Gordon, who, after joining the navy, was now booked to leave for candidate school in Newport, Rhode Island, in mid-July. At Gordon's mother's apartment, they spent most days and some evenings together: they listened to classical music, discussed *Finnegans Wake*, and marveled at recordings of Dylan Thomas reading his poetry. To Gordon, who left as planned on the 13th, Sylvia maintained a carefree, "golden-girl" persona, but, to Dick, she had shown her disquiet. In a letter in early July, she complained about her severe unhappiness; Dick responded on the 7th by saying that, even though he was "saddened" by her "intense unrest," he wanted her to remember that it was "one thing to be concerned with aliveness and sincerity and creativity, and quite another to remain more or less deeply troubled and rootless and uncertain."

Following Gordon's departure, Sylvia's depression worsened. Writing in her journal on the 14th, she sounded dangerously disturbed. "All right, you have gone the limit," she wrote, adding that all of her friends were either married or "being creative." "You saw a vision of yourself in a straight-jacket, and a drain on the family, murdering your mother in actuality, killing the edifice of love and respect built up over the years in the hearts of other people." One subject that occupied her subconscious, which she did not write about in her journal—she could not admit this until she entered therapy years later—was her father. Dead now almost thirteen years—how she remembered *The Tempest*'s "Ariel's Song," which began "Full fathom five thy father lies"—he haunted her memories.

Bored and unable to write, Sylvia searched out distractions. She gave up shorthand after four lessons, because the squiggly characters confused her. At her mother's suggestion, she took a mornings-only part-time nurse's-aide job at the Newton-Wellesley Hospital; the staff placed her in charge of feeding patients too weak or too near death to feed themselves. But, despite her activities, she sank deeper into a depression. She still could not sleep. She went to the local drugstore to buy popular psychology books, in which she found ample evidence that she was "losing my mind." And she desperately believed that, if she had a nervous breakdown, her family would be ruined financially. One morning, after Gordon left for candidate school, as Sylvia dressed in the bedroom she again shared with her mother (Warren had come to Wellesley for the summer and taken over his old room), Aurelia noticed partially healed scars on Sylvia's legs. Questioning her, Aurelia got the answer: "I just wanted to see if I had the guts!" Then Sylvia became near-frantic. "Oh, Mother, the world is so rotten! I want to die! Let's die together!"

Taking her in her arms, Aurelia tried to calm her. Within hours, Aurelia had Sylvia in the office of Dr. Francesca Racioppi, the Plath family physician, who strongly recommended that Sylvia consult the psychiatrist Dr. J. Peter Thornton. After he had seen Sylvia at home on the 18th, Thornton advised Aurelia to bring her into his Commonwealth Avenue office in Boston on Tuesday, and following that appointment Thornton scheduled another.

One night over the weekend of the 25th, Gordon, home on leave, ate supper with Sylvia at Elmwood Road. During the evening—indeed, throughout the whole weekend—Sylvia appeared so like her old self that Gordon would never have guessed that she had lately been considering suicide. On July 27, the Monday after Gordon left, Sylvia saw Thornton a third time, again in his office. Then, Thornton reported his diagnosis to Aurelia: Sylvia suffered from a severe depression that would leave her hovering on the brink of nervous collapse unless she received the medical treatment believed at that time to intervene most dramatically with emotional distress—electroshock therapy. Aurelia, who felt more alone now than she had in all the years since Otto's death, hesitated at first. She considered the doctor too young and could not forget Sylvia's comment that he reminded her of an ex-boyfriend she didn't care for. But eventually she gave in. As soon as he could make arrangements, Thornton told her, the sessions would begin on an outpatient basis at the Valley Head Hospital. Full hospitalization did not seem necessary.

That evening, the Plaths—Aurelia, Warren, and Sylvia—visited Olive Higgins Prouty's. They strolled through her gardens, drank Old Fashioneds on the terrace, and ate supper. But they did *not* openly discuss Sylvia's depression and impending shock treatments. On the sly, Aurelia did confess to Prouty—to quote letters Prouty would subsequently write—that Sylvia "seemed deeply depressed because she could not write or do any constructive work on her senior thesis," and that she (Aurelia) feared Sylvia "was having what might be a nervous breakdown." Sylvia, though, did not talk about her sickness with anyone besides her immediate family and doctors. Not even Gordon, to whom she felt closer now than ever.

On the 29th, Sylvia's reluctance to discuss her depression became academic. On that day she received her first round of electroshock therapy, which caused her to cease communication with other people almost entirely. The day's routine would be repeated for all future sessions. A neighbor drove Aurelia and Sylvia to Valley Head Hospital, after which Aurelia, at the doctor's request, sat with her friend in a waiting area while Sylvia underwent the procedure in a treatment room. Metal probes were placed on Sylvia's temples so that powerful dosages of electricity—"shocks"—could be shot through her body. Following the session, the staff returned Sylvia to Aurelia, and the two of them left the hospital. On that first day and on three additional days, Thornton oversaw the session. At some point in August, he went on vacation and left a Dr. Tillotson to oversee several more sessions.

In later years, standard medical procedure would demand that doctors administer electroshock therapy only after the patient was given a muscle relaxant and a general anesthetic. Also, a doctor or a nurse would stay with the patient during the recovery period, to provide support and counseling. In the case of Sylvia Plath, none of this happened. Because she had taken no muscle relaxant, her body was rigid with fear. Because she had received no anesthesia, she was, in effect, nearly electrocuted. Because no doctor or nurse accompanied her in recovery, she experienced a painful, numbing loneliness as she lay on the table by herself. With her psyche ripped open by raw wattage, she was more vulnerable than she had ever been. And to whom could she turn in this ultimate moment of need? No one. Rather, she became haunted by thoughts of abandonment. In theory, electroshock therapy lowers a patient's level of anxiety by interfering with the brain's normal functions and by creating temporary memory loss. Yet, in a very real sense, Plath's level of anxiety *increased* with electroshock therapy, if for no other reason than the manner in which her doctors conducted the sessions.

As a side effect of shock therapy, Sylvia's sleeplessness turned into acute insomnia. In August, night after night passed during which she did not sleep at all. It seemed she had become immune to the sleeping pills she now took. By the third week in August, as she continued her shock treatments, Sylvia had not slept all month. Now desperate, Aurelia began putting the sleeping pills under lock and key in the family "safe"—actually a metal lockbox that she kept in the bedroom she shared with Sylvia.

On the night of August 21, Sylvia took two sleeping pills (out of a new bottle of fifty) and slept fretfully on and off through the night. The next day, Saturday, she felt well enough to go on a double date to the beach with Dick Linden, an acquaintance of Gordon's. As the two couples lay in the afternoon sun, Sylvia questioned her friends about the best way to commit suicide. At that time, Dick and the other couple did not take Sylvia seriously. Yet, on this day, as she would later tell Eddie, she *did* flirt with suicide: she swam out into the ocean alone and tried to drown herself. She was saved, she said, because she finally could not force her body to give in to the destructive wishes of her mind. Later that night, the two couples went dancing at The Meadows. Nothing unusual happened.

August 23rd seemed to pass uneventfully, but Sylvia—in truth— had reached a low point. After an exhausting academic year, after a disillusioning month in Manhattan during which she came to see herself as a failure, after enduring the insult of O'Connor's rejection, after being subjected to poorly executed electroshock therapy—which she feared might continue—Sylvia decided that she did not want to live. On Monday, August 24, around 2:00 P.M., she waited for her mother to leave with a friend to watch a film of the coronation of Queen Elizabeth II, and for her grandparents, just returned from a vacation, to go sit in the backyard (Warren was at his summer job). Sylvia dressed in a blouse and a pair of dungarees, broke into the metal lockbox, and, with the sleeping-pill bottle and a blanket in hand, proceeded down- stairs to the dining room. There, against a bowl of flowers on the dining- room table, she propped a note: "Have gone for a long walk. Will be home tomorrow." Then, in the kitchen, she drew herself a small jar of water at the sink, crossed to the door leading to the cellar, and, shutting the door behind her, descended the stairs. On the other side of the cellar, she put down the blanket, water, and pills long enough to shove to one side the stack of firewood that blocked a tiny two-and-a-half- foot entrance to the crawl space under the front porch. Next Sylvia gathered up the blanket, water, and pills, put them beside the firewood, and hoisted herself up into the space—it was about five feet off the ground—before she restacked the wood so that it appeared untouched. Finally, secure in the crawl space, she lay down. Wrapping the blanket around her, she opened the pill bottle. Because she had only taken two, forty-eight pills remained—more than enough. One by one, Sylvia placed each pill on her tongue and washed it down. She did not know how many were left in the bottle—there were some—when eventually the pills she had swallowed took over and she quietly passed from consciousness.

7

In the theatre, Aurelia could hardly watch the coronation's slow, plotless ceremony unfold on the screen. An indefinable dread filled her so completely that she began to perspire. She forced herself to stay until the movie ended, then asked her friend to drive her straight home. As soon as Aurelia entered the house and discovered Sylvia's note on the table, she was certain that something bad had happened. Once she related recent events to her parents, who had been vacationing on the Cape and did not know how sick Sylvia was, they, like Aurelia, feared she had not gone on a walk at all. Telephoning Sylvia's friends, Laurie Totten among them, Aurelia learned that none had seen her. By five o'clock, Aurelia imagined the worst. She contacted the police, who, on hearing about Sylvia's medical history, placed a missing-person bulletin on the radio. In the radio spot, Sylvia was described as five feet nine inches tall, brown-haired, brown-eyed, and 140 pounds. When last seen, the police said, she wore a light-blue skirt and a white sleeveless blouse.

At twilight, Sylvia had not come back. The police had searched 26 Elmwood Road from attic to cellar without discovering any clues. Hoping that they might locate her at one of her favorite haunts in Boston, Aurelia, Warren, and Colonel Rex Gary, a friend of the family who had been affiliated with United States Army Intelligence, drove into Boston and searched predictable areas. They eventually gave up and returned to Wellesley, as rain began to fall. After a sleepless night, the Plaths and the Schobers awoke on Tuesday morning to the sound of the telephone ringing. Friends and neighbors had read stories about Sylvia in the newspapers and wanted to know more. The Boston *Globe* morning edition printed a front-page story under the headline BEAU- TIFUL SMITH GIRL MISSING AT WELLESLEY; the Boston *Herald* named its story TOP RANKING STUDENT AT SMITH MISSING FROM WELLESLEY HOME. As the telephone continued to ring—soon the newspapers started calling for comments from Aurelia—police officials and vol- unteers mounted an all-out manhunt, though they were hampered by the night's rain. Search parties scoured the shores of Morse's Pond and Lake Waban as well as the woods near Elmwood Road. Post 80, the Explorer Scouts, lead by Bradford Gove, a neighbor of the Plaths, combed the area between Dover Road and the Sudbury River aqueduct. Perhaps due to the rain, the Andover State Police bloodhound, Lieutenant Sid, could not turn up Sylvia's scent in the area off Worcester Turnpike, where search squads made up of police, neighbors, and members of the American Legion conducted a foot-by-foot examination of the grounds. At its peak, the dragnet included at least one hundred people.

The afternoon editions of the newspapers updated the story that the Associated Press now sent out over its nationwide wire. The *Globe*'s evening edition published a front-page article, BOY SCOUTS HUNT MISSING SMITH STUDENT, in which Aurelia Plath was quoted. "It sounds peculiar," Aurelia said, "but [Sylvia] has set standards for herself that are almost unattainable. She's made almost a minor obsession of fulfilling what she believes to be her responsibility to her sponsors, and I am gravely concerned for her." By the end of Tuesday, Aurelia's fear heightened when, searching the house yet again, she discovered that the metal lockbox had been pried open and the sleeping pills were gone. The steady flow of friends through 26 Elmwood Road—William Rice, the Unitarian church minister, and Max Gaebler, a family friend, were two of many—tried to console Aurelia without success. She decided that Sylvia had stolen the sleeping pills, sneaked away from the house, and, finding some appropriate hidden place, overdosed. If she was not found soon, it would be too late. Perhaps it already was.

On Wednesday, Aurelia's outlook was not helped by the *Globe* morning edition, which ran the front-page article DAY-LONG SEARCH FAILS TO LOCATE PLATH GIRL. Illustrated by a photograph of the Plath family—Sylvia, Warren, Aurelia—in hopes that it might prompt Sylvia to "report her whereabouts," the article contained another quote from Aurelia. "For some time [Sylvia] has been unable to write either fiction, or her more recent love, poetry. Instead of regarding this as just an arid period that every writer faces at times, she believed something had happened to her mind, that it was unable to produce creatively any more. . . . Although her doctor assured us this was simply due to nervous exhaustion, Sylvia was constantly seeking for ways in which to blame herself for the failure, and became increasingly despondent." That same morning, the *Globe*'s front-page SLEEPING PILLS MISSING WITH WELLES-LEY GIRL added a new twist to the story for the public. "It doesn't look good," Wellesley Police Chief McBey declared in the article.

Distraught, the Plaths and the Schobers gathered for lunch. Then, because they had to get on with their lives, Grammy went down to the cellar to do laundry. It was while she stood at the washing machine that she heard a low moan from behind the stack of firewood. Immediately, she summoned Warren, who raced down the steps and, at her direction, unpiled the logs. As she and Warren peered into the dark crawl space, they saw Sylvia—wrapped in a blanket, covered with her own dried vomit, dazed but alive. Hurrying upstairs, Warren and Grammy told the news to Aurelia and Grampy. The police were called, and Officer Theodore McGlone, who happened to be in the neighborhood searching for Sylvia in garages, arrived within minutes. After he and Warren pulled Sylvia from under the porch, she was taken by ambulance to the Newton-Wellesley Hospital, the very place she had worked earlier in the summer. While Sylvia received medical treatment, Chief McBey, now at Elmwood Road, recovered from the crawl space an empty water jar and a medicine bottle containing eight sleeping pills. From this evidence, and from Aurelia's testimony that Sylvia had previously taken only two of the pills, McBey concluded that Sylvia had swallowed forty pills before she had passed out. Which had *saved* her life: she had consumed so many that she became ill and threw up a significant number of them.

Back in the hospital emergency room, doctors described Sylvia as being "semicomatose," her condition "fair." Externally, her only visible deformity was an open wound on the upper right cheek, which she had apparently inflicted by bashing her face into a slab of concrete in the crawl space when she roused from her drugged state and tried to sit up. Later, doctors placed her in her own room and allowed only four people—Aurelia, Warren, Grammy, and Reverend Rice—to see her. By then the updated story had already hit the newsstands. The *Globe* evening edition announced: SMITH STUDENT FOUND ALIVE IN CELLAR. FOUND AT HOME, SMITH SENIOR IN 'FAIR' CONDITION, read the headline with which the Associated Press began the article that it broadcast over its wire service to newspapers all across the country.

More front-page articles appeared on Thursday. The *Globe* pronounced, WELLESLEY GIRL FOUND IN CELLAR; the Wellesley *Townsman*, SYLVIA PLATH FOUND IN GOOD CONDITION. Also, Aurelia was besieged by telephone calls, letters, and telegrams. No communication was more cherished than the one from Olive Higgins Prouty, who the day before, while vacationing at the Spruce Point Inn in Boothbay Harbor, Maine, had accidentally run across an article about Sylvia's disappearance in the morning edition of the Boston *Herald*. Telephoning the Wellesley Police Department, Prouty had discovered that after that story ran Sylvia was located. "HAVE JUST LEARNED SYLVIA HAS BEEN FOUND AND IS RECOVERING AT HOSPITAL," Prouty wired. "I WANT TO HELP. AM WRITING."

Doom of Exiles

1

In late August, letters continued to pour in to Aurelia at 26 Elmwood Road. "She demanded . . . far too much of herself. But plenty of people have been through such crises, and come out of them strengthened," wrote R. G. Davis, adding that he would be willing to do "anything [that] would in any way be helpful" in assisting Sylvia's rapid return to Smith, from which she was now on medical leave. On the 28th, Elizabeth Drew confessed: "Had I known she was in this very serious depression, of course I should have written differently to her before. . . . I *did* think it was a bit odd that she sent me a special delivery letter about her long paper topic, but students so often get panicky about their subjects . . . that I didn't think anything of it." But the most welcome letter came from Olive Higgins Prouty. At that time, Aurelia's Boston University annual salary was thirty-nine hundred dollars, a sum that barely covered her family's living expenses. The Plaths had a total cash "emergency" savings of only six hundred dollars. Once Aurelia had forwarded her this information, at Prouty's request, Sylvia's sponsor responded by offering to pay up to five hundred dollars for Sylvia's hospitalization at Newton-Wellesley. This was merely a first step, she wanted Aurelia to know. Prouty, who sympathized with Sylvia in part because she herself had had a breakdown twenty-five years ago, would continue to give her full support—both financial *and* emotional. Already Prouty had requested that her own psychiatrist, Dr. Donald McPherson, consult on the case at her expense. Naturally, Prouty would be available to help as soon as she returned to Brookline, the day after Labor Day. With this letter, Aurelia saw two burdens lift from her shoulders: she would not have to endure the ordeal of Sylvia's recovery alone, nor would that recovery bankrupt her financially.

As for Sylvia, after the Newton-Wellesley Hospital's medical staff had stabilized her condition on the 26th, she was moved to a private room, turned over to Racioppi, and placed under a twenty-four-hour nurse's watch. Her overriding physical ailment was an acute infection, caused by the open wound on her face, which made her run a fever that doctors held in check with penicillin injections. As soon as possible, Warren or Aurelia (who occasionally slept nearby, at the Cantors' house) replaced nurses on the twenty-four-hour watch to cut expenses. Looking at her daughter lying in the hospital bed, Aurelia felt a blend of thankfulness and apprehension. Sylvia was alive—and for that Aurelia could not express her gratitude—yet she was also still seriously mentally sick. What, then, should Aurelia's next move be? A friend offered the use of her Provincetown summer home for an extended convalescence. Finally, Sylvia's condition was much too threatening to be cured by relaxation, so Aurelia decided to consult experts in the field. McPherson was available, but, at the suggestion of Reverend Rice, Aurelia also contacted Dr. Erich Lindemann, head of Massachusetts General Hospital's psychiatric wing, who examined Sylvia on September 1. Without question, he believed, Sylvia should be transferred to a psychiatric facility—soon. He would be happy to admit her to Massachusetts General, if Aurelia approved.

Lindemann had reached this conclusion even though Sylvia showed slight signs of improvement. Her spirits had been lifted in large part by the support of friends like Gordon, who, arriving in Wellesley on August 29, wrote her a long letter, which Aurelia delivered by hand. (Sylvia could still have no guests besides family and Reverend Rice.) Gordon ended his letter, which described an episode of disappointment he had endured at Amherst, by saying: "Talking to you makes living worthwhile. Sharing anything I have with you gives me the greatest pleasure, because I feel I have faith in you, and you speak my language—mine." On the 31st, Sylvia answered Gordon's with her own moving letter in which she said that she was unsure about her future but that she *was* sure that his was one of the most important letters she had ever received.

Sylvia was coherent enough to write Gordon, but she remained very sick. So, on September 3, after her eighth night in the Newton-Wellesley Hospital, doctors transferred her to the psychiatric ward of the Massachusetts General Hospital. There Lindemann carried out an extensive psychiatric examination. By the 9th, when he met with Prouty, who was back from Maine (from now on, Aurelia involved Prouty in all discussions regarding Sylvia's medical care), Lindemann stated that he believed Sylvia had no mental disease or psychosis but had suffered an adolescent nervous illness from which she should recover fully. Three days later, McPherson examined Sylvia to provide Prouty and Aurelia with a second opinion. "The symptoms suggest an acute schizophrenic episode in a highly endowed adolescent girl," McPherson wrote Prouty. (At the time, "schizophrenia" did not imply an extreme pathological state, as the diagnosis later would in clinical usage; instead, it denoted a period of dissociation from which a patient usually emerged.) "This is not at all a hopeless situation as many recover with or without treatment. The time factor is unpredictable and it is greatly to her advantage to have intelligent supervision. Insulin and shock therapy are often indicated and seem to be of real value in this kind of trouble."

On the whole, Sylvia did not respond to her ward setting at Massachusetts General as well as Lindemann might have hoped. Her exposure to patients significantly more depressed than she tended to affect her negatively. Over time, it became clear that she needed to be in a private institution. Lindemann suggested McLean Hospital, a part of the Massachusetts General system that also enjoyed a reputation for being one of the country's best mental facilities. On the other hand, Prouty wanted Sylvia to go to Silver Hill, a country-club-like sanitarium in New Canaan, Connecticut, where through the years both she and her husband had undergone treatment. Prouty had already contacted Dr. William Terhune, director of Silver Hill, who assured her that Sylvia would be admitted and that her expenses could be paid for by a foundation to which Prouty was a major contributor. In the end, Aurelia followed Lindemann's advice, although her decision did not sway Prouty from her conviction to sponsor Sylvia's recovery. On the 14th, Prouty drove with Aurelia and Sylvia from Massachusetts General to nearby Belmont, the small town in which McLean was situated atop a high wooded hill. Soon after checking into her private room, Sylvia met her personal psychiatrist, a brilliant and sympathetic twenty-nine-year-old woman named Ruth Tiffany Barnhouse. Related to the jewelry-store Tiffanys, Barnhouse, who had been educated at Barnard College and Columbia Medical School, also claimed as a relative Philadelphia Presbyterian minister Donald Grey Barnhouse, the first evangelist to broadcast a nationwide religious radio program. As a mother of two, the result of an elopement that ended in divorce, and the present wife of fellow doctor William Beuscher, Barnhouse was just what Sylvia needed—an Ivy League woman who had lived a life out of the "Ivy League." For the first time in her brief but turbulent psychiatric history, Sylvia had found a doctor whom she could trust.

Meanwhile, Prouty dealt with Sylvia's medical expenses. Because of the Plaths' financial straits, Prouty asked doctors and hospitals to reduce or waive their fees. Lindemann agreed to a reduction; Massachusetts General cut its fee in half. Tillotson, in charge of some of the ill-fated Valley Head electroshock treatments, waived his. And when Prouty approached Thornton, he halved his $155 bill (which broke down to twenty-five dollars for one house call, fifteen each for two office visits, and twenty-five each for four shock treatments). This gesture, however, did not satisfy Prouty. On the 26th, she wrote Thornton a stinging letter in which she boldly accused him of driving Sylvia to suicide.

> Unfortunately the shock treatments at Valley Head proved disastrous, as you know. Sylvia was not hospitalized during the treatments and her experience and memory of the shock treatments led to her desperate act. I realize that you left on a vacation during the course of the treatments, but the fact remains that she was not properly protected against the results of the treatments, which were so poorly given that the patient remembers the details with horror. I feel very strongly that Sylvia should have been guarded against what happened, while she was undergoing the shock treatments. I think her attempt at suicide was due largely to the horror of what she remem-

bers of the shock treatments, and the fears aroused. . . . I would like to hear from you in regard to this. . . . Have you no interest in a case that had such a disaster following your treatment of her?

On the 29th, Thornton shot back his reply. After he called Prouty "poorly misinformed" and "psychiatrically ignorant," he defended his decision to administer the electroshock treatments on an outpatient basis and described Sylvia's response to them as "favorable." Calling Prouty's opinions "worthless," Thornton told her that he trusted his letter would "help" her with her dealings with doctors in the future and "stimulate" her to search out information about psychiatry. He closed his letter by admonishing Prouty not to "burden" his office with "any further communications."

During the last half of September, while Prouty squared away the cost of Sylvia's treatment (Prouty herself had put down the four-hundred-dollar deposit required by McLean for Sylvia's admission), Barnhouse concentrated on becoming acquainted with Sylvia and her case. Barnhouse remembers:

She wouldn't talk. She was furious. She was angry at her mother. She had too much plain living and high thinking—her words. She had been raised with this intense focus on the thinking function, on intellectual performance, which was not her nature. Using the Jungian categories of psychological types, she was an intuitive, feeling type; she just had an extremely high IQ, that's all. Moreover, she had been traumatized by her month in New York. There had been all these girls who had been encouraged to use a more affective part of themselves than she had ever been encouraged to use—and yet what she saw was a low-level, stereotypical, superficial version of that. This left her with no place to go. She didn't have any appropriate models. I was interested not only in her head and her performance but also how she felt. I wasn't telling her how she was supposed to feel. This was the side I wanted to bring out in her—eventually.

At McLean, Barnhouse allowed Sylvia few visitors. Besides Prouty—who came about once a week—and Aurelia—who in the wake of Sylvia's hospitalization moved into Prouty's house, where she remained on and off until May, but who was often driven to McLean for her weekly visit with Sylvia by Margaret Cantor—Sylvia received only Wilbury Crockett. Yet his recollection of his early sessions with her indicates the severity of her sickness. "Sylvia had lost touch with words," Crockett remembers. (She had obviously suffered a severe reversal since writing Gordon a letter.) "So I brought along a game called Anagram, a word game. And I can see us now: sitting in the hospital visiting quarters, I would spread out the letters on a card table. I sat at one end of the table, Sylvia at the other. And I would take her finger, place it on a letter, and say, 'Sylvia, this is an A.' And she would say, 'Yes, an A.' Then I would take her finger and reach for an N. 'Sylvia, this is A-N. *An* apple.' Next I would take her finger and reach for a D. 'A-N-D, this spells *and.*' " It took a month or so for her ability to read and write to return. When it did, it did so quickly and completely. However, one byproduct of her recent ordeal did not go away. In the months following Sylvia's breakdown—following, in particular, her poorly administered shock treatments—Aurelia noticed that her daughter's personality, which had previously been integrated, seemed to be split. In the past, Sylvia could be "up" or "down" but was usually a blend of the two. Now the extremes became apparent: she was either manic or depressed, with little in between. Aurelia hoped that Sylvia's treatment at McLean might integrate those personality traits. Otherwise, she envisioned her future mood swings reaching even more drastic polar opposites.

The method of treatment for Sylvia that Barnhouse employed, and that McLean officials endorsed—daily psychotherapy sessions, regular insulin injections, and unstructured free time during which she could engage in occupational therapy if she chose—did not meet with Olive Prouty's approval. After she visited with Sylvia for two hours on October 6 and took her for a drive on the 13th, Prouty wrote Barnhouse a terse letter. Sylvia had complained about "the long objectless hours spent in her room," had admitted that she was "not mixing well with other patients," had longed for some activity to "make her isolation more bearable." Despite Prouty's complaints, Barnhouse did not change Sylvia's treatment radically, but encouraged Sylvia to type some of Prouty's manuscripts—Aurelia brought a typewriter from home—that Prouty supplied for that purpose. On the 21st, when she took Sylvia to lunch at the Hartwell Farms, Prouty noted that Sylvia had typed the documents flawlessly and that she now wanted to read a book on contract bridge. To Prouty, the expert typing job had led to the desire to read about bridge: a routine and the performance of menial tasks *do* improve a patient's mental outlook. At Silver Hill, where Prouty still wanted Sylvia to go if only as a follow-up to McLean, Sylvia would receive this type of structured treatment, since Terhune believed in providing patients with schedules he expected them to follow. Barnhouse did not agree with Prouty; nor, for that matter, did Lindemann, who now saw Sylvia weekly. As a result, Sylvia remained at McLean—on McLean's terms. In mid-October, while everyone concerned discussed how best to treat Sylvia, Smith, from which Sylvia remained on medical leave, sent her a telegram announcing that she had just been elected to Phi Beta Kappa. Otherwise, Sylvia had little contact with Smith, though she did occasionally see a young woman named Jane Anderson, a Smith acquaintance who was also hospitalized at McLean.

During the first half of November, Prouty and Aurelia continued to visit Sylvia regularly. Early in the month, even if *they* did not see signs of improvement, McLean doctors did. Around the 7th, after this (supposed) change for the good, her insulin injections were stopped. However, Sylvia had by no means recovered. "She continues getting psychotherapeutic treatment which I believe is the main approach," Psychiatrist-in-Chief Paul Howard wrote to Prouty at mid-month. "Her cheek"—as yet unhealed—"continues to get better and a surgeon advises me that it is well to let these things alone. . . . Although electroshock therapy is . . . a possibility I do not believe, considering her improvement, that it would be good to think of [it] at this time."

The debate regarding Sylvia's treatment continued into November. On the 16th, Prouty arrived at McLean to find Sylvia "terribly depressed and discouraged" because she could not "escape idleness"—an obvious downturn, if she had in fact improved earlier in the month. On the 23rd, when she wrote to Director Franklin Wood to pay him a monthly bill of $790—the last bill she would be willing to pay, she said—Prouty told him that, during the eleven weeks Sylvia had been a patient at

McLean, Prouty could see "little change in her depression, attitude or . . . ideas." Prouty went on: "I usually find Sylvia wandering listlessly up and down the corridor and when I leave she says she will do the same, as there is nothing else for her to do." This aimlessness, according to Prouty, contributed to Sylvia's lack of improvement. On the 25th, by way of defending McLean, Wood evaluated Sylvia's condition. He wrote Prouty:

> There are things about for her to do and people to interest her in them. It is more of value to her to do these things with her own feelings than by schedule. . . . We notice if under pressure or ex- pectation she seems to feel worse, further confirmation that the pressure of a schedule would not be supportive as it is with some people. And in this connection I do not think that visits with relatives or friends should especially be the occasion of an examination of any sort, either as to the progress of her ideas or the number of her accomplishments. . . . This girl has been an accomplisher, and living in the atmosphere of accomplishment, and is excessively self con- scious in her depressed state; and usually tries to put her worst foot forward saying that anything she is doing or thinking is "nothing."

At the moment, Wood continued, Sylvia had been put on chlorprom- azine, known to reduce tension in patients. If that drug did not work, electroshock therapy was a last resort.

Though Prouty had said she would stop paying for Sylvia's treatment, she did not. Instead, she decided to place her in another hospital. Prouty and Aurelia conferred at tea on December 2, and Prouty toured the Boston Psychopathic Hospital alone the next day; she took Aurelia to see the facility on the 5th. Boston Psychopathic's director, a Dr. Solomon, set in motion the process to admit Sylvia within a week. Then, upon discovering from McLean that Sylvia had experienced "a distinct turn for the better," Prouty told Solomon that she would delay moving her until after Christmas. She also wrote McLean that, as of January 1, she would no longer be responsible for Sylvia's expenses there—and now she meant it. It was at this point that the McLean staff modified both Sylvia's schedule and the standoffish manner in which they had dealt with Prouty and Aurelia. Barnhouse had a long meeting with Aurelia—the longest conversation the two women had had since Sylvia was admitted—and the staff concluded that Sylvia would have to undergo electroshock therapy again. Finally, McLean offered to treat Sylvia free of charge after January 1. Because of this, Aurelia left Sylvia at McLean for the time being.

Soon after December 15, Barnhouse began giving Sylvia the shock treatments, which ended before Christmas Eve. Barnhouse recalls:

> I convinced her that she had to have shock treatment because she was persisting in this depression and she had to get out of there. I didn't want her to become chronic. She was still suicidal. We had worked on the preparation for the shock treatments for months. When she had the treatments—I don't think she had more than two or three—she recovered so fast that it was obvious that the shock treatment itself had a psychological significance, apart from whatever shock treatment does to people. What I mean is, it was almost as though she had to be punished for something. So she finally got it. I mean, that's one interpretation.

Following the shock treatments, Sylvia improved dramatically. During the Christmas holidays, her depression appeared to evaporate. By New Year's, the old Sylvia seemed to have emerged. On various occasions, doctors described her as "cheerful," "vivacious," able to gain "good insight into her problems." By January 13, McLean officials, who had begun treating Sylvia without charge, decided that her recovery was so remarkable that she did not need to stay in the hospital. They concluded—amazingly—that she was ready to return to Smith as a special student. When Prouty heard about this, she was angry and astonished. She wrote bitterly to William Terhune, Silver Hill's director: "The fact is they [McLean officials] are not going to send Sylvia to Silver Hill at all. In spite of the nearly $4,000 I have sent McLean Hospital since September it has failed to lead to the period of 're-education' at Silver Hill which I desired so much for Sylvia and which I was willing to finance." Prouty never realized her wish. Later in January, McLean released Sylvia to go home in preparation for her upcoming return to Smith.

It was not the first time she had been to Wellesley since her breakdown. In late December and January, McLean had allowed Sylvia occasional visits home. One day, she had actually traveled to Harvard with Philip McCurdy. (The night before, she had explained to Philip why she had tried to kill herself—she feared she had, lost her talent to write—and told him that she had attempted it before—when she was ten she slit her throat, she said, and showed him a scar which, whether she invented the story or not, he could plainly see.) After the visit to Harvard, they returned to Philip's Wellesley home for supper, then went dancing at the Totem Pole. Tired but excited to be together, they drove to Sylvia's house. Sitting in his car in front of 26 Elmwood Road, Sylvia suddenly stopped talking and made romantic advances towards him. Confused at first, Philip gave in. Their necking heightened their passion, and they soon ended up, as Sylvia had referred to the act throughout high school, "having sexual intercourse"—her first time.

Barnhouse believed that Sylvia should no longer suppress her sexual desires. In therapy, she had encouraged her to consider experimenting with sex when she had the opportunity. Sylvia had wasted no time in doing just that; Philip happened to be party to her experimentation. As it turned out, Sylvia and Philip had been Platonic friends for too long to set out on a romantic relationship. They had a second night of awkward sex in the front seat of his car, but decided not to try it a third. Rather, they would go back to their close friendship.

Barnhouse may have placed part of the blame for Sylvia's emotional problems on sexual frustration, yet another possible cause surfaced at this time. In the wake of Sylvia's release from McLean, Aurelia received word from one of Otto's sisters that in the Plath family their mother, a sister, and a niece all suffered from depression. Otto's mother had become so sick that she had been hospitalized. Perhaps Sylvia's illness did not result from outside factors at all. Perhaps she had simply inherited the disease from her father.

2

The start of Plath's return to Smith was inauspicious. The very auto-
mobile trip to Northampton—Warren had volunteered to drive her
there before he went back to Harvard for his own spring term—almost
ended in disaster. While they were driving down a snow-covered hill
next to Paradise Pond, as Sylvia wrote to Gordon, "the car plunged
into a skid the likes of which I never hope to see again—speeding
downward sideways. . . ." The car could have crashed into a tree or
another car—or Paradise Pond itself—but fortunately it merely skid-
ded into an embankment. Shaken by the memory of the near car-crash,
which strangely terrified her even though she had just survived the
more frightening ordeal of her own suicide attempt, Sylvia spent her
first days at Lawrence familiarizing herself with her new room, a big
maroon-gray-and-blue-painted single overlooking Green Street. Because of Sylvia's general physical and mental condition, Smith gave her
special considerations for the term. First, the single room—a rarity.
Second, Lawrence reduced her house workload to a single duty: de-
livering the housemother's breakfast tray each morning. Third, as a
special student, she enrolled in only three courses: George Gibian's
Tolstoy and Dostoevsky, Elisabeth Koffka's Nineteenth Century Intellectual History, and Newton Arvin's American Fiction 1830–1900.
Naturally, Smith had not retained her scholarship monies for the year;
to help Sylvia study worry-free, Aurelia cashed in an insurance policy
to finance the spring semester. Sylvia's adviser, Kenneth Wright, implored her to relax and enjoy her courses. As for her concern about
earning low marks, Wright remembers telling her that "a person of
her intelligence need have no such fears." Finally, her doctors and
Smith officials expected Sylvia to see the school's psychiatrist, a Dr.
Booth, once a week.

With her lightened schedule, Sylvia could concentrate on readjusting
to college life. On February 6, 1954, one week into the term, she
attended a tea at the home of Elizabeth Drew, who embraced her and
welcomed her back to Smith. The night before Valentine's Day, Sylvia
took in a reading given by Esther Forbes at the Hampshire Bookshop.

On Valentine's Day itself, she went to the dance drama *Green Mansions;* the day after, a lecture by Mary Ellen Chase. In those first two weeks, Sylvia read for her classes as well, finishing *Sister Carrie, Crime and Punishment,* and a collection of Hawthorne short stories. And to try her hand at boys, she went on a blind date one Saturday night with an attractive but shallow Amherst College student. Amid all these distractions, she did not feel disappointed that she would not be graduating with her class, Smith '54. Or so she reported to Gordon in the airmail letters she sent to him now that he had graduated from Newport and begun his service aboard the battleship U.S.S. *Perry*. The ship's tour of duty in European waters, a special communications mission, was scheduled to last through May.

At the start of Sylvia's new life, she enjoyed a burgeoning friendship with Nancy Hunter, the girl who had taken over Sylvia's spot in her second-floor double room, just down the hall from the single Sylvia currently occupied, when Sylvia had not returned to Smith in September. As they became acquainted, the young women realized that despite key differences (a transfer student from Wooster College in Ohio, Nancy was a true Midwesterner) they had a lot in common. Intellectuals, both had come from humble backgrounds, studied hard, and tried to fit into the college's mainstream by not appearing to be "scholarship girls." Before long, Sylvia and Nancy were spending many hours in each other's rooms. Surprisingly, Sylvia did not avoid discussing events from the summer and fall. In their rambling conversations, Sylvia recounted her suicide attempt and, more important, the reasons behind the breakdown that caused the attempt. "A brief expedition into the New York world of fashion journalism triggered a spiraling depression from which she could not extricate herself as the summer wore on," Hunter would write, recalling Sylvia's version of the story. "What should have been a stimulating, exciting round of gala festivities produced only a mounting tedium that did not subside even at the chance to meet and interview outstanding figures in the literary world. She found the work artificial and banal. [Soon she believed] that she could do nothing well except study and compile a superior academic record. When she began an earnest, unproductive study of Joyce's *Ulysses* for her honor thesis . . . , the last shred of self-confidence withered. 'I was a nothing,' she exclaimed. 'A zero.' " Even more noteworthy, in their conversations Sylvia felt comfortable enough with Nancy to discuss her father's death, a topic about which she had been close-mouthed for years. "She talked freely about her father's death . . . and her reactions to it," Hunter would write. " 'He was an autocrat,' she recalled. 'I adored and despised him, and I probably wished many times that he were dead. When he obliged me and died, I imagined that I had killed him.' And then she added, 'The strangest part of the suicide attempt was regaining consciousness in the hospital. I don't believe in God or in an afterlife, and my first reaction when I opened my eyes was "No, it can't be. There can't be anything after death." ' "

In her early days back at Smith, Sylvia received numerous letters inquiring about her health. One arrived from Eddie Cohen. Telling her that "in my own little way, I love you" and that he had learned about her suicide attempt by reading the Associated Press stories in his local papers, he confessed: "When I was writing you that you should see a psychiatrist"—and he had, of course, as early as Christmas 1952—"I don't think I conveyed to you the sense of desperation I felt about the matter. Actually, I was thinking much more than I said, and held long ethical debates with myself and a psychiatrist friend about the propriety of writing your mother and suggesting that you be put under convalescent care. I permitted myself to be talked out of it." Sylvia answered Eddie, who had not been available to her in her time of crisis during the summer because he had married and gone on an extended honeymoon in Mexico where she could not reach him by mail, with a long recapitulation of the last several months of her life that did not differ drastically from the one she told Nancy. On the whole, she composed fewer letters these days, since she devoted almost all of her energy to schoolwork.

March became so busy—she attended an I. A. Richards lecture, studied hard, and dated several boys—that by the end of the month she needed a break from her routine. Lately, she had begun corresponding with Ilo Pill, the Estonian artist whom she had known at Lookout Farm. Now living in Manhattan with his mother, Ilo suggested Sylvia visit him there during her spring vacation; she could stay with him at his

139 · DOOM OF EXILES

mother's apartment. Weighing the situation—this would be her first trip to New York since her breakdown—Sylvia decided to go. When her vacation arrived, though, she first spent a weekend at home during which, on the 25th, she traveled into Cambridge to lunch with Warren and meet his Radcliffe girlfriend; saw Barnhouse, who approved the New York trip; and took in the Cabaret Dance at Harvard's Adams House. There she met "Scotty" Campbell, the assistant director of Harvard Summer School, who encouraged her to apply for a scholarship for the coming summer. Would *last* summer be held against her? she wanted to know. Absolutely not, Campbell assured her—much to Sylvia's astonishment.

Excited by the news, Sylvia flew to New York on March 28—her first commercial flight. (Even though money was scarce, Aurelia had insisted she fly.) At LaGuardia Airport, Ilo and his mother greeted her warmly, then drove her to their apartment—a gloomy third-floor walk-up at Lexington and 123rd Street, the heart of Harlem. That evening, Ilo treated her to T. S. Eliot's *The Confidential Clerk.* The next morning, he revealed that he was not going to work that day; at this point, Sylvia told him that she was engaged to be married and so she and Ilo could only be friends. She remembered all too well the embarrassing episode in the barn loft during her Lookout Farm summer and must have questioned her decision to come see Ilo in the first place. In fact, Ilo may have thought that by accepting his invitation Sylvia was implicitly agreeing to the physical relationship he had wanted years ago. When she made it clear that she wished to keep their association strictly Platonic, which she did by inventing the story about the fiancé, Ilo dressed and went to work.

Relieved, Sylvia had lunch with Cyrilly Abels in the Ivy Room at the Drake Hotel. Later, she did go through with her plans to meet Ilo at the Metropolitan Museum, where they saw a show of the American painters Sargent, Whistler, and Cassatt. That night, again treated by Ilo, they took in William Inge's play *Picnic,* which starred Sandra Church and Paul Newman. On Tuesday, after visiting the Museum of Modern Art, Sylvia ate supper with a friend of a friend named Atherton Sinclair Burlingham (nicknamed Bish), whom she was supposed to look up in New York and whom she would describe as being a Union

Theological Seminary student. The next morning, a serious strain developed in her friendship with Ilo, who continued to manifest an interest that Sylvia did not approve of, and Sylvia announced with some ceremony that she intended to go back to Wellesley. Then she packed and left. But instead of returning home, she stayed in New York and called on friends, especially Bish. On her way to Wellesley by train on Saturday, she stopped off briefly in New Haven to see Melvin Woody, a boy whom she had met through Marcia in New York the summer before.

Back at Smith the next week, Plath tried to write a poem, something she had not done since last May. On April 16, once she had warmed up by revising "The Dead," an old sonnet, Plath attempted a new poem, "Doom of Exiles," also a sonnet. Their voice at times richer and more confident, these poems, though they finally fail to do so, strive to achieve a greater level of maturity than her earlier poetry.

Plath's work also began to appear in print again. The Spring 1954 *Smith Review*, the journal of which she would have been editor if she had not had a nervous breakdown, published four Plath poems—"Admonitions," "Never to Know More Than You Should," "Verbal Calisthenics," "Denouement." Also, in May, *Harper's* ran "Doomsday."

In the academic and creative areas of her life, Plath was now functioning as efficiently as ever. After Eddie had written in late April to ask if he had not heard from her because she had "run off with a handsome Czarist pretender [to live in] sensual and satisfying sin with him while he runs blow-darts to the Maumaus"—or had she been "popped back in an institution"?—Plath, who still hoped to write a short story based on their extensive correspondence, replied with a new plea for him to give up her letters. Eddie answered:

I suggest, flatly, that my letters have much more value than yours. Not as literature, certainly, but at least in terms of your facing the world, and yourself. Strong language, I admit, and you have never been particularly good at taking it before. It remains to be seen whether you are now capable of picking yourself off the floor and flinging it back in my teeth. When you are capable of doing that instead of pouting in silence for six months, you will have come a long way toward being a whole personality. As of now, or at least six months ago, you were no more capable of giving in anger than giving in love.

In her response, Sylvia ridiculed Eddie, radical bohemian that he used to be, for marrying into a mindless middle-class life. "How much free-lancing will you be doing when there are three kids around the house wanting, respectively, to be diapered, fed and have the funnies read to them?" he shot back. "And will your husband, whoever he may be, find contentment in talking to you or making love to you while you are banging on a typewriter? You can't plan your life out on paper and expect it to behave that way. I suspect that this tendency of yours contributed to your trouble. You didn't know what to do when something happened that wasn't in the blueprint."

In this spring of 1954, one obvious symbol of Sylvia's past trouble lingered—the brown scar under her right eye, from which she tried to distract attention by bleaching her hair platinum-blond. Or so she would tell her mother and others. In fact, she may have been trying to make herself more glamorous, which the platinum-blond hair definitely did, since during the spring term two boys—roommates, no less—had assumed a notable place in her life. In Calhoun College at Yale, Melvin Woody shared a room with Dick Wertz and Richard Sassoon; the former was a past boyfriend of Nancy's, the latter a friend of Marcia's. Mel regaled them with such glowing descriptions of Sylvia that Sassoon had convinced Wertz to go with him to Northampton to see her. As soon as Sylvia and Sassoon met, on the weekend of April 17, they were drawn to each other immediately. Sylvia was especially intrigued by Sassoon, a Paris-born British subject who had sophisticated tastes in music, literature, and wine. Moreover, even though he was nineteen, thin, and on the short side, Sassoon exuded a dark, lustful sexuality which deeply appealed to Sylvia. Also, she did not overlook the fact that Richard's father's cousin was the well-known British poet Siegfried Sassoon.

Their first date might have ended in calamity—Sassoon's car became stuck in mud as they drove through the countryside and a tow truck had to be called to pull it out—but they still saw each other weekly from mid-April until the end of the semester. At this same time, Sylvia dated Sassoon's roommate, Mel. In fact, their relationship had advanced to the point where intercourse was the next logical step. With Woody, though, Sylvia never went as far as she had with Philip and would in the future with others. A philosophy major, Woody wrote Sylvia in early May a tortured letter in which he complained of feeling an agonizing lack of completion in their relationship. He knew she was afraid of getting pregnant, yet he longed to have sex with her—and not just for the physical release but for the psychological and mental involvement that being intimate with someone can produce. He could not continue like this, he said; it was too emotionally painful for him.

On the face of it, Sylvia's almost Byzantine romantic involvements, combined with the sexual frustration her dates expressed, implied that she was a tease. But by the moral standards of the day her behavior was understandable. With no reliable birth control available, no legal abortion, and the certain promise of social rejection should their affairs result in pregnancy, Sylvia and other young women and men suffered the constant stress of aroused and unresolved sexual tensions. In Sylvia's case, because every one of her boyfriends fell in love with her, the tensions were magnified.

Despite her involvement with Mel, Sylvia went with Sassoon to New York for a weekend in early May. Afterwards, she felt excited over the trip—and the chance of a romance with Sassoon. Then again, much in her life seemed to be going well lately. On April 30, Smith awarded her a twelve-hundred-dollar scholarship for the next year—the college's largest. Also, she finally selected her senior thesis subject—Dostoevsky, not Joyce—which allowed her to choose as her adviser George Gibian, her Russian-literature professor, whom she admired. Best of all, she received a Harvard Summer School scholarship. At the end of the semester, after she was elected president of Alpha Phi Kappa Psi, won a twenty-dollar poetry prize for "Doom of Exiles," and earned excellent grades (American Fiction, A; Russian Literature, A; European History, A−), Sylvia returned to Wellesley. Only months before, she had been anguishing in a suicidal depression. Now, on top again, she was writing, publishing, and excelling in school just like the golden girl she once was.

3

When Sylvia arrived home at the end of May with platinum-blond hair, her mother was shocked. Sylvia explained by saying that she was simply trying out a new adventuresome personality. Aurelia decided not to argue with Sylvia about the hair—or anything else, for that matter— for Sylvia's sake and for her own. Aurelia's ulcerous stomach, which had flared up in response to Sylvia's breakdown, had become even worse of late. It had forced her to pass up teaching summer school and instead to rent a cottage on the Cape with her parents. Aurelia had not yet left Wellesley during the first five days in June, when Nancy Hunter—Sylvia's twin, as she now referred to her—arrived for a stay. Nancy's visit contained two high points. One afternoon she and Sylvia called on Mrs. Prouty. In a gesture that showed that, even though they were young women, they could still be girlish, Sylvia and Nancy became giddy with silliness and ate first one tray and then, once Prouty ordered it, a second tray of cucumber sandwiches—much to the horror of the butler who served them. The girls said that they had never before eaten cucumber sandwiches, although, of course, Sylvia had—*at* Mrs. Prouty's. Prouty, a soft-spoken but forceful woman who dressed in tweed suits, silk blouses, and cashmere sweaters, and who seemed to carve out time from her busy schedule to give Sylvia her undivided attention when she visited, overlooked the girls' behavior and talked with them on their own terms. The next day, Nancy's birthday, Sylvia gave Nancy a copy of *Alice in Wonderland*, inscribed with the phrase "A classic, read-aloud heirloom to be taken in small, mirthful doses at bedtime." Later, Sylvia drove Nancy to the Cape, where Nancy, a Midwesterner, saw the ocean for the first time in her life.

After Nancy's visit, Sylvia tried her best to relax in preparation for her upcoming stint in summer school. She played tennis with Philip, dated Perry Norton (whom she had not seen in a year), attended an art festival and a Robert Frost reading, and at mid-month traveled to Hanover to serve as a bridesmaid for Marcia, who was marrying Mike Plummer. She also enjoyed visiting Gordon, who was back from his five-month tour of Europe. On the 10th and the 18th, she drove down to Newport, where the *Perry* was docked, to have lunch on board ship with her "Ensign Lameyer." In the middle of this peaceful period, tragedy struck on the 21st, in Winthrop: Ruth and David Freeman's father, William, died suddenly of a heart attack. Immediately, Aurelia, Sylvia, and Warren went to console the Freemans. While she walked through the town on this trip, Sylvia felt the passage of time more than she ever had before—the events of the last eighteen months almost overwhelmed her—and concluded that her days of youth had finally lost their idyllic luster. Following supper at the Freemans', Sylvia helped David wash the dishes; she then strolled past her old house, which was now surrounded by, as she wrote to Gordon, the bushes her botanist father had planted. Eventually, because he needed to talk to her, David drove Sylvia home. If anyone could sympathize with David over the loss of his father, Sylvia could. After all, Sylvia had been consoled by David on the afternoon of her own father's funeral, fourteen years ago.

In late June, as the Plaths and the Schobers vacationed on the Cape, in Eastham, Sylvia saw Dick Norton in nearby Orleans. Talking to him, she realized that she could never date him again. When she left that day, Sylvia actually felt sorry for him. Seeing Dick only furthered her conviction that she loved Gordon—a fact that she did not evade in the many letters she now wrote to him.

Around July 1, Sylvia, Nancy, who had also received a Harvard Summer School scholarship, and two other Lawrence girls rented a one-bedroom flat in the Bay State Apartments on Massachusetts Avenue in Cambridge. In an informal arrangement, all four girls contributed a dollar a day for food, which, because they had taken the bedroom and left the other girls to sleep on a dingy hide-a-bed in the dining room, Sylvia and Nancy agreed to prepare, each cooking every other night. Together in Cambridge, only a "T" ride away from Boston, Sylvia and Nancy resolved to live the summer to the fullest. They shopped at Filene's, ate in cafés, wandered through bookshops, went to concerts on the Esplanade, and whiled away many an afternoon sitting on the bank of the Charles. Early on in Boston, since they shared a bedroom, Nancy noticed the way Sylvia folded, stacked, and arranged her clothes with a sort of studied, military precision. When Nancy questioned her about this, Sylvia gave her a strange answer: "Yes, if anyone ever disarranged my things I'd feel as though I had been raped intellectually." Neither girl—perhaps they were too young—mentioned the broader emotional issue this behavior suggested: that some people who suffer catastrophic losses in childhood feel an overpowering compulsion to control all areas of their life later on, even down to the way they fold and stack their clothes.

In summer school, Sylvia signed up for two courses, German and The Nineteenth Century Novel. The latter—taught, ironically, by Frank O'Connor—had a challenging syllabus, which included Austen's *Emma* and *Pride and Prejudice*, Stendhal's *The Charterhouse of Parma*, Balzac's *Eugénie Grandet*, Dickens's *Bleak House*, Trollope's *The Last Chronicle of Barset* and *Phineas Finn*, Flaubert's *Madame Bovary*, Tolstoy's *The Cossacks*, Turgenev's *On the Eve*, and Twain's *Huckleberry Finn*. In July, as she studied German and read novels, Sylvia dated Gordon, either in Massachusetts or in Newport. Sylvia and Gordon might have become an item—the word marriage had actually been brought up—but Sylvia made a pact with Nancy to date other young men that summer. They tested their agreement one day, two weeks into the term, when, leaving the Widener Library, they encountered a tall, balding man who wore glasses. Striking up a conversation, the man—Edwin—told the girls that he was a professor from an Eastern school, doing research at Harvard for the summer, and that he wanted to take them to coffee. In the coffee shop, Edwin talked about his life and work—like many professors, he tended to speak in monologues— as Sylvia and Nancy wondered which of the two he would ask for a date. Later, at the apartment, they got their answer. Edwin telephoned and, though Sylvia answered, asked to speak to Nancy.

On the night of July 19, when Edwin picked her up in his yellow sedan convertible, Nancy learned that their evening out would actually be a steak dinner cooked by Edwin at his apartment. After supper, Edwin became obvious with his sexual overtures. Nancy was just as obvious with her refusals. At one point, in a scene reminiscent of a bad Hollywood comedy, Edwin was literally chasing Nancy around the sofa. Eventually, in light of her demands to go home, he complied. At the apartment, while they lay in bed in their darkened bedroom, Nancy recalled for Sylvia Edwin's escapades, which, perhaps because of their boldness, fascinated Sylvia. Over the next few days, as she screened Edwin's calls, Sylvia became drawn into the conversations he would strike up with her. Ultimately, he asked *her* out, she went, and this date led to some involvement. On the afternoons of the 26th, 29th, and 30th, it was Edwin who drove Sylvia to appointments with Ruth Barnhouse, her McLean psychiatrist, whom she was seeing privately. Before long, Sylvia had a key to Edwin's apartment.

Up to that point, Sylvia had not been involved with a seasoned lover. Now, though, she was. One night towards the end of their first week of dating, Sylvia and Edwin consummated their physical relationship. The end result was both terrifying and confusing for Sylvia. During the act, which she would vow she had been opposed to, Sylvia experienced a vaginal tear, which hemorrhaged. When the blood would not stop, Edwin took her to a neighborhood hospital. Sylvia signed in under a pseudonym, for fear that the newspapers might pick up the story— she could not forget last year's media spectacle over her failed suicide attempt—and was examined and released by a gynecologist. After she spent what remained of the night with Edwin, she skipped her classes the next day to go with him to the beach—and, she hoped, to recover from her trauma. At five, he dropped her off at her apartment, but no sooner had he left than she collapsed in the bathroom, blood puddling on the tile floor around her. Rushing to her side, Nancy heard Sylvia say, "I think I'm bleeding to death. You have to help me." "Of course I'll help you," Nancy answered. "But I have to know what's wrong. What's causing the bleeding?" "He raped me," Sylvia said.

When the bleeding became worse, Nancy telephoned the doctor who had examined Sylvia the night before. He told Nancy to attempt a particular home-remedy procedure on Sylvia; it did not work. Nancy then called Edwin and demanded that he drive them to the hospital. The treatment the doctor administered there finally stopped the bleeding. Later, as Sylvia and Nancy got out of his car to go into their apartment, Edwin said, "I'll call tomorrow to see how she is." To which Nancy responded, "Don't bother. You've done enough."

Otto Plath, 1924
(Rare Book Room, Smith College)

Sylvia, age two *(T. B. Conlin)*

RIGHT: Sylvia and Warren
(Lilly Library, Indiana University)

BELOW: Sylvia and Warren, August
1940, in Winthrop *(Lilly Library,
Indiana University)*

BELOW: The Plaths—Warren,
Aurelia, Sylvia *(Lilly Library,
Indiana University)*

ABOVE: Sylvia, February 1947, at the Powleys' country home in East Colrain, Mass.
(*Betsy Powley Wallingford*)

RIGHT: Betsy Powley, 1947
(*Betsy Powley Wallingford*)

Sylvia, a leggy teenager, in Wellesley
(Lilly Library, Indiana University)

Wilbury Crockett, Sylvia's teacher, in the late
1940s *(Gamaliel Bradford High School)*

Sylvia and Marcia Brown on a skiing vacation, February 1951, in New Hampshire
(Rare Book Room, Smith College)

Sylvia and Joan Cantor at the beach, August 1952
(Rare Book Room, Smith College)

Sylvia, 1952. Aurelia later sent a print of this photograph to Sylvia's children, and wrote on the back: "To Frieda and Nick/Fall of 1952/Sylvia—your mummy, who loved you with all her heart." *(Rare Book Room, Smith College)*

RIGHT: Sylvia in her dormitory, Haven House, at Smith *(Barbara Sugarman Cohen)*

Lynne Lawner
(© *Pino Abbrescia*)

Plath reading in the
Glascock Poetry Contest at
Mount Holyoke College
(*Mount Holyoke College
Library/Archives*)

BELOW: Sylvia Plath interviewing Elizabeth
Bowen for *Mademoiselle*, summer of 1953
(*Lilly Library, Smith College*)

ABOVE: Edward Cohen in the
early 1950s *(Edward Cohen)*

Sylvia with Richard Norton at
the Yale prom
(Lilly Library, Indiana University)

RIGHT: Peter Davison, 1955, rehearsing for The Poets' Theatre in Cambridge, Mass.

Philip McCurdy, December 1953, in his room at Harvard. Sylvia was standing behind the photographer, waiting to be taken out to dinner. *(Philip McCurdy)*

BELOW: Sylvia and Gordon Lameyer *(Gordon Lameyer)*

OPPOSITE: Sylvia in her bridesmaid's dress, with Ruth Freeman, just before Ruth's marriage to Arthur Geissler *(Ruth Freeman Geissler)*

Sylvia in Paris, 1956 *(Gordon Lameyer)*

BELOW: Ruth Barnhouse with her first two children, February 1953, shortly before she began treating Sylvia *(Ruth Barnhouse)*

Newnham, Sylvia's Cambridge College

RIGHT: The Beacon—Ted's family home in Heptonstall, Yorkshire

Sylvia Plath and Ted Hughes in Paris just after their honeymoon in Benidorm, Spain, in 1956
(Rare Book Room, Smith College)

ABOVE: A street in Heptonstall

The moors behind The Beacon, where Ted and Sylvia went walking

Court Green,
North Tawton, Devon

BELOW: Ted Hughes and
Sylvia Plath, 1956 *(Rare
Book Room, Smith College)*

Ted Hughes and Sylvia
Plath in Concord, Mass.,
December 1959 (*Rare
Book Room, Smith College*)

The hedgerow-lined lane
near Court Green down
which Plath rode when
she was taking horseback-
riding lessons in 1962;
the experience would be
reflected in her *Ariel*
poems.

ABOVE: Sylvia Plath's grave in Heptonstall in late 1988. When a third tombstone was removed from Plath's grave because, as had happened with the previous two stones, vandals chiseled off the name "Hughes" from "Sylvia Plath Hughes," a local resident erected a handmade cross that bore only "Sylvia Plath."

23 Fitzroy Road in London, formerly Yeats's house. Sylvia hoped that living there would make her work blessed.
(Elaine Henderson Duble)

Aurelia Plath with Sylvia's letters, at the time of the publication of *Letters Home*
(© Arthur Grace/Sygma)

Within a week, Sylvia was dating Edwin again. Either Sylvia accepted more of the responsibility for the episode than she wanted to admit and therefore did not blame Edwin or she felt drawn to men whose behavior towards her tended to border on abuse. Just as she now continued to date a man who she said had "raped" her, she would soon become deeply involved with someone who would hit and spank her. Ultimately, there would be one man who, in part because of his violent nature, the brunt of which she often felt, captivated Sylvia so completely that only months after their meeting she had married him.

On Sunday, August 1, Sylvia ate supper with Gordon and his mother. When Sylvia and Gordon talked alone before supper, she explained her recent illness to him: Edwin had manually assaulted her—he had not, Sylvia reassured Gordon, gone any further—and had torn the skin of her vagina with his finger. Gordon accepted Sylvia's explanation without asking what it said about *his* and Sylvia's relationship, which had become so serious that Gordon considered them unofficially engaged. (He expected they would marry after his discharge from the navy.) While Gordon was away for the next two weeks on a tour of duty off the Virginia coast, Sylvia wrote sexually suggestive letters to him that did little to dispel the idea that she now loved him dearly.

Though she wrote love letters to Gordon and dated Edwin, Sylvia also occasionally saw another man, a Harvard professor whose wife, assuming that Sylvia and her husband were having an affair—they were not—referred to her as "the blonde bitch." When Gordon returned from Virginia, he and Sylvia spent the August 14 weekend together and, for the first time in their months-long courtship, made love. In the following days, as the anniversary of last summer's suicide attempt approached, Sylvia started to worry that because of their single sexual encounter she had become pregnant. Gordon, of course, was more than happy to propose marriage, but both he and Sylvia felt relieved when she finally got her period. Never again would Sylvia and Gordon be so close to marriage as they were in late August and early September of 1954, or so intimate.

4

For the first three weeks in September, Sylvia relaxed in Wellesley. She dated Gordon, read some, and considered what she would do after she graduated from Smith in May. She felt pulled in two directions: she hoped to have a family (with Gordon or someone else) but she also wanted to establish a career in writing or academics. Either way, she knew for certain that she would go to graduate school. Remembering her conversation with Mr. Crockett, she decided to apply to Oxford and Cambridge Universities, which she hoped to finance with a Fulbright Scholarship. (To play it safe, she would also apply to American universities and for additional scholarships.) So, when Plath returned to Smith to begin her senior year, which she did by settling into her (and Nancy's) new room at Lawrence and by starting her classes—Esther Cloudman Dunn's Shakespeare, Anita Luria Ascher's Intermediate German, and senior thesis unit—she also drafted her statement of intent for a Fulbright. But the excitement of the term's early days tired her out and, coming down with a respiratory infection, she—again—checked into the infirmary, where Gordon stopped by to see her on the 30th. Once released, she worked on her senior thesis, which would discuss, she and Gibian had concluded, Dostoevsky's use of the double in the novella *The Double* and *The Brothers Karamazov*. The opening chapter, they further agreed, would be due by October 22.

As she drafted her thesis chapter, studied, and worked odd jobs to make money, *The Smith Alumnae Quarterly* asked Plath to write an article about Alfred Kazin, that year's English-department Neilson Professor. Once he had met Sylvia and discovered that she was talented and had already chalked up an impressive list of publications, Kazin invited her to sit in on his creative-writing section. Following the first class, in which Plath stood out among the other ten students as she offered opinions on the stories up for discussion, Kazin suggested that she join the group permanently. The author of *On Native Grounds* and *A Walker in the City*, Kazin had a reputation too impressive for Sylvia to resist studying with him, so she added his course. "The teacher can help the student in two ways, Mr. Kazin points out: first, to have confidence in her own individuality; and, second, to learn that all literature is discipline," Plath wrote in her article (which she finished by the end of October and *The Smith Alumnae Quarterly* published in its fall issue). Plath took Kazin's advice to heart and wrote a short story—her first in nearly two years. "[Kazin] told me it's my holy duty to write every day, spill out all, learn to give it form," Sylvia wrote to Gordon at this time. "He is extremely critical and encouraging, and the fortuitous accident of interviewing him is something I'll praise fortune for all my life long. I adore him!"

By mid-semester, Sylvia had once again pushed herself to the limit. Besides keeping up with her classwork, now fifteen hours' worth, she busily applied to graduate schools, submitted her work to magazines, and served in extracurricular organizations like Alpha Phi Kappa Psi. Indeed, she felt so pressed for time, she wrote to Gordon, who was now living temporarily in Wellesley while the navy repaired the *Perry*, that she would not be able to see him—not even on weekends. In one letter, Sylvia begged Gordon to have patience with her and to accept her weaknesses and limitations. When, in late October, he asked to visit her anyway, she told him that she would not have any free time for around eight months.

In a way, Plath really did have a full schedule. Professor Joyce Homer interviewed her for Oxford on October 28, Mary Ellen Chase for Cambridge on November 9. To create the proper image, Sylvia had dyed her platinum-blond hair walnut-brown. In November, the interviews behind her, she relished the publication of her poem "Go Get the Goodly Squab" in *Harper's*, an occasion significant enough—her third poem in the magazine in a year—to warrant a Wellesley *Townsman* article. In mid-November, Cyrilly Abels wrote Plath to tell her that her poem "Parallax" had won honorable mention in *Mademoiselle*'s Dylan Thomas Poetry Contest. And, over Thanksgiving break, she had so much to do—work on her thesis, read Shakespeare—that Sylvia could be with Gordon, still living in Wellesley, only at Thanksgiving dinner. Soon after this, Gordon lost his patience. "Although I know you are not thinking of leaving me for another man (unless for the time being it is Fyodor [Dostoevsky]), your attitudes toward me have changed and mine toward you," he wrote on December 2. "Last summer the reality of a fissure in our relationship seemed like an impossible bad dream; we wondered what there could be which we could disagree about and which we could not settle peacefully in words." But now the "impossible" seemed to have happened. He was hurt by her refusal to see him, Gordon let her know, and he disliked "some of [her] disconcerting remarks." Why *had* their relationship deteriorated?

In a word, Sassoon. During November, as she put off Gordon, Sylvia had become preoccupied with Richard Sassoon. By December, she hoped to have an all-out love affair with him. On the weekend of the 10th, they went to New York together. If they had not been physically intimate before now, they were during this trip. On the 18th, Sassoon wrote to Sylvia—his characteristic ornate English-mixed-with-French prose pulsed on the page, even when its sentences' syntax sometimes rendered its meaning incomprehensible—to chide her for bossing him. "Worst, what no woman has dared, you tell me what to do! Yet fetch and carry for the future like an American rattle-snake stung female hound in the hunt and the spring, when lame laddies are in love the way the cloud is in the sky by the grace of God, the ocean and the sun and cannot tell if [it] floats." Later in the letter, Sassoon joked that he was "scolding" her, because "one must always be inventing new ways of scolding when one is conceiving new ways of loving." His parting passage would have rivaled any written by Sylvia's previous boyfriends. "Darling, darling, my darling, my very darling," he gushed, "I think you will never die or be old, because I love you too much and there is a force and a fire and a fury of life in my love."

Plath may have been falling in love with Sassoon, but she still worked to further her career. In December, she entered *Vogue*'s Prix de Paris competition, finished the rough draft of her thesis, and published her poem "Circus in Three Rings" and her short story "In the Mountains" in *The Smith Review,* on whose editorial board she again served. Also, beginning in December and continuing into January, she lined up individuals to write letters of recommendation for her various scholarship (Fulbright, Radcliffe, and Woodrow Wilson) and graduate-school applications. Had she ever been able to read these private documents, she would have been deeply heartened. "If any graduating senior deserves an opportunity to study abroad," Mary Ellen Chase stated, "[Sylvia] most surely does." Elizabeth Drew offered similar acclaim: "I have known Miss Sylvia Plath intimately as a student for the past three years, and I have never had a more brilliant and a more charming student to teach. . . . I can truthfully say that I cannot think of any American student that I would choose above Miss Plath to represent America in my country [Drew was British]." Newton Arvin said he believed that "[Sylvia] will prove to be a really original teacher and writer," while Kazin called her "someone to be watched, to be encouraged—and to be remembered." And Gibian, who thought Plath was "the outstanding student in my experience at Smith College," felt that "we shall hear further of her as a scholar, short story writer, and poet."

The challenge facing these recommenders—and Plath—was not complicated. They had to convince graduate-school and scholarship committees to support the candidacy of a student who had a record of serious mental instability. Logically, Ruth Barnhouse, Plath's psychiatrist, could best address this issue. Regarding Plath's breakdown, treatment, and present academic pursuits, Barnhouse wrote:

In my opinion, at the time of hospitalization Miss Plath was suffering from a state of mental turmoil which is highly unlikely ever to recur. Some of the qualities most obvious in her illness were the very ones which, properly channelled and maturely balanced, contribute to her undoubted superiority as a person. She has a great sense of responsibility, not only to others who may depend on her, but also to herself, and to her integrity. She is extremely quick and sensitive in her relationships with others, and this, combined with her natural intelligent curiosity, leads her to seek experience almost for its own sake. In my opinion she is perfectly capable of handling the difficult situations into which these attitudes sometimes lead her. . . . She has confidence in her abilities without seeming over-confident. Her chief fear is that having had an emotional upheaval sufficiently severe to provoke her hospitalization will be held against her as evidence of basic instability. While in many cases this might be a valid conclusion, in the case of Miss Plath, I feel that anyone refusing her for a position on those grounds would be depriving not only Miss Plath, but also depriving themselves.

Oddly, the only negative comments made about Plath in these letters of recommendation came from Lawrence House, whose housemother filed in the Vocational Office an evaluation as disparaging as Plath's teachers' were laudatory. "Sylvia Plath is a girl of unquestionable character," Estella Kelsey wrote. "Her appearance is quite striking. She has a pleasant voice and pleasing, correct deportment. [But she] is self-centered and very selfish. Her talent for writing has made her difficult for the girls to live with."

5

After she spent Christmas in Wellesley, Sylvia returned to Smith in early January. As soon as she got back, she developed her worst sinus infection yet. During a near week-long infirmary stay, she wrote five poems and entertained a handful of guests. One, sent to her by Alfred Kazin, was a young Harcourt, Brace assistant editor named Peter Davison who told her to keep him in mind if she ever finished a novel. Released from the infirmary, Plath submitted her new poems (along with two others) to *The New Yorker*, dropped off to a typist the draft of her thesis, *The Magic Mirror: A Study of the Double in Two of Dostoevsky's Novels* (in accepting it Gibian had called it a "masterpiece"), and focused on her classes. For the semester, her last, she enrolled in Dunn's Shakespeare, Helene Sommerfeld's Intermediate German, Kazin's Twentieth Century American Novel, Alfred Young Fisher's one-hour independent-study course Theory and Practice of Poetics, plus Honors hours. Not long afterwards, *Vogue* announced that she had reached the finals of the Prix de Paris, which meant that she had next to write a ten-page treatise on Americana. Despite her recent illness and her more remote nervous breakdown, Plath seemed to be as highly motivated—and as busy—as ever.

On January 22, Plath interviewed at Harvard with a screening committee for the Woodrow Wilson Fellowship. In the meeting, it became apparent that the four-man-and-one-woman panel frowned on Plath's application, not because of her résumé but because of her gender.

Following the interview, having told her mother she planned to see a recently married Smith friend in New York, Sylvia went to Logan Airport and flew to New York, to meet not a Smith friend but Sassoon. (Curiously, Sylvia now seemed to have enough money for periodic air trips, even though her budget remained tight.) Over the next three days, she tried to forget the Wilson interview, which she felt she had little chance of passing, and absorbed herself in New York's cultural and social life. Besides seeing the Japanese film *Gate of Hell* and the Russian Jewish play *The Dybbuk,* Sylvia and Sassoon ate at several French restaurants—Le Gourmet, Café Saint-Denis, and Le Veau D'Or. Back at Smith, Plath received the bad news she expected. On January 27, she opened a letter from Francis M. Rogers, who informed her that her "name [had] been withdrawn from the list of nominees who [were] still being considered for National Woodrow Wilson Fellowships." Rogers also suggested that Plath "consider applying to a graduate school that is not most likely to be overcrowded with applicants in your field." In disbelief, Sylvia underlined this section of the letter. More forthcoming on her calendar, she wrote next to this date "refusal from WWilson" and "SHOCK!" Sylvia now feared that she would also be turned down for a Fulbright and that her application for a Radcliffe would be blocked by Rogers, a dean at that college.

Life looked much better for Sylvia in February. At mid-month, she was accepted in the honors bachelor's program (the equivalent of an American master's) at both Cambridge and Oxford Universities. Overjoyed, she wrote her mother about the acceptances, saying that she thought British men were wonderful. No doubt, she was thinking of Sassoon, with whom her relationship had become more complicated. On the 8th, they had slipped away to New York for another quick trip, and it was at this time that their involvement took on darker colorings. Returning to New Haven, Sassoon wrote Sylvia—his "very dearest": "Do not think I am scolding you, my love, for I have recently decided that you are a quite grown up child and that I may not henceforth chide you in the manner to which I am used, nor even probably spank you. Such it is that if you ever anger me greatly I shall have but two alternatives, one of which is to beat you, which is a very different thing from spanking." At the end of the letter, Sassoon added an afterthought:

"Do not take me too literally about not spanking you anymore. . . ." (Eventually, Sylvia would tell a friend that one time at Rahar's Sassoon had become angry at her and slapped her.) If she was searching for an affair more complex than the one she had had with Gordon, she had certainly found it with Sassoon.

March was as bustling—and draining—as any recent month. For school, Sylvia studied German, read Shakespeare, and wrote about five poems a week in Fisher's directed-study course. For *Mademoiselle*, she reported on Smith's symposium "The Mid-Century Novel," which Chase chaired, and which featured such speakers as Kazin and Saul Bellow. Although Sylvia had supper with Gordon on the 6th—a pleasant evening—she was so exhausted by mid-month that she checked into the infirmary for two days. As of March 23, she felt well enough to date Peter Davison, the young Harcourt, Brace editor. In Northampton for his quarterly trip to bookshops, Davison took her to lunch at Rahar's; then she drove with him to drop in on stores in Holyoke. Sylvia found out that Peter, a Harvard graduate and a Fulbright fellow, was the son of the British poet Edward Davison, who taught at Hunter College and who spoke on the women's club lecture circuit. Also, Peter could be charming—the sort of young man she would like to go out with more in the future.

At home on spring break for the first two weeks in April, Sylvia saw Philip McCurdy, visited her friend Sue Weller in Cambridge, and worked on typing her poetry manuscript *Circus in Three Rings*, which she was assembling for Alfred Young Fisher. Refreshed, Sylvia returned to Northampton at mid-month, then two days later left for Mount Holyoke, where she was to compete in the Irene Glascock Poetry Contest, a student literary competition whose past winners included Muriel Rukeyser, James Agee, and Robert Lowell. On arriving at Holyoke, Plath checked into the dormitory room that had been reserved for her. Later, in the dormitory, she met Lynne Lawner, a brilliant and classically beautiful young woman in her sophomore year at Wellesley College, who was also a contestant. Soon, the two went over to an informal reception and joined the other four Glascock contestants, all of whom were interviewed by *The Christian Science Monitor* and *Ma-*

demoiselle and photographed with contest judge Marianne Moore, whom Plath had never met.

Following supper, everyone moved on to the main event. In an oak-paneled room, the contestants seated themselves at a long table. Behind them rose a wall of bookshelves filled with poetry volumes. Before them sat the judges—John Ciardi and Wallace Fowlie were the other two—and an audience of about two hundred, mostly Mount Holyoke students. Beginning the ceremony with a brief opening speech, Moore advised the poets to "write what you are impelled to write," to be resilient to "rebuffs and unfavorable comments," and "to do something else for a living—something that doesn't grate on your nerves too much—[so that] you can do your writing in evenings and on weekends." The house lights dimmed, a hush fell over the crowd, and each poet read. From her portfolio, Plath chose "Winter Words," "Epitaph," "Lament," "Verbal Calisthenics," "April Aubade," "Love Is a Parallax," "*Danse macabre,*" and "Two Lovers and a Beachcomber by the Real Sea." When Plath finished, the audience applauded enthusiastically.

At a party after the reading, Plath met Ciardi and Fowlie, both of whom she adored. Saturday morning, breakfast in bed was served to each contest participant. Then the six student poets recorded poems for the campus radio station, listened to a forum on translation presented by the judges, and attended a luncheon in their honor. At Smith on Monday, Plath glowed when she saw *The Christian Science Monitor.* In it, her "April Aubade" appeared alongside the article "Judges Hear Glascock Poetry Contestants" and several photographs—small shots of the contestants and a large one of Moore sitting on a sofa chatting with Plath. Three days later, Sylvia received from a contest spokesman a letter that contained some of the judges' comments. "[Moore] commends your spirit, patience, craftsmanship, and strong individuality," the spokesman wrote. "Her main adverse criticism is of a too adjectival manner at times bordering on formula." Confusing signals—but Plath accepted them. She had become inured to hearing mixed news. In mid-April, for example, *The Atlantic Monthly*'s Edward Weeks accepted a poem—sort of. Though he regarded the second stanza of Plath's "Circus in Three Rings" as "a perfect beauty," he believed "neither the first nor the third are up to it." Therefore, he suggested

Plath take the second stanza, build a poem around it, call it (because of its controlling metaphor) "Lion Tamer," and resubmit it to him. To tempt her, Weeks enclosed a check for twenty-five dollars and hinted at including the poem in the magazine's August "Young Poets" section.

Surely Weeks did not mean to, but he disturbed Plath greatly with his letter. Indeed, Sylvia told her mother that the letter, which she considered paternalistic, made her feel ill and disillusioned. She resented Weeks's attempt to alter her work in any way. But he did present her with the chance to appear in *The Atlantic Monthly,* so, after discussing her problem with Fisher, Plath decided to submit to Weeks the original "Circus in Three Rings," a newly composed "Lion Tamer," and five other poems. In her cover letter, Plath told Weeks that she preferred "Circus in Three Rings," that his magazine was among the very few in which she wanted to publish, and that she had been chosen, which she had just learned, one of the winners of the Glascock competition. (She had tied with William Key Whitman; the two split the one-hundred-dollar prize.) All bases covered, Plath mailed Weeks her package.

As she waited for a response, she received more distinctions. In late April, she won the Alpha Phi Kappa Psi Award, the Alpha Award in Creative Writing, and a one-hundred-dollar Christopher Prize. In the middle of all this success, though, Sylvia faced near disaster: her mother suffered yet another gastric hemorrhage. With Aurelia's future prognosis unclear—major stomach surgery seemed unavoidable—Sylvia demanded that she take the coming summer off, rent out 26 Elmwood Road, and convalesce on the Cape.

Sylvia herself now felt the term's wear and tear. To relieve some of the pressure, she withdrew from a course—German—which she did not need to graduate. (That she was dropping one of her father's favorite subjects did not appear to occur to her.) Life was a neverending struggle between emotional demands and physical energy, she wrote to Gordon, who had himself become an emotional demand on Sylvia. This tension had developed not because of any rift between the two of them but because Sylvia and Sassoon had fallen in love. Soon after they spent a Saturday night together at Elinor Friedman's house in Longmeadow, at which time Sylvia had prepared him a lamb chop supper, Sassoon wrote, "[Y]ou will torture tonight! It will do no good, I shall only wake tired and angry and incompetent to deal with the world . . . but you *will torture* . . . because I love you." To put off Gordon so that she could see Sassoon, Sylvia still maintained that she was too busy for Gordon to visit her. As a result, one April weekend, Gordon went on a skiing trip to Canon Mountain with two girls from Pembroke College. On a particular run, he bolted head-first into a woodpile and broke the metacarpal in his hand, an injury serious enough to require minor surgery at a naval hospital. Before long, just as Sylvia had interpreted her fractured fibula as her "break" with Dick, Gordon identified his cracked metacarpal as his "break" with Sylvia.

Though she was trying to end her affair with Gordon, Sylvia mailed him, towards the end of April, a letter in which she enclosed her "Sonnet for a Green-eyed Sailor," a wild, hypnotic love poem she had written for him. Sylvia might have preferred Sassoon, but she obviously could not let go of her feelings for Gordon. After all, she had loved—and no doubt did love—Gordon too. Many years later, towards the end of her life, evidence of her love for him would resurface. Then, if not now, she saw the loss of that love as tragic.

Seemingly, with each passing day of her last month at Smith, Plath received greater acclaim. On May 4, she appeared at a literary festival in Kingston, New York. She judged a creative-writing contest and read her poems to an audience of seven hundred students from across the state. On the 12th, she won an honorable mention, one of twelve, in *Vogue*'s Prix de Paris. A follow-up letter suggested that she apply for a job at Condé Nast. At Last Assembly, on May 18, she was awarded the Elizabeth Babcock Poetry Prize, the Ethel Olin Corbin Prize for her poem "Second Winter," the Marjorie Hope Nicholson Prize for best senior thesis (she shared it with another student), and the Academy of American Poets Prize, voted to her by the English department on the basis of an anonymous manuscript of ten poems. The next day, *Mademoiselle* bought "Two Lovers and a Beachcomber by the Real Sea" as a companion to an article on the Glascock which the magazine planned to run in August. Two days later, *The Atlantic Monthly*'s Weeks accepted not "Lion Tamer" but "Circus in Three Rings," also to come out in August. And, finally, the Spring 1955 *Smith Review* contained her poem *"Danse macabre"* and her story "Superman and Paula Brown's New Snowsuit." But the best news of all arrived on the 20th. On that date, Plath read a letter from the State Department's International Educational Exchange Service: she had been granted a Fulbright Scholarship to study literature at Cambridge University. She especially wanted a Fulbright because that grant, unlike others, covered almost all tuition, travel, and living expenses. Overjoyed, Sylvia telephoned her mother, who was in Newton-Wellesley Hospital being given intravenous feedings to reconstitute her system for the subtotal gastrectomy which doctors had decided she needed.

During the next few days, Sylvia lived in a state of wonderment. When she wrote to Lynne Lawner, with whom she had become pen pals after Glascock, she described herself as "walking on air" due to her Cambridge acceptance—sure to fail her finals because of this "feather-headedness." She would sail for London in September on the *Queen Elizabeth,* she continued, a dream come true.

In May, as Gordon faded from the picture, Sassoon had become the focus of Sylvia's affection. She had visited him one weekend at Yale, and he had written her nine long letters. He ended one with his now standard "Darling, I love you," before he lapsed into a splattering of French punctuated with the word "LOVE" printed in letters three inches high. In another, he stated: "[M]y love lies in waiting still and stealthy . . . as a tiger, that can be taught to be gentle, I think." In yet another, he confirmed plans to celebrate the end of Plath's finals by meeting her in New York. Following that trip, during which she took in *Desperate Hours,* several films, Central Park, and the Museum of Modern Art and lunched with Cyrilly Abels, Plath described the event to Lawner as "magnificent." Her Manhattan fling with Sassoon behind her, graduation awaited.

For someone who had led such an active undergraduate career, Plath did not appear prominently in her senior yearbook. Listed as "not pictured" under the photograph of *The Smith Review*'s staff, she showed up only in the group shot of Lawrence House members, except, of course, for her senior portrait, which depicted a smiling collegiate Plath—a true Smithie—in pageboy hairdo, white blouse, and cashmere sweater. However, at the end of the year she received several awards that distinguished her. By Last Chapel on June 3, Plath had been given the Clara French Prize (for being the outstanding student of English) and selected both as a member of Phi Beta Kappa and as a *summa cum laude* graduate, one of only four in her class.

Graduation ceremonies took place on Monday, June 6, a beautiful, crisp New England late-spring day. On the stage sat the honorary-degree recipients, among them Marianne Moore. In the huge audience sat Aurelia Plath, who had checked out of the hospital and arranged for a friend to drive her to Northampton. (Along the way, Aurelia lay on a mattress in the back of her friend's station wagon.) The centerpiece of the ceremony, which occurred on the college's quadrangle, was the commencement address given by former Illinois governor Adlai Stevenson, whose son, coincidentally, was engaged to be married to Nancy Anderson, another Smith '55 graduate. Standing at the podium before Smith's six hundred seniors, these women who had just completed one of the most rigorous undergraduate programs in America, Stevenson, himself divorced, informed the graduates that their "highest vocation" in life, as Plath would recall his wording, was to achieve a "creative marriage." At the end of his speech, the audience applauded: Stevenson had not said anything at all alien to the crowd that day. After all, women were *expected* to marry, have children, run a home, volunteer in the community. If a woman wanted a career, she pursued it *in addition* to her domestic life. As Polly Longsworth, Smith '55, remembers: "I think we were in a condition of mind where we could hear Stevenson's message—we'd been brought up on it—but not believe it. Smith had told us differently for four years. It was only later, when his words began to prove true, that most of us got mad." On that day in June, Sylvia Plath was surely not mad as she took her place in the alphabetical roll call of names and proudly accepted her Smith diploma.

6

One person who did not attend Sylvia's graduation was Gordon. "I have taken all you had to give—and you gave more than anyone," he wrote to her in early June. "We diverge now, you set on a bramble path in the middle of a lemon forest, and I drifting on a balancing craft over a liquorish, clouded sea. Though I am cast up now out of the round belly of the whalewhite night upon the headland of the bloodrock shore, I will taste still the sea on my tongue and feel the tempest wind swim through my hair." After she read Gordon's letter, Sylvia did something odd: she tried to make up with him. In late June, they played tennis and went to Crane's Beach twice. As she rekindled this affair— it did not become sexual—Sassoon grew impatient. In June alone, he wrote her ten letters. "I and the sky are both pretending and hiding a very terrible fire. . . . [I]t burns tremendous deep and the brand is a beam and gleams with a rage beyond redness—in a bomblike between sorrow and gladness—a tenor like before screaming scaring sound to slight in a frozen blare—burns. . . . I long for my Sylvia." After graduating from Yale and moving off campus, Sassoon even described his apartment as belonging to "Sylvia's Lover." By the end of the month, though, he knew things were terribly wrong. "It's an awfully long time since I asked a girl to write me," he said in one letter, before he told her to send him a card "to let me know if you are quite well."

In June, Sylvia distracted herself from Sassoon by keeping busy. She visited her mother, still in the hospital, who had been operated on during the week of the 13th. She submitted poems to *Harper's*, *Harper's Bazaar*, *The Ladies' Home Journal*, and *The Nation*, which accepted "Temper of Time." And, on the 11th, she served as maid of honor at the wedding of Ruth Freeman and Arthur Geissler at Saint John's Episcopal Church in Winthrop. Also, during that month, she ate supper, separately, with Wilbury Crockett and Patsy O'Neil and wrote to the Academy of American Poets to thank them for her prize. But her biggest diversion was the prospect of a new boyfriend. In June, Peter Davison quit his job at Harcourt, Brace in New York to accept the position of assistant to the editor at Harvard University Press in Cambridge. "I hope to see a bit of him," Plath wrote to Lawner about Davison, now a candidate for an affair.

At the end of June, on the same day Sassoon wrote his letter asking to hear from her, Sylvia dropped him a note. "At last a whiff of perfume in my mailbox . . . in my whitewalled damnably odourless home," Sassoon wrote back. "I love you, Sylvia. A madness I am strong enough to live with—even alone." To compensate further for her neglect, Sylvia telephoned Sassoon early one Sunday morning. In a long letter which he wrote just after they hung up, Sassoon said: "I want . . . very much to see you again soon, my darling . . . [but] I must stop my mouth and stopped it is until my pretty Sylvia smiles and the lights change and . . . my God, I fear it will be a very dangerous moment." Then, Sylvia invited Sassoon to Wellesley for the July Fourth weekend. "Darling, darling, thank you for inviting me," Sassoon answered. "I was afraid that . . . you wouldn't . . . because you were doubtless calculating . . . how many beach hounds [Sylvia had been sunning at the lake] severely wounded by the lack of bronze, how . . . Dids't count swounds, wretched woman?! . . . [Anyway,] two days with my love is worth the world the wretched ways of which are payment for it."

Following her weekend with Sassoon, Sylvia drove her mother, just released from the hospital, to the Cape so that the family could celebrate Grammy and Grampy's fiftieth wedding anniversary on the 10th. Afterwards, Sylvia returned to Wellesley alone, while Aurelia remained to convalesce. Later in the month, Sylvia traveled to New Haven. Sassoon had hoped her visit would be pleasurable, but midway through the weekend, they got into a heated argument—at one point, Sylvia accused him of faithlessness—which apparently Sylvia, not Sassoon, started. Sassoon could not figure out why Sylvia wanted to fight. In retrospect, one reason suggests itself. Like Eddie, Dick, and Gordon before him, Sassoon had fallen in love with Sylvia. As they discussed their future life together, Sylvia became uneasy. How could she give herself to Sassoon? In fact, she found him lacking in such basic areas as looks and temperament. When she had located character flaws in her previous boyfriends, she always first abruptly pulled away, then instigated a slow dissolution of the relationship. (Gordon was currently in the slow-fade stage.) In short, during the spring term, as Sassoon had become more in love and less aggressive with her, he had turned into a weak figure in her eyes. Now his shortcomings seemed even worse. It was only a matter of time before Sylvia lost interest—and dropped him.

Sassoon was left reeling. "I tried very hard . . . the last 24 hours we were together to reach you," he wrote the Monday after she left. "I tortured you in my attempt and I also failed. I wanted more than anything in this world to bring you back to me, and I may someday be cut to think that was why I failed. But perhaps, the reasons lie more profound within us." Despite their argument, Sassoon still loved her. "I do not believe I shall ever love another woman so heartedly, so deeply, so happily, so sadly, so confidently, so desperately, so fully, as my love for you has been." He continued his line of thinking, using much more lyrical prose, in his next letter, written on Tuesday. "I promise you now, when you are ready for me, when you are really ready, ready so that if you were again by chance not ready . . . then I shall be waiting for you and ready to meet you—ready . . . for you even if you are not ready."

Indeed, Sylvia was *not* ready. Apparently, she put Sassoon completely out of her mind and immersed herself in writing. As of the Tuesday following New Haven, she had finished a lighthearted article about her first tea with Olive Higgins Prouty which she hoped to sell to *Reader's Digest*. The next morning, she started "Platinum Summer," a story she aimed to send to the "slick" magazines. That night, Mrs. Lameyer took her to supper and to *Henry IV, Part I*, staged at Theatre-on-the-Green. (Sylvia was reluctant about going, though she did not show her apprehension to Mrs. Lameyer.) But the high point of the week was a date with Peter Davison on Saturday night. After cocktails at Peter's and supper at Chez Dreyfus, they went to *Henry IV*—Sylvia's second time to see it in a week. She did not complain, for she now regarded Peter as a potential serious boyfriend. His boyish handsomeness matched his easygoing personality. His credentials were good too: born in New York, then raised in Miami and Colorado, he had been educated at

Harvard and Cambridge. And she found him sexually appealing. Sylvia more than reciprocated when, in the living room of his apartment after *Henry IV,* Peter made a pass at her. She was so willing, in fact, that she readily followed Peter into his bedroom.

Over the next few days, Sylvia worked on "Platinum Summer," helped her mother, who had returned from the Cape, around the house, and dated Peter. Gordon wrote to ask if he could see her on the weekend of August 6. Since she had already agreed to go with Peter to Martha's Vineyard, she quickly sent him back a letter, by airmail, which said that a friend of Alfred Kazin—a "Mr. Davison"—was taking her to the Vineyard to be interviewed by an agent, that this was her *only* opportunity to meet the agent, but that she desperately wanted to see him—Gordon—before she sailed to England. On her weekend with Peter, which they spent at Barn-House, a cooperative located on South Road near Chilmark, Sylvia met Roger Baldwin and Ann Hopkins, attended a champagne party given by a German baron and baroness, and learned even more about Peter—his father was close friends with Robert Frost, she noted—although no agent interviewed her. Nor was one supposed to. From the start, Peter intended the weekend to be strictly social.

August was a banner month for Plath. *The Atlantic Monthly* printed "Circus in Three Rings"—Plath's most satisfying publication to date; *The Nation* ran "Temper of Time"; and *Mademoiselle* included "Two Lovers and a Beachcomber by the Real Sea" as a sidebar to its article "Poet on College Time," the Glascock piece, which mentioned Plath prominently. Because of these accomplishments, Plath heard not only from friends like Gordon and Mrs. Prouty but from Henry Volkening, an agent whose clients had included Thomas Wolfe and Saul Bellow and who possibly wanted to represent Plath. With August's publications amounting to a kind of milestone, Plath could look back over her fledgling career. So far, she had written at least 220 poems—an enormous quantity for a young woman not yet twenty-three—as well as numerous short stories, newspaper articles, and magazine pieces. And now, as of August 1955, some of that work had found its way into national periodicals. But with acceptance came a never-ending flow of rejection slips. Most of the poems and stories she mailed out that summer were returned. *The New Yorker* and *The Atlantic Monthly* rejected poems; *Collier's* and *Woman's Day*, stories. Yet Plath would simply not give up. Until the very end of her life, each rejection she received fueled in her a stronger desire to publish.

On August 14, on a date with Peter Davison, Plath talked about her writing, especially her poetry. "I was far less impressed by the poems she was actually writing at that time"—he would call them "sedulous villanelles and acrobatic caprices"—"than by the furious intensity of her preparation," Davison later wrote. "She had studied contemporary poetry like coastal charts before a voyage, and she enthused about makers I had never heard about—Isabella Gardner, George Barker, Theodore Roethke."

Over the last month or so, Sylvia and Peter had dated about a half-dozen times. Davison remembers that on almost every occasion, as they had on their first date, they ended up sleeping together. At some point on their date on the evening of the 19th, Sylvia finally felt comfortable enough with him to tell him about the summer of 1953. No doubt because the second anniversary of her suicide attempt was approaching, memories of the summer weighed heavily on her mind. That night, Sylvia confessed to Peter that she had considered either shooting herself or drowning herself before she finally settled on taking sleeping pills. In the wake of their intimate conversation, Peter believed that Sylvia had revealed to him some private part of herself. So, he was stunned when, on the evening of the 23rd, after supper at 26 Elmwood Road, where Peter met Aurelia for the first time, Sylvia took him on a long walk and told him that she did not want to see him again. She "spoke in such a way as to retract any tenderness that had infused our lovemaking," Davison would write. "She was on the lookout for a man whose strength and gifts would anchor her instability, and I was at best a leaky life preserver."

On August 28, her summer affair with Peter over, Sylvia went to Washington, D.C., to see her friend Sue Weller, who was working for the government. During her stay, Plath visited several traditional tourist attractions—the Washington Monument, the National Gallery, the White House, the Supreme Court, the Capitol; and the Library of

Congress. On September 2, she took the train to Baltimore to meet up with Gordon, who drove her back to Wellesley. In the car, they discussed various topics, among them literature and writing, but mostly they reminisced. Yet it became clear that Sylvia was trying to bring some sense of closure to their relationship, which had now essentially ended even though she would have supper with him on September 3 and with him and his mother the day after.

In early September, Sylvia spent time with Warren (one day they swam in the icy waters off Crane's Beach); talked with Peter on the telephone twice; saw Olive Higgins Prouty and Mary Ellen Chase, separately; and had supper one evening with the Harvard professor whom she had dated the previous summer. On the 12th, Warren drove her to New York. The next day, she wandered about the city, shopping at Bloomingdale's and sightseeing at Rockefeller Center. On the 14th, she kissed Warren good-bye and boarded the *Queen Elizabeth II*, which set sail for England at nine o'clock in the evening. From the deck of the ship, Sylvia told Manhattan farewell—she would actually write that word on her calendar—as she watched the city slowly recede into a gray wash of twilight.

Abroad

1

For the three days she sailed on the *Queen Elizabeth II,* Sylvia often socialized with a boy named Carl Shakin. During the day, they sat out on deck; at night they went ballroom dancing, which gave Sylvia the chance to use the Fred Astaire dance lessons—a gift from Aurelia—she had taken just before her departure. Soon their friendship turned into what Sylvia called a shipboard romance. On September 20, the *Queen Elizabeth II* docked in Cherbourg, France, where Sylvia and Carl went ashore for a pleasant afternoon. Then the ship cruised on to Southampton, England, its port of entry; here the Fulbright students caught a train into London's Waterloo Station. From there, a bus took them to their temporary residence at Bedford College on Regent's Park. On their first night in London, Carl took Sylvia to *Waiting for Godot.* Over the next four days, Sylvia saw three more plays and the French film *Rififi,* and generally explored the city, usually with Carl. She also attended a reception for Fulbright English-literature students. At the reception, she met David Daiches, but because of (to her mind) poor hostessing, she was not introduced to John Lehmann, C. P. Snow, or Stephen Spender. On the 24th, Sylvia moved to a fourth-floor room at a YWCA, which she shared with three other Fulbright girls. After that, she spent less time with Carl and more with an old boyfriend of Sue Weller's who took her to out-of-the-way spots, like a Dickensian pub called The Doves. Sylvia stayed in London until October 1, the date on which her Cambridge college—Newnham—opened and she took the train north to begin the Michaelmas term.

In England, the universities were made up of free-standing colleges which were defined not by academic affiliation (Business, Engineering, Arts and Science) but by general mission. A student remained within his home college, unable to move from one to another. With names like King's, Saint John's, and Pembroke, several colleges formed Cambridge University. At Cambridge, the academic year was divided into trimesters, separated by two long vacations. Students, who wore black university robes to class, chose their triposes—the examinations they had to pass to graduate at the very end of their years of study—and prepared for them by attending lectures and tutorials on a volunteer basis.

Early on in Cambridge, Sylvia became acquainted with the school and the town. She strolled through the university's beautiful courtyards; hiked along the River Cam, which compared in width to Wellesley's Linden Street; and, on the bicycle she had imported, snaked her way down the town's tiny cobblestone streets lined with an assortment of cafés, public buildings, and shops. The walk from the university to the town was short (the two entities actually seemed to merge into one another), so Sylvia made the trip often. Each time, she noticed some new sight—a rose garden, a fish-and-chips store, an apothecary, a church.

In those first days, Sylvia unpacked the clothes and books from her Samsonite luggage, which she had bought just for Cambridge, and arranged her things in her room. She had been assigned to live in Whitstead, a large ten-woman graduate-student residence house located on Barton Road, near Newnham. An attic single, her room had a gas fireplace, a gas ring on the hearth, bookshelves, and a cozy window seat on which she could sit and, when she was not reading or writing, stare over the treetops onto the Whitstead gardens below. Venturing out, Sylvia checked into the campus's social life and learned that the university sponsored a club for almost everything, from "Esperanto to wine-tasting to Gepettos (puppetry) to tiddleywinks!" She introduced herself to her director of studies, Kathleen Burton, with whom she selected the triposes for which she would read, and went to her first lectures, which started on October 7. This term, Miss Burton would tutor her weekly; Sylvia would also go to lectures on tragedy. To prepare for her optional exams, Sylvia decided to sit in on F. R. Leavis's lectures on the English moralists, Basil Willey's on the history of literary criticism, and Joan Bennett's on the seventeenth-century metaphysical poets.

Immediately, Sylvia hated the weather in Cambridge. The temperature was colder than Boston's, the British heating inferior to American. In the morning when she ate breakfast and dressed in her robe to go to lectures, she could actually see her breath.

From the beginning, Sylvia read numerous books as background for her lectures and tutorials. Yet she also tried to strike up a social life, which did not promise to be too difficult since men outnumbered women ten to one at Cambridge. On the 10th, she dropped in on a Labour Party dance and met Mallory Wober, a nineteen-year-old Londoner who had lived for years in India. Before long, Sylvia and Mallory were friends, often sharing tea in each other's "digs." With his black hair, blush-red cheeks, and tall rugged build, Mallory was a welcome exception to other British men, whom Sylvia now regarded as washed-out and fragile. One evening, after a concert in King's College's dining hall, Mallory took Sylvia to supper at an Indian restaurant, the Taj Mahal, where he introduced her to mangoes and bindhi quaht, dishes familiar to him from his nine years in Darjeeling.

To expand her social life further, Plath joined the Amateur Dramatic Club, for which she auditioned by reading the parts of Rosalind in Shakespeare's *As You Like It* and Camille in Tennessee Williams's *Camino Real*. By October 12, not two weeks into the term, what with dating, attending classes, and studying dramatics, Sylvia had come down with a sinus infection. As had been her custom at Smith, she checked into the campus hospital, whereupon she discovered that instead of Smith's treatment of penicillin and cocaine spray she was to receive nothing stronger than aspirin. Also, she had to eat tasteless meals, unlike Smith's delicious food, and deal with rude nurses who, if Sylvia asked for a tissue, offered to tear up a sheet. After a day of this treatment, Sylvia left the campus hospital and went downtown to her National

Health Services physician, a Dr. Bevan, who prescribed appropriate medication and promised to X-ray her head within a week if she did not feel better.

In time, Sylvia recovered from her sinus infection. Returning to her studies, she initiated a friendship with Jane Baltzell, a Whitstead resident with whom she shared tutorials with Miss Burton, and performed, in mid-October, in an Amateur Dramatic Club one-night-only showcase of a Pope play in which she delivered fifteen wordy speeches. Around this time, Sylvia also saw the royal couple—a rare sight for the British, much less an American. In Cambridge to christen the opening of a veterinary laboratory, Queen Elizabeth and the Duke of Edinburgh were scheduled to come by Newnham for sherry and a presentation ceremony. After they were delayed by rain on the morning they were supposed to visit, the royal couple finally showed up. As they strolled between two greeting lines formed by the Newnham girls, Sylvia—so thrilled that she fell into *Mademoiselle* prose when she wrote about the episode later—thought the Duke "enchanting," the Queen "quietly radiant in a Kelly-green princess-style coat and hat." Following the brief ceremony, which left her "speechless with excitement," Sylvia hurried out into the pouring rain to glimpse the royal couple getting into a car that would take them, she learned, to lunch at Trinity College.

Several days later, still excited by the royal visit, Sylvia celebrated her birthday—her first abroad—by opening presents mailed to her by her family. She also set out on a new friendship with a charming "light-skinned Negro," Nathaniel LaMar, to whom she had been introduced by boys from Pembroke College. A student of Archibald MacLeish's at Harvard and an acquaintance of Warren's at Exeter, LaMar, who had just published his story "Creole Love Song" in *The Atlantic Monthly*, would eventually become one of Plath's best friends at Cambridge. By the end of October, when she wrote to Olive Higgins Prouty, who in her last letter had called Sylvia her "most wonderful-of-all scholarship girls," Sylvia described her life as pleasant and full of activities. Indeed, she had been so pressed for time, she told Prouty, that she had postponed writing stories and poems until December.

In early November, Sylvia saw *I Am a Camera*, engaged Nat LaMar in long literary chats in a local coffee house, and auditioned for a large part in Ben Jonson's *Bartholomew Fair,* for which she was turned down. Though not writing, she still submitted work to magazines. When she had shown a batch of poems to the editor of *Chequer,* one of Cambridge's literary journals, he had accepted "Epitaph in Three Parts" and " 'Three Saryatids Without a Portico' by Hughes Robus: A Study in Sculptural Dimensions." Yet as she read, attended lectures, and saw her friends, Sylvia became anxious. She felt Smith had trained her well in Chaucer, Shakespeare, and the moderns, but, she now decided, she was ignorant about many other periods of literature. She knew nothing of the classics or of any literature produced in England in the sixteenth, seventeenth, and eighteenth centuries. Because of her poor preparation, she could never attempt a doctorate, something she had considered doing.

Around November 20, Sylvia had tea with Dick Wertz, Sassoon's Yale roommate, who was reading in theology at Cambridge. As they talked, Sylvia realized she missed Sassoon, then studying at the Sorbonne. To take her mind off Sassoon, Sylvia dated several boys. One was David Buck, a resident at Christ's who was reading in English and who had landed a major part in *Bartholomew Fair.* (In the end, Sylvia had been offered a five-line bit part as a prostitute which she accepted because she wanted the experience of performing in a Cambridge production.) Another was John Lythgoe, a kind-hearted biology student. But mostly, she saw Mallory, whom she now considered her "Jewish God." On the weekend of the 18th, they attended Tennessee Williams's *The Glass Menagerie,* read aloud Dylan Thomas and Oscar Wilde in his room, and went punting on the Cam. On one other occasion, after Sylvia had mentioned she regretted that she did not have a phonograph in her room, Mallory showed up with a stack of records, a gramophone, and—hard to believe—a Hammond organ that he had rented for a week.

Starring Raymond Massey's son Daniel, *Bartholomew Fair* ran from November 24 to December 3. Throughout rehearsals, Sylvia enjoyed playing a prostitute, although she had made up her mind to quit the Amateur Dramatics Club if she did not get bigger parts in the future. The opening-night audience included several critics (one long, negative

notice eventually appeared in the London *Times*), and Mallory met
Sylvia at the stage door after the premiere to congratulate her. By early
December, the grind of the term—the academics, the dates, the
play—had taken a toll. Sylvia succumbed to another sinus infection
and a fever that became so bad she was bedridden, causing her to miss
the last three performances of *Bartholomew Fair*.

On December 4, she had recovered enough to have lunch with—
of all people—Sassoon, who had flown to England to visit relatives and
dropped by Cambridge to see Dick Wertz. After lunch, Sylvia served
Dick and Sassoon tea in her room. Before Sassoon left, he and Sylvia
agreed to meet in Paris over Christmas vacation. One reason Sylvia
decided to resurrect her relationship with Sassoon was that, as she
wrote in her journal, she found most British men to be pallid, neurotic
homosexuals—a development she blamed on segregated schooling. She
was also disgusted by British boys' poor dental hygiene; they all seemed
to let their teeth rot until they had to be pulled. Mallory did not
resemble such British boys, but Sylvia looked forward to seeing Sassoon
nonetheless.

On December 9, the Michaelmas term ended and Mallory left for
London. Alone in Cambridge, Sylvia, when she was not catching up
on her letter writing, filled out her Fulbright renewal papers. As she
did, she also began to reflect on her personal shortcomings. The hardest
thing in her life, she wrote to her mother, was accepting that she could
never be perfect. She *so* lacked perfection she was sure that her Fulbright would not be extended (only about 10 percent were). Obviously,
it was time for a vacation.

2

Though Mallory had asked Sylvia to come to his home in London
during Christmas break, Sylvia had previously accepted an invitation
from John Lythgoe. On December 20, after a three-day visit with John
during which she also set aside a few hours one afternoon to stop by
Mallory's and meet his parents, Sylvia went to the London airport,

where she expected to board a prepaid charter flight to Paris. In the airport waiting room, she spotted Jane Baltzell. The two had gradually become good friends, even though Sylvia was afraid Jane could be her *doppelgänger*. Both German-American, Ivy League–educated Whitstead residents who were reading English in Newnham, they were possibly too similar, Sylvia had warned Jane. Nevertheless, today they seemed happy to see each other.

Hours passed—no plane. Bad weather had grounded all aircraft in Paris. Eventually, because no airplane was forthcoming, the travel company bused the passengers to the ferry docks. After another two or three hours, everyone was boarded onto a boat to cross the Channel. Halfway through the trip, a winter storm passed over. As a numbing drizzle fell, choppy waters tossed the boat to and fro so badly that many passengers began vomiting in the enamel basins provided on deck for that purpose. Huddling under Jane's Burberry raincoat, the two young women sipped brandy to settle their stomachs. By the time the boat landed on the French coast and Jane and Sylvia had made the train ride into Paris, it was eleven o'clock—too late for Jane to find a hotel room. So, Sylvia offered to share the room Nat LaMar had arranged for her.

At the hotel, Jane, exhausted by the nightmarish trip, collapsed into bed, but Sylvia, delighted over being in Paris and by the prospect of seeing Sassoon, decided not to go to sleep just yet. Without mentioning Sassoon, she told Jane she wanted to explore the city—and left. She walked to Sassoon's flat to find him waiting for her there. They had an hour together before Sylvia returned to the hotel, only to discover that her room door was locked. No matter how hard she knocked, Jane would not answer. Exasperated, Sylvia explained her predicament to the concierge, who could not open the door with a passkey, as it turned out, because Jane had left the key in the keyhole and turned in the locked position. Finally, the hotel manager let Sylvia sleep in a room with two girls from Switzerland, all three in the same bed.

When Sylvia knocked on the door the next morning, Jane answered. "How could you?" Sylvia blurted out furiously. At which point Jane, who assumed Sylvia had stayed out all night, realized her mistake: she was so worn out, she said, that she must have slept through Sylvia's knocking. "Rarely have I felt more hopelessly embarrassed," Baltzell later wrote. "My fault was the more grievous, of course, in that she had been doing me a kindness. At the same time, I found the peculiar intensity of her anger inappropriate. I had not, after all, locked her out on purpose; but she was angry just as though I had. She somehow conveyed as much, alluding to her *doppelgänger* theory." To save the friendship, not to mention their nerves, they struck a truce. All would be forgiven if Jane would be more careful with the key in the future. Yet, astonishingly, when Jane left for Italy a few days later, she again locked the key in the room. The episodes with the key would be the beginning of the end of Sylvia and Jane's friendship.

Over the next week and a half, Sylvia saw as much as she could of Paris, a city she grew to love even more than London. In her short time there, Sassoon introduced her to many of the city's sights, among them the Champs-Elysées, the Seine Chapel on the Ile de la Cité, the Rue de la Paix, the Place Pigalle prostitutes, and the Louvre, where Sylvia marveled at Brueghel, *Winged Victory,* and the *Mona Lisa.* With Sassoon, she mingled with children at the Garden of the Tuileries, saw an Impressionist exhibit at the Orangerie, strolled along the Seine, and went to two French films and two plays. On Christmas morning, her first away from home, Sassoon took Sylvia to Notre Dame Cathedral. Sitting on a pew in the soothing morning light, Sylvia, as she would later write, thought of her mother and her brother and all the other people she loved.

On the 31st, Sylvia packed her suitcases, checked out of the hotel, and, with Sassoon by her side, boarded the midnight express for Nice. Along the way, they celebrated New Year's, enjoying a delicious breakfast as they watched the scarlet sun rise over the Mediterranean. In Nice, located on Angels' Bay, Sylvia spent her first day relishing their magnificent view of the snowcapped Alps, groves of orange and olive trees, and the green palms. During their week in the south, Sylvia and Sassoon wandered the streets of Nice; motorbiked around nearby inlets to Monte Carlo (in one casino Sylvia lost three dollars at a roulette table and left in a rush) and on into Ventimiglia, Italy; and, the two of them exhausted, rested in their hotel room by reading *The Autobiography of Alice B. Toklas.*

One day Sylvia and Sassoon motorbiked to Vence, a small, uncommercial town that was home to a Matisse chapel Sylvia wanted to see. But when they found the chapel in Vence, it was closed. A sign on the front gate said the building was open only two days a week. For some time, Sylvia sat nearby and sketched the small church; eventually, she returned to the front gate. Standing there, she started to cry, because she could imagine the sunlight falling in streaks through the blue, yellow, and green stained-glass windows—a sight she was not going to be able to see. Then, while she cried, the mother superior suddenly appeared, as if from nowhere, and, saying, *"Ne pleurez plus, entrez,"* unlocked the gate to allow Sylvia in. Slowly Sylvia entered and "in the heart of sun and the colors of sky, sea, and sun, in the pure white heart of the chapel" lowered herself to her knees.

On January 8, 1956, Sylvia and Sassoon returned to Paris by train. In the fall, Sylvia had dated several young men. Just before Christmas, though, she decided that she really only wanted to be with one—Sassoon. Consequently, Sylvia was devastated when, as she finished packing to leave Paris, Sassoon told her that he intended to go out with other women once she was gone. In fact, he and a Swiss girl had become so involved lately that they had actually discussed marriage. Distraught, Sylvia flew to London on the 9th in a blur of anger and confusion. Back at Whitstead the next day, she could hardly get excited over the gift from Gordon she found waiting for her there—an autographed copy of Richard Wilbur's *Misanthrope*. She tried to put the ugliness of her final hours with Sassoon behind her. She rewrote her Fulbright renewal application, composed an article about her trip to France, and drew pen-and-ink sketches of Cambridge. The activities did not help. Writing to her mother in mid-January, she complained with bitterness about not being happy at Cambridge.

When the second term started, on January 17, Plath decided to buckle down, stop socializing, and pour all of her energies into academics and creative writing. To experience the spiritual calm that she believed the act of writing produced, she would write at least two hours a day. And though she realized that writing did not necessarily lead to publishing, she resolved herself to sell something to *The New Yorker,* since she appreciated the magazine's beautiful, crafted style. She spent the last week of January working on "The Matisse Chapel," a twenty-five-page story inspired by her Vence trip. In early February, she submitted it to *The New Yorker,* which turned it down two weeks later with a standard rejection slip.

As she battled what was turning into a full-fledged depression, a result of her falling-out with Sassoon, Sylvia also tried to decide how she was going to live her life in the future. Because she saw herself as becoming no more than a minor writer, because she had so much love to share with another person, and because she did not really *want* a career, Plath, not yet twenty-four, concluded that she was *meant* to marry a man, have children, keep a home, and write in her spare time. After all, the next-oldest generation's women writers—Jean Stafford, Hortense Calisher, Phyllis McGinley—conducted their lives in this way. There was just one problem: Sylvia had no one to marry. Mallory was too young and naive, she decided; John was actually just a Platonic friend; and Sassoon, even if he had not rejected her, suffered from periodic depression and poor health. To find an appropriate candidate for marriage, she would just have to keep on searching.

Through most of February, Sylvia had neither the energy nor the desire to date; instead, she gradually sank deeper into her depression. At the beginning of the month, she heard news from America that saddened her even more. Grammy, who in late January had become sick with—her doctors believed—gastritis, had now been diagnosed as having stomach cancer. Deeply shaken, Sylvia wrote her grandmother a heartfelt letter in which she told her how much she loved her. Then, later in February, Plath's poems, which appeared in that month's *Chequer,* received bad reviews. She was so disappointed that she discussed the reviews with Christopher Levenson, the editor of *Delta, Chequer*'s competition. Much as Sylvia delighted in such lectures as Daiches's on Virginia Woolf and James Joyce, her schedule started to wear on her. As the month progressed and the relentless cold English weather became more inclement, Sylvia slipped into an all-consuming depression which caused her to relive memories of her breakdown. She now believed she had become suicidally depressed that summer because of the hysterical stresses that tore her apart—a conflict between wanting and fearing to take action, between longing for and being able to achieve perfection. By the 24th, Sylvia had developed insomnia. Desperate over the frigid weather—she fed her heater shilling after shilling but still had to wear several sweaters, wool pants, and knee socks just to keep warm—she came down with a cold and a sinus infection.

This was not her only bout with illness in February. Recently, she had visited the university's infirmary for a complete physical examination, after which, at the suggestion of the medical staff, she set up an appointment with the school psychiatrist. In their session, which did not take place until the morning of the 25th, Sylvia revealed to the psychiatrist her greatest resentment about Cambridge: she had no older friends in whom she could confide. At the university, she had found extraordinary dons and mature men (she used this language as she wrote her mother that afternoon), but so far she had not become friends with any of them. "Wanted to burst out in tears and say Father, Father, comfort me," she confessed in her journal about her session with the psychiatrist, echoing a passage she had written days before when she had said, "And I cry so to be held by a man; some man, who is a father."

Sylvia did not discuss her father with the psychiatrist. Nor did she tell her doctor something else. Lately, she had become so obsessed with Sassoon—lost to her, he was probably having his way with some prostitute, she imagined—that she regularly visited a statue of a boy and a dolphin, which stood in one of Newnham's gardens, because to her it had somehow come to represent Sassoon.

On the night of February 25, Sylvia ate supper with Nat. Afterwards, she did not linger too long, since she had a party to go to. A new magazine—*The St. Botolph's Review*—had started up to rival the two established Cambridge literary journals, and the editors were giving a party to celebrate their first issue. Sylvia had read the magazine earlier in the afternoon—and admired it tremendously. So she had decided to drop in on the party, if only to take her mind off her problems.

3

Sylvia had bought *The St. Botolph's Review* from Bertram Wyatt-Brown, a friend (and frequent date) of Jane Baltzell. Taking one copy from his stack of seventy-five, Sylvia had gone back to her room and studied its contents page, which promised stories by Than Minton, E. Lucas Myers, and George Weissbort, and poems by Myers, Daniel Weissbort, Daniel Huws, Ted Hughes, and David Ross, the magazine's editor. The names were familiar to Sylvia, although she knew none of the contributors personally. Huws had been the author of an attack on her *Chequer* poems, and Myers, Huws, and Hughes had published poetry in *Chequer* and *Delta*. Since it was a small volume, only about thirty pages, Sylvia read it quickly. Finished, she remarked with awe the poetry's powerful veracity. Of the poets, Sylvia most admired Myers and Hughes; in particular, she liked Myers's "Fools Encountered" and, because they were so violent, all three of Hughes's, "Fallgrief's Girl-Friends" and two untitled pieces. More excited by the poems than by any she had read in *Delta* or *Chequer*, Sylvia rushed out and found Bert, still selling his magazines. When she asked him how she could meet these poets, Bert told her that they would be at a party for the magazine that night at the Women's Union.

By chance, on her way back to Whitstead, Sylvia bumped into a friend, Hamish Stewart, who recently had asked her for a date. As soon as she suggested that he take her to the *St. Botolph's* party, he agreed. In her room, Sylvia passed the time before her supper with Nat by writing in her journal, making the observation at one point that Hamish—clearly on her mind—often filled his idle hours with drinking, a vice she considered deplorable. Then again, lately she herself had been drinking wine and sherry alone in her room at night. She liked the feeling it produced—sex-charged, joyful. Left to her own devices, she could easily become an alcholic, she admitted to her journal. Since coming to England, she had been drinking a lot; in France, she and Sassoon had consumed a steady flow of wine. If liquor could heighten the good times, she thought, it could also blunt the bad. And so she drank in her room, often to forget about her depression—and, now, Sassoon.

Eventually, Sylvia dressed in a cute "American" outfit, which she accessorized with silver earrings, a red hairband, and a pair of red shoes. After supper with Nat, she returned to Whitstead, where Hamish picked her up in a cab. At Miller's Bar, a stop they made on their way to the party, Sylvia stood at the counter and quickly downed several whiskeys. Soon the whole world floated around her. When they left after an hour, Hamish had to help Sylvia walk.

By the time they reached the Women's Union, a foreboding building on campus just off Falcon Yard, Sylvia was very drunk. Still, as they entered the huge second-floor room in which the party was located, she took the scene in. To the back of the nearly dark, smoke-laden room, a jazz combo improvised; in front of the band, couples mingled—some dancing, some talking, all drinking. Tonight, most of the boys wore jeans and turtlenecks, the girls stylish black dresses. Their attire, like the party itself, projected a studied "hip" feel. Sylvia ran into Bert, but they could barely carry on a conversation. The music was too loud; they were both drunk. Bert could—and did—point out the *St. Botolph's* crowd. About the room stood Huws, Ross, Weissbort, Myers, and Minton. Saying good-bye to Bert and abandoning Hamish as well, Sylvia, drink in hand, confronted Huws to argue about the bad review he had given her *Chequer* poems. Afterwards, she approached Luke Myers, also drunk, yet not so badly that he could not dance with Sylvia. Over the band's blaring music, she shouted how much she liked his poems—and quoted all of "Fools Encountered." The song ended; Luke returned to his girlfriend.

Then, as Sylvia would later write, "the worst thing happened." Standing there in the hall, she saw him—"that big, dark, hunky boy, the only one . . . huge enough for me." Though he had been "hunching" over other women, Sylvia had wanted to know who he was the instant she spotted him. Now, while she studied him, he fixed his stare on *her* and headed across the room. When he came nearer to her, Sylvia could see more clearly his tall frame, his broad shoulders, his youthful, sensual face. He stopped, close enough for the two of them to touch. Her body rigid with fear and expectation, Sylvia looked at him, knowing in her heart who loomed before her—Ted Hughes.

Now, Sylvia began quoting to Hughes one of his poems from the magazine, an untitled piece the first line of which was "I Did It, I." After she finished, Hughes said, "You like?"—and offered her a brandy. Guiding her into a side room, Hughes shut the door and poured Sylvia the drink. While she sipped the brandy, they talked about Sylvia's *Chequer* poems, Hughes's poems, his London job, and his "obligations" in the other room—a girlfriend. Dreamily, Sylvia looked at his face, noticing his demure lips, his wide forehead, his soulful eyes. Then, as if to acknowledge the palpable sexual charge that had formed between them, Hughes leaned down and kissed Sylvia on the mouth. Pulling away, he tore the red hairband from her head and yanked off her silver earrings. "Ah, I shall keep these," he said.

Sylvia felt pleasantly dazed. As soon as Hughes made a move to kiss her on the neck, Sylvia, ready to show that she could hold her own in such matters, reached up and bit his cheek so hard her teeth broke skin, causing him to flinch. Somehow it did not seem possible to continue, so they stepped apart. Certainly Sylvia had found her match, though Hughes had found his too. Moments later, as Hughes left the room, Sylvia could see blood trickling down his cheek.

Now that she had met the only man who could make Sassoon pale by comparison, Sylvia had no reason to stay at the party, especially since she could not be with him. She found Hamish, who was more than willing to go. Outside, in Falcon Yard, Hamish coldly referred to the *St. Botolph's* poets as phonies. But what about Ted Hughes—is he a phony? Sylvia wanted to know. And, in a statement that sounded more like a warning than a comment, Hamish replied, "He is the biggest seducer in Cambridge."

Still drunk, Sylvia and Hamish walked through the night. When they reached the gates of Queens, Hamish's college, they climbed over a wall, sneaked through the yard, and crept into his residence hall. Up in his room, they were soon lying on the floor beside a fire Hamish built in the fireplace. When he kissed her, his mouth felt nice, Sylvia would remember. And after he rolled on top of her, his body pressing down heavily against hers, she begged him to scold her—because, she said, she was a whore and a slut. "You're only a very silly girl," he said, between kisses.

At two-thirty, afraid that she would be caught out after hours, Sylvia asked Hamish to take her back to Whitstead. She crawled into bed at three, then awoke the next morning at nine with a hangover. To soothe her nerves, she wrote in her journal, lingering on an impassioned account of her meeting with Ted. That night, after plodding through Racine in the afternoon, she ate supper with Mallory—who was no Ted Hughes, she now realized. (In a reversal of her pledge to do nothing but write and study, a regimen that had probably made her more—not less—depressed, she had decided to go on dates again.)

The following afternoon, she sat in her cold Whitstead room and wrote a poem that she dedicated to Hughes. Remembering "Jaguar," his poem about a savage jaguar that she had read in a back issue of *Chequer,* Plath composed her poem, the central focus of which is a woman being stalked by a panther. Fleeing the animal, the woman believes that she has become his "bait." A second afternoon of work, and she had finished the poem, which she entitled "Pursuit." Right away, Plath submitted it, along with others to fill out a batch, to *The Atlantic Monthly.*

In the coming days, Sylvia chatted with friends to find out more about Hughes. Having read English in his first two years and archaeology and anthropology in his third, he graduated from Pembroke College at Cambridge in 1954. Between June 1954 and February 1956, he held a series of menial jobs: a rose gardener; a night watchman; and, at present, a reader at J. Arthur Rank's Pinewood Studios, for whom he sought properties to be adapted into screenplays. When he was unemployed or had days off work, Hughes returned to Cambridge. He hated the university's conservative traditions, but he loved the town. In Cambridge, he wrote, read in the library, and caroused with his friends at a local pub called The Anchor. Essentially, these friends composed the group of young men who would one day publish *The*

St. Botolph's Review: E. Lucas Myers, an American from Tennessee and a cousin of Southern poet Allen Tate; Daniel Huws, "just over six feet tall and Celt dark," Myers would write of him, "[his] lips slightly pursed in a physiognomy of marked sensitivity"; David Ross, Daniel's suitemate, whose father was a graphic designer in London; Than Minton, a talented prose-writer; and Daniel Weissbort, an American poet and fiction-writer who would years later write an unpublished sequence of short stories including one—"only slightly fictionalized"—that dealt with the interplay of the young men in this group. In the story, the narrator's psychiatrist tries to explain the give-and-take of the young men. The group is, according to the doctor, "homosexually collusive"— a term that cast, the narrator says, "a somewhat ambiguous light over what I had regarded as a peculiarly heroic and male collection of individuals."

At the time Sylvia met Hughes, his best friend was Luke Myers, whom he had known since January 1955. Myers, Huws, and Hughes had all published poems in *Chequer*. On one of Hughes's trips to Cambridge, the magazine's editor had taken him around to Myers's room. Myers's initial glimpse of Hughes would linger in his mind for years. "He was an inch or so taller than Daniel and wore . . . the brown leather greatcoat that had been issued to an uncle in World War I," Myers would write. "His brown hair fell across the right side of his forehead and his voice modulated curiously at certain significant points in his speech. His eyes and his mouth were powerfully expressive." Instantly, the two men formed a rare, intimate friendship. Their opinions and tastes coincided so completely that it seemed they inhabited the same body. The next time he came to Cambridge, Hughes, who usually spent nights with various friends, stayed with Myers, even though Myers lived in the Saint Botolph's Rectory's refurbished chicken coop, a space so tiny it held only a bed and a desk. When they were not holed up in the hut rehashing life and literature, Myers and Hughes drank with the rest of their friends at The Anchor. Often enthralling his listeners with tales from myths he had memorized, Hughes played his role, the center of the circle, for all it was worth. Once David Ross had decided to finance a literary magazine, Hughes, Myers, and the others offered to contribute poems and stories. They all seemed happy to name the magazine for the address of Luke's hut. After all, if Hughes, the group's undisputed poetic genius, was in Cambridge—or so it was until university officials forced Myers to move into a residence hall— the hut in the garden behind Saint Botolph's Rectory was his home too.

4

Despite Hughes, Sylvia was still obsessed with Sassoon. On the night of March 1, only days after *The St. Botolph's Review* party, Sylvia wrote Sassoon a letter in which she asked if she could go with him to Italy over her spring vacation; the trip, she said, would "save [her] from death." She admitted she could not extricate herself from "that abstract tyrant"—Richard—who had stolen her soul and murdered her flesh. The letter, which she never mailed, set the tone for March.

Early in the month, Sylvia reflected back over the term. Already, she had read fifty plays; among the writers she had studied were Racine, Ibsen, Strindberg, Chekhov, Synge, Yeats, Corneille, Chapman, and Marlowe. On the 4th, she had a blowout with Jane, who returned five books, which she had borrowed, without erasing her penciled notes from their pages. Apparently, Jane assumed that, because Sylvia had already underscored passages in black ink, she—Jane—could write in the books in pencil. On the contrary, Sylvia felt as if "my children had been raped, or beaten, by an alien." Livid, she rushed to Jane's room. "In a very vehement and dreadful way . . . she protested my marks in her books," Baltzell would write. "I have never seen rage like it. More directly than in the [Paris] hotel incident she put it to me that I had acted *maliciously*." After dressing Jane down, Sylvia left, somewhat mollified. But from then on, the two women were no longer friends.

Not long afterwards, Sylvia received a letter from Sassoon that disturbed her. He had decided to return to America, he said, and—of all things—enlist in the army. Sylvia interpreted his move as yet another rejection. Reading his letter, she confessed to her journal that she loved him deeply—perhaps more than any of her other boyfriends. Happy she had not mailed the last letter she had written him, Sylvia composed a second. In this one—long, rambling, pleading—she stated that even if he had taken countless mistresses she would still love him and that she wanted to have his baby. She planned to come to Paris during spring vacation, Sylvia continued; was there any reason why she could not see him? Later that night, rereading Sassoon's letter to her, Sylvia became disconsolate. She returned to her journal and wrote: "[I]t hurts, Father, it hurts, oh, Father I have never known; a father, even, they took from me." Two nights after that, as she drank sherry alone in her room, she continued. "I rail and rage against the taking of my father, whom I have never known. . . . I would have loved him; and he is gone. . . . I must beware, beware of marrying for that [reason]"—that is, to have a boy "become" her father. Only now, as she wrote to herself, could she admit a fact about her personality that would become even more obvious to her in the future: when she felt abandoned by a male romantic figure, she subconsciously experienced the sense of loss she harbored over the death of her father.

To help fight her depression, Sylvia tried to remain active. As often as possible, she attended the lectures given by Dorothea Krook, a Cambridge professor for whom she held deep admiration. On March 9, the day on which *The New Yorker* rejected another batch of poems, Sylvia mailed her mother a letter in which she enclosed "Pursuit." Though she had written her mother six days earlier about Hughes— in that letter, she had described him as the only man in Cambridge who could match her intellectually and creatively—she did not reveal that he had inspired "Pursuit," her new, sexually charged poem. Instead, she brought up Sassoon, who was "saintly," she told her mother. In this letter Sylvia avoided any mention of his rejection of her, her resulting depression, or the memories of her father now surfacing in her mind.

That evening, on a date with Hamish, she drank five or six whiskeys. The next day, on her way to the college library, she ran into Bert, who told her that Hughes and Myers had come by Whitstead the night before and thrown stones at her window. She must have still been out drinking with Hamish, for she had heard nothing. But, as a result of Bert's story, she stayed in her room that night, hoping that Hughes might return. He didn't—or so she thought: downstairs the following morning, Sylvia learned that he *had*. Throwing mud instead of stones on the wrong girl's window—yes, mud!—he had repeatedly called out Sylvia's name.

On March 13, a letter arrived that cheered Sylvia up considerably. Her Fulbright had been renewed—and for a whole year. This meant that she could stay in England for the summer without worrying about expenses. The letter also prompted her to make other career moves. Now, she would definitely apply for a Eugene Saxton Fellowship, with which she hoped to support herself for a year while she wrote a novel.

Excited and encouraged, Sylvia momentarily forgot about a splinter of glass that, in a freak accident, had lodged in her eye the day before. By the end of the week, though, the pain had become unbearable. When her friend Gary Haupt took her to the casualty ward at Addenbrooke Hospital, a doctor determined that removing the splinter would require an operation. After anesthetizing her eye with drops, he cut the splinter from the tissue, an excruciating procedure whose aftermath was equally painful: for the next twenty-four hours, she had to stay awake to apply medicine to her eye so the hole would heal. On the 18th, she was exhausted as she wrote to Gordon, who had recently asked her to go with him to Europe during her spring break (he was coming to screen graduate schools in Germany). Agreeing to the trip, Sylvia suggested that they meet in either Paris or Munich.

Before she could go to Europe, she had a rendezvous to keep. At coffee on the 13th, Myers had asked her to visit him and Hughes in London on her way to Paris. They would be staying near Bloomsbury, on Rugby Street, in a flat that Daniel Huws's father kept, Myers said, and Sylvia was welcome to spend the night. Following her last week of lectures, she took the train from Cambridge to London. When she and Hughes met at the Rugby Street flat, a grungy, run-down place that did not have adequate lavatory facilities, their attraction to one another was even stronger than it had been during the *St. Botolph's* party. All that night they made love. And the sex they had was so rough, Sylvia noted on her calendar the next day, that her face was left battered with purple bruises, her neck raw and injured. Yet only one thing truly upset her: at five in the morning, either because his mind was blurred by their hours of sex or because, as Sylvia suspected, he was ruthless and wanted to humiliate her, Ted called her "Shirley," the name of his last girlfriend. If she had been excited by Sassoon's spanking—and seemingly she had been—now she was involved with a man who so eclipsed Sassoon in power and strength that she had to pause, horrified yet fascinated.

The next day, weary from lack of sleep, Sylvia traveled by car and ferry from London to France, sharing the ride with a fellow Fulbright student and his girlfriend. She arrived in Paris in the early evening and checked into the Hôtel Béarn on Rue de Lille, near the Louvre and one street away from the Seine. Over the next two weeks, she again saw the sights of Paris—the Tour Eiffel, the Champs-Elysées, Notre Dame—but this time without Sassoon. For, true to his promise, he had left the city, for Spain. On her first day in Paris, Sylvia had walked down the Rue du Bac beyond the Place des Invalides to Rue Duvivier and rung the bell for Number 4. The concierge broke the news: Sassoon would not be back until after Easter—well beyond the time Sylvia would be in Paris. Weeping, she sat in the concierge's living room and wrote Sassoon an incoherent letter.

Though Sassoon was gone, Sylvia did not have to see Paris alone. She frequently enjoyed the company of Giovanni Perego, a communist newspaper reporter (who was, to Sylvia, like a father) whom she had met this trip on her first night in Paris; or Anthony Gray, a British boy she had met before leaving England; or Gary Haupt, her Cambridge friend. Nor were these *merely* Platonic escorts. Following an afternoon on the town, Tony Gray ended up in Sylvia's hotel room. Kissing at first, they were soon undressed and in bed. As they lay there, Sylvia admired his sensual and muscular body, but when she got up to go to the bathroom, Tony changed his mind and put on his clothes. In the future, they continued to see each other—but only as friends.

On April 4, Gordon arrived in Paris. Immediately Sylvia realized that meeting him had been a mistake. After one night, which they spent at the ballet, Sylvia and Gordon began to argue bitterly; soon Sylvia was considering going back to London early. Ultimately, she did not, and on the 6th she and Gordon left Paris by train for Munich.

They were barely out of the city before they were fighting again, this time over whether John Malcolm Brinnin could have saved Dylan Thomas from drinking himself to death in New York City. Interestingly, Sylvia thought so, Gordon not.

As the train finally pulled into the Munich station, snow was falling heavily. Once they had checked into separate rooms at the Bahnhof Hotel, Sylvia and Gordon started to dress for supper, and Gordon sliced his thumb with a razor blade while shaving. The moment she heard him cry out in pain, Sylvia rushed into his room to help. She wrapped a towel around his thumb to stop the bleeding; then she sat down beside him on the bed. Eventually, without speaking, Sylvia rested her head on his shoulder. The quiet—overwhelming and poignant—spoke for itself. Whereas great love and compassion had once existed between them, now there was only silence.

Sylvia and Gordon stayed in Germany, their fathers' homeland, only one day. On the 7th, they boarded a train headed from Munich through Austria (Sylvia's grandparents' homeland) and the Tyrolean Alps to Venice, where they stopped for two days. On the 9th—Rome. There they discarded all pretense of friendship and went their separate ways. During the next four days, they rarely saw each other outside their pension on the street above the Piazza di Spagna, a site near the house in which Keats died. On her own or with Don Cheney, a Choate friend of Gordon's now at Oxford, whom the two had bumped into at the American Express office, Sylvia visited the Etruscan art exhibit, the Sistine Chapel, Saint Peter's, and the Vatican. On Friday the 13th, following a miserable week, Gordon took Sylvia to the airport, lent her money for a ticket, and told her good-bye. They were both relieved that their ordeal had finally ended.

In London, Sylvia went straight to Ted, who had mailed her a brief note in Paris in care of the American Express. After he remarked the smoothness of her body, the thoughts of which still lingered in his memory, Ted told her that, if she did not come to him in London, he would come to her in Cambridge. Sylvia agreed on London, for the 13th. At his flat, they fell into bed for another sleepless night of sex. The next day, Sylvia took the train to Cambridge. The past three weeks had been disturbing yet clarifying. Sassoon had deserted her—for good. Gordon had disappointed her—to her way of thinking if not his. And, as bookends to these weeks, she had spent two nights in London with Ted—"the strongest man in the world," she told her mother, a man who possessed "a voice like the thunder of God."

5

In mid-April, to spend more time with her, Ted followed Sylvia to Cambridge. They lounged around Sylvia's Whitstead room, ate supper with Luke, and often took long walks through the nearby countryside. On these hikes, Ted would point out different types of birds, leaves, and flowers that Sylvia had never noticed before. Eventually, Sylvia found herself falling more directly under Ted's influence. She wrote about him in her letters, journal, even poems. Of Ted's many interests, one in particular intrigued her. His familiarity with horoscopes—how to read them, what they meant, how they predict (and control) one's life—was equaled only by his fascination with the paranormal and the powers of the mind. Sylvia began to wonder where he had learned so much about the occult. After all, she considered herself a curious person, and she knew almost nothing about the subject. On the other hand, Ted seemed to have studied it all his life.

But in her letters to her mother, Sylvia did not dwell on Ted's taste for the supernatural. Instead, she rhapsodized about him, almost to the point of comic exaggeration. Ted was tall and "hulking," had a "large-cut" face set off by blue-green eyes, possessed a Dylan Thomas-esque voice that "boomed through walls and doors." Violent and arrogant, he commanded one's attention, "like a blast of Jove's lightning." And, most dangerously, he was a "breaker of things and people," someone who wildly caroused with his friends. He was this way, Sylvia believed, because he felt trapped by the claustrophobic country in which he had been born and raised. If he lived in a country large enough for him, a country like America, surely he would become a different man.

While she saw Ted, Sylvia also tried to get on with her life at Cambridge. She attended lectures and sat in on Dorothea Krook's supervisions, which she found intellectually stimulating. On April 21, the Cambridge newspaper *Varsity* published "An American in Paris," an article by Plath about her spring vacation. Then, on the 24th, she and the *Varsity* features editor went to a London reception for Soviet leaders Nikolai Bulganin and Nikita Khrushchev. When *Varsity* wrote up the event in its article "Vodka and Caviar," the reporter alluded to Plath in passing. "Sylvia Plath, American undergraduate at Newnham, took the Marshal's hand—'You must come to Cambridge.'"

One sorrow, though, continued to cloud Sylvia's life—her grandmother's failing health. Grammy's illness recalled for Sylvia "my father's slow long death." She implored Aurelia—who had "borne daddy's long, hard death," "taken on a man's portion in [her] work," and endured ulcer attacks, stomach operations, and Sylvia's breakdown—to watch *her* health. Sylvia hoped her mother would be able to come to England in the summer, as Aurelia then planned to do. On April 26, Aurelia's fiftieth birthday, Grammy lapsed into a coma from which she did not recover. Three days later, she died. The death forced Sylvia to contemplate how she would feel if Aurelia died, leaving her with no one to turn to for love and advice.

By early May, even though they had known each other for less than eight weeks, Sylvia and Ted began to discuss marriage. That month, they spent almost every day together in Cambridge. On May Day, they punted up a nearby river to Grantchester for a picnic under an apple tree. On the 3rd, in Sylvia's room, Ted read *The Catcher in the Rye* while Sylvia wrote articles—she had never before been able to work in the presence of a boyfriend—about the Russian reception, which she planned to submit to *The New Yorker,* and Paris, which she would try on *The Christian Science Monitor.* And, on the evening of the 19th, Sylvia took Ted, dressed in an old worn-out suit—his only one—to a Fulbright reception in London. At mid-month, Sylvia wrote to tell her mother that, next June, she and Ted wanted to come to America, marry, and celebrate their wedding with a huge barbecue. Sylvia also said that she and Ted wanted seven children so that the seventh child of their seventh child could be a rare white witch—an indication of just how much Ted now influenced her thinking.

One afternoon, Ted and Sylvia spent hours sitting out in Whitstead's garden. While Ted looked on, Sylvia typed copies and carbons of Ted's poems that she planned to submit to American magazines like *The New Yorker, The Atlantic Monthly,* and *Harper's.* She did this, she wrote to her mother, because Ted had just appointed her to a new job: she was to be his official literary agent.

In May, besides seeing Ted, Sylvia studied and wrote for *Varsity.* One of her articles, which previewed upcoming summer fashions, was illustrated with photographs of her modeling clothes and swimsuits. She also endured rejections—*The New Yorker* turned down her Russian-reception article—and sat in on tutorials and lectures. In Dorothea Krook's philosophy supervision, she wrote two papers on Plato. Slowly, Plath had come to see Krook as her mentor in poetics, much as Barnhouse had been her mentor in psychology. Krook thought highly of her pupil as well. "Sylvia was extraordinarily modest, self-effacing, unassuming, unspoilt," Krook would write years later. "[She seemed] to want only [a] selfless intellectual relationship. I remember noting and appreciating it at the time; I think of it now—now that I know the full extent of the personality that refused to claim attention—with the utmost tenderness and admiration."

In America, Mary Ellen Chase, Plath's Smith professor, heard glowing reports—like this one—about her former student. When she visited Cambridge in mid-May, Chase had a two-hour coffee with Plath. She hinted that, once Plath had finished Cambridge, Smith might be willing to offer her a teaching position. Sylvia was honored, but, as she wrote her mother, she could not imagine teaching at Smith without a husband.

Recently, in a letter to Prouty, she had discussed marriage—and Ted. Early in June, Prouty mailed Sylvia her no-holds-barred response. "I can see you are going through the thrilling early stages of being again 'in love,'" Prouty wrote. "Too bad the early stages are of limited duration." She then launched into a stinging attack on Ted. "You anticipated that I would feel skeptical. I think 'skeptical' isn't quite the word. Fearful more closely describes it. [Ted] sounds too much like Dylan Thomas for me to think he would make a satisfactory husband and father. Thomas's attitude toward women was much like that you describe, his fascination to them and their fascination to him are similar. Thomas's wife was marvellous about his various love affairs and came to his rescue when he broke down physically and morally. Are you ready to do this for this second Dylan Thomas?" Prouty expressed deep concern about Ted's violent behavior. "You don't really believe, do you, that the characteristics which you describe as 'bashing people around,' unkindness and I think you said cruelty, can be permanently changed in a man of 26?" She advised the obvious: "Your own experiences with the several men with whom you have felt you were 'in love' are warnings, don't you think?"

Actually, she did not. Recently, she and Ted had made up their minds on the issue: they were going to get married—soon. So, when she traveled by train to London on June 13 to greet her mother, who had that day landed by ship in Southampton, Sylvia was ecstatic. That night, Sylvia and Ted took Aurelia to supper at a restaurant called Schmidt's and told her their decision. They loved each other; why postpone the inevitable? Aurelia agreed. Now that she had met this young man about whom she had heard so much in Sylvia's letters, she understood Sylvia's enthusiasm. Handsome and sensual, he exuded a charm she herself found difficult to resist.

But there were problems. Sylvia feared Newnham College might argue that marriage would distract her from her academics. She also expected serious misgivings on the part of the Fulbright committee, who could terminate her grant renewal. As a result, Sylvia and Ted agreed that they should keep their marriage a secret. Next June, after Sylvia had graduated, they would stage a formal wedding at the Wellesley Unitarian Church. Warren would serve as best man and Sylvia's Uncle Frank would give the bride away. According to this plan, they could have the best of both worlds: they could be married now, without jeopardizing Sylvia's position at Cambridge, and later have a public ceremony.

On the morning of June 16, Ted and Sylvia purchased two gold wedding rings. Then they bought a marriage license and, because

Ted was required to marry in the parish in which he at present resided, Sylvia, Ted, and Aurelia went to the Church of Saint George the Martyr, near Queen's Square. In the church, while a steady rain fell outside, Sylvia Plath married Ted Hughes at one-thirty in the afternoon. Sylvia wore a pink knitted suit, a gift from her mother. In her hands, she held a pink rose, a gift from Ted. A pink ribbon adorned her hair. The curate stood as second witness; Aurelia was the only guest. Because Ted had not told them he was marrying, Ted's parents did not attend the ceremony. Once he had pronounced the couple man and wife, the minister leaned down and kissed Sylvia's cheek, wet with tears.

Later that afternoon, Aurelia returned on the train to Cambridge, where she stayed for the next five days at the Garden House Hotel. After they spent their honeymoon night in the dingy Rugby Street flat, Sylvia and Ted joined her there. At Whitstead, Sylvia collected her mail and discovered that *Poetry* had bought Hughes's "Bawdry Embraced"— his first American acceptance. On the 18th, Hughes left Sylvia long enough to go to Yorkshire to store some of his personal belongings at his parents' home. By the 21st, he had come back to Cambridge, and the three of them—Sylvia, Ted, and Aurelia—boarded the train for London. The following morning, they all flew to Paris. There they amused themselves by sightseeing for several days, before Aurelia set out on her own to tour Europe. Remaining in Paris, Ted and Sylvia wandered about the city, wrote, and mailed their poems to American magazines. Finally, on July 5, they went on a grueling twenty-four-hour train trip that placed them in Madrid at nine o'clock on the evening of the 6th.

In Madrid, Sylvia and Ted rented a seventh-floor hotel room at $2.75 per night, a price that Sylvia considered expensive but worth it, since their room had a private bathroom with a tub and a shower, and a balcony on which she sunned in the morning and typed in the afternoon. The tub was a luxury for Ted, who, growing up in Yorkshire, had never before had regular access to such private facilities. He became so overjoyed as he took his shower each day that Sylvia could hear him squawking riotously in the tub. But Sylvia did not complain. These were the first baths Ted had taken since the morning of their wedding.

After three days in Madrid, during which they attended a bullfight (Sylvia was sickened and angered by the sight of the slaughtered bull), Plath and Hughes boarded a bus for Alicante, where they remained for two days before continuing on for Benidorm, a small town on the Spanish coast. On the bus ride, as olive orchards, desert hills, and patches of scrub grass flashed by the window, Sylvia and Ted struck up a conversation with a woman who rented out rooms for the summer in her home in Benidorm. In town, the woman led them through the slender streets, past row upon row of shops, to her house, huge and painted brown, which was built directly adjacent to the sea. In the house, Ted and Sylvia rented a room that contained two new maple beds, which they shoved together and turned to face French doors that opened out onto a balcony terrace overlooking the Mediterranean.

Their Benidorm honeymoon began poorly when, on their first day, Ted succumbed to sunstroke and Sylvia came down with a severe case of dysentery. Hypnotizing her, Ted planted in her mind a subliminal message: she should sleep soundly that night and wake up feeling better the next day. (They had recently been experimenting with hypnosis; Ted believed that the process helped him tap into his imagination.) The mind control worked. In the morning, Sylvia awoke with no symptoms of her illness whatsoever.

Once both had fully recovered, they took up a planned schedule of writing. Around the 18th, it was upset so that they could move. Upon realizing that their present living arrangements would not provide the privacy they wanted, Ted and Sylvia rented instead a small house that featured stone-tiled floors, white plaster walls, dark walnut furniture, a front porch roofed by a grape arbor, and, like their last room, a view of the mountains and the sea. Now, their days in Benidorm became quiet and simple. Rising at seven o'clock, they ate breakfast: Sylvia had *café con leche*, Ted brandy-milk with wild bananas and sugar. (Eventually, Sylvia realized how much sugar appealed to Ted, who sometimes ate it by itself.) Breakfast done, they walked down to the peasant market to buy their daily supply of fish and vegetables. On these outings, Sylvia could observe the town firsthand. In a village where only the rich owned iceboxes, and displayed them proudly in their living rooms, she noticed that ordinary citizens lived, as she would write in a two-part article for *The Christian Science Monitor,* "as simply and peacefully as they have for centuries, fishing, farming, and tending their chickens, rabbits, and goats." Plath liked the townspeople's modest life-style, even if it meant that she too had to get by without a refrigerator and to cook on a one-ring petrol stove. By eight-thirty each morning, Plath and Hughes were back at their house, writing. At noon, they broke for lunch. In the afternoon, they swam in the sea and slept for two hours. After that, they both wrote for two additional hours, between four and six; ate a supper that Plath prepared; studied languages, between eight and ten; and (usually) took a stroll by the sea or through the village before they went to bed.

Certain images of Benidorm would stay with Plath for years. "Every evening at dusk the lights of the sardine boats dip and shine out at sea like floating stars," Plath wrote in her *Monitor* article, her beautiful, subtle language reflecting the love she felt for her present surroundings. "In the morning counters are piled with silvery sardines [in the fish market], strewn with a few odd crabs and shells"—the food she bought fresh. One day, Plath simply sat down in the village and observed the town's buildings. "The design of windows in a row of houses began to interest me. Some windows were dark, some boarded-up, some full of stained glass, some oblong in shape, some with a Moorish keyhole outline. In fact, I spent a whole afternoon discovering that the windows, balconies, doors and chimneys of the houses at the fishing harbor formed a kind of mosaic, with the oblong white walls balanced, broken and tilted in harmonious patterns."

In this landscape, Plath found inspiration. As July melted into August, she wrote steadily. By mid-August, she had completed one story about the Madrid bullfights; was well into the writing of "That Widow Mangada," a story about the strange woman from whom they had rented the room during their first week in Benidorm; and had come up with the idea for two more—"The Fabulous Roommate," which would rely on Nancy Hunter as source material for the main character, and "The Hypnotizing Husband," which would include what she was learning about hypnosis from Ted. Plath also wrote poems—"Alicante Lullaby," "Dream with Clam-Diggers," "Epitaph for Fire and Flower," "Fiesta Melons," "The Goring," "The Beggars," "Spider," and "Rhyme."

Only one episode, in Sylvia's account of it, marred the well-ordered, productive rhythm of their days in Benidorm. Years later, she told a close friend that one afternoon while she and Ted sat on a hillside Ted was overtaken by an inexplicable rage. As Sylvia had described it, his face whitened, his body contorted, his gaze intensified. And, according to Sylvia, before she knew it, he was on top of her—not kissing her, as he usually did, but choking her. At first, she said, she fought him. Then, eventually, she merely gave in and allowed his superior strength to dominate her, his fingers to tighten more and more around her neck. Finally, at the moment when she began to lose consciousness—the moment she said she resolved herself to die—Ted released his grip and stopped his assault as abruptly as he had started it. When Sylvia told this story, her marriage to Ted was under enormous stress, and she claimed that this episode had made her question the wisdom of her decision to marry him. Whatever the case, whatever happened on the hillside in Benidorm, Sylvia did nothing.

As August dragged on, money ran out, and Sylvia and Ted had to cut their honeymoon short. On August 21, five days after their two-month wedding anniversary and four days after Ted's twenty-sixth birthday, they loaded their suitcases onto a bus that would take them to Barcelona, one stop on their way to Paris. Sitting on the bus, Sylvia thought back over the past two months. In many ways, her honeymoon had been joyous and intellectually fulfilling—for years she would remember Ted reading Shakespeare to her while she cooked, the sight of the purple mountains at midnight, the smell of the fish she bought in the town's open market—but it also contained the choking incident. She herself had described Ted as a "breaker of things and people." But the scene on the hill scared her. Sylvia had known Ted barely three and a half months when she married him; seven months ago, they had not even met. Had she chosen a man who was too much for her? Should she tell someone about the assault? *Was Mrs. Prouty right?*

Sylvia had gone too far to turn back. To family and friends, she had announced her love for Ted so emphatically that, if she cast him in a bad light now, she would look like a fool.

6

On August 23, Sylvia and Ted arrived in Paris. Checking into the Hôtel des Deux Continents, they tried to rest up from their travels. The next morning, Warren, then in Austria as a member of the Experiment in International Living, arrived for a visit, his first with Sylvia since she had left America. For four days, they explored the city and caught up on what was happening in each other's lives. On the 28th, Sylvia saw Warren off. The following morning, the Hugheses left on a rough Channel crossing to London, where they stayed to recover only one night before heading by train to Yorkshire, far to the north. For the first time, Sylvia saw the stark rolling landscape of the moors, the cold terrain that had pressed itself so vividly on the imaginations of the region's most famous literary figures, Charlotte and Emily Brontë. In Yorkshire, Sylvia also met her in-laws, who did not know until now that Ted had married.

Over time, Sylvia learned about the Hugheses' family history. Ted's mother, Edith, descended from the Farrars, a West Yorkshire family that included Nicholas Farrar, who established the religious settlement Little Gidding. Ted's father, William Henry, came from a family with roots in Spain and Ireland. When Edith and William married, they settled in the Calder Valley, a beautiful section of Yorkshire. Ten years after their son, Gerald, and four years after their daughter, Olwyn, the couple had their youngest child, Edward James Hughes, born on August 17, 1930. Then the Hugheses lived in Mytholmroyd, a village in Yorkshire where William worked as a carpenter. In 1938, they moved to the mining town Mexborough, after William had purchased a newsagent-tobacconist shop there. Years later, the children grown, Edith and William bought their final home—The Beacon—in Heptonstall, a hamlet in Hebden Bridge, Yorkshire. Meanwhile, Gerald had emigrated to Australia. Olwyn, who earned a degree from the University of London, had ended up in Paris to work as a secretary for, at different times, the North Atlantic Treaty Organization and a theatrical agency. And Ted had served as a ground wireless mechanic in the Royal Air Force for two years; graduated Cambridge; and worked as a chauffeur, gardener, and night watchman. What a brief history did not reveal, Sylvia soon learned, was the Hugheses' involvement in the occult and witchcraft. Not unlike many inhabitants of Yorkshire, an isolated region in which the average citizen frowned on progress and clung to religion and superstition, Edith, it was rumored, studied magic, passing her knowledge on to her children. Finally, this explained Ted's avid interest in horoscopes, hypnosis, and mind control.

In Yorkshire, Sylvia marveled at the lush countryside. She loved to stare out from Ted's bedroom windows onto the curving hills broken up by stone walls into the pastures in which sheep and cows were put out to graze. Sylvia did not especially like the cold weather, which required her to bundle up in wool sweaters, pants, and knee socks, but she tried to adapt. During the day, if she was not admiring the landscape from The Beacon or tramping through the moors with Ted, Plath wrote. Usually, while Ted worked downstairs in the parlor on his children's book, *How the Donkey Became and Other Fables*, which he had started in Spain, Plath worked upstairs in Ted's bedroom on her poetry or prose. Early in September, she finished her Benidorm article (which *The Christian Science Monitor* would buy) and a ten-page sketch about Hardcastle Crags, an area landmark. By mid-month, Plath had produced a poem, "November Graveyard," and a story, "Remember Stick Man." At the end of the month, she completed the story "All the Dead Dears" even as she started notes for another, "Dream Man." In this flurry of writing, Plath often took time out to type Ted's manuscripts, which he dictated to her from handwritten notes. Also, she conducted her and Ted's literary business. After *The Atlantic Monthly* accepted her poem "Pursuit" on September 1, Plath submitted her poems to *The New Yorker* and *Poetry*, her stories to *Mademoiselle*, Ted's poems to *The Nation, Poetry, Encounter, The London Magazine*, and Ted's stories to *The New Yorker*. Finally, Plath was pleased to see in the Fall 1956 *Smith Alumnae Quarterly* her "B. and K. at the Claridge," the article about the Russian reception that *The New Yorker* had turned down.

As September progressed, life at The Beacon became increasingly difficult for Sylvia. On the 4th, she observed on her calendar that she and Ted had not made good love since Paris, that she felt isolated and lonely, and that she resented Ted's reluctance to understand her unhappiness. She described the 10th as an oddly depressing day, the 18th as a nightmare because of horrible feelings of jealousy and forces of witchcraft and black magic within the Hugheses' household. But the 21st was the worst of all: on that day, Ted's mother blundered into Ted's bedroom while Ted and Sylvia were making love. After this, Sylvia became more than eager to leave The Beacon. On the 26th, she happily accompanied Ted on a trip into London so he could audition at the BBC. That day, Ted read so well that the BBC invited him to record a program on Yeats. On returning to Yorkshire, Sylvia resolved herself to stick it out there until the Michaelmas term began. She was distracted, in part, by the idea of writing a novel. The book would center on the experiences of a young American coed who comes to Cambridge to study; its structure would be episodic, almost like a set of interconnected short stories. She would work on the novel in earnest this fall, she decided, when she was not reading and studying.

Plath's letters indicate that, during September, she did not leave England. But one reliable eyewitness account places her on the *Queen Elizabeth II*, sailing from America to England. Kenneth Pitchford, a first-year Fulbright student at Oxford and himself an aspiring poet, struck up a brief friendship with Plath on the ride over. "She was accompanied on the boat by a very tall broad-shouldered American football player sort. Rugged and square-cut and dark," Pitchford remembers. "I didn't know who it was; it was certainly not Hughes. He was with her all the time, as if he had some special function." Pitchford did not learn the reason Plath was on board the ship until years later. "Of course, she and Hughes spent the summer in Spain after they were married at which time Plath learned that she was pregnant. And then she came back to America for an abortion because she could not be known as married yet, for fear that she would lose her Fulbright. So she came back, got the abortion, and was permitted to ride over on the boat with the first-year students. This is how I met her."

On the ship ride, Sylvia was not forthcoming about why she was there. Nor did she ever openly discuss this pregnancy, if she *was* pregnant, with friends. But years later, when she listed in her journal emotions and situations she had known—among them love, hate, and madness—one she included was abortion.

Plath and Pitchford's short acquaintance ended in mystery as well. Plath continued with the Fulbright students into London. "After a welcoming lecture one day, she and I were walking across Regent's Park," Pitchford recalls, "when I said to her, 'I've heard there's a new movie playing—*War and Peace*. Would you like to go?' My question had sort of extracted her from this guy who still escorted her and she looked at me and said, 'Listen, some day I'll marry a poet like you and kill myself.'"

From wherever she came, Plath arrived in Cambridge on October 1— alone. Ted remained at home with his parents. At Whitstead, Sylvia found an acceptance letter from *Poetry*'s Henry Rago, who bought all six poems she had submitted to him. Thrilled, Plath mailed off more poems to *The Atlantic Monthly*, on whose staff Peter Davison now worked, having left Harvard University Press. Over the next few days, Sylvia received from Ted long passionate love letters in which he characterized himself as restless and eager to be with her. He also offered advice about Plath's writing, telling her to create poems that would startle the reader. In October, a month during which she saw little of her husband, Plath finished two short stories, "The Invisible Man" and "The Wishing Box," and several poems, among them "Spinster" and "On the Plethora of Dryads." Towards the end of the month, she met with more literary success. *Granta* published her story "The Day Mr. Prescott Died," *The Nation* accepted Ted's poem "Wind," and *The Christian Science Monitor* bought her "Sketchbook of a Spanish Summer." All of this did not blunt the pain of two more *New Yorker* rejections—one for Ted and one for her. Defiantly, she mailed the magazine three new stories.

Despite her activities at Cambridge, Sylvia missed Ted too. During the summer, they had "shared" themselves night and day. Now separated, they became so lonesome that they met for a quick weekend in London on the 12th. Back in Cambridge on Monday, Sylvia fell into a depression that lessened only on the 23rd, when Ted came to Cambridge. Because they were so unhappy living apart, they started to have second thoughts about the whole idea of a secret marriage. Sylvia had learned that three women Fulbright students were married, and Dorothea Krook, whom Plath had told about her marriage, had vowed to defend her at Newnham. Soon after Ted recorded his program on Yeats for the BBC—a session, for which he was paid seventy-five dollars, that went so well that the BBC invited him back for a second session at the same price—Sylvia met with Fulbright and Newnham officials, who, when she told them she was married, only congratulated her.

For her birthday, Ted gave Sylvia a pack of tarot cards, which she planned to put to good use: she now believed that her horoscope indicated she should become a practicing astrologist. Lately, she and Ted had frequently read a Ouija board they had constructed from cutout letters, a coffee table, and a wineglass. Some nights, as they worked the board, they met an assortment of spirits, with names like Keva, Pan, and Jumbo. She and Ted, Sylvia wrote to her mother, one day hoped to equal Mr. and Mrs. W. B. Yeats. Ted would be the astrologer, she the tarot expert. And later, when the money came rolling in from their writings, she would buy a crystal ball with which to tell their future.

In the days following her birthday, Sylvia and Ted searched for a place to live. They settled on 55 Eltisley Avenue, where, for four pounds per week plus utilities, they rented all of the first floor of a row house. The flat had only one drawback: they had to share a bathroom with the upstairs couple, who just happened to be Siegfried Sassoon's only son—Richard's distant cousin—and his wife. Ted would move into the house immediately, but Sylvia would wait until December 7, the end of Michaelmas term.

With their private lives in order, Plath and Hughes focused on their careers. On November 5 and 6, the *Monitor* ran Plath's article on Benidorm, each installment illustrated by her pen-and-ink drawings. Afterwards, *Granta* published Plath's poem "Ella Mason and Her Eleven Cats," a piece Ted had assigned her to write, and *Lyric* ran two of her poems, *Chequer* four. As one of his poems was printed— "Wind" in *The Nation*—Hughes had two more accepted, "The Drowned Woman" by *Poetry* and "The Hawk in the Storm" by *The Atlantic Monthly*. With several publications to Hughes's credit, Plath now submitted large batches of his poems to magazines like *Harper's,* the *Kenyon Review, Nimbus, The Paris Review*, and *The Virginia Quarterly Review*. In mid-November, the Atlantic Monthly Press, the house to which Plath had submitted Hughes's children's book, *How the Donkey Became,* rejected it. "There is too much viciousness—the animals are portrayed as beasts rather than animals to respect and be comfortably afraid of," wrote Emilie McLeod, editor of children's books. "Also the rather cavalier treatment of God might well strike horror into the soul of librarians." However, if Hughes wanted to rework the fables, McLeod assured him, she would reconsider. Plath too received her share of rejection letters in November—from *The Nation, Mademoiselle, The Atlantic Monthly,* and *The New Yorker,* which she now considered disdainful.

Undeterred, Plath continued to plot out their professional lives. She typed her poetry manuscript, *Two Lovers and a Beachcomber by the Real Sea,* which she planned to submit to the Yale series, and Hughes's *The Hawk in the Rain,* which she intended to enter in a first-book contest sponsored by the Poetry Center of the Ninety-second Street Y in New York City. Its winner, to be chosen by Marianne Moore, Stephen Spender, and W. H. Auden, would be published by Harper and Brothers. Plath felt sure that Hughes would win, since the volume represented, as she wrote her mother, the "most rich, powerful" poetry since Yeats and Dylan Thomas.

While Plath mailed out their poetry, which translated into little cash when it was accepted, she and Hughes worried about money. Their most innovative scheme to produce income centered on the Ouija board. They had recently contacted a new spirit, G.A., who assured them of his ability to predict the weekly British football pool, which had pots of up to seventy-five thousand pounds. Beginning in November, Ted and Sylvia bet in the pools, sure that they would win with G.A.'s help. To establish a more reliable cash flow—G.A.'s first predictions were wrong—Ted landed a teaching job in a local school for wayward boys. The modest salary would at least pay for the rent on their flat. Nevertheless, because cash was tight, Sylvia became angry when Olwyn dropped by for a weekend, since she could see firsthand how Olwyn foolishly wasted money on expensive clothes and cigarettes, this while she owed Ted fifty pounds. Sylvia's displeasure with Olwyn underscored a larger concern in her own life: though she had now been married for almost six months, she still felt a drive to establish herself as Ted's wife.

To do this, Sylvia moved into 55 Eltisley Avenue promptly in December. Soon afterwards, when she wrote R. G. Davis, Smith's present English-department chairman, to inquire about a teaching position for the next year, she used that letter as an opportunity to announce her marriage. She even signed her name "Sylvia Plath Hughes," something she had just now started to do. Finally, she revealed her marriage to family and friends, even ex-boyfriends. Besides Peter Davison, with whom she now corresponded in his post as editor at the Atlantic Monthly Press, she told Sassoon, to whom she referred to her wedding as "the crime." The contents and tone of Sassoon's response testified to his shock. Sassoon wrote:

> There is really no reason for me not to believe that you are happier now than you ever were or could have been with me, or indeed that you have now found the man that you really desire in spite of all difficulties to make a home with and that joy is yours. Except your letter to me was not the letter of a happy woman. At least, not to me, and as you . . . are a good letter writer I may accept my reactions as feasible. And so it is that night after night I am with, amongst all that there is between us to accept and to accept the less of, and as you say to have the guts not to damn (which is hard enough in itself), there is in the midst the final . . . fact of a bitter and unhappy letter. Doubtlessly I deserve it. But you are wise and woman enough to know that I—above all I—am not one who needs to be blamed for the attitude. Indeed, however you might have put it, even if you

had not chosen to speak aptly of "the crime," I shall have my years to live in the structure of loss, in regret and even in shame. For the angel is dead, the red god dead and I am like a carcass from which the interior has been taken.

7

After Christmas, her first one with Ted, Plath saw several pieces of her work published. In January 1957, *Poetry* printed six poems, *The Atlantic Monthly* "Pursuit," *Granta* her story "The Wishing Box." Plath also began, at Ted's suggestion, to memorize one poem by an established poet each day. This, Ted believed, would help improve her writing. During January, besides a poem, she finished two love stories, which she planned to try on the New York "slicks." In addition to her writing, Plath typed both Hughes's *How the Donkey Became,* which he had revised for the Atlantic Monthly Press, and her *Two Lovers,* which she was going to submit to the Yale series. Then, in late January, as she started her next term, Plath wrote to Radcliffe, Tufts, and Brandeis to ask about jobs. From those colleges, she received only form letters telling her that all positions were filled. Because of this, she felt relief when R. G. Davis wrote from Smith, in response to her recent letter, and encouraged her to "definitely . . . make formal application for an appointment here." Following a January 28 coffee date with Mary Ellen Chase, who happened to be in Cambridge, Plath became even more confident that Smith would offer her a position for the coming year. Though Plath never knew it, after the coffee date, Chase wrote Davis a letter in which she guaranteed him that "Sylvia would be a fine addition to our staff." However, Chase could not be so approving about Hughes, whom she still had not met. According to his former instructors, Hughes was "solitary" and unlikely to become "a scholar." Indeed, Chase had already formed an overall negative opinion of him. While Plath waited for Smith's decision on her application, she finished the poems "Sow" and "The Lady and the Earthenware Head" and brainstormed on her novel, which she had not yet started but described in her journal as the journey of a young woman who endures "destruction, hatred and despair" on her search for the "redemptive power of love."

On February 23, just two days before the anniversary of what Sylvia called "that fatal party where I met Ted," the Hugheses' lives were permanently changed. For on that date, at ten-thirty in the morning, a telegram arrived for Ted:

OUR CONGRATULATIONS THAT HAWK IN THE RAIN
JUDGED WINNING VOLUME POETRY CENTER FIRST
PUBLICATION AWARD. LETTER WILL FOLLOW.

Signed by John Bleibtreu, of the Ninety-second Street Y, the telegram stunned Plath and Hughes, who started jumping about their tiny flat and shouting. Impulsively, they telephoned Aurelia in Boston, forgetting that it was well before 6:00 A.M. The next day, Plath wrote her mother a nostalgic letter in which she recalled reading Ted's poems in *The St. Botolph's Review* for the first time. Even then she envisioned that she could do much for and with him. And now this—the acceptance of his collection, which she believed would be a "best-seller." "I am more happy than if it was my book published!" Sylvia said. "I am so happy *his* book is accepted *first.*"

Days later, when Hughes received Bleibtreu's letter, it contained one unpleasantness. "The only difficulty facing us at the moment is a request from Miss Moore," Bleibtreu wrote. "In her letter announcing *The Hawk in the Rain* as her first choice, she praised your work, saying the 'talent is unmistakable'; 'The work has focus, is aglow with feeling, with conscience; sensibility is awake, embodied in appropriate diction. Besides The Hawk there are three striking pieces: The Thought Fox, Griefs for Dead Soldiers, The Martyrdom of Bishop Farrar.'" But, Bleibtreu pointed out, Moore had also included the following sentence: "HOWEVER, I would ask, if not insist, that The Little Boys and the Seasons, The Drowned Woman, and Bawdry Embraced be omitted." Hughes responded to Bleibtreu with a detailed letter in which he agreed to the deletion of "The Little Boys and the Seasons," which he had written early in his career, but opposed the elimination of "Bawdry

Embraced" and "The Drowned Woman" since they represented an important (yes, sexual) part of his poetic vision. This said—and he stated it in a way that sounded final—he moved on to other matters. He wanted the new poems "The Horses" and "The Ancient Heroes and the Bomber Pilot" included, four other poems replaced with updated drafts, and the dedication page of the book to read "To Sylvia."

Soon after Bleibtreu's letter came, R. G. Davis offered Plath a job at Smith. To teach three sections of Freshman English each term, she would earn an annual salary of forty-two hundred dollars. Plath accepted the position immediately.

At the same time as Plath's term ended, Hughes began to question the wisdom of sending his letter to Bleibtreu. It might be foolish to buck Moore, regardless of whether his own position was right. So Hughes wrote Bleibtreu a second letter. His new—but final—verdict was this: besides "The Little Boys and the Seasons," Hughes now wanted to cut "Bawdry Embraced" and "The Drowned Woman," the two other poems that bothered Moore. These poems certainly reflected an important part of his poetic voice, Hughes stated, but each book did not *have* to stand as a complete articulation of the mind that had imagined it. On April 8, Elizabeth Lawrence, Hughes's editor at Harper and Brothers, wrote Hughes to implore him to keep all three poems that Moore disliked, should he wish to stand by his original manuscript. Even so, Hughes allowed the poems to be omitted. In short, he changed his mind because he did not want to jeopardize the successful publication of his book. For, though he and Plath had calculated that the book could not be expected to earn them much money—at his royalty rate of 15 percent of 43 percent of the retail price, he would earn only about ten cents per book—Hughes understood that the American publication of *The Hawk in the Rain* would open countless doors for him.

In April, the Hugheses received more rejection slips—from *The Paris Review*, the *Sewanee Review*, and *The Saturday Review*. The harshest, however, came from the Atlantic Monthly Press's editors, who decided Hughes's revised children's book was "too sophisticated" for children but not sophisticated enough for adults. Before long, the Hugheses' disappointment was lessened: *The London Magazine* bought

Plath's "Spinster" and "Black Rook in Rainy Weather" and Hughes's "Famous Poet"—their first professional British acceptances. Throughout much of April, when she did not attend her final term's lectures and he was free from teaching, Plath and Hughes wrote. Plath finished the story "All the Dead Dears" plus—finally—a substantial chunk of her novel. As of April, she had produced approximately eighty single-spaced pages of a planned three-hundred-page rough draft. Also, she decided that *Hill of Leopards,* the novel's working title, would be controversial, since it would expose numerous people and places in Cambridge. At the end of the month, with only about five weeks to go before examinations, Plath stopped writing in order to devote her full energies to reading as much as she could of the Greeks, Corneille, Racine, Ibsen, Strindberg, Webster, Marlowe, Tourneur, Yeats, Eliot. To work more on the novel, she would just have to wait until summer: for their wedding present, Aurelia had rented them a cottage on the Cape for seven weeks. Ted too anticipated a summer of creative work. On May 10, he received a vote of support when Faber and Faber, to whom *The Hawk in the Rain* had been submitted, accepted the book for publication in England. "Mr. [T. S.] Eliot"—one of the company's directors—"has asked me to tell you how much he personally enjoyed the poems," the letter of acceptance read, "and to pass on to you his congratulations on them."

In May, Plath had to sit for her written examinations. "I [bike] home for lunch between my daily intellectual safaris at the Univ. Library where I am crystallizing my opinions on 2000 years of tragic drama (that started to be trauma) and 2000 years of moral philosophy from Socrates to D. H. Lawrence...," Plath wrote Lynne Lawner, who had just been granted a Henry Fellowship to Cambridge. In ten days, her examinations would start, Plath continued, and the idea of writing all day for three days seemed overwhelming, although she would have to be up to the task. "I should be practising penmanship even now," she added.

Between May 27 and 31, Plath wrote her exams. By the time she finished, she was so exhausted she could hardly work up any excitement over *Two Lovers* reaching the finals of the Yale competition. (Auden would select a winner during the summer.) After Plath received her results—she earned a II-i, the equivalent of a high B in America— she and Hughes packed their belongings and traveled to Heptonstall, to visit Ted's parents before leaving for America. In Yorkshire, when they were not reading and writing, Sylvia and Ted corrected the proofs of the American *Hawk in the Rain,* examined the syllabus for Smith's English 11, and socialized with Olwyn, there on a ten-day holiday from Paris.

On June 16, their first wedding anniversary, Sylvia awoke to the sight of Ted lugging a huge vase of pink roses into their bedroom. Later that afternoon, they had tea with Ted's family, who gave them presents, the most impressive of which was a gift of fifty pounds from Ted's wealthy Uncle Walt. Sylvia was again contemplating her novel, which she had renamed *Falcon Yard,* but only with half a mind. Homesick, Sylvia longed to sail to America, to an old life that she knew would be changed in many ways, now that she would be bringing a husband with her.

Fixed Stars

1

They had arrived in New York only after she had endured a horrendous case of *mal de mer* on the trip over, Plath wrote on July 1 to Lynne Lawner, for whom she had left in Cambridge her bicycle and black gown; Ted lugged off the ship their thousand pounds of trunks and suitcases. In Wellesley, Sylvia and Ted were greeted by family and friends, all anxious to see her and meet Ted. On June 29, Aurelia hosted a catered reception for the couple in the backyard of 26 Elmwood Road. Because their marriage had become public knowledge, a second wedding seemed unnecessary, so the reception took on the quality of a welcome-home party. In total, over seventy guests attended, among them Gordon Lameyer and his mother, Philip McCurdy, the Crocketts, the Cantors, the Freemans, Elly Friedman, Marcia and Mike Plummer, and Peter Davison. To Gordon, Sylvia appeared "cordial but understandably distant"; to others, effusive and happy. Either way, she was proud of the opportunity to show off Ted, and stood by his side through much of the afternoon. Since Ted displayed the good humor and charm of which he was capable, most of Sylvia's friends appeared to like him.

Following the party, Sylvia and Ted visited for two weeks with Aurelia, who had just been promoted to associate professor at Boston University. Also, Sylvia arranged for Ted to see her dentist, who was, according to Ted, an improvement over British dentists. While in Wellesley, Hughes received a telegram telling him that the London

Poetry Book Society had selected *The Hawk in the Rain* as its autumn choice, an honor that meant a sale of eight hundred books and excellent publicity within the poetry community. Finally, the time arrived for the couple to take advantage of Aurelia's wedding present—seven weeks alone on the Cape. On July 13, Warren, who had been awarded his own Fulbright, drove Sylvia and Ted from Wellesley to Eastham in the family car, their bicycles strapped to the car's roof.

During their writing vacation in Eastham, Ted's poems appeared in numerous periodicals in England and America—*The Spectator, The Nation, Poetry, Harper's*, and the *Times Literary Supplement*. Also, *The New Yorker*, who had received an advance copy of *The Hawk in the Rain* in late July from Harper and Brothers, bought "The Thought-Fox," even though the magazine had rejected the same poem a year before, when Plath had submitted it for him. Because of these accomplishments, Hughes worked that much harder on a second collection of poems. Meanwhile, Plath, who had neither written a poem in the last six months nor published a short story in a national magazine in the last five years, met with mixed results when she tried to write. At first, she eased into what she hoped would be a productive period by following a comfortable reading schedule, finishing novels by Wolfe, Faulkner, and Henry James. Even so, she composed only one story, "The Trouble-making Mother," and rewrote another, "The Laundromat Affair." (Neither was accepted for publication.) Completing these stories, she then tackled "Dialogue over a Ouija Board," a long poem consisting of dialogue between two people arguing as they sit around a Ouija board. But when Plath read the final draft, she realized that she had produced a poem so odd—nearly six hundred lines of rhymed dialogue between its two characters, Sibyl and Leroy—that no magazine would print it. She did not even bother to mail it out.

Following "Dialogue," Plath dabbled with her novel, which brought her more frustration, because she felt the book was bogged down. Then, on August 8, anxious and upset, Plath received the worst insult of her career. After holding *Two Lovers* for almost six months, the Yale Series of Younger Poets glibly informed her in a letter that her manuscript had not won that year's competition. Devastated, Plath became angry not only at Yale but at herself, for in her mind she had already decided she would win the prize.

In early September, leaving the Cape behind, Sylvia and Ted moved to Northampton, where, for the coming academic year, they would rent a small apartment at 337 Elm Street, not far from campus. A "rear" apartment attached to a larger main house, it stood across the street from the Blessed Sacrament Catholic Church and Northampton High School, buildings Plath passed each day when she walked or drove to school. (The Hugheses had acquired a secondhand car for the year.) On campus, Plath shared an office on the library's top floor with one other professor, a Miss Hornbeak; all three of her Freshman English classes met in Seelye Hall. Her responsibilities required several days of faculty meetings, orientations, and welcoming teas. She met her first class on September 25, an event that the *Daily Hampshire Gazette* previewed nine days earlier in an article about Plath entitled "Ex–Gazette Writer Returns as Smith Faculty Member."

From the start, Plath found teaching painful. She felt inadequate for the task, overwhelmed by the material, and intimidated by the girls. Also, she did not understand why her fellow faculty members, these same instructors who had encouraged her so when she was a student, treated her coldly. By October 1, Plath was nearing a state of panic. "Last night I felt the sick, soul-annihilating flux of fear in my blood switching its current to defiant fight," she wrote in that date's journal entry, which she titled "Letter to a demon." She lay in bed unable to sleep, her nerves "shaved to pain & the groaning inner voice: oh, you can't teach, can't do anything. Can't write, can't think." Continuing, she named "this murderous self"—the part of her personality that tore down her confidence and made her feel inferior—"my demon." Her demon, she wrote, wanted her to believe that she was "so good" that she "must be perfect. Or nothing." Instead, she viewed herself as someone who becomes exhausted and who has trouble "facing people easily." Her demon would destroy her, she decided, unless she fought it, which she could do only by carving out victory after victory. And she *had*. The first was accepting Smith's job offer; the second, actually beginning the school year; the third, teaching her classes following a sleepless night; the fourth, confronting her demon the night before with Ted and "spitting in its eye." Though "Letter to a demon" summed up her emotional state, it also demonstrated a larger psychological concern. Part of her needed to control every aspect of her existence, which meant being the perfect wife-teacher-writer, while another part wanted simply to live life as it came.

As she struggled from day to day with her teaching, Plath lost all drive to write; an emotional—not a physical—exhaustion set in. Because she wrote only in fits and starts, she mailed out fewer of her manuscripts. During the whole fall term of 1957, she made only one sale, two poems to *The London Magazine*. She enjoyed some successes—*Accent* printed her poems "Recantation" and "Tinker Jack and the Tidy Wives," *The Grécourt Review* ran "All the Dead Dears," and, in early October, *Poetry*'s Henry Rago wrote her that she had won the magazine's one-hundred-dollar Bess Hokin Prize that year—but mostly Plath produced little and received few acknowledgments.

At the same time, Hughes wrote and published with a vengeance. Early in September, after minor achievements (his poems appeared in *The London Magazine* and *The Spectator*), he reached a watershed in his career when Faber and Faber issued *The Hawk in the Rain* in England, Harper and Brothers in America. And though he was confident about the quality of the poems, he could not possibly have anticipated the critical acclaim the volume would receive. *Library Journal* contended that Hughes's poems had a "striking field of vision"; *The New Statesman* called Hughes a "clearly remarkable poet." In the months following the book's release, *The Hawk in the Rain* was reviewed, almost always positively, in countless periodicals, among them *The New York Times*, the London *Times*, and the *Times Literary Supplement*.

While Hughes basked in the glow of this critical praise, Plath, in a hell of lecturing and paper-grading, became jealous of him for the first time. To help divert her mind from the drudgery of teaching, Plath forged new friendships, most notably with Paul and Clarissa Roche. A one-time cleric and former protégé of Bloomsbury painter Duncan

Grant (for whom in his twenties in London he had frequently posed nude), Paul Roche had published *The Rat and the Convent Dove and Other Tales and Fables* (1952) and the novel *O Pale Galilean* (1954). In the mid-fifties, Paul left England and Duncan, married Clarissa, and, after an aunt in Clarissa's wealthy family had lined up a job for him there, came to Smith College to teach English and creative writing. When Plath arrived in Northampton, Roche was entering his second year of teaching. "Paul and I saw Ted and Sylvia quite often, and we were friends," Clarissa Roche would write. "Paul and Ted had their Englishness in common. And they were both poets who had been trawled across the Atlantic by willful young wives. Sylvia and I were much the same age, we shared an affinity to Europe, particularly England, and we were both disdainful of the culture we were supposed to revere."

Despite her friendship with the Roches, Plath became more depressed as October began. "I have been exhausted, frustrated, etc. and find it very different to 'teach' a story than to 'know' it in my own head . . . ," Plath wrote to Lynne Lawner, now studying at Cambridge. Also, Plath went on, she felt buried by paper-grading and class preparation, alienated from the faculty, and "chomping at the bit to do my own writing." She ached "to cook pineapple upside-down cakes & write on a book of poems," both of which would have to wait until June. Plath's spirits were hardly improved by a trip to New York so Hughes could give a thirty-minute reading at the Poetry Center of the Ninety-second Street Y on the afternoon of the 20th. At the postreading reception, the purpose of which, like the reading itself, was to commemorate the Harper and Brothers release of *The Hawk in the Rain,* Plath met Ted's editor, Elizabeth Lawrence, and members of the Poetry Center's staff. As she talked to these people, all there to celebrate a book that would not have been published if she had not submitted it to the Y contest, Plath had to wonder if *she* would ever have a book accepted.

In November, Plath became more distressed. She wrote to her mother that, because she squandered the energy she needed to write by teaching, her talent was deteriorating. On the 5th, after she had graded a set of sixty-six papers on two Hawthorne short stories, Sylvia wrote Warren a letter in which she characterized herself as hovering in a dark mood caused by her unsuccessful attempts to teach Smith's coeds, whom she called bitches. Now, she considered herself so inadequate in her role as instructor, she told Warren, that she did not want to teach next year—she might even quit at Christmas. "If I fainted, or paralyzed myself"—or told Mrs. Hill, acting department chairman, that she could no longer teach—"I'd probably escape all right: but how to face myself . . . after that?" she wrote in her journal. *That* trauma would be even more damning, "although escape looked very sweet & plausible." Other people, however, did not share Plath's poor opinion of her teaching abilities. Generally, her students enjoyed her classes and respected her as an instructor; years later, some would even remember her as brilliant. Then, in late November, the English department voted unanimously to renew her contract. In short, Plath had allowed her groundless feelings of inferiority to dominate—and ruin— her life. Not surprisingly, she declined the department's offer. By doing so, she angered many of her sponsors, in particular Mary Ellen Chase, who through the years had been one of her strongest advocates at Smith.

Secretly, Sylvia wanted to leave Northampton for a second reason, one that had less to do with teaching than with Ted. Writing her mother from England, Sylvia had confessed to Aurelia that she feared exposing Ted to Smith girls, since she remembered all too well the way many Smithies availed themselves of male professors—young and old. Apparently, Sylvia had reason to worry about Ted. "[Hughes] would be seen walking along Paradise Pond communing very seriously with a very attractive blonde pageboyed student—there were several of them—and the gossip was that he was going to replace Fisher, who was the Chairman of the Department and who had married [numerous] Smith wives [students]," remembers Lee Camp, a student of Plath's that year. "And we all thought that it was rather rotten. Here they were newly married, [and we thought] he should mind his p's and q's and at least not embarrass her publicly. He just lapped [the girls' attention] up. Incredibly egotistical. [There was a lot of student gossip about faculty affairs, but] whenever we talked about seeing Ted Hughes walking along Paradise Pond Road with yet another blonde pageboyed wonder, it was always in very hushed tones. We really didn't want anybody else to hear us talking about it. I think we were tremendously protective of [Plath]. Somehow we instinctively felt some kind of fragility in all this."

As much as possible, Plath tried to forget about this new, threatening development. Just before Thanksgiving, she recorded a group of her poems in Boston at the Beacon Hill studios of Stephen Fassett. For the holidays themselves, Sylvia and Ted joined Aurelia in Wellesley; the highlight of their vacation was a Wednesday-night supper at the home of Olive Higgins Prouty, who liked Ted immediately and promised to arrange for him to appear on American television. After Thanksgiving, Sylvia and Ted returned to Northampton while Aurelia checked into the hospital for still another stomach operation. As Aurelia recuperated at her sister's, Sylvia worked hard to finish out the term. Oddly enough, now that she had reached the decision not to return to Smith, she took teaching more in stride. She would eventually revise her opinion of Smith's students; they were not bitches at all but hard workers. Nevertheless, before the semester was over, Plath became sick. On December 15, lethargic and feverish, she canceled the rest of her classes—five days' worth—and drove with Ted to Wellesley. The moment Sylvia walked in the front door, Aurelia, who had just returned from her sister's, knew her daughter was seriously ill. She took her temperature (it was 102 degrees), then Aurelia telephoned their family doctor, who examined Sylvia at home and diagnosed her as suffering from viral pneumonia and physical exhaustion. Placed on antibiotics, Sylvia improved enough to join in with other family members as they trimmed the tree on Christmas Eve.

2

While Sylvia suffered from pneumonia, Ted met with more professional accolades. For the spring term, Chairman Max Goldberg offered him a position teaching English and creative writing at the University of Massachusetts at Amherst. The *Sewanee Review* and *The New Yorker* accepted poems, and *Jack and Jill* bought one of his children's stories, "Billy Hook and the Three Souvenirs." Though Plath said that she was happy over Hughes's accomplishments, she still had to fight off jealousy. On January 14, 1958, to cheer herself up—magazines were rejecting her poetry and *Two Lovers* could not find a publisher—she typed a whole stack of Ted's new poems. But a week later, Plath read the work of the six women poets in *New Poets of England and America,* and became angry. None had published more than she had, she complained to her journal, except maybe May Swenson and Adrienne Rich. She had written better poems than other women who had more established reputations—without comparable recognition.

In February, Plath's publishing drought lifted somewhat. *The Smith Alumnae Quarterly* ran her poem "Spinster" alongside a photograph of her sitting out in a field typing. "No spinster is Sylvia Plath Hughes," stated the picture's caption, "who teaches English at Smith, here shown typing out of doors in Yorkshire." Also, *ARTnews* made her a proposal—it would pay her fifty to seventy-five dollars to write a poem about a piece of art—which sent her to the library to pore over books of reproductions of paintings by Gauguin, Matisse, Rousseau, Klee, and De Chirico. Finally, *Mademoiselle* bought her poem "November Graveyard," her first acceptance in about a year.

Two Lovers had fared so poorly with publishers that Plath decided to eliminate all of the poems written in her old—she thought sweet—voice and keep only those she had produced lately—poems for which she had either consciously or unconsciously used Ted's as a model. Then she would rename the collection *The Earthenware Head* and submit it to other presses. To divert her thoughts from the failure of her poetry manuscript—its fate certainly contrasted with that of Ted's book—she also contemplated (although she did not work on) her novel. From what she had written so far, she particularly admired "Friday Night in Falcon Yard," a thirty-page chapter which she considered the book's core. She hoped to have a rough draft of the novel finished soon after Christmas.

She and Ted may have decided what to do next year—spend it writing in Boston—but Sylvia still had sleepless nights, which left her so tired that she had to take naps when she came home from school in the afternoon. Sylvia also realized that she was again drinking more than she would have liked, usually with friends but sometimes at home by herself. And, of course, she still could not write. As her emotional state worsened, she depended on Hughes more and more. In one journal entry, she recorded that on that day alone she sought out Ted in the apartment some one hundred times, on each occasion to kiss or, merely, smell him. Soon she concluded that her desire to be near Ted had become as fundamental to her as eating. On his good days, Ted indulged her even when she was complaining about familiar subjects, like her job. Alfred Kazin, now teaching at Amherst College, noticed this psychological interplay between the two of them on the night he ate supper with the Hugheses in early March. "From being the proud boast and great love of the English Department she had become just another overworked and overlooked junior instructor," Kazin later wrote; "she could not wait to get away. But on the surface she was a cheery young newlywed, studying the latest cookbook, and eager to give a good dinner to her old teacher, to whom she owed nothing whatever. At dinner we talked, we prattled, and the dark Yorkshire poet, her ferociously talented and surly husband, listened with contemptuous patience to her woe in teaching at Smith and my woe in teaching at Amherst."

Finally, at the end of the month, Smith recessed for spring vacation and Plath broke out of her writer's block. On her first free morning, March 20, an unstoppable urge to write overtook her. With the paintings of Paul Klee firmly in her mind, she produced not one but two longish poems, "Virgin in a Tree" and "Perseus." The next day, she finished two more Klee-influenced poems, "Battle-Scene" and "The Departure of the Ghost" (later retitled "The Ghost's Leavetaking"). Over the following six days, she completed four additional poems— "The Disquieting Muses," "On the Decline of Oracles," "Snake-charmer," and "The Dream." The first two were informed by De Chirico, the latter by Rousseau. In eight days, possessed by a manic energy she had not experienced since summer, she had written eight poems, all of which came to her so effortlessly she seemed to be transcribing—not writing—them. The poems were among the best she had written to date. As a result, Plath concluded that she had happened upon her deepest source of inspiration—art—and through that inspiration broken new ground in her poetry. Certainly, the poems' voice represented one wholly different from any she had used in the past.

On the night of the 28th, after she had mailed five of the eight poems to *The New Yorker* (three were sure things, she believed), she celebrated by drinking martinis with Ted. The next morning, hungover though still emotionally charged by her recent writing, Plath listed in her journal the poets whom she considered rivals. In history: Sappho, Elizabeth Barrett Browning, Christina Rossetti, Amy Lowell, Emily Dickinson, Edna St. Vincent Millay. Of her own generation or of the one before: Edith Sitwell, Marianne Moore, May Swenson, Isabella Gardner, and Adrienne Rich. At the time of this journal entry, Sylvia Plath, twenty-six years old, had not released a book, had not in fact published a single poem in almost a year. But for her these eight March poems had put to rest, at least temporarily, any doubts she felt about her ability to write.

The writing stopped the day she resumed teaching in early April. Though she planned various future projects (in one scheme she would churn out slick women's-magazine short stories under the pseudonym Sylvan Hughes), Plath could do no more than plan.

On the 11th, she accompanied Hughes to a reading he gave at Harvard University. In March, Hughes and Harvard's Jack Sweeney had agreed that Hughes would speak at the school on a Morris Gray readership, which paid one hundred dollars plus expenses. But neither could have foreseen the April 11 winter storm that left much of Massachusetts covered with snow and ice. The Hugheses drove down from Northampton to Boston as sleet pounded the car's windshield. When they met Jack Sweeney in Cambridge, the three took a taxi to Radcliffe's Longfellow Hall. Because of the bad weather, Plath was sure they would find a vacant auditorium. In fact, the room held a smallish crowd, made up primarily of Sylvia's family and friends.

As Hughes began his reading, which would include "The Thought-Fox," "To Paint a Waterlily," "Acrobats," and "The Casualty," among others, he looked out onto the sparse crowd, most of whom he recognized from Aurelia's welcoming party—Mrs. Cantor, Olive Higgins

Prouty, Marcia and Mike Plummer, Carol Pierson, Peter Davison, Gordon Lameyer, Philip McCurdy, and Aurelia. The audience also contained a handful of people from Harvard: Harry Levin, a Joyce scholar; Philip Booth, the poet; Al Conrad, an economist; and Conrad's wife, Adrienne Rich. Hughes stood at the podium before them. A dark, compelling figure, he spoke in a voice, warbly and off-pitched, that seemed to defy the body from which it came. Though understated, his delivery conveyed the energy and violence of his poetry. After Hughes completed his last poem and the audience's applause faded, Plath took her place down front beside him to greet her friends. Sylvia spoke briefly to McCurdy, Lameyer, and Davison, no conversation moving beyond salutations. Olive Prouty stopped by to gush, "Isn't Ted *wonderful*." Then, once Plath and Hughes had chatted with Aurelia, the couple retired to Jack and Mairé Sweeney's, where they met Al Conrad and Adrienne Rich for a drink. Afterwards, they all went on to supper at Felicia's Café with Philip Booth.

Later in the month, Plath met with more mixed career news. On the 17th, the Hugheses traveled to Springfield, Massachusetts, and Plath recorded first an interview with Lee Anderson, who had set up the session for Yale, and then a selection of thirteen of her poems. The next day, Anderson conducted a similar program with Hughes. Plath enjoyed being Hughes's equal on this trip, but she felt a new surge of discouragement on her return to Northampton, for there she discovered a letter from *The New Yorker* rejecting her latest submission—those sure things. Suddenly this refusal caused her to doubt the very skill she was so confident about only a month ago. Whereas many publish in *The Saturday Evening Post* and *The New Yorker*, Plath wrote in her journal, "[M]aybe [I] can't." Her lack of belief in herself swayed her overall mood, which affected the way she dealt with Ted, whose confidence, bolstered by the reception of *The Hawk in the Rain*, had never been stronger.

Lately a noticeable friction had developed between Plath and Hughes. Initially, the scrimmages had been minor. Sylvia would complain about his manners—the way he scratched himself or picked his nose—and Ted would accuse her of nagging. By late April, their disagreements had escalated. One Sunday night, Ted claimed Sylvia had thrown away an old set of his cuff links and one of his books about witches (because she could not stomach reading the parts about torture, he said)—an accusation Sylvia denied. Finally, Ted would not stop complaining, so Sylvia stalked out of the apartment. When she returned, he was gone. Soon Sylvia had to get out for a while and walked to a neaby park, where, eventually, in the distance, she spotted Ted wandering down a street under the lamplights. Sneaking along a row of trees, Sylvia approached him. Then he stopped and glared at her, she later wrote, and if he had not been her husband she would have "run from him as a killer."

Early in May, the friction between Plath and Hughes lessened a bit. They visited Leonard Baskin, the sculptor (and a friend of Ted's) who lived in Northampton. They attended a poetry reading given by Robert Lowell at the University of Massachusetts. And Plath—again—renamed and reordered her poetry manuscript. She now called it *Full Fathom Five* after a recent poem. Using a line from *The Tempest*'s "Ariel's Song," Plath had approached a subject that would soon dominate her poetry more and more—the death of a father. In this poem, the narrator mixes memories of her dead father with those of the ocean. The two clusters of imagery blur at the end of the poem, when the speaker declares that she will "breathe" water.

At mid-month, Plath and Hughes began to quarrel again. Their differences peaked on May 21, the date on which Hughes had agreed to participate in a public reading of Paul Roche's translation of *Oedipus*. Sylvia had not confronted Ted about his walks around Paradise Pond with students, nor had he mentioned them to her, but when, mysteriously, Ted insisted that Sylvia *not* come to the reading, she became suspicious. Rushing to campus, Sylvia sneaked into the auditorium once the reading had begun. When he saw her slip in, Ted became so furious that his performance deteriorated into an unrecognizable mumble, causing more than one person to wonder what had gone wrong.

The next day was to be Plath's last day of teaching, so she wanted Ted to meet her after she had finished her final class. Because Ted had said that he would, Sylvia was puzzled when she walked through the parking lot to their car to find it empty. She thought momentarily about driving home to see if Ted had gone to the apartment by mistake, but, as she would later write, she had not happened upon anything unseemly in the apartment yet—she had, though, prepared herself for it—and did not want to today. Instead, she checked in the library reading area—no Ted. Then, emerging into the cool May air, she felt a compulsion to rush to Paradise Pond and walked quickly across campus. She arrived at the road to which Smith girls took their dates to make out on weekends, and there she saw, coming up the road, her husband strolling with a young Smith student dressed in khaki Bermuda shorts. How she remembered Hamish's description of Ted Hughes— "the biggest seducer in Cambridge." And now she had caught him red-handed.

When she approached the couple, the student ran off, leaving Ted face to face with Sylvia. Who was *she* and what was *he* doing with her? Sylvia demanded. Her name was Shila, he thought—he wasn't sure— and they had been taking a walk, *only* taking a walk. Sure that Ted was lying, Sylvia tried to force the issue—to no avail. He stood by his story, regardless of her questioning. Finally, Sylvia bolted off, heading for the apartment alone. That night, writing in her journal, she could not control her rage. To whom would Ted dedicate his *second* book? His navel? His *penis?* In her mind he had become a "smiler"—nothing more. Yet she would not "jump out of a window or drive Warren's car into a tree, or fill the garage at home with carbon monoxide and save expense, or slit my wrists and lie in a bath," Sylvia wrote. Even so, Ted's behavior *had* caused her to think about suicide.

Several nights later, Ted and Sylvia, still mad, got into a physical fight. Sylvia ended up with a sprained thumb, Ted raw fingernail marks on his face. "I got hit," Sylvia remembered, "and saw stars—for the first time—blinding red and white stars exploding in the black void of snarls and bitings." The aftershock of the fight lasted for days. As a result of the confrontation, Sylvia understood something disturbing. Under certain circumstances, she could become so violent that she could kill another person, or herself.

3

In early June, once she had concluded her official duties at Smith, Sylvia patched things up with Ted enough to make a five-day trip to New York. In the city, they had an expensive supper with Ted's editors at the Biltmore; attended a Fifth Avenue party at which Plath met Lionel and Diana Trilling and Ralph Ellison; had a drink— Drambuie—at the home of Oscar Williams, best friend of Dylan Thomas and husband of Gene Derwood; dropped in on Babette Deutsch, who had written glowingly of Hughes's work; ate lunch with Dave Keightley, an editor at the World Publishing Company who wanted to read Plath's poetry manuscript (eventually he too rejected it); and visited Brooklyn to see Marianne Moore, who served them strawberries and sesame-seed biscuits while she chatted about how much she admired Ted's poetry. For Plath, none of these meetings compared with one that occurred completely by accident. One night, as she and Ted headed for the subway, Sylvia spotted Dick Wertz, to whom she was about to speak until she noticed the person *he* was walking with—Richard Sassoon. For an instant, Sylvia did not know what to do. Since neither Wertz nor Sassoon had seen her, the move remained hers to make. Clutching Ted's hand, she pressed on hurriedly towards the subway, leaving Sassoon—and her old life—behind.

A few days after they returned to Northampton, the Hugheses went to Wellesley for a long weekend. In Boston, after Plath recorded poems for Jack Sweeney at Harvard and she and Ted ate with Olive Higgins Prouty, they searched until they found an affordable apartment to rent. In an elevator building that faced the Charles River, they located a sixth-floor, two-room apartment which was available for one year at $115 per month.

On June 16, the Hugheses celebrated their second wedding anniversary, in Wellesley, with a supper prepared by Aurelia. It was at this quittime that Aurelia voiced her dissatisfaction over Sylvia and Ted's decision to quit their jobs to write full-time. Since Otto's death, Aurelia had scrimped and saved to make ends meet, yet she somehow saw to it that both of her children had the best educations America and England could offer. And she had supported her family by working for years in a job that, truth be told, she considered far beneath her talents. Now Sylvia and Ted, who had acquired enviable and lucrative jobs (their combined income for the next year would have been over six thousand dollars, a handsome sum at the time), had simply walked away from positions that other young writers would have given anything to have. Sylvia interpreted Aurelia's comments as both an attack and an attempt to control her and Ted's lives. Though harsh words were never exchanged, each knew the other's view of the matter.

In June, Plath witnessed demonstrable evidence that she had made the right decision. First, *The London Magazine* published "Spinster" and "Black Rook in Rainy Weather"—encouragement enough, but nothing compared with what came on the 25th. While she sat at her typewriter that morning, she glanced up from her work to see the mailman, rushed out to the box as she always did, and extracted some envelopes. When she did, she noticed a thin envelope with *The New Yorker's* address printed in the top lefthand corner. Immediately she ripped open the envelope and scanned the letter. Certain phrases caught her eyes—"Mussel Hunter at Rock Harbor," "marvelous poem," "happy to say we're taking it," "Howard Moss." Thrilled, she dashed upstairs, told Ted, and began leaping up and down. Only after she calmed down and read the letter again did she realize Moss had accepted a second poem, "Nocturne" (later renamed "Night Walk" by the magazine). For these two poems, because no magazine pays better than *The New Yorker*, Plath earned a stunning $338. As she proudly pointed out to her mother, the amount was sufficient to cover three months' rent on their Boston apartment. She might have had to endure ten years of rejections, Plath wrote to Prouty, but she had finally done it. She had cracked the magazine in whose pages she most wanted her work to appear.

Despite this acceptance, Plath sensed another depression coming on, in large part because she was still not able to write. At the end of June, she observed that her life seemed "magically run by two electric currents"—"joyous positive and despairing negative." She also understood that whichever one seemed in control at any given time "dominated [her] life." As July unfolded, she was controlled less by the positive, more by the negative. She tried to work—she ground out one poem, "Lorelei," after she and Ted had done the Ouija board one night and Pan, who predicted she would publish a book of poems with Alfred A. Knopf, suggested that she write about the subject—but did not achieve the kind of results she wanted.

She cried easily, frequently with no provocation. Minor daily tasks sometimes overwhelmed her. Once, unable to fix a veal-chop supper, she turned to Ted and burst into tears. Since this behavior made her too dependent on Ted, she resolved to change—and not to rely on him as much. Around the 25th, she broke out of her slump somewhat and wrote at least four poems, two of them about Benidorm.

On August 9, *The New Yorker* published "Mussel Hunter at Rock Harbor." When she first saw the poem in print at the home of a Northampton friend who had telephoned as soon as her issue arrived in the mail, Plath simply marveled at it. Soon afterwards, the *Sewanee Review*'s Monroe Spears accepted "The Ghost's Leavetaking." Then, on the 14th, *The Christian Science Monitor* ran Plath's article "Beach Plum Season on Cape Cod," which it had accepted earlier that month. Illustrated by two of her pen-and-ink drawings, the article concluded: "And perhaps even those who have simply spent long afternoons under blazing Indian summer skies, picking beach plums from the waist-high bushes and hearing them ring with a pleasant metallic sound in the bottom of tin pails, can once more savor the fragrant grasses and the richness of the early harvest air in the clear red sweetness of homemade beach plum jelly—preserved not only as breakfast food but as food for memories of a Cape Cod summer also."

Sylvia did not visit the Cape in the summer of 1958. She remained in Northampton until early September when she and Ted packed their car, said good-bye to their friends, and moved into their tiny apartment on Beacon Hill in Boston.

4

"Two rooms, each with a big bay window overlooking rooftops, chimney pots, mosquito trees, and the blue of the Charles & the Harvard Bridge. . . . At my right, the pruned & plumed trees of Louisburg Square, at my left, the towering structure of the estimable John Hancock building. . . ." So began Plath's description of Boston, her colorful language reflecting her love of the city, in a letter to Lynne Lawner. Since they owned no car, Plath continued, she walked everywhere— from the docks to Hanover Street to Blockstone Street, which "outdoes anything I've seen in England & Europe."

Plath's first two weeks in her new apartment at 9 Willow Street were so hectic and event-filled (among other things, there was a visit from Luke Myers) that they seemed to evaporate. Before long, Plath relegated herself to a daily routine of studying languages and writing, but by the end of September, she had become impatient with her inability to write at the level she wanted. She also worried about money, even though in September alone Ted earned upwards of one thousand dollars by selling poems to magazines and winning first prize in a poetry competition in England sponsored by the Guinness Brewery.

Because of her financial concerns, in early October Plath registered at a Boston employment agency. On her first job interview, she landed the position of part-time secretary at Massachusetts General Hospital's adult psychiatric clinic, the same facility to which she had been admitted after her breakdown in the summer of 1953. Her duties included answering the telephone, assisting doctors, and typing patients' records. Working again, she had an excuse for not writing. Yet, as the days passed, she drifted into another depression. She could not churn out fiction at the rate she had planned, and poems came sporadically, if at all. Even the appearance of "Night Walk" in *The New Yorker* on October 11 did not help. In time, Plath sought targets on whom she could vent the anger. She complained to Ted about money, his poor hygiene—she could not abide his dirty hair, his ragged fingernails, his disinclination for bathing—and her inability to become pregnant, something she now desperately wanted. In response, Ted either ignored her or, once again, accused her of nagging. Her unhappiness over her failure to conceive was self-evident. Her disgust with Ted, especially considering how physically attracted to him she had been when they first met, was more difficult to explain. It would seem her troubled emotional state had affected the very way she viewed the people whom she most loved.

Ted was not her only victim. She also attacked Aurelia—privately, not to her face—and came to consider her one cause of her depression. To help alleviate some of her emotional pain, Sylvia requested private sessions with Ruth Barnhouse, her McLean psychiatrist, then practicing in Boston. Barnhouse readily agreed and even lowered her regular fee to five dollars per session so that Plath, always strapped for money, could afford the therapy which Barnhouse realized she badly needed.

From the first session, Barnhouse forced Plath to examine the feelings she had for her husband, mother, and—most important—father. In early December, after they had discussed Aurelia at length, Barnhouse told Sylvia: *I give you permission to hate your mother.* As soon as Barnhouse had said the words, or so it seemed, Sylvia began to re-evaluate Aurelia. Casting both Aurelia's motives and her own reactions to them in loosely Freudian terms, Sylvia decided that her mother was a chronic worrier who agonized about everything—the man Sylvia married, Sylvia's yearly finances, how she and Ted would support children. It was Aurelia's worrying, Sylvia decided, that made her angry. And repressed anger, Sylvia learned from Barnhouse, leads to depression. To Sylvia, this explained why she had become chronically depressed. As she sat through her weekly sessions, Sylvia actually began using the phrase "I hate my mother" to describe the way she felt about Aurelia.

Around the Christmas holidays, a time of year when one often thinks about family, Sylvia began to wonder why she felt that her mother did not love her when through the years so much practical evidence existed to indicate that she *did*. She might hate her mother, Sylvia wrote in her journal the morning after she had welcomed her into her apartment for Christmas, but that wasn't all. "I pity and love her too." In fact, though she no doubt disapproved of much of her mother's behavior, in particular her recent compulsion to offer unwanted advice, Sylvia did not harbor anything as strong as hate for Aurelia. Anger, impatience, resentment—yes; but on some level she could not hate the person in her life to whom she had been closest.

In their late-December sessions, Plath and Barnhouse addressed Plath's writer's block. Since moving to Boston, Sylvia had not even attempted the novel she had hoped to finish by Christmas; the random poem she turned out hardly encouraged her. Again, Sylvia wrote in her journal, the answer to her problem seemed to lie in Freud, specifically his *Mourning and Melancholia.* In his work, Freud used a vampire metaphor to suggest that an overbearing person—in Sylvia's case, her mother—was guilty of sapping the ego of a lesser person, who was often injured by this behavior. When Aurelia had voiced dissatisfaction over Sylvia's quitting her job at Smith, she had indirectly implied that Sylvia could not make a living as a writer. In effect, she was *willing* Sylvia's writer's block to prove her—Aurelia—right. For Sylvia, the solution was obvious: she had to write in order to *defy* her mother. Finally, she did. Encouraged by the publication of her poem "Second Winter" in *The Ladies' Home Journal* and the purchase of three poems by *The London Magazine,* and inspired by the case histories that she had typed at the psychiatric clinic earlier in the fall (she had quit the job after two months), Plath tapped into subject matter—suicide and mental illness—from which she produced the short story "Johnny Panic and the Bible of Dreams"—the best she would ever write.

In mid-December, she and Ted attended a Truman Capote reading. At this time, Capote, who had lived in Northampton in the late forties when he had had an affair with Newton Arvin, one of Sylvia's Smith professors, was settling into the fame that books like *Other Voices, Other Rooms* and the recently published *Breakfast at Tiffany's* had brought him. Plath responded to Capote with a mixture of emotions. She admired his work, yet felt jealousy over his fame, which in a perverse way impelled her to try to write even more. Ted hated, Sylvia observed, "the homosexual part of [Capote] with more than usual fury."

Though she saw this, she did not speculate what Ted's attitude revealed, nor did she specify what kind of man is threatened by another man's obvious displays of the feminine side of his personality.

"Second Winter," Plath's poem in the December 1958 *Ladies' Home Journal,* is spoken by a narrator who realizes that her love is "gone." When this poem appeared, Sylvia's own romantic life was floundering. Lately, she and Ted had been arguing more than usual, although these fights had not become physical. Ted had recently humiliated Sylvia in front of Marcia and Mike Plummer; he accused her of refusing to sew buttons on his shirts and of tearing up his worn-out socks. Later, in private, when Sylvia demanded to know why he had degraded her in front of her friends, Ted told her that by scolding her he hoped to force her to perform these minor tasks in the future. On a broader level, Sylvia had come to believe that much of their friction derived from her (and Ted's) fear of running out of money. If she suggested to him that he should find a job, though, Ted became angry. In therapy, Sylvia had made one major breakthrough regarding her relationship with Ted. After considering why she had become so furious with him in Northampton when he did not meet her on her last day of class, she confided in her journal: he was aware of her love for him, but he wasn't there for her. "Isn't this an image of what I feel my father did to me?"

During that fall in Boston, Plath had rekindled a friendship with Lucie McKee, whom she knew from Smith. Both living in the city, they had run into each other one day at the Public Garden. Soon after this, Sylvia visited Lucie, who had just had a baby boy. At one point during her visit, as they stood by Lucie's son's crib, Lucie noticed a "dark look" about Sylvia. "It was a look that didn't coincide with what Sylvia was talking about and what was going on between us," McKee remembers. "It appeared to come from thoughts and feelings, unexpressed at the back of her mind. It didn't last long, but it made an impression on me. It had an ominous quality about it—an expression of seeming foreboding, like the brief pulling away of a curtain from an inner vision of something morbid that clung to her consciousness and that she could not hide at that moment." Afterwards, Sylvia and

Lucie occasionally got together for coffee. "As she seemed glad to see me, my husband and I invited Sylvia and Ted and one or two other couples for dinner one evening." All went well. Ted impressed the group with tales from his boyhood about a tomcat whom he, McKee remembers, "admired for his aggressiveness and prowess in the neigh-borhood." Much later, Lucie ran into Ted walking on the Boston Common. "He told me about some records he had just bought. 'I've had a record orgy!' he said. It was a brief conversation and he didn't bring up Sylvia. I found Ted easy to talk to. He was warm and amusing, but had something to do with contained violence about him, in the way he expressed himself, his interests; that tom cat, for instance. I don't remember him asking me about myself, but he talked about himself in a way that swept me up with his exuberance, so that I didn't notice being ignored."

5

In January 1959, *Mademoiselle* published Corinne Robins's article "Four Young Poets," which featured Plath and Hughes. The article focused on the various ways fledgling poets found to write poems *and* pay their bills. One new segment of the poetry scene consisted of the "bohemians," who were, according to Robins, "swelling the ranks of the sound-deafened beat generation and building makeshift nests in the sacrosanct ivied schoolyards." As alternatives to the beats, Robins presented Plath and Hughes, university poets who sometimes found higher education a "solution to the economic problem." On the subject of teaching, Plath remained circumspect. " 'Ted and I had similar reactions,' " the article read. " 'It was exciting and rewarding to intro-duce students to writers one particularly enjoys, to stimulate discussions and to watch students develop, but it takes time and energy. Too much, we found, to be able to work at length on any writing of our own.' " So, they gave up teaching to live in Boston and write—together. " 'The bonuses of any marriage—shared interests, projects, encouragement and creative criticism—are all intensified,' " the article continued, still quoting Plath. " 'Both of us want to write as much as possible, and we do. Ted likes a table he made in a window niche from two planks, and I have a fetish about my grandmother's desk with an ivy and grape design burned into the wood. In the morning we have coffee and in the afternoon tea. That's about the extent of our differences. We do criticize each other's work, but we write poems that are as distinct and different as our fingerprints themselves must be.' " To show that difference, *Mademoiselle* ran Plath's "The Times are Tidy" and Hughes's "Pennines in April."

Of course, the Hugheses' lives did not exactly resemble the rosy picture *Mademoiselle* painted. Some days, Sylvia tired of cooking meals—especially breakfast, for example—and let Ted fix his own, even though she believed this was probably a mistake. More drastically, they continued to quarrel about finances. Sylvia now boldly confronted Ted—"Get a job," she would snap—which only made him leer at her. That she could not write intensified her unhappiness about Ted. (After "Johnny Panic," she had only been able to grind out one story, "The Shadow.") On bad days, she had begun concocting a new plan. Perhaps she would get into a graduate school, earn a doctorate, and make a steady income by going back into teaching. Lately, she was crying often, and not only in therapy sessions, where she routinely broke down, but at home, alone or with Ted.

In late January 1959, Plath's life started to look up—somewhat. On separate occasions, *The Nation* ran her poems "Frog Autumn" and "Two Views of a Cadaver Room." One evening, she and Ted had a supper party for the Stephen Fassetts, Robert Lowell, and his wife, Elizabeth Hardwick. And *The Spectator* published her poems "The Companionable Ills" and "Owl." Plath also finished two poems, "Point Shirley" and "Suicide off Egg Rock." Still, Ted had been writing so well that he now approached the end of his *second* book. While she fought a more contrary muse than Ted's, she wrote to Lee Anderson, she dutifully reshuffled her poetry manuscript, renamed it *The Bull of Bendylaw,* and again submitted it to the Yale Series of Younger Poets.

Plath's main source of creative encouragement at present came from a course she had begun auditing at Boston University, Robert Lowell's creative-writing seminar. Following Lowell's example, Plath now wanted her poetry to deal with matters closer to the bone. Instead of writing about subjects like goblins, the Lorelei, and fairy-tale characters, she would confront weighty issues—issues of the self. In therapy, Plath had learned that she most feared failure. Previously, she had chosen topics that presented her with little challenge. Now, she hoped to tackle difficult subjects: her husband, her mother, her dead father— and herself. She would attempt this departure even though, in March, eight of her "old" poems appeared in print in *The London Magazine, Audience, The Nation,* and *The Christian Science Monitor.* Plath described her new resolve to Lawner. She would reject the "Feminine (horror) lavish coyness," she wrote, but would aspire to create poems that were "grim, antipoetic." As for *Falcon Yard,* the Cambridge novel with which she had been dabbling for years, she had all but abandoned it. It existed only in fragments and in notes, daring her to finish it. She tried to write a novel, Plath confessed to Lawner, but had run into nothing but difficulty because she could not force the "material [to] take off from what did happen."

Sylvia also struggled for a breakthrough in her emotional life. Without a doubt, the most cathartic episode of her entire residence in Boston took place on Sunday, March 8. For the last several therapy sessions, Barnhouse had suggested that Sylvia do something she never had before: visit her father's grave. Sylvia finally decided she would. On that Sunday morning, she and Ted dressed, ate breakfast, and boarded a trolley bound for Winthrop. In the small town, as she walked along one street and then another on her way to the graveyard, Sylvia became more and more apprehensive. Finally, she and Ted arrived at the Winthrop Cemetery. Sylvia's father was buried in the third (and newest) section in a grave located on Azalea Path, not far from the front gate. Because his grave was close, Sylvia spotted the marker right away: "Otto E. Plath: 1885–1940." Staring at the marker, Sylvia was torn with emotion. "Felt cheated," she would write in her journal. "My temptation to dig him up. To prove he existed and was dead." Barely able to cope with her sorrow and anger, she turned to Ted and they left. To calm her down, they took a long walk along Winthrop's rocky shore and eventually ended up on Deer Island. There a prison guard told them that they could not continue on, so they headed back to Boston.

At home, Plath worked on a poem. Ten days later, the visit to her father's grave still haunted her memory. To purge herself and to better understand her feelings, she wrote another poem, "Electra on Azalea Path." In it, the narrator, a young woman in her twenties, visits the grave of her father, who had died, according to the narrator's mother, from gangrene. Now the daughter, who had previously attempted suicide, has come to the father to ask his forgiveness; the narrator never reveals to the reader *why* she believes she must be forgiven. Once she has asked the father to "pardon" her, the speaker declares the climactic confession: *her* love killed him. On the day Plath finished this poem—the same day she completed another, "Metaphors"—she posed in her journal the question: if she had "killed and castrated" her father, were her "dreams of deformed and tortured people" a result of "guilty visions of him or fears of punishment for me?"

In the spring, still worried about money, Plath accepted another part-time job, this one as a secretary for the chairman of the department of Sanskrit and Indian Studies at Harvard. In late March, Hughes received a letter from the award committee for the John Simon Guggenheim Foundation, to which he had applied for a grant. Without making a firm commitment, the committee requested additional information, such as a proposed budget. If Ted won a Guggenheim, which would bring him about five thousand dollars, they could subsist well beyond September, the month when Plath now projected that their money would run out.

Somewhat relieved, Plath continued to work, read, and write. She and Ted also entertained. The Hugheses regularly visited with the Fassetts, the Booths, and Robert Lowell and Elizabeth Hardwick. Of her schedule, Plath most enjoyed Tuesday afternoons, the time when she attended Lowell's creative-writing class. As the semester had progressed, she slowly gravitated towards two fellow students—a chain-smoking young woman who used her shoe for an ashtray and the man with whom she appeared to be romantically involved, Anne Sexton and

George Starbuck. Plath had been drawn to them in large part because she admired their poetry; compared with other students', it was lively and innovative. Once she came to know them, she discovered that they both had interesting lives. An editor at Houghton Mifflin, Starbuck had published poems widely. Sexton, a mental-hospital "graduate"—as Plath called her—and a favorite of Lowell's, had also published well, even in *The New Yorker*. Born in Wellesley, she, like Plath, went to Bradford High School, though Bradford marked the end of her education, since she had not gone on to college. (Younger than Sexton, Plath had not known her in Wellesley.) According to Plath, Sexton possessed the nonchalance of a person who was writing at a level she had never dreamed of.

As March gave way to April, the three young poets struck up a close friendship. After sitting in Lowell's class for two hours, Plath, Sexton, and Starbuck would hurry from the building, squeeze into the front seat of Sexton's dilapidated Ford, and weave through the zigzagging Boston streets to the Ritz-Carlton Hotel. "I would always park illegally in a LOADING ONLY ZONE, telling them gaily, 'It's okay, because we are only going to get loaded!' " Sexton would write years later in an essay. "Off we'd go, each on George's arm, into The Ritz to drink three or four or two martinis." While they drank and ate bowls-ful of free potato chips in the hotel's mezzanine-lounge bar, they talked about their private lives enough for Plath to figure out that Sexton and Starbuck *were* having an affair. Sexton would remember that on more than one occasion she and Plath broached the issue of suicide as well: Sexton had tried once. As they discussed their earlier attempts (neither saw this line of conversation as morbid), Plath and Sexton felt a kind of release. Once they had finished their martinis, the three of them wandered over to the Waldorf Cafeteria, where each could eat supper for seventy cents.

On April 10, Hughes received official notification: he had been granted a Guggenheim. More good news followed. First, Yaddo, an artists' colony in Saratoga Springs, New York, invited the Hugheses to work there during September, October, and November. Next, The *Sewanee Review* accepted Plath's "Point Shirley," *The New Yorker* her recently

finished "Watercolor of Grantchester Meadows" and "Man in Black."
Also, *The London Magazine* published three of Hughes's poems, *Horn
Book Magazine* and *The Christian Science Monitor* one each of Plath's.

Then, on the weekend of the 18th, Plath served as one of the
judges—John Crowe Ransom was another—for the Glascock Poetry
Contest, the Mount Holyoke competition that she had won as a student.
Late in April, Plath decided to write a children's book. On May 2, after
she thought about it for a few days, Plath sat down at her typewriter
and wrote *The Bed Book;* a series of ten poems about beds, it involves
two main characters, Wide-Awake Will and Stay-Uppidy Sue. That
same day, Plath mailed the book to Emilie McLeod at the Atlantic
Monthly Press. In her cover letter, she told McLeod that Ted was also
finishing a children's book, *Meet My Folks!*

In May, Plath began to feel jealous of Sexton and Starbuck. Sexton
had submitted a poetry manuscript to Houghton Mifflin, Starbuck's
employer; Plath decided not to try her book there as she had planned,
since the company would probably not accept hers *and* Sexton's. Also,
Starbuck, like Plath, had entered a manuscript in the Yale competition.
In mid-May, Houghton Mifflin signed up Sexton's book. Hearing this,
Plath sulked. With her luck, she would find out any day that Starbuck
or Maxine Kumin, a friend of Sexton's, had won the Yale, Plath wrote
in her journal; feeling sorry for herself, she even begrudged Sexton
her champagne celebration.

Near the end of the month, Plath and Hughes got into another
argument; afterwards, they did not speak to each other for days. When
she had moved to Boston in September, Plath had hoped she would
be happy in the city. Now she counted the days until their lease expired.
Since January, Ted had been talking about returning to England. With
all of her problems in Boston, Sylvia had tentatively agreed, but only
if Ted bought her an icebox and guaranteed her access to a good dentist.

Plath met with more rejection in June. On the 6th, Dudley Fitts,
editor of the Yale series, wrote that her manuscript had been chosen
as that year's alternate. It had "lost by a whisper," Fitts contended,
because the poems lacked "technical finish." Plath could hardly believe
Fitts's letter. All but a handful of the poems had been published in or
accepted by some of the leading periodicals in England and America,

and over the years her poetry had been criticized for being *too* crafted, not too *poorly* crafted. Infuriated, Plath lashed out at Fitts in her journal, calling him a fool who couldn't recognize a syllabic verse if he had to. Fitts's rejection fueled her ambition. Renaming the manuscript *The Devil of the Stairs,* she submitted it to trade publishers—Knopf, Viking, and Harcourt, Brace. It was not until the 12th, when he called to chat on the telephone, that Plath discovered who *had* beaten her out for the Yale—George Starbuck! Furious, she wrote to Ann Davidow, her Smith friend, with whom she kept in touch. Blowing off steam, she called Starbuck a "louse" and dismissed his poetry as light verse.

In June, William Maxwell at *The New Yorker* turned down two stories, although he did offer to meet with her to discuss fiction in general, and *The Atlantic Monthly* returned both poems and stories. Amid all this frustration, Plath did receive some encouragement. *The Christian Science Monitor* ran her article "A Walk to Withens," the *Sewanee Review* two poems; and *The London Magazine* bought two poems, *The Hudson Review* four. Most important, however, Emilie McLeod wrote Plath: she admired *The Bed Book* but wanted changes. "I would very much like to have you take out the connecting narrative [including the poems' characters]," McLeod said, "and just make this more or less a listing and description of beds—farfetched and exotic." Within a week of receiving her letter on the 11th, Plath rewrote the book and mailed it back to McLeod.

Though she liked McLeod, Plath had become leery of Peter Davison, who, Plath concluded, now blocked her work at *The Atlantic Monthly*. In March, Davison had married Jane Truslow, a classmate of Plath's, who shared numerous biographical facts with her. She had lost her father when she was young, attended Smith because of her widowed mother, lived in Lawrence, majored in English, studied with Kazin, worked as a *Mademoiselle* guest editor, suffered a breakdown at Smith, and graduated with honors in 1955. "I was grateful as a puppy that I had finally, at thirty, found the only woman I had ever unhesitatingly wanted," Davison would one day write. But Plath believed that Davison resented her—Sylvia—because of their ill-fated affair; he was sabotaging her work as revenge. Naturally, Plath had no concrete proof. All she had was Editor Weeks's last letter of rejection. " 'Alicante

Lullaby' has a lot of audible fireworks in it but no very clear plan," it read in part; "The Eye Mote with its change of rhythm also held our attention, but I question if the interest in it holds up all the way."

Plath read much in June—J. D. Salinger's *Seymour: An Introduction,* which appeared on the 6th in *The New Yorker,* Virginia Woolf's *The Years,* and short stories by Jean Stafford, Lowell's former wife, whose prose Plath considered more human than Elizabeth Hardwick's—but she wrote little herself. By late June, Plath could hardly wait to leave Boston. At the moment, she and Ted planned to set out by car on July 1 and tour America. They had just one obligation: to arrive at Yaddo in September to begin an eleven-week residence. At present, omens were good. In June, Faber and Faber—in the person of T. S. Eliot, no less—bought Hughes's *Meet My Folks!* Sylvia noted in her journal at the time that, because she had still not become pregnant, Ted unfortunately would have no child to whom he could dedicate his children's book. In the spring, fearing she was barren, she had visited a gynecologist to have her tubes "blown out" (her phrase). The procedure had worked. Although she did not know it, Sylvia was already pregnant on the day in early July when she and Ted began their tour of America, in a car they had borrowed from Aurelia.

As they headed for California, where their destination was Sylvia's father's sister Frieda (whom Sylvia called "Aunt Frieda," even though they had never met), Sylvia and Ted stopped at points along the way— Sault Sainte Marie in Michigan, Yellowstone Park in Montana, and the Great Salt Lake in Utah. In Yellowstone Park, one night as they slept in their tent, loud clangs coming from the direction of their car woke them. When they peered out the tent's flap, they saw the source of the commotion—a bear had broken in their car's rear window and was rummaging through their food. Unable to do anything, Sylvia and Ted glared at the animal from their tent. Finally, they tried— unsuccessfully—to fall back to sleep. In the morning, they emerged to survey the damage, which was considerable. During the day, they reported the attack to other campers, prompting one to tell them about a woman in a nearby camp who had been mauled to death by a bear.

That night, Sylvia and Ted covered both their car-window frames and their tent with kerosene and red-pepper flakes, the two substances known to ward off bears. Later, Plath would use this episode as the basis for the short story "The Fifty-ninth Bear." Between the real-life incident and the imagined incident, however, there is one drastic difference: in the story, the bear mauls the husband—and kills him.

Finally, Sylvia and Ted reached California. On August 1, they visited Sylvia's Aunt Frieda and Uncle Walter in Pasadena. Though she had been close to her mother's relatives, Sylvia had known few if any of her father's. Coming on the heels of a year during which she had dredged up feelings about her father in weekly therapy sessions, had stood at the foot of his grave for the first time, and had attempted to deal with the pain of his loss in her poetry, this meeting did not leave Sylvia unmoved. "It is amazing," Sylvia wrote to her mother, "how Frieda resembles daddy—the same clear, piercing, intelligent bright blue eyes and shape of face." After two days in California, Sylvia and Ted headed back east. Along the way, they stopped in Luke Myers's hometown of Sewanee, Tennessee, where a local socialite gave a party for them. One of the numerous guests they met was the *Sewanee Review*'s editor, Monroe Spears. The magazine's summer issue contained Plath's "The Ghost's Leavetaking" and "Point Shirley." Because Plath had also recently submitted her story "The Fifteen Dollar Eagle" to Spears, she was happy to meet him and his wife, Betty, who, Plath would remember, welcomed them to the South.

On August 25, once Plath and Hughes had left, Spears accepted "The Fifteen Dollar Eagle." "[It] seems to me a remarkable tour de force and a very fine story," Spears wrote. His letter awaited Plath when she and Ted arrived in Wellesley on August 28. The acceptance helped soften the disappointment Plath felt over yet another rejection, that of *The Bed Book*. "I'm sorry there has been such a delay in sending you word on *The Bed Book*," Emilie McLeod wrote in a letter dated August 17. "Unfortunately, Little, Brown does not share my enthusiasm. It was their feeling that the book is not simple and basic enough, that some of the beds are too farfetched, and that it has more appeal to adults than to children." She suggested that Plath try other pub-

lishers, then told her to send the manuscript back to her, if she did
not place it elsewhere. Perhaps in the future she might be able to push
it through. "I do hope you and Ted enjoyed your trip," McLeod concluded. "I'm sorry I could not have better news."

6

In early September, the Hugheses arrived at Yaddo. In a grand Victorian manor house, residents met, attended concerts and readings,
and ate breakfast and dinner. West House, a smaller building, had been
divided into artists' quarters and studios. Cabins, no two alike, were
set in among the colony's heavily wooded grounds. After checking in
with Acting Director Polly Hanson, the Hugheses proceeded to their
living quarters, a spacious ground-floor West House bedroom, complete with a bath and a huge closet. Hughes would write during the
day in a cabin just a short walk from the grand manor, while Plath
worked in a third-floor studio in West House. When she saw her studio,
Plath could not have been more pleased. Containing a cot, a rug, and
an enormous wooden desk on which she could write, the room had
four big windows that, facing east, looked out onto towering green pine
trees.

During their stay at Yaddo, Plath and Hughes maintained a simple
schedule. After breakfast in the mansion's dining hall, at which Plath
normally had eggs, a coffee roll, toast, jam, orange juice, and coffee,
she and Ted picked up a boxed lunch (no community lunch was served),
retired to their studies, and worked without interruption until they
wished to stop. At night, residents reassembled in the dining hall for
a semiformal supper. Then, following the meal, they often attended
readings given by the writers in residence (Hughes read on September
9, Plath on September 23). In the summer, Yaddo housed some thirty
residents, but, because it was fall and most writers had returned to
university jobs, Plath and Hughes were two of only about twelve artists.
(By mid-October, the number had dwindled to a half-dozen.) The staff
carried out all practical duties—cooking, cleaning, and the like—so

Plath felt free to read and write at will, roam the grounds, or accompany Ted on fishing trips. At first, she read mostly, studying stories she admired by Eudora Welty, Jean Stafford, and Katherine Anne Porter. She also scanned—and dismissed—the work of John Updike and Nadine Gordimer. Eventually, Plath moved on to Ezra Pound, who captured her imagination; Elizabeth Bishop, for whom she developed a deep admiration; and Iris Murdoch, whose prose had behind it an overpowering intellect. The longer Plath remained at Yaddo, the less she read. For, once she had adjusted to her surroundings, she started to write, again under Ted's tutelage.

Sylvia allowed Ted to control more areas of her life than her poetry-writing. "Despite the strength of her poetry, Sylvia seemed to hide behind Ted," remembers Sonia Raiziss, one of the other residents then at Yaddo. "She always seemed to allow him to take the lead in conversations; she even let him enter a room first. They were both very imposing in looks—very tall, almost godlike in their physical aspect. Nevertheless, *he* was the important person in their household, although she didn't seem to resent it. In fact, in an odd way, she had a confidence about herself. It was almost as if she were saying, 'You'll hear from me one day.'"

At Yaddo, Plath wrote despite a string of rejections. In late September, *The New Yorker* returned a batch of poems, keeping only one "for further consideration." In early November, *New World Writing* turned down a recent story. In late November, after it had refused three short stories under separate submission, *The Atlantic Monthly* mailed back a group of poems—more rejections Plath blamed on Peter Davison. Even worse, in early October, both Henry Holt and Harcourt, Brace refused her poetry manuscript. Plath had become so certain of her manuscript's doomed fate that, when she mentioned it to Malcolm Cowley at Yaddo at the end of October, she read his reaction as a sign that he too had rejected it, or would in the future.

Between September and November, some good news did arrive. Plath's poetry appeared in the *Partisan Review, Poetry, The London Magazine, The Christian Science Monitor,* and the *Times Literary Supplement.* Also, in October, *The New Yorker* bought "A Winter's Tale" and John Lehmann at *The London Magazine* accepted her story "This Earth Our Hospital," which at Lehmann's prodding Plath renamed "The Daughters of Blossom Street." Best of all, in that same month, Plath received a letter from James Michie, an editor at the British publishers William Heinemann; Michie inquired about the possibilities of acquiring a book of Plath's poems. "Seeing two new poems of yours in this month's *London Magazine* has reminded me how good your poetry is," Michie wrote. "Have you an English publisher arranged for your first volume? If not I should be very glad if you would consider us as candidates. Being a poet myself I should be delighted to look after you here." Finally, after so many publishers had turned down her poetry manuscript, Plath had something to be excited about, although she remained guarded in her optimism: she would celebrate when Michie *accepted* her book.

Certainly, Michie's letter motivated Plath to write. While she churned out more prose pieces—three short stories and the memoir "A Prospect of Cornucopia"—and considered starting another novel—because her life had been filled with, she believed, so much love, madness, and hatred—Plath also wrote several poems. At Yaddo, Plath and Hughes, as was their custom, routinely hypnotized each other. Good work sprang from deep within the imagination. To tap into that source, one could try mind control, hypnosis, stream-of-consciousness experiments, and Plath and Hughes tried them all. As they did, Plath met with startling results. In late September and early October, she produced three minor poems. On October 19, she warmed up by practicing Ted's concentration exercises (breathing deeply, she focused her mind on a series of free-flowing objects); Plath then wrote "The Manor Garden" and "The Colossus." The latter, one of the more intellectually satisfying and poetically mature poems she had yet written, depicts a daughter's fruitless efforts to reassemble a crumbling statue that is her father. Finishing the poem, Plath renamed her poetry manuscript yet again. This time, choosing her newest effort as the title poem, she called the volume *The Colossus and Other Poems.*

In late October, Plath envisioned a long "Roethke-influence[d]" poem that would be a meditation on a number of subjects as divergent as greenhouses and madhouses. To be called "Poem for a Birthday," it became a seven-section poem, more a mosaic than a narrative, which took her two weeks to write. Though it does not follow in story line any of the poem's previous six parts, the final section, "The Stones," is narrated by a patient in a hospital that Plath surrealistically describes as being "the city of spare parts." The bulk of this section details how the narrator, severely hurt by an unnamed injury, has her body sewn back together with catgut stitches. Finally, at the end of the poem, the narrator is "good as new," although the stitches itch. Hughes would come to regard "The Stones" as the most significant poem Plath had written, a turning point in her canon. Calling it "unlike anything that had gone before in her work," Hughes would write in an essay years later:

> In its double focus, "The Stones" is both a "birth" and a "rebirth." It is the birth of her real poetic voice, but it is the rebirth of herself. That poem encapsulates, with literal details, her "death," her treatment, and her slow, buried recovery. And this is where we can see the peculiarity of her imagination at work, where we can see how the substance of her poetry and the very substance of her survival are the same.

Early on in her Yaddo stay, Plath had asked herself when she would "break into a new line of poetry." By Thanksgiving, she had—if not in "The Colossus," in "The Stones." Plath did not care about describing in critical language exactly what she hoped to attempt in her "new" poetry. She cared only about *writing* it. But critics had begun to invent a vocabulary to discuss the embryonic style of poetry represented by Plath's latest work and Robert Lowell's recently published *Life Studies.* Reviewing the book in the September 19 *Nation,* M. L. Rosenthal contended that "[t]he use of poetry for the most naked kind of confession grows sparse in our day." Whitman had taken American poetry to "the very edge of the confessional, in his *Calamus* poems," but Pound and Eliot had employed "a certain indirection [to mask] the poet's actual face and psyche from greedy eyes." Lowell, however, "removes the mask" in *Life Studies,* for "[h]is speaker is unequivocally himself and it is hard not to think of *Life Studies* as a series of personal

confidences, rather shameful, that one is honor-bound not to reveal."
To place his achievement in perspective, Lowell credited his inspiration
as being *Heart's Needle,* a volume written—before *Life Studies*—by
W. D. Snodgrass, a student of his at the University of Iowa's Writers'
Workshop.

Towards the end of her stay at Yaddo, as she had for some time,
Plath suffered from insomnia. For the last two months, when she did
sleep, she had also been haunted by dreams. Without a doubt, one of
her strangest dreams at Yaddo occurred in early October. Marilyn
Monroe came to her one night as a "kind of fairy godmother," Plath
wrote in her journal on the 4th. "I spoke, almost in tears, of how much
she and Arthur Miller meant to us. . . ." Then, after Marilyn gave her
a manicure, Sylvia asked Marilyn, because Sylvia "had not washed [her]
hair," about hairdressers, saying, "they always imposed a horrid cut on
me." Finally, in the dream, Marilyn invited Sylvia to visit her during
the Christmas holidays, promising a "new, flowering life."

With thoughts of a "new, flowering life," and with a resolve to learn,
under Ted's guidance, more about hypnosis, astrology, and tarot cards,
Plath left Yaddo with Hughes for a Thanksgiving in Wellesley. Following the holidays, Ted and Sylvia remained until their scheduled departure for England. During those weeks, Sylvia packed downstairs
while Ted wrote upstairs in her bedroom. Sylvia also had a medical
examination which confirmed what she had learned at Yaddo: she was
pregnant, now five months along. On December 12, the date on which
her poem "A Winter's Tale" appeared in *The New Yorker,* Plath and
Hughes boarded a Boston train to New York, where they would sail
for England on the S.S. *United States.* "On the day they left, Sylvia
was wearing her hair in a long braid down her back with a little red
wool cap on her head, and looked like a high school student," Aurelia
Plath would write. "As the train pulled out, Ted called, 'We'll be back
in two years!'" It was the last time Sylvia Plath ever saw Wellesley.

England

1

In London, the Hugheses stayed briefly with Daniel and Helga Huws, Ted's Cambridge friend and his wife. By December 17, they were in Yorkshire to visit Ted's parents and Olwyn, on holiday from Paris. With her hair recently cut and curled, Olwyn looked chic to Plath, who liked her a great deal. Unfortunately, Sylvia could not work up the same enthusiasm for Ted's mother, Edith. On previous trips, Sylvia had not criticized Ted's family, in deference to Ted; only days into this outing, though, Sylvia told her mother in a letter that, because she could not eat Edith's awful food, which Edith prepared in a kitchen that always seemed to be somewhat dirty, she worried about her unborn baby's health. Sylvia became further disaffected when the Hugheses observed Christmas but did not, to her amazement, put up a Christmas tree. All in all, her reintroduction to England did not go as smoothly as she would have hoped.

At The Beacon, Plath read, thought about new poems, and fumed over the latest rejection letter for her poetry collection, this one from Farrar, Straus. Angered by that refusal, Plath retyped the manuscript, still called *The Colossus and Other Poems,* and prepared to submit it to Heinemann. While she worked, she also tried to get along with the Hugheses. Specifically, Sylvia attempted to establish a cordial relationship with Olwyn, who, overprotective of Ted, seemed threatened by the presence of a wife in his life. Olwyn had felt similarly towards Gerald's wife, right after Gerald had married. On this issue, Sylvia would hear rumors in the future; apparently, Gerald had moved to Australia to escape Olwyn, who, as the story went, was so jealous that she repeatedly interfered with his marriage. For whatever it was worth, Olwyn seemed to be warming up to Sylvia.

On Sunday, January 3, 1960, the Hugheses took the train to London to start looking for an apartment. Staying in an extra room in the Huwses' Rugby Street flat, they searched for a week with no luck. When she learned of their problem, Dido Merwin, the wife of W. S. Merwin, whom Plath and Hughes had met in Boston, lined up some small but nice flats for them to consider. "Nice" implied hot water, central heat, and a refrigerator—all extras in some apartments. Finally, the Hugheses located a functional if tiny flat just off Primrose Hill, near Regent's Park and the Chalk Farm tube station. A third-floor (fourth in America) unfurnished walk-up in a five-story building, the flat, which overlooked Chalcot Square and a miniature park named Chalcot Square Gardens, was within a short walk of shops, a laundromat, and the doctor to whom Dido had introduced Sylvia. Consisting of a cramped living room, a modest bedroom, a bath, and a kitchen (which contained a sink—nothing else), the place was too small, but because the rent was affordable—eighteen dollars per week plus gas and electricity—the Hugheses happily signed the three-year lease, which stipulated that they could move in after February 1. They then returned to Heptonstall to begin packing.

While she was in London, Dido's doctor, John Horder, and Horder's obstetrician partner, Christopher Hindley, had examined Sylvia, who was, both doctors agreed, in excellent health. Since patients in England spoke for hospital beds eight months in advance, and since most British women delivered their babies at home under the supervision of a midwife, Sylvia resolved herself to giving birth at Chalcot Square—an outdated notion to Americans. In Yorkshire, fortified by the iron tablets and nonbarbiturate sleeping pills her doctors had prescribed, Sylvia enjoyed her first bath in two weeks. (The Huwses' flat did not have a private bathroom.) Over the coming days, when they were not packing, Ted and Sylvia took walks along the moors, read, and anticipated Faber and Faber's publication of two new books by Hughes. His second collection of poems, *Lupercal,* named after the Roman fertility festival, was scheduled for release in March, his children's book, *Meet My Folks!,* the following winter.

Ted and Sylvia moved to London on February 1. Initially, they spent most of their time unpacking and overseeing the delivery and installation of a new stove, refrigerator, and bed. They borrowed furniture from the Merwins, who lived only a five-minute walk away and with whom they had become friends. To be accurate, Ted had become friends with Bill, principally because, as Ted wrote Olwyn, they praised each other's poems and Merwin had Leo rising in his astrological chart—an appealing aspect to Ted. On the other hand, Sylvia and Dido struggled to maintain a superficial acquaintanceship. To Plath, who wrote about her to Lynne Lawner, Dido was "older, very energetic, very British, very thrice-married." Other people were wary of Dido as well. "She had this feeling of being superior to everyone," remembers Anne Stevenson, the poet and biographer. "She was European. She quoted French and Latin at the drop of a hat—in fact, she sort of weaved it into her conversations—in an effort to make you feel like a fool who doesn't know anything, and make herself look superior. Dido considered Sylvia 'the ugly American.' Also, she was slightly jealous of Plath's being a poet. While their hostility was not open, it was unspoken, under the surface."

Regardless of Dido and Sylvia's misgivings, the Merwins helped the Hugheses enormously. Bill, who often worked for the BBC, introduced Ted to Douglas Cleverdon, the legendary "Third Programme" producer best known for his radio presentation of Dylan Thomas's *Under Milkwood,* which starred Richard Burton. More practically, Bill offered Ted the use of his study when the Merwins left in April to spend the summer at their country home in France.

In early February, Plath anticipated the birth of her child, now so close that she was seeing her midwife, Sister Hannaway. While she tried to ignore the clanging and hammering of builders working on the house, Sylvia also helped Ted, in her own limited way, as he painted walls and floors and hung pictures. Mostly, she savored the arrival of a letter from James Michie. "I like your poems and Heinemann would like to publish them," Michie wrote on February 5, referring to *The Colossus.* "Can you ring me here and drop in to see me any time, any day this month?" Joyous, Plath set up an appointment with Michie and signed a contract for the book on February 10. She accepted the offer of the first British house to read her manuscript because Heinemann, the publisher for Somerset Maugham, Evelyn Waugh, and D. H. Lawrence, released a small number of poetry collections and would therefore—she hoped—print the book well. As part of their deal, Heinemann would submit *The Colossus*—which she had dedicated to Ted and which contained, among its forty-eight poems, all of her Yaddo poems, about one-third of the text—to various houses in the United States. She had suffered nothing but "cold shoulders" from American publishers, Plath wrote Lawner. The worst blow had come when she lost the Yale to "old cold gold" George Starbuck, she continued. So she would just remain an "exile" in England, never to return to the "land of milk & honey & spindryers." Still, she would have to deal with American magazines. On February 22, she mailed out "Poem for a Birthday," which *Poetry* had recently turned down because it displayed "too imposing a debt to Roethke." Eventually, the *Sewanee Review* rejected it as well, finding it too long.

In late February, Hughes, who admired the six author's copies of *Lupercal* he just received, read at the Oxford Poetry Society. Sylvia made this trip with him, because she had never been to Oxford. In the days after the reading, the Hugheses met social obligations. Visiting in London, Luke Myers often stopped by Chalcot Square to see Ted and remained for hours when he did. On February 29, the Hugheses went to a buffet with David and Barbara Ross; since Luke and Daniel and Helga Huws were also there, the occasion amounted to a *St. Botolph's Review* reunion. The next day, the Hugheses had lunch at a Soho Greek restaurant with Hughes's editors, who discussed with him possible choices for an illustrator for *Meet My Folks!* The day after that, the Hugheses were guests at a cocktail party given by John Lehmann, the editor of *The London Magazine,* who had accepted Plath's poems "The Sleepers" and "Full Fathom Five." At the party, Sylvia met the writers Elizabeth Jennings, Roy Fuller, and Christine Brooke-Rose.

Then, during the first weekend in March, Olwyn arrived in London from Paris. Although she slept at a friend's, she, like Luke, spent long stretches of time at Chalcot Square. By March 10, Plath, eight months pregnant, had become fed up with parties and, even more so, with houseguests. After an exhausting crossing to England, a horrid January, and an even more tiring February, Sylvia simply did not have the patience to deal with Ted's friends and family holed up in her flat for hours. Writing to her mother, Sylvia confessed to being worn out from sitting hours on end in stuffy, smoky rooms, unable to take even a nap. These days, with the baby's birth so close, Sylvia wanted only to rest and sleep.

On the 18th of March, Faber and Faber released Hughes's *Lupercal*, a collection of forty-one poems which he dedicated to Sylvia. The reviews echoed those of *The Hawk in the Rain*. Of the many notices that ran in such periodicals as the Oxford *Times*, the *Times Literary Supplement*, and *The Spectator*, Donald Hall's in *The New Statesman* was representative. "Ted Hughes's *Lupercal* is better than *The Hawk in the Rain*, which was a superb first book. With energy and confidence, Hughes has extended the subject matter which his habitual turbulence of language can control. He is now the master of his metaphors and not their servant. His drive, his power and his gusto particularly delight me here." On March 24, partly as a result of the book's critical reception, Hughes won the prestigious Somerset Maugham Award, which brought with it a five-hundred-pound cash prize earmarked to be spent on travel abroad. With these achievements to his credit, Hughes merited even more public attention. A personality profile of Hughes—one of the first—appeared in *The Observer* in London not long after *Lupercal*'s publication. Written by *Observer* poetry editor A. Alvarez, who had interviewed Hughes at Chalcot Square, the piece praised Hughes at length.

> The new winner of the 500 pound Somerset Maugham award, Ted Hughes, is a tall, craggy Yorkshire poet of thirty, who is not afraid of Strong Feelings.
> He was at Cambridge with last year's Maugham prize winner, Thom Gunn, and between them, Gunn and Hughes, although they

do not know each other well, are two of the most exciting British poets.

They both represent a more romantic revolt against the dry, cerebral verse of the Movement of the fifties (Conquest, Larkin, Amis, Wain, etc.), though Gunn still partly belongs to the Movement; but their romanticism is tougher and stronger than the stuff of Dylan Thomas and the forties people.

Hughes is more earthy and emotional; more close to the land and farm. He comes from Brontë country and still breathes the Yorkshire moors. In London where he lives in Chalcot Square, near Camden Town, he has the look of a countryman, in gangling contrast to his tall, trim American wife, Sylvia Plath, who is a *New Yorker* poet in her own right.

Because of good publicity and strong reviews, *Lupercal* sold well. As of June, it had already entered a second printing. Mail for Hughes poured into Chalcot Square—letters from friends, requests for poems from editors, and invitations to give readings. When the correspondence piled up, Plath had to answer it, because, as she wrote her mother, if she didn't Ted never would.

At the end of March, Sylvia could do little besides write letters, for she had reached full term. Finally, on the night of March 31, after she and Ted had taken a walk along Primrose Hill and Regent's Park that had tired her enough so she fell asleep immediately, Sylvia awoke to labor pains. Then everything happened quickly. By two o'clock, when Ted called the midwife, Sylvia's contractions were violent. By five, she was fully dilated. By five-thirty, when the nurse called the doctor, Sylvia believed the baby would come any minute. And it did—at five-forty-five. A girl, she weighed seven pounds and four ounces and measured twenty-one inches in length. Sylvia called her Frieda Rebecca, and the source of the name was clear. It was Otto's sister Frieda, Sylvia's aunt whom she had described as "resembl[ing] daddy—the same . . . blue eyes and shape of face."

During labor and the actual birth, Ted remained at Sylvia's side; he often held her hand and rubbed her back. As he had hypnotized her over the past few weeks, Ted had offered a posthypnotic suggestion that she have a quick and painless delivery. Though by no means painless, it was—at four and a half hours—relatively quick. Recovered somewhat, Sylvia placed a transatlantic telephone call to her mother, but the line was disconnected, so she called back an hour later. After telling Aurelia about the details of the birth, Sylvia hung up and went to bed. She fell into a heavy sleep, from which she did not wake for about two hours. That day, Ted served her breakfast and lunch in bed. They now began to think about who to name as godparents; Olwyn was one logical choice. The midwife stopped by at eleven and at teatime to check on both Sylvia and the baby. Because she now saw herself and Lynne Lawner as "emotional sisters on the other side of the moon," Plath started her next letter to her by confessing that "[t]he whole experience of birth and baby seem[s] much deeper, much closer to the bone, than love and marriage."

In England, for the first fourteen days of a baby's life, the National Health provided the services of a midwife free of charge, just as it had prenatal care and delivery. In all, three different midwives saw Sylvia and Frieda. On April 3, Sylvia got out of bed to have a candlelight supper with Ted; it featured a casserole cooked by Dido. The next day, Sylvia took her first bath since the birth. Usually, the baby cried between midnight and 4:00 A.M.; Sylvia napped during the day so that she could care for the baby at night and let Ted sleep. On the 6th, Sylvia and Frieda received their first guest, Bill Merwin, who dropped in to see the baby and to confirm with Ted that he was coming over that evening to meet Bill's publisher.

After two weeks of recovery, Plath tried to write, but she did not have enough energy. On April 9, *The New Yorker* published "Man in Black." At mid-month, *The Atlantic Monthly* bought "The Manor Garden" and "A Winter Ship" for seventy-five dollars each. Certain that it *had* been Peter Davison who had been blocking her acceptances at the magazine, acceptances that she had started earning while at Smith and had continued to receive until he came to work there, Plath mailed her last batch of poems directly to Edward Weeks. This way, she could circumvent, as she called it, Peter's "Iron Curtain."

Yet, despite these successes, Plath could not write; she was still too tired. She could barely attend a handful of social functions with Ted.

On the 19th, they had lunch with a woman from the BBC and Karl Miller, literary editor for *The New Statesman;* two days later, they went to a cocktail party at Faber and Faber; the following day, they ate dinner with Lee Anderson, currently in England to record British poets for Yale. Normally, the Hugheses would employ the Babyminder Service, for which they paid fifty cents an hour, but on Sunday the 17th they took Frieda on her first outing, a ban-the-bomb march. When she told her mother about it, Sylvia implored Aurelia not to vote for Richard Nixon in the upcoming presidential elections. To Plath, Nixon was a dangerous Machiavelli. Vote Kennedy, she demanded.

Up until now, the Hugheses had not openly embraced politics, although as early as her high-school years Plath had shown evidence of a growing political awareness. Perhaps their friendship with the Merwins, both of whom endorsed liberal causes, had provided the catalyst needed to get them to act on their beliefs. But none of their present activities compared to the event to which the Hugheses had been invited for May 4. That evening, they were scheduled to have supper, along with the Stephen Spenders, at the home of Mr. and Mrs. T. S. Eliot.

2

The Eliots lived on the first floor of a drab brick building in a functional, but expensive, flat. After they met Eliot's wife, Valerie, the Hugheses were joined by Eliot himself in the living room for sherry; slowly Plath felt at ease, as Eliot talked about traveling through America. Eventually, Stephen Spender arrived with his wife, Natasha Litvin, the concert pianist, and the group's conversation turned to gossip about friends of the Spenders and the Eliots, among them Stravinsky, Auden, Virginia Woolf, and D. H. Lawrence. Next, they all moved on to supper, where Plath sat between Eliot and Spender. Not only did Plath have a new baby and a book contract for *The Colossus,* but here she was socializing with the Spenders and the Eliots, talking about Stravinsky and Woolf. She had certainly come a long way from that frightened Smith freshman who had actually received a B + in English.

On May 2, the Hugheses ate supper with Jane and Peter Davison, paid for by *The Atlantic Monthly*. The meal became uncomfortably anxious: Sylvia decided Peter was furious with her for mailing her last poems to Weeks, not him. His anger, although mostly concealed, only convinced Sylvia that he *had* in fact blocked her poems. After supper, as the Hugheses got onto the bus to go home, Peter shouted, "Look for *The Hudson Review;* I have a long poem coming out in it." Sylvia would write her mother that pity prevented her from calling back that she had *four* poems forthcoming in the same magazine.

In May, when they had free time from their active social calendar and from caring for Frieda, Plath and Hughes also worked. With the Merwins in France, Hughes put in a morning and an afternoon shift in Bill's study, accomplishing much on his third book of poems and on a play. He recorded his short story "The Rain Horse" for the BBC as well. Meanwhile, Plath corrected the *Colossus* proofs and saw the publication of her story "The Daughters of Blossom Street" in *The London Magazine* and her poem "Watercolor of Grantchester Meadows" in *The New Yorker*.

During June, Plath's list of publications continued to grow, with her poems appearing in *The Critical Quarterly, The London Magazine*, and the *Partisan Review*. More important, by late June, Plath had finally returned to writing. To date in 1960, she had produced only one eighteen-line poem, "You're." But with life regaining some normality, Plath stole a few moments on June 27 and wrote "The Hanging Man." Just six lines, it displays a power of language and voice as formidable as that of "The Stones." The month's most memorable event, though, occurred on the 24th. To commemorate the publication of W. H. Auden's *Homage to Clio*, Faber and Faber hosted a cocktail party to which the Hugheses were invited. Midway through the party, Charles Monteith, a Faber editor, called Plath out into the hallway. There she saw Hughes standing, drink in hand, between four other Faber poets—Eliot, Auden, Spender, and Louis MacNeice. As the men posed nonchalantly, a photographer snapped away. "Three generations of Faber poets," Monteith had said, predicting the sentiment of Philip Day's London *Times* article "A Pride of Poets," which ran on Sunday the 26th. Of Hughes, a member of the "younger" crowd, Day commented: "Ted Hughes from the Pennines, whose muscular verse has won him this year's Somerset Maugham award, [was at the party along with] his poet-wife Sylvia Plath."

In July, a month when her poems appeared in *Harper's* and *The Atlantic Monthly*, Plath began to write poetry in earnest. Working mornings in Merwin's study, Plath finished "Sleep in the Mojave Desert," "On Deck," and "Two Campers in Cloud Country." Immediately she mailed a batch of poems to Howard Moss, who bought "On Deck" and "Two Campers" for *The New Yorker*. Still, Plath was not satisfied with the amount of money she and Hughes earned by writing. In July, she requested help in finding a job from Cambridge University's Women's Appointment Board. Hughes, who had finished his play *The House of Aries*, which the BBC produced in early July, concentrated on writing poetry.

In August, the month *The New Yorker* published Plath's "The Net-Menders," the Yale Series of Younger Poets turned down another of her poetry manuscripts—the third one. Hurt, Plath told her mother in a letter that she was especially angry that no American publisher wanted her collection because it was better than the majority of first books. How ironic that her British husband could find success in her country—Harper and Brothers released *Lupercal* on August 3 to excellent reviews—and she could not.

Following a ten-day vacation in Heptonstall in late August, the Hugheses returned to London to work. Ted began writing in the upstairs flat of their neighbor Mrs. Morton while she was gone during the day; he found Mrs. Morton's less distracting than the Merwins' study. In the meantime, Plath finished four poems during September and October. She also continued to publish; in the early fall her poems appeared in *The Hudson Review*, the *Kenyon Review*, and *The Atlantic Monthly*. Late in October, the BBC, who had turned down everything she had submitted from *The Colossus*, accepted two new poems, "Leaving Early" and "Candles."

Of course, for Plath, the major professional event of October—indeed of the entire year—was the publication of *The Colossus and Other Poems* by William Heinemann. Plath had asked Michie to release the book on her birthday, but because Heinemann only issued books on Mondays, *The Colossus*'s official publication date became October 31. As she waited for reviews, Sylvia kept active. She and Ted attended a supper at the Stephen Spenders' where the guests, among them Louis MacNeice and Rosamond Lehmann, gossiped about Lloyd George's jilting of Spender's father. Then, only days after her birthday, she and Ted went to a November 1 champagne party for the Guinness Awards, the prize Ted had won last year while in America. As it happened, Plath would have quite a wait for reviews. None appeared in October. In November, only three minor notices came out, in *John O'London's, Time and Tide,* and the Manchester *Guardian.* Plath became so disheartened that, in November, she stopped writing poetry and concentrated on grinding out women's magazine fiction; she even lined up a London agent to try to sell the stories.

During December, three more reviews were published. After *Punch*'s piece on the 7th, the next to appear—the first truly significant notice—was A. Alvarez's "The Poet and the Poetess," which *The Observer* ran on the 18th. In it, Alvarez wrote:

> Miss Plath neither asks excuses for her work nor offers them. She steers clear of feminine charm, deliciousness, gentility, supersensitivity and the act of being a poetess. She simply writes good poetry. . . .
>
> She is not, of course, unwaveringly good. At times, her feeling weakens, the language goes off on its own and she lands in blaring rhetoric. At other times she hovers close to the whimsy of fairy stories. . . . But it would be a strange first book that had no faults; *The Colossus* has more than enough excellent poems to compensate for them.

Plath read Alvarez's piece while she, Ted, and the baby spent Christmas holidays in Yorkshire, where they planned to stay until New Year's Day. This visit to The Beacon turned out to be anything but pleasant for Plath.

3

Sylvia and Ted's week in Heptonstall had passed calmly, even though the Yorkshire winter bore down hard on The Beacon, and the house itself was too small to accommodate gracefully everyone staying there. The powder-keg atmosphere finally erupted one day when, according to Sylvia in a letter home to her mother, Sylvia asked Olwyn to stop degrading her and Ted, which she had done for much of the week, and Olwyn flew into a tirade. Calling Sylvia a "nasty bitch" and accusing her of overeating at Christmas dinner, Olwyn criticized Sylvia for acting as if The Beacon were *her* house, for defaming a poet whom Olwyn admired, and—of the three, this seemed the worst affront—for not putting her up at Chalcot Square when she was in London in the spring. Throughout the episode, Olwyn announced that she— *Olwyn!*—was the daughter of the house; she even referred to Sylvia as "Miss Plath"—an indication, to Sylvia, that Olwyn had never truly accepted Ted and Sylvia's marriage. Also, Olwyn claimed Sylvia was intolerant, selfish, inhospitable, and immature—words she flung at her out of hatred. Finally, when Olwyn stopped, Sylvia, stunned and speechless, took Frieda from Olwyn, who had been holding her through all this, and fled upstairs. Early the next morning, Sylvia, Ted, and Frieda—at Sylvia's urging—left The Beacon several days early. It was the last time Sylvia would see Olwyn. Years later, Olwyn would defend her actions by saying that Sylvia had merely overreacted to their charged dialogue.

On January 1, 1961, at home in London, Sylvia nursed a "grumbling" appendix and the flu, which she and Ted had come down with following a heatless train ride back from Yorkshire. Sylvia also tried to find some logic in Olwyn's tantrum. Only one explanation seemed reasonable. Obviously, Olwyn was extremely jealous of Sylvia. Writing to her mother, Sylvia speculated why. Ted and Olwyn were abnormally close, she said. One could even describe their relationship as incestuous, since they had slept in the same bed until Olwyn was a young teenager.

Sylvia believed that, specifically, the immediate cause of Olwyn's attack was the release of *The Colossus*. Sylvia's accomplishments naturally increased her standing in Ted's eyes; this filled Olwyn with jealousy. Whatever the reason was, Sylvia decided that she would never stay in the same house with Olwyn again—ever. From now on, she and Ted would visit Yorkshire only if Olwyn was not there. And, finally, Olwyn would *not* be Frieda's godmother.

Over the next ten days, Sylvia tried to forget Olwyn. She thought about the supplement of American poetry *The Critical Quarterly* had arranged for her to edit. She set up an appointment with a surgeon to advise her on her appendix. And she and Ted had lunch with Thom Gunn, whom she considered genuine and caring. She wished that Gunn lived nearer (he taught at the University of California at Berkeley) so that she and Ted could see more of him. The Hugheses also had Dido Merwin over to supper; Dido, who had recently had a face-lift, was alone in London while Bill traveled across America on a reading tour. Because Dido had been so generous with Frieda—on this night she gave her the first in the series of Beatrix Potter's Peter Rabbit books— Sylvia concluded that Dido would be an ideal godmother.

Sylvia believed that Olwyn, still in Yorkshire, was now criticizing her to the Hugheses. Edith had mailed Sylvia and Ted a curt note which said that they should have expected to get the flu if they took the train on a Saturday during holiday season. Ted tried to reassure Sylvia. According to Ted, Olwyn had acted the way she did because of her— Olwyn's—own jealousy.

Plath's overall state of mind improved on January 13 with the publication of John Wain's review of *The Colossus* in *The Spectator*. Wain wrote:

> Sylvia Plath writes clever, vivacious poetry, which will be enjoyed most by intelligent people capable of having fun with poetry and not just being holy about it. This policy [of crafting poems] ought to produce quaint, over-gnarled writing, but in fact Miss Plath has a firm enough touch to keep clear of these faults. Here and there one finds traces of "influences" not yet completely assimilated ("Snake-charmer," for instance, is too like Wallace Stevens for comfort, and the sequence "Poem For a Birthday" testifies too flatly to an ad-

miration for Theodore Roethke), but, after all, this is a first book, and the surprising thing is how successful Miss Plath has already been in finding an individual manner.

Wain's observation about "Poem for a Birthday" surfaced in another commentary. When Heinemann had submitted *The Colossus* to Alfred A. Knopf, the book was given to Judith Jones, one of the house's young editors. In her in-house report on *The Colossus,* Jones had written, "This girl is a poet, there is no question about it, and I think one of the most exciting young ones that has emerged in a long time." Her first manuscript had arrived at Knopf unsolicited about a year earlier, Jones went on, but Jones felt it was "too slim." Now, from Heinemann, came this impressive—and significantly different—volume. "I have [only] one reservation about her work and because of that I would like to get the opinion of someone like Stanley Kunitz to try to find out whether the pros here would be apt to bear down too heavily on what I would call her imitativeness. This is most pronounced in a long poem that seems to be so deliberately stolen from Roethke's 'The Lost Son' that I would almost fear the charge of plagiarism."

In London, Sylvia, unaware of Jones's interest, celebrated a different sort of good news: she was pregnant again. She went on a crash program of relaxation and diet reorganization to improve her health, which had declined since midwinter. Also, she planned to have her appendix removed in February, because the "grumbling" had worsened noticeably. First, she had to complete a part-time, afternoons-only job she had taken at *The Bookseller,* a London-based publication that advertised forthcoming books in two large biannual issues. Plath had been hired to copyedit and lay out the entire children's section of the spring issue. While working at *The Bookseller,* she thought about babies' names. She leaned towards Nicholas Farrar or Megan Emily. Megan would be shortened to Meg, Sylvia wrote her mother, and Emily, besides being for Brontë and Dickinson, was a feminization of her father's Emil.

At the time, Plath was also keeping a hectic social and literary routine. The February *Encounter,* a magazine edited by Spender and Melvin J. Lasky, contained Plath's poem "A Winter Ship"; the February *London Magazine* ran her story "The Fifty-ninth Bear." On January 31,

Plath and Hughes listened to themselves on the BBC radio program "Two of a Kind," a show that featured interviews with married couples who worked in the same field. This week's program, which the Hugheses had taped on January 18, was entitled "Poets in Partnership." On the program, an extended edition of which was also broadcast on March 19, Plath commented that she believed she had lived a happy childhood until the age of nine, although she did not elaborate on air about the probable cause of the end of that happiness. As for Hughes, one of his more intriguing discussions involved a description of how he could write about Sylvia's experiences as well as his own. It was as if he were a medium for her thoughts, he said; theirs was such a "sympathetic" relationship that he could read her mind at any given moment. They felt they made up, in essence, one person, one *single* shared psyche. Hughes believed, as he told the interviewer, that a "telepathic union"—like theirs—can and does exist between two people. Following the broadcast, the Hugheses received much fan mail. One letter was from a woman in Devon, Elizabeth Compton, whose husband, David, was also a writer. Should the Hugheses ever come down to Devon, Compton wrote, she would be honored to have them over for lunch.

On February 1st, Plath and Hughes went to a party for Theodore Roethke, the American poet whom Plath now ranked second only to Robert Lowell. Roethke extended to Hughes an open invitation to teach at the University of Washington, Roethke's longtime employer, whenever he liked. On the 5th, in response to a card from Anne Sexton, Plath wrote her that she admired *To Bedlam and Part Way Back*, the new book of Sexton's that Lowell had said would place her alongside Pasternak; that she was mother to a comedienne named Frieda, a child who had made Sylvia and Ted want to forge a dynasty; that she relished the reception her work had received in England; and that she had met Spender, MacNeice, Auden, Gunn, and, just this week, Roethke.

The next day, Plath miscarried. To comfort her, her doctor told her that one in four women did so; if she wanted to, she could also become pregnant again right away, he said. Still, Sylvia was saddened and depressed. To help cheer her up, Ted bought February 10 tickets for

Webster's *The Duchess of Malfi,* starring Dame Peggy Ashcroft. Plath herself tried to divert her thoughts from the incident by spending time with Frieda—and writing. In the days following her miscarriage, Plath turned out seven poems. The first, "Parliament Hill Fields," is spoken by a woman who has just lost a child—the word "miscarriage" is never used—but who finds solace in the fact that she has another child at home. Her grief over the dead child and her joy over the one who survives create a push-pull of emotions that colors all the narrator sees and does as she wanders through Parliament Hill Fields, a section of London's Hampstead Heath. Three days later, Plath wrote two poems, "Whitsun" and "Zoo Keeper's Wife," neither of which concerns babies or miscarriages. The next day, Plath finished "Face Lift," inspired by Dido's recent surgery. In the poem, a woman attempts to recapture her youth by submitting to cosmetic surgery. Whereas babies are mentioned only metaphorically in "Face Lift," the poem she wrote four days later, "Morning Song," directly addressed the issue of motherhood. Awakened by her baby's crying, the speaker gropes from bed, "cow-heavy and floral / In my Victorian nightgown," and heads for the child. Beautiful, simple, touching, "Morning Song" was Plath's—then—definitive statement on motherhood.

After "Morning Song," Plath wrote "Barren Women," which states flatly that a woman without a child is like an empty museum, and "Heavy Women," which implies that conceiving a child is almost a divine act. These two poems, and "Face Lift," seem directed at Olwyn and Dido, who were childless and—to Plath—manipulative. (Plath saw Dido's face-lift as a desperate ploy for Dido to keep Bill.) Because poems like "Barren Women" and "Face Lift" are indictments of their subjects, several of the February poems appear to have been triggered, on some level, by Olwyn's attack on Sylvia at Christmas. If Plath could not adequately defend herself in person, then she would get revenge in print. When Olwyn read "Barren Women" and other, similar poems, she could not deny the obvious: Plath was writing about women like *her.*

In February and March, more reviews of *The Colossus* appeared. In *The London Magazine,* Roy Fuller attacked Plath for echoing established poets. "The language of this poetry is unusual but not eccentric," Fuller wrote. "How excited we would be about Miss Plath if we—and she—had never read Mr Ransom and Miss Moore." Plath felt comforted, though, by Howard Sergeant's notice in the spring *English*. In a long piece on several books, Sergeant devoted two sentences to *The Colossus:* "Miss Plath . . . is unusually reserved and precise in *The Colossus*, withholding sufficient to create almost an air of mystery about her subjects, yet not too much to destroy the balance or the tension of the poems. Indeed, what few defects there are in this distinguished first volume are due more to her sudden descents into fantasy than to any failure of craftsmanship."

4

Plath read these reviews in a bed at Saint Pancras Hospital. Because the miscarriage had aggravated the soreness in the area of her appendix, Sylvia's doctor recommended that she have an operation right away. Sylvia baked extra food for Ted, who alone would take care of Frieda for the two weeks of Sylvia's hospitalization. Then, on February 26, the day the BBC rebroadcast the Hugheses' episode of "Two of a Kind" on the weekly roundup, which doubled their initial seventy-five-dollar fee, Plath checked into Saint Pancras. She expected to be operated on the next morning, but Monday came and went and she did not have surgery. Ted arrived on Monday night with an airmail letter containing the best remedy to brighten her mood: a *New Yorker* first-reading contract. By signing the enclosed document, the cover letter said, Plath would agree to submit each new poem she wrote to *The New Yorker* before she showed it to any other magazine. For this right to exclusivity, *The New Yorker* would pay her one hundred dollars—the check was included—on signing the agreement; 25 percent more for each poem the magazine purchased; a cost-of-living bonus for all work accepted; and an even more lucrative rate for work the editors considered exceptional. Overjoyed, Plath signed the contract, even if, as she told her mother, the point was moot: she mailed *The New Yorker* all of her work first anyway, with or without a contract.

Sylvia finally underwent surgery at eleven o'clock on Tuesday morning. After a nurse gave her a shot to dry up her saliva and make her drowsy, attendants wheeled her into an anteroom to receive a second shot, which blacked her out. She had no further memories until she awoke following the operation. For the rest of that day, drugged with painkillers, she dozed on and off. On Wednesday, considerably more alert, she sat up in bed, wrote letters, and observed the twenty-eight-bed ward. Over the next several days, Sylvia tried to cope with hospital living. She read Agatha Christie mysteries; admired the flowers that arrived from Ted, Ted's parents, Helga Huws, and Charles Monteith; and, beginning Friday, added to a diary she kept on the ward. Hospital food tasted flat to her, so Ted brought her one good meal each day— fresh orange juice, creamy milk, a steak sandwich. A week after surgery, on the day doctors removed her stitches, Sylvia felt better than she had in a year. The appendix had probably been poisoning her system for some time, she decided. Her condition had improved so much that doctors released her from the hospital on the 8th, earlier than expected.

At Chalcot Square, Sylvia continued to recover. Under strict doctor's orders, she rested in bed and refrained from lifting anything, no matter how light. The day's major outing was usually a short stroll on Primrose Hill. Soon, she felt a drive to write. On the 18th, in the Merwins' study, Plath wrote a poem on the back of pink Smith College memorandum stationery. Initially named "Sickroom Tulips in Hospital," she shortened the title to "Tulips" on the third draft. Employing long iambic lines and fat seven-line stanzas, she described a bouquet of red tulips in a hospital room from the point of view of a woman who is sick. For much of the poem, the speaker paints a picture of the setting—the doctors, the nurses, herself. Then, finally turning to the tulips, she sees them as a rival for her health.

On March 21, Sylvia's doctor examined her and reported that she was improving. A week later, Hughes received a letter from Lord David Cecil awarding him the Hawthornden Prize for *Lupercal*. The honor, which took the form of a gold medal and a one-hundred-pound cash prize, would be given to him at a public ceremony. On the 31st, three days after she wrote another poem, "I Am Vertical," *The New Statesman* published Plath's "Magi" on the same page as Roethke's "In Evening Air." All of this good fortune for the Hugheses was eclipsed by a letter from Judith Jones dated March 29. Knopf was interested in *The Colossus,* Jones told Plath. "One reason . . . that we have brooded so long over our decision is my uncertainty about one particular poem which seems frankly too derivative to me not to invite a good deal of criticism," Jones wrote. "['Poem for a Birthday' is] in terms of imagery and rhythmic structure . . . so close to Theodore Roethke's 'Lost Son' that people would be likely to pounce on you." If Plath would cut "Poem for a Birthday," Jones said, Knopf would accept *The Colossus.*

On April 5, Plath responded. She would drop five sections of "Poem for a Birthday" if Jones would let her print, as separate poems, "Flute Notes from a Reedy Pond" and "The Stones." Also, she wanted to run "The Stones" last, since the act of being "mended" seemed like an appropriate way to conclude her volume. Finally, because Plath admired Stanley Kunitz—who believed the manuscript should be cut considerably, Jones had told her—she would omit "Point Shirley," "Metaphors," "Maudlin," "Ouija," and "Two Sisters of Persephone." Hopeful, Plath mailed Jones the letter.

The following day, Faber and Faber officially released Hughes's *Meet My Folks!*—a book, illustrated by George Adamson, which he dedicated to Frieda. Over the coming weeks, because of excellent publicity and good reviews, the book sold well. Later that month, Plath sat in the audience of a live BBC television broadcast featuring Ted. With each passing month, Ted seemed to become more respected—and well known—among both the literary community and the general population of England. On April 26, in a letter to Alfred Kazin, Plath described Hughes as a famous man whose stories and poems appeared widely. Without mentioning her fame (or lack of it), Plath asked Kazin to recommend her for a Saxton grant. She was writing seven days a week, she told him, in a borrowed study down the street from her flat. The dust in the room was so thick you couldn't hear a pencil drop.

In late April, Jones answered Plath's letter about *The Colossus.* She agreed wholeheartedly with Plath's suggestions to end the book on "The Stones" and to cut "Metaphors," "Maudlin," "Ouija," and "Two Sisters." But instead of dropping "Point Shirley," Jones preferred that Plath eliminate either "The Ghost's Leavetaking" or "Black Rook in Rainy Weather." It was now, once she had read Jones's letter, that Plath realized Jones *was* going to offer her a contract. "ALFRED KNOPF will publish *The Colossus* in America!" Plath shouted on the page to her mother on May 1, adding that she had not told her before because she wanted to make sure the deal did not fall through. After all, Knopf had asked her to drop ten poems—to make a forty-poem book, she said. (Sylvia did not tell her mother half the cuts were made because "Poem for a Birthday" borrowed too heavily from Roethke.) To make sure that they did agree on the ten poems eliminated, Plath wrote back to Jones on May 2 to confirm that she would be happy to keep "Point Shirley" and drop "Black Rook in Rainy Weather."

Now, Plath's two May publications—*The Listener* printed "A Life," *The Observer* "Morning Song"—were that much more satisfying. In some way, Plath perhaps felt that she was even keeping pace with Hughes, who finished his first five-act play, *The Calm.* Knopf's acceptance encouraged her as she wrote each morning in the Merwins' study. For some weeks, she had been at work on a secret project—a novel. Its protagonist was a young girl who has a nervous breakdown one summer after she exhausts herself holding down a guest editorship at a *Mademoiselle*-like magazine in New York. Following the breakdown, which culminates in a failed suicide attempt, the young character, who would eventually be named Esther Greenwood and who feels more than passing anxiety about her confused romantic situation with her boyfriend, Buddy Willard, is confined to a mental hospital and subjected to a series of electroshock treatments. Familiar territory for Plath—maybe *too* familiar. She told few people about the book. One was Ann Davidow. She was about a third of the way through a novel concerning a college coed approaching and then enduring a nervous breakdown, Plath wrote to Davidow in April, but she did not go into detail.

In early June, Hughes was awarded the Hawthornden Prize. Since custom dictated that the previous year's winner attend the public ceremony, Alan Sillitoe, the British novelist best known for *The Loneliness of the Long Distance Runner* and *Saturday Night and Sunday Morning*, was also present. Like Hughes, Sillitoe was married to an American poet, Ruth Fainlight, who was there as well. Plath enjoyed meeting them both, especially Fainlight.

The day before the Hawthornden ceremony, Plath recorded a twenty-five-minute reading of her poems for "The Living Poet," a monthly BBC series that in the past had featured, among others, Lowell, Roethke, and Kunitz. Also in June, Plath published "You're" in *Harper's* and "I Am Vertical" and "Private Ground" in *The Critical Quarterly*. In that same *Critical Quarterly*, A. E. Dyson reviewed the Heinemann *Colossus*. Criticizing Plath for being "reminiscent" of Roethke and—curiously—Ted Hughes, Dyson ultimately offered the book high praise. "*The Colossus* is a volume that those who care for literature will wish to buy and return to from time to time for that deepening acquaintance which is one of the rewards of the truest poetry. It establishes Miss Plath among the best of the poets now claiming our attention; the most compelling feminine voice, certainly, that we have heard for many a day." Finally, after a drought of critical attention, Plath was receiving *some*, though not so much as she would have liked.

For Sylvia, June's major event was the arrival in London of Aurelia, who had been planning for some time to come visit. Nothing could have prepared Aurelia for the joy she felt at holding Frieda for the first time. Sylvia was, of course, happy to see her mother. Two years had passed since Ted and Sylvia's departure for England, so they had much to catch up on. First, though, Sylvia and Ted would take a short vacation. With Aurelia there to baby-sit, they set out for France. Their initial stop was Douarnenez, a fishing port in Finisterre from which they could explore rocky terrain and swim in the Atlantic Ocean. The stay proved restful and reinvigorating. So, on July 5, tanned from hours of sunbathing and more relaxed than they had been in months, Ted and

Sylvia traveled to the Merwins' farm in Par Bretenoux. There they ate generous portions of the Merwins' home-grown produce, continued to relax, and generally enjoyed life on a working farm. On Friday the 14th, after a week in the country, Sylvia and Ted returned to London; they arrived at Chalcot Square in time to eat supper, which Aurelia had prepared. Over the weekend, as Sylvia visited with her mother, who moved into the Merwins' flat now that Ted and Sylvia were back, they spoke of Plath and Hughes's BBC work, their current writing projects (Sylvia alluded to a novel but gave no details), and, of course, Warren, who hoped to come see Sylvia in the fall.

On July 17, Plath read "Tulips" live over the BBC from the Mermaid Theatre, the site of a festival. The next day, Sylvia and Ted, accompanied by both Frieda and Aurelia, made the seven-hour trip from London to Yorkshire in a new Morris station wagon they had bought. They passed through what Aurelia would call some of the "ugliest cities in the world" to arrive at The Beacon. Sylvia introduced her mother to Ted's parents, and the three of them hit it off—a good sign, since bad feelings still existed between Sylvia and her in-laws because of Olwyn's scene at Christmas. Aurelia wrote Warren that the Hugheses even "exceed[ed her] most optimistic expectations." During the next week, Aurelia and Sylvia chatted with the Hugheses, played with Frieda, and took a side trip to West Riding. On the 26th, the four of them—Ted, Sylvia, Aurelia, Frieda—went back to London, whereupon Plath discovered in the mail a letter informing her that she had won first prize in the Cheltenham Festival.

Ted and Sylvia stayed in London only one night. The next morning, they drove for five hours to Devon, where they would look for a house to buy. They had reached the end of their patience with the tiny Chalcot Square flat. They needed space: studies for Ted and for Sylvia, and more room for Frieda to play. With the prices in London prohibitively high, they could only afford to buy a house in the country. The arrangement would *not* be ideal. Sylvia loved the cultural activities and amenities in the city. Nor did she relish the idea of moving to the boondocks now that her career seemed to be gathering some momentum. Yet if she wanted a home—and she did—she had little choice.

Anyway, Ted wished to live in the country again (or so he said), far away from the city's distractions.

On Friday at midnight, after they had looked at eight houses, only one of which was a possibility, Plath and Hughes drove back to London. That one potentially suitable estate, Court Green, was located in North Tawton, which was one hour by car from Exeter or from the coast. A typical Devon hamlet, North Tawton consisted of little more than a main street lined with shops and pubs around which a few houses had been built through the years. Surrounding the town in all directions was a lush countryside divided, usually by hedgerows, into pastures, where sheep and cattle grazed. Going into and out of town, a visitor traveled along a narrow two-lane road, also lined with hedgerows. Situated in North Tawton itself, Court Green, currently owned by a titled couple named Arundel, was comprised of three acres of land on which sat a two-story, twelve-room thatched-roof house, a two-room servants' cottage off the main house's cobblestone court, and stables. All structures desperately needed major repairs, just as the grounds, which featured a seventy-two-tree apple orchard, cherry trees, and blackberry and raspberry bushes, begged tending. Life in North Tawton would be the antithesis of the Hugheses' life in London, since in the town, essentially a farm community, they would be landowners. Their nights at cocktail parties and suppers at the homes of such literary figures as T. S. Eliot and Stephen Spender would be replaced by early mornings of potato-digging and strawberry-picking. So, Court Green's price would have to be right before the Hugheses would consider such a drastic move.

When Aurelia left London for America on August 4, Sylvia and Ted had not made a commitment. Soon afterwards, the Arundels presented them with a price—thirty-six hundred pounds (about ten thousand dollars)—that the Hugheses decided was too good to pass up. Sylvia mailed the Arundels, as a deposit to hold the property, a check in the amount of 10 percent of the asking price. Then, because they did not want to pay what Sylvia considered to be an astronomical interest rate—6.5 percent—they set about accumulating cash. They withdrew all of the nearly six thousand dollars from their savings account in

Boston; borrowed interest-free five hundred pounds (about fourteen hundred dollars) each from Aurelia and Ted's parents, which they promised to repay through $280 reimbursements made every September; and took out a small bank loan to cover the difference. This way, they could essentially pay cash for Court Green, into which they wanted to move by the end of August.

On August 16, Plath signed a contract with Knopf for *The Colossus*. Two days later, almost ten months after the book's publication, the *Times Literary Supplement* reviewed the Heinemann *Colossus*. "Miss Plath tends to be elusive and private . . . , as if what the poem were 'about' in a prose sense were very much her own business," wrote the anonymous critic in a piece entitled "Innocence and Experience." "Thus this first volume is a stimulating one but also, combining as it does fine surface clarities with a deeper riddling quality, it is a teasing one."

The most dramatic development in Plath's life during this time took place at mid-month, when her doctor informed her that, for the third time in two years, she was pregnant. In some way, for Sylvia, this seemed to compensate for her miscarriage. She only hoped that nothing would go wrong with this pregnancy, due to reach full term around the first of the year.

Before they could move to Devon, the Hugheses had to sublet their flat. Because of London's housing shortage, they did not expect trouble, yet they were still somewhat surprised by the eight calls they received on the first day the newspaper ran their listing. Of those eight parties interested, two couples stopped by at the same time, and both wanted the flat badly enough to pay the $280 fee for "fixtures and fittings" which Plath and Hughes were asking. One couple immediately wrote out a check, but Ted and Sylvia liked the other couple better. That night, the Hugheses called the first couple and told them that they had decided to remain in London. Next, they called the second couple, "a young Canadian poet" and his wife, a "German-Russian," as Plath wrote her mother, and gave the flat to them. The Hugheses also asked them to supper the following week. Though the poet, David Wevill, was by no means as famous as Ted Hughes or Sylvia Plath, he had published poems in numerous literary magazines. His wife, Assia Gutmann, was a woman whose beautiful elegant face more than compensated for what one friend remembers as "hips like the rear end of a 158 bus." Wevill was her third husband.

5

On August 31, 1961, the Hugheses moved from London to Court Green. For one hundred dollars, they hired movers, which they needed, since Sylvia, four months pregnant, could not lift boxes or carry furniture. As they settled into the house during their first days there, Ted and Sylvia spent little time out of doors, although Sylvia did pick some fruit and vegetables and visit her neighbors Rose and Percy Key, who lived at the end of Court Green's driveway. In the middle of their move-in, Sylvia and Ted welcomed their first houseguest on September 9—Warren. Thrilled to see him in England for the first time, Sylvia showed Warren Devon—when, that is, Warren was not helping Ted rearrange furniture or make repairs around the house. Sylvia and Warren, sometimes joined by Ted, explored the Exeter Cathedral, picnicked at Tintagel, attended an auction, and ate at the local inn. As expected, Warren left by train on the morning of the 15th.

No sooner was Warren gone than Helder and Suzette Macedo, a pleasant Portuguese couple the Hugheses knew from London, arrived for a weekend visit. When they left, Plath established a regular schedule: she wrote in the mornings while Ted minded Frieda, minded Frieda in the afternoons while Ted wrote, and cooked supper before an evening of reading and rest. Since March, Plath had written only a handful of poems: "Insomniac," "Widow," "Stars over the Dordogne," and "The Rival." But in North Tawton, in September alone, she would produce four substantial poems. After finishing "Wuthering Heights," a poem in which the narrator identifies the difference between herself and the moors by depicting her body as "the one upright / Among all horizontals," Plath continued her examination of the subject—man in nature—by writing "Blackberrying." The poem, one of Plath's best, documents the narrator's movement down a lane lined by blackberry bushes so laden with berries that she can pick them at random. (During Warren's visit, Sylvia and he had picked blackberries on a lane similar to the one Plath describes in the poem.) As she reaches the end of the lane, she walks between two small hills until she arrives at the edge of a cliff overlooking the ocean. And there the poem ends. For one of the first times, Plath fused the movement of the poem's character with the movement of the language itself. The narrator of "Blackberrying" is finally in awe of the landscape, its richness and dominance. The poem's success lies in Plath's ability to summon the language to convey that awe to the reader.

Life at Court Green, like life in London, was demanding for the Hugheses. Plath was assisted in her domestic chores by Nancy Axworthy, Lady Arundel's maid, who for one dollar per day ironed and cleaned two days a week. Dr. Webb lived three houses up the road, and Plath, her pregnancy beginning to show, regularly consulted with him and his midwife, Winifred Davies. At this time, Plath heard from her agent: she had finally sold one of Plath's short stories to a women's magazine in London. Hughes too kept busy, driving thirty-five miles on four separate occasions to the BBC studios in Plymouth to record shows for "Women's Hour." He also finished a play for "Third Programme" and wrote a series of assignments for the *Times'* "Children Pages."

By October, the Hugheses had settled into a productive routine. In that month, Plath solicited each of the magazines that had printed her poems to secure permission for Knopf to reprint them; wrote Judith Jones to ask her to include in *The Colossus*'s acknowledgments Elizabeth Ames and Yaddo, where many of the poems had been written; and began attending, along with Rose and Percy Key, the neighborhood Anglican church. But each morning, regardless of what she did in the afternoon, Plath wrote in her study. The month's most successful poem, "The Moon and the Yew Tree," started as an exercise given to her by Ted, who suggested that she write a poem about a yew tree that stood near the house. Ted continued to exert an influence over Plath's creative life. As she tapped into her subconscious through mental exercises which Ted showed her how to do (one of his favorites involved free-associating on a particular object, like a yew tree), she opened herself up to write more innovative—and better—poetry.

Plath finished three other poems in October. Towards the end of the month, however, a flurry of activities hampered her writing. She submitted to James Michie a draft of *The Bell Jar*, the novel she had just finished. *Poetry* accepted five of her new poems. Then, after celebrating her birthday on the 27th, she took the train into London on the 31st for a three-day, two-night trip during which she stayed with the Sillitoes. Her first evening there, she attended the Guinness ceremonies at Goldsmith's Hall, where she accepted her seventy-five-pound prize and read her poem. The next day, she met with a women's-magazine fiction editor who encouraged her to write more magazine fiction. Next, because the Hugheses felt they needed every penny they could earn, Plath dropped off her original manuscript of *The Colossus* to the bookdealer who had recently sold two of Ted's original manuscripts to Indiana University. Finally, that evening, Plath saw two one-act plays, *The American Dream* and *The Death of Bessie Smith*, written by the young experimental American playwright Edward Albee. On the afternoon of November 2, Ted and Frieda met Sylvia at the Exeter train station and drove her back to Court Green.

In November, Plath could hardly keep up with her career. Early in the month, *The New Yorker* bought "Blackberrying"; *The New Statesman* published her review of three children's books, *The Observer* her poem "Sleep in the Mojave Desert." On the 9th, she opened a letter from the Eugene F. Saxton Foundation telling her that she had won a two-thousand-dollar grant. Previously, the selection committee had turned down Plath's application in the field of poetry; this time, Plath had applied in fiction—and won. She would receive the first of four quarterly payments in about two weeks. To reassure her mother that she would feel no pressure to crank out a novel just to fulfill the grant guidelines, Sylvia revealed that she had already completed a "batch of stuff" that was "tied . . . up in four parcels" and ready to be mailed to the Saxton "bit by bit as required." In fact, *The Bell Jar* was much more than a "batch of stuff." Michie had now accepted it at Heinemann. So, when William Koshland, of Knopf, wrote to Elizabeth Anderson, of Heinemann, to ask about a Plath novel (in *The New York Times'* announcement of Saxton winners, Plath's project was listed as a novel), Anderson told Koshland that Plath's novel was forthcoming. But, she added, Koshland needed to know something. Concerned that the novel, which might be read as autobiographical, could anger family and friends, since some characters were based—very loosely—on living people, Plath had decided to play it safe and release the novel under a pseudonym.

In December, Plath realized just how bad winter in Devon would be. The enormous two-story house, seemingly as big as a castle now that winter approached, remained next to impossible to heat, even after the Hugheses installed space heaters. The temperature in unheated rooms hovered around thirty-eight degrees, in heated rooms fifty-five. Still, Plath put up a strong front, though she had always been depressed by the cold. On the 18th, she told her mother that, because the Maugham committee did not want its prize money back (Ted had never taken the three-month trip abroad demanded of him), she would pay off their six-hundred-pound bank mortgage and save them, as she put it, a substantial amount in interest. Eleven days later, she wrote her mother again, this time to describe their Christmas tree and to congratulate Warren on his engagement to his girlfriend, Margaret Wetzel. In the letter, Sylvia also recalled their Christmas Day at Court Green. Before she spent the morning preparing a turkey dinner and her evening sitting beside a fire raging in one of their fireplaces, Sylvia and Ted had taken Frieda into the living room to see their Christmas tree for the first time. How her little face had blossomed with delight as she gazed up at those sparkling ornaments—the silver birds, the tinsel!

6

The first mild contraction hit at four in the morning, early on January 17, 1962. By eight-thirty, contractions came some five minutes apart—sufficient reason for Ted to call Winifred Davies. Soon Davies showed up with a cylinder of air and gas, which Sylvia breathed through a mask during particularly strong contractions. The day wore on. With Ted sitting by her side, Sylvia endured the afternoon and early evening. Finally, when Sylvia had been in labor for eighteen hours, Davies became concerned and called Dr. Webb, who arrived at Court Green at five minutes before midnight, just in time to see, as Sylvia later wrote her mother, "this great bluish, glistening boy sho[o]t out onto the bed in a tidal wave of water that drenched all four of us to the skin, howling lustily." Immediately Sylvia sat up in bed, anxious to hold her baby. Weighing a hefty nine pounds eleven ounces, the boy had dark features—black eyes, black hair. Studying him, Sylvia decided that he bore an uncanny resemblance to Ted. Even so, Sylvia, who beamed with delight, saw that Ted responded to his son's birth in a peculiar way: for some reason, he did not appear to be pleased that the baby was a boy.

Over the coming days, Sylvia tried to rest, although the baby, whom she and Ted named Nicholas Farrar, often woke her up with his crying. So he would be fresh to care for Frieda during the day, Ted slept in his and Sylvia's bedroom alone while Sylvia moved to the guest room, Nicholas in a carry-cot beside her. Because of this arrangement, whenever Nicholas cried, Sylvia awoke instantly. Winifred Davies stopped by regularly to check on Nicholas; she always made sure to involve Frieda in the examinations so that she would not feel neglected. Neighbors also visited, among them Rose Key, who brought Nicholas a knitted suit. On the 24th, Sylvia spent her first whole day out of bed, only napping in the afternoon. Then she came down with a serious case of milk fever, which required additional bed rest and penicillin.

Plath needed to regain her strength quickly, for she had work to do. In January, Judith Jones informed her that *The Colossus* would be published in April, probably on the 23rd; she would be receiving page proofs in the last week of January. Meanwhile, *The Critical Quarterly* released the anthology Plath had edited; because of good reviews, it sold well. Finally, late in the month, *The Observer* published "The Rival," *The New Yorker* mailed her two checks for cost-of-living adjustments, and she and Hughes received notification that their work would be included in *New Poets of England and America*, Meridian Books' forthcoming contemporary-poetry anthology. Relatively satisfied with her professional life, Plath had only one true worry: Nicholas. Specifically, she felt troubled that, as the days passed following Nicholas's birth, Ted's dissatisfaction over the baby's sex seemed to increase. Ted appeared much more standoffish with Nicholas than he had been with Frieda, uneasy even about holding or cuddling him. Ted's coldness towards Nicholas so bothered Sylvia that, while showing him off to her neighbor Mrs. Hamilton on Nicholas's first day out of the house, Sylvia confided that Ted appeared "reluctant" the baby was a boy. Mrs. Hamilton, a gray-haired woman who was followed about by an old dachshund named Pixie, replied stoically that Ted was probably jealous for Frieda.

In February, *The London Magazine* ran Plath's "In Plaster" with Hughes's "Still Life." In that same issue, the editors published a selection of comments by contemporary poets on the day's vital literary and social issues. Each contributing poet wrote a fifteen-hundred-word *ars poetica*, and the editors grouped these under the title "Context." Both Plath and Hughes presented commentaries they had written back in the fall. Hughes tried to explain how poets grow as artists—or, rather, fail to grow, having burned out in youth. He did not seem to recognize that he was possibly writing about himself—and Plath. "The poet's only hope is to be infinitely sensitive to what his gift is," Hughes wrote, "and this in itself seems to be another gift that few poets possess. According to this sensitivity, and to his faith in it, he will go on developing as a poet, as Yeats did, pursuing those adventures, mental, spritual and physical, whatever they may be, that his gift wants, or he will lose its guidance, lose the feel of its touch in the workings of his mind, and soon be absorbed by the impersonal dead lumber of matter in which his gift has no interest, which is a form of suicide, metaphorical in the case of Wordsworth and Coleridge, actual in the case of Mayakovsky."

In a reflection of her political sensibilities not unlike those which she displayed when she implored her mother to vote Kennedy, not Nixon, Plath set out in her essay to pinpoint recent political trends that most affected her thinking. "The issues of our time which preoccupy me at the moment," Plath wrote, "are the incalculable genetic effects of fallout and the documentary article on the terrifying, mad, omni-

271 · E N G L A N D

potent marriage of big business and the military in America"—"Juggernaut, The Warfare State" by Fredrick J. Cook, published in *The Nation*. Did this have an impact on her work? In a manner of speaking. Her poems did not directly address Hiroshima, she said, but "a child forming itself finger by finger in the dark." They did not address world annihilation, but "the moon over a yew tree in a neighboring graveyard." They did not concern "the testaments of tortured Algerians, but . . . the night thoughts of a tired surgeon." Then, once she had listed the poets who delighted her—Lowell in *Life Studies*, Roethke in his greenhouse poems, Elizabeth Bishop on occasion, Stevie Smith almost all the time—Plath commented on the importance of the craft of poetry. "I am not worried that poems reach relatively few people. As it is, they go surprisingly far—among strangers, around the world, even. Farther than the words of a classroom teacher or the prescriptions of a doctor; if they are very lucky, farther than a lifetime."

Eighteen months after the release of the Heinemann *Colossus*, the *Sewanee Review* finally ran a review of the book, written by Lucas Myers. Stating that "there is not an imperfectly finished poem" in the volume and that he was "struck . . . by her posture vis-à-vis her material, which is one of considerable objectivity, even when the material is her childhood, her Muses, her pregnancy," Myers wrote:

> Poems should be criticized as they are, not as the critic thinks they might have been, and these poems, as they are, merit anybody's reading; but I can not help wondering what will happen if, in Miss Plath's second volume of poems, the emotional distance is shortened—no melting of the moulds her craftsmanship has created, I think, but a lesser frequency of phrases like "Now, this particular girl," "Mark, I cry," "gimcrack relics," and more of the pressure of "Lorelei," of the close of "The Colossus," or of "Departure," which is an example of her finest writing.

More than one critic had commented on the distance that Plath kept between herself and her subject matter. Ted too, by hypnotizing her and continuing to insist that she try mental warm-up exercises, had hoped to produce greater spontaneity in her poetry. Hughes's efforts seemed to be working. Her best recent poems had been, in point of view, more subjective, less distanced. In March, when she had recovered from Nicholas's birth enough to begin writing in her study two hours each morning, Plath decided to undertake a piece spoken by invented characters who address subjects about which she knew much—pregnancy, miscarriage, childbirth. Set in a maternity ward and featuring three unnamed women, the piece, a radio play titled *Three Women* written for the BBC's "Third Programme" at the request of Douglas Cleverdon, Ted's producer, and inspired by the Bergman film, was subtitled *A Poem for Three Voices*.

When Plath and Hughes were not writing in March, their lives progressed at a fairly quiet pace. Ted gardened, Sylvia started horseback-riding lessons at one of the local stables, and the two of them decided that both children should be baptized on March 25. Plath approved of this even though she had stopped attending the town church. One Sunday, the minister had told the congregation that Christians, unlike those "educated pagans" who feared dying, should be *happy* about the atomic bomb, for it was a sign of the Second Coming. If she were back in Wellesley, she would still worship at the Unitarian church, Sylvia told her mother. She was not, so she would send the children to the town church's Sunday school but not attend the church herself.

In April, Plath filled her afternoons with domestic duties. Since the weather had now turned nice, she spent hours out of doors, often picking daffodils from Court Green's massive flower beds. Each week during April, she and Ted gathered from six hundred to a thousand daffodils to sell through a local market. When not outside, Plath helped Ted oversee workmen who were covering the house's concrete floors with linoleum; was interviewed at home for a BBC series on Americans who came to England and did not leave; and greeted or planned for guests. Ted's Aunt Hilda and Cousin Vicky drove down for Easter, although they did not bring Ted's parents—a surprise.

These were her afternoons; her mornings, she wrote. Now that Nicholas slept through the night, Plath did too, so she could rise at six o'clock and write for at least four hours without interruption. She began

April by producing "Little Fugue," another poem about "my" father, the first to tackle head-on the subject of his death. As the poem's narrator remembers the father's blue eyes and one leg, she also recalls his death when she was seven. In his absence, all she can do is try to get by. On the 4th, Plath wrote first "An Appearance," then "Crossing the Water." A poem that describes two people rowing a boat across a lake at night, "Crossing the Water" is reminiscent of "Wuthering Heights" and "Blackberrying" in that it portrays a character's response to a memorable landscape. The next morning, Plath wrote "Among the Narcissi," a poem in which the narrator observes an octogenarian named Percy who, recovering from an operation, stands in his garden. Though the poem grew from fact (Plath's neighbor, Percy Key, who had recently undergone surgery on his lung, did often stand among his narcissi), it addresses, on a larger level, the contradictory nature of life by depicting the image of a dying man engulfed by the bright, lively flowers. Her next poem, "Pheasant," was inspired by an image as well—a pheasant standing on a hill—but the effort finally lacks the linguistic energy that her best poems now possessed.

Not true her poem of the 19th—"Elm." Based on a fragment she had written previously, the poem uses as its focus an elm tree not unlike the wych-elm near the cemetery next door to Court Green. The poem's elm, however, is hardly real, for "Elm" is a monologue whose metaphorical strategy is so precise that the elm speaking is at the same time equivalent to a woman speaking. And it is through this voice, these synchronous voices, that the emotional power of the poem emerges. The speaker discovers herself in a love affair that is ending; she expresses her mental state through a sort of maniacal longing. After she describes her strained frame of mind, the poem's narrator confesses that she is searching desperately for someone to love. Because of this hysteria, she realizes that some deadly force within her has been triggered into action by this loss of love. The disintegration of love, the poem says, is a sure death warrant for the speaker. The poem's language may be subtle in its clarity, but its meaning is painfully obvious. Love, or the absence of love, destroys.

"Elm" is a powerful, urgent statement spoken by a narrator who has been abandoned by the person she loves. As far as Plath knew, Ted was not drifting away from her. On the surface, their marriage appeared to be as stable as ever. But over the next several weeks events would unfold that would prove that Hughes's affection for Plath was not nearly as strong as she had hoped.

The summer of 1962 would be a long, bitter season.

The Bitter Season

1

When they were not fixing up Court Green, watching the children, or writing, the Hugheses spent much of the early spring planting a huge vegetable garden, since they hoped to live the next year off the food they would grow. Each also anticipated the release of a book: Plath awaited the Knopf *Colossus*, Hughes his Faber and Faber *Selected Poems*. (He would share the volume with Thom Gunn, as each poet was too young for a "selected" of his own.) In early May, the Hugheses interrupted their busy routine to host the Sillitoes, down from London. During the brief visit, Plath and Fainlight often left their husbands, who entertained themselves, and engaged in long, absorbing conversations—in the morning over coffee at the kitchen table before Plath retired to her study to write, in the afternoon during tea, at dusk while they sat outside beside the flower garden. The two women had always enjoyed one another's company, but now they felt closer, perhaps because each had recently given birth to a boy. They talked about their newborn sons, although they touched on other subjects as well—Plath's horseback-riding lessons, London friends, and, most often, of course, poetry.

One morning, after they had breastfed their babies, Fainlight described her recent poems and Plath read aloud her newest one, "Elm." After Plath finished, Fainlight was overwhelmed. Moved by the poem's haunting sentiments and impressed by Plath's skillful use of language, Fainlight raved. Plath did not comment. She merely put the poem away, and they carried on their conversation. When the Sillitoes were leaving, though, Plath told Fainlight that, because she liked the poem so much, she was dedicating "Elm" to her.

Following the Sillitoes' visit, the Hugheses resumed their normal schedule. They wrote—Ted poems, Sylvia a *New Statesman* review of four books written for or about children—and they had lunch one day with Elizabeth and David Compton. Later in the month, they received more houseguests. On May 14, Sylvia wrote to her mother that, on the coming weekend, she and Ted would entertain the "nice young Canadian poet"—David Wevill—and his "attractive, intelligent wife"— Assia Gutmann: the couple subletting Chalcot Square. From all indications, Plath eagerly awaited the Wevills. She did not feel the same way, however, about the trip to Court Green that Ted's family had planned for the first part of June. Since Ted's mother, Edith, in Sylvia's eyes, did little to help out around the house (Sylvia described her to Aurelia as a lazy woman who lay in bed until noon), Sylvia had to assume the burden of cooking and cleaning not only for her family but for her guests. Besides, because of the scene with Olwyn, Sylvia still felt awkward around the Hugheses.

As expected, David and Assia arrived on Friday. Like Ted, Sylvia had always been drawn to the Wevills, whom she considered exceptionally bright and energetic. They were certain to realize their dreams, she thought: David worked hard to develop as a poet and Assia, at present employed by an advertising agency, hoped to become a poet too, or possibly a translator. Early in the weekend, the two couples talked about the Hugheses' new home, the London literary scene, and poetry in general. Yet as the weekend progressed, an odd chemistry formed between Ted and Assia: their interaction began to take on obvious sexual overtones. This should not have been surprising. Ted had been the object of women's flirtations in the past (Sylvia could not forget the anonymous girls at Smith), and Assia—a beautiful if thick-waisted woman who disguised her figure by wearing long, flowing coats—had the reputation of having affairs, especially with poets. Her marriage to Wevill had evolved out of an affair the two had started while Assia was married to another man.

Strong-willed and determined, Assia—apparently—made the first move with Ted. On one morning of the Wevills' stay, as Sylvia would later contend, Assia came downstairs to discover Ted sitting alone at the kitchen table drinking a cup of coffee. Creeping up behind him, she lifted her nightgown to her chin, released it to flutter down over his face and torso, and trapped him inside the nightgown with her. Though Plath never saw anything so flagrant as Ted and Assia strait-jacketed in her nightgown together, she did pick up on unmistakable clues—a prolonged glance, a subtle body gesture, a suggestive insin-uation. Nevertheless, she did nothing.

In person, that is. On Monday after the Wevills left, Plath locked herself in her study and wrote "Event" and "The Rabbit Catcher," poems that deal with dying relationships. In the brief slice of life captured in "Event," one learns that the narrator's mental, even phys-ical, well-being depends upon love—above all else. The loss of love, the poem implies, impairs. "The Rabbit Catcher" also deals with a couple's strained romance. At the end, the narrator reveals that the "we" of the poem are in a relationship so confining that it is killing her. The poem's stifling tone paralleled the anxiety Plath experienced, now that, once again, a source of tension had emerged between her and Ted. When the marriage that is supposed to be perfect—made in heaven, as she once called it—begins to break up, the disintegration becomes magnified many times over. At the moment, Plath was reacting to her perception of trouble in her marriage on nothing more than hunches. The concrete evidence would come soon enough, although one piece, about which Plath did not yet know, had already occurred. On the day the Wevills left Court Green, Ted had sneaked to Assia a private note: "I must see you tomorrow in London."

After delaying the book in April, Alfred A. Knopf finally released *The Colossus and Other Poems* officially on May 14. With the deletions Plath and Jones had made, the volume contained forty poems, a size with which Plath was genuinely pleased. When Heinemann had brought out the book in England, *The Colossus* had, if nothing else, been reviewed by the major periodicals, even if it took six months or longer for some of the notices to appear and, once they did, they were not so unqualified as Plath would have hoped. But the reception of *The*

Colossus in America was drastically worse than imagined by either Plath or the Knopf staff, who, according to in-house routing sheets, had expected to sell one thousand copies of the book.

In May, June, July, and August, only one review appeared—in *Library Journal*. In August, *The Christian Science Monitor* and the New York *Herald Tribune* mentioned the book briefly in round-up pieces. Eventually, in the fall, three more notices appeared—in the *Kenyon Review*, *The Hudson Review*, and the Charleston *Miscellany*. That, however, would be it. *The Colossus* was never reviewed in *The New York Times*, *The New York Times Book Review*, or any other major city newspaper—not the Chicago papers, the Washington *Post*, the Los Angeles *Times*, not even—and this was most surprising—Plath's hometown newspapers, the Boston *Herald* or *Globe*.

Plath had worked hard on *The Colossus*, which had gone through draft after draft. Had she wasted all the years she spent writing these poems? With the prospect of receiving no fame and no money from the book, now out in both England and America, Plath could not help concluding that she probably *had* wasted her time. *The Colossus*'s reception was a blow to Plath—one of many, as it turned out, that she endured in the summer and fall of 1962.

2

During the first week in June, Ted's family arrived in Devon. His mother, father, and Uncle Walt remained six days in all; Edith spent the nights at Court Green, while Ted's father and uncle lodged in the village, at the Burton Hall Hotel. This was a pleasant visit, marked by long conversations about family matters, suppers out (four in six days, which solved the problem of Plath's having to cook for her company), and drives through the countryside in the Morris. Plath had prepared herself for a bad jolt, but it did not transpire: no one brought up Olwyn. Still, Plath felt relieved when the Hugheses were gone; in fact, she seemed almost content. For the first time in months, she tried to appreciate life's simple things. She coddled her babies, read books, and strolled through the countryside. As of June 7, she had not been in her study for three days; during her writing time, she had weeded her garden instead. "This is the richest and happiest time of my life," Plath wrote to her mother. One reason for her happiness, Sylvia implied, was Ted's success. His first two poetry collections had brought him respect and adulation in the literary community; his children's book and BBC broadcasts had expanded his popularity. Already, at the young age of thirty-one, he ranked the release of a "selected" poems (though shared with Gunn), which Faber had published on May 18. In fact, Hughes now wielded so much power that on his recommendation alone, a whole career could be made—or resurrected. He had proved his clout in late May by broadcasting over the BBC a radio show on Keith Douglas, a British poet killed at age twenty-four in Normandy during World War II. "Keith Douglas was born in 1920," Hughes stated in his prepared text. "By the time he was killed . . . in 1944, he had produced what is to my mind a more inexhaustibly interesting body of poetry than any one of his generation has produced since, in England or America." On the basis of Hughes's single broadcast, Faber decided, provided that Hughes would write an introduction, to issue a "selected" edition of Douglas's poems, much to the delight of Douglas's impoverished mother, who wrote Hughes to thank him.

Before long, Plath returned to her study. If critics and readers were going to ignore *The Colossus*, then she would just write poems so startling, so innovative, that they could *not* be overlooked. She began to consider a new, ambitious poem, "Berck-Plage." She would draw much of her inspiration for the poem from the Devon landscape, she decided, which occupied her mind a great deal these days. In her recent letters to her mother, Plath had lingered on descriptions of the local countryside (she loved the laburnums and the orchard of blossoming apple trees) and told her at one point that she longed to see Court Green "through your eyes." She was referring to Aurelia's upcoming six-week vacation to England, which had her arriving in Devon during the third week in June.

Before that, Sylvia saw Alvarez, who, with his American friend John Nesselhof, stopped at Court Green briefly on his way from London to Cornwall over the Whitsun weekend. Instantly, Alvarez recognized a change in Plath. The move to the country and Nicholas's birth seemed to have produced in her a new confidence and fulfillment. But there was something else. "I'm writing again," Plath told Alvarez privately. "Really writing. I'd like you to see some of the new poems." She *was* writing too. After producing little poetry between October 1961 and February 1962, Plath had written, in March, the lovely and strange *Three Women;* in April, six poems, including "Elm" and "Crossing the Water"; in May, three shorter poems. Now, in June, she was working on "Berck-Plage." Happy for her success, Alvarez told her to send some of her recent work to *The Observer*. (When she did, he accepted "Crossing the Water.")

Alvarez made another observation. "No longer quiet and withheld, a housewifely appendage to a powerful husband, she seemed made solid and complete, her own woman again," Alvarez would write. "Since [theirs] appeared to be a strong, close marriage, I supposed [Ted] was unconcerned that the balance of power had shifted for the time being to [Sylvia]." Mistaking Plath's false security for true strength, Alvarez never guessed that she and Ted were drifting apart. Like Fainlight before him, Alvarez had been taken in by Plath's apparent joy. He had believed what Plath had *wanted* him to believe—that all was well, even blissful—not what was actually occurring.

Recently, Sylvia and Ted had gone to a town meeting of beekeepers. At it, they wore masks and watched a Mr. Pollard make three hives out of one by transferring queen cells. Because of the meeting, Plath ordered some Italian hybrid bees, which Pollard delivered to Court Green on the 15th. Even though Pollard placed the box out in the orchard, well away from the house, in the days following the installation the bees swarmed Ted, stinging him six times. Ted was still nursing his bee stings on June 21, when Aurelia arrived in Devon, after flying from Boston to London and taking the train south from there. Sylvia, Ted, and both children greeted her at the train station and drove her to Court Green in the Morris. Aurelia would later recall her early hours in North Tawton. "The welcome I received when I arrived . . . was heartwarming. The threshold to the guest room I was to occupy had an enameled pink heart and a garland of flowers painted on it. Frieda recognized me; 'Baby Nick' "—whom she had never seen—"went happily into my arms."

Over the next day or so, Aurelia settled in. She and Sylvia played with the children, wandered Court Green's grounds, and talked about Warren and Margaret's wedding, which Sylvia had missed on June 2. Sylvia spoke passionately about how, at that moment in her life, she had everything—beautiful children, a successful husband, a nice home (or it would be eventually), and her own career. But while Aurelia listened to her daughter's monologues, she could not help thinking that, below the illusion of bliss which she projected, Sylvia was worried and depressed. Aurelia's suspicions resulted from the "tension," as she called it, between Ted and Sylvia. Although she recognized this from the start, she did not confront Sylvia. After all, to hear Sylvia talk, life was perfect.

The first real blow of the summer came in late June. While Aurelia kept the babies at Court Green, Sylvia and Ted traveled by train into London to record appearances for the BBC, Hughes for "Children's School Hour" and Plath for "The World of Books." In London, Sylvia telephoned home to check with her mother. When she did, she learned that what she and Ted had feared before they left had occurred: their neighbor, Percy Key, had died (on the night of the 25th). Lately, Percy had appeared to be giving in to his lung cancer; he sometimes became so ill, in fact, that he would hallucinate. His illness must have reminded Plath that, twenty-two years ago, her father had mistakenly diagnosed himself as dying from this same disease. In past weeks, Percy's condition had deteriorated dramatically; on occasion, Rose had to ask Ted to carry him from room to room. Plath and Hughes had dropped in on Percy the morning they were going to London, and they both knew then death was upon him. Now it had happened—just as it had with Sylvia's father so many years ago.

Returning to Devon, Ted and Sylvia attended Percy's funeral services; he was buried in a cemetery on a hill near Court Green. When Sylvia first saw Rose following Percy's death, she hugged her; Rose kissed Sylvia and burst into tears. The entire ordeal affected Sylvia deeply. Images of Percy's death and funeral worked themselves into "Berck-Plage," which Plath finished on June 30.

Plath had recorded an essay, "A Comparison," for "The World of Books." Its subject, the difference between writing a poem and writing a novel, was informed by *The Bell Jar* (she had sent her final progress report to the Saxton Foundation in early May) and by a second novel she was writing. (In the program, Plath did not use the books' names.) In fact, Plath had completed a large portion of this new manuscript, which was a sequel to *The Bell Jar*. "This was a joyous book, dealing with her experiences as a young American girl in England," Aurelia Plath would remember Sylvia revealing to her on this trip. "It told of her romance, her return to this country [America] with her husband, when she taught and traveled with him, and ended with the birth of her first child. The hero of that book was her husband. It was to be given to [Ted] in rough draft form as a birthday gift [in August]."

As June progressed, Sylvia again experienced second thoughts about her husband's character. By July 2, well into her mother's stay, Plath wrote another poem about a failing relationship. Her first poem since "Berck-Plage," "The Other" tries to identify the catalyst for a doomed love affair. Alluding to adulteries, the poem's narrator, never clearly revealed, speaks directly to the "other." The poem remains purposefully vague, and Plath plays with the anonymity of pronouns throughout, but the main concern of "The Other" is beyond conjecture. In the poem, the rival is not a family member—mother, sister, brother. It is another woman.

3

On the morning of July 9, 1962, Sylvia lay in the bed she shared with her husband. Already, the day was hot, but Sylvia did not think of the heat. Almost two months had passed since David Wevill and Assia Gutmann's visit to Court Green. Over these two months, Ted's behavior had become increasingly odd. Sometimes, Sylvia did not know where he was, for Ted now regularly went into London alone. When they were together, they often argued, more so than they had in the past. But this morning, Sylvia tried to take her mind off Ted. With her mother at Court Green, her pace had been busy. Yesterday, they had visited the Adamsons'; tomorrow, they would have tea with Mrs. Macnamara, a neighbor. Today they planned to shop in Exeter while Ted took care of the children. Soon Sylvia got out of bed, dressed, and proceeded down to the kitchen. After breakfast, ready for the day, Sylvia and her mother headed for the Morris.

On the way to Exeter, Sylvia sounded even more optimistic than usual. As she steered the Morris, she chatted with her mother. At one point, she made a remark that echoed something she had said days before: "I have everything in life I've ever wanted—a wonderful husband, two adorable children, a lovely home, and my writing." Again, Aurelia listened to Sylvia without commenting, even if she did not fully believe her. "[T]he marriage was seriously troubled," Aurelia Plath later wrote. "There was a great deal of anxiety in the air." A few hours later, events would prove Aurelia right.

After they went shopping, Sylvia and Aurelia enjoyed a pleasant lunch. Originally, they had planned to remain in Exeter·all afternoon, but following the meal they both agreed to call it a day. Driving back to North Tawton, Sylvia again seemed in good form; her talk was upbeat and spirited. When they arrived at Court Green and had parked the car, she and Aurelia got out and headed towards the house. Then the moment Sylvia opened the front door, she heard it—the telephone ringing on the other side of the room. Instinctively, she rushed for the phone to answer it before it stopped ringing. As she did, Ted arrived at the top of the stairs. Startled by Sylvia's presence, he too made a dash for the phone. But halfway down the stairs, he missed a step and—awkwardly, harshly—fell backwards. His momentum carrying him down the rest of the stairs, he hit his butt on each of a half-dozen steps before he landed with a thud on the floor. His giant bulk sprawled out near Sylvia's feet. Calmly, she picked up the receiver and said hello.

To Sylvia's surprise, the caller—without question a woman—drastically lowered her voice, trying to sound like a man, and asked to speak to Ted. Despite the woman's obvious attempt to disguise who she was, Sylvia identified her immediately. The voice belonged to Assia Gutmann.

Sylvia could not move. Ted lugubriously struggled to his feet, and Sylvia handed the receiver to him. After talking briefly, Ted hung up. Then Sylvia jerked the telephone wire from the wall socket. A silence fell over the room. Even Aurelia, who stood motionless in the doorway, recognized the moment's drama. Like Sylvia, Aurelia understood the full implications of the telephone call.

Asking her mother to look after Frieda, Sylvia spent the rest of the afternoon in torment. Later that evening, she gathered up Nicholas and his baby things and bolted from the house. Leaving in the Morris, she considered where she could go; finally, she decided to visit a couple whom she had seen a lot that spring—Elizabeth and David Compton. Driving over, she became more and more angry. When she looked at Nicholas sitting in the carry-cot beside her on the front seat, she became filled with rage and hatred. How could Ted do this to the children? To her? Back at Court Green, Aurelia tried to calm Frieda by reassuring her that everything would be all right. For Aurelia, though, the problem was dealing with her son-in-law. After all, how was she to treat Ted, now that the unthinkable had happened?

Eventually, Sylvia arrived at the Comptons'. By the time she reached Elizabeth, a woman who she believed would sympathize with her dilemma, Sylvia was almost unable to cope. Her mental condition, which had deteriorated considerably as she drove, would shock Elizabeth, who years later remembered the night in graphic detail:

> Then suddenly, late one evening, Sylvia arrived with Nick in his carry-cot, and the change in her was appalling. She kept saying "My milk has dried up, I can't feed Nick. My milk has gone."
>
> At last she told me that Ted was in love with another woman, that she knew Assia and was terrified of her. She wept and wept and held onto my hands, saying, "Help me!"
>
> What could I do? I have never felt so inadequate in my life. She claimed, "Ted lies to me, he lies all the time, he has become a *little* man." But the most frightening thing she said was, "When you give someone your whole heart and he doesn't want it, you cannot take it back. It's gone forever."

Still despondent, Sylvia returned to Court Green the next morning. It was then Aurelia decided that, to be out of the way, she should stay with Winifred Davies. Afterwards, Aurelia visited Court Green daily to care for the children, which allowed Sylvia and Ted a chance to go about their routines with as much ease as possible. But each night Aurelia returned to Davies's.

Sylvia would not have been much company for her mother anyway. She continued to appear more disturbed than she had in years. She piddled about in the house or garden, except for the mornings, when she was in her study.

Actually, though, she didn't write much. In the three weeks after July 9, she produced only two short poems. On the 11th, her first day home after the night at the Comptons', Plath wrote "Words Heard, by Accident, over the Phone." Previously, when Plath had used life experiences as source material for her work, she had chosen events that had occurred in the past. She needed the episode to reinvent itself in her subconscious before she could capture it on the page. Not so with "Words Heard." The poem opens as the narrator is shocked by a voice on the phone that asks—"Is he there?" The implied answer is, he is. Throughout, the poem's language is coded—direct statements are always avoided—and it is through this misdirection that "Words Heard" achieves its own weird tone.

When the poem's confrontation is over, the narrator has two revelations. First, the seeds of some future event have been laid. Second, she decides that if she did not have a telephone, then she could not have received the call, and therefore her life would not be in a state of disaster. In short, the cause of the problem is the telephone, or so the narrator has decided. Neither the "he" nor the "I" of the poem apparently has anything to do with it. It is an interesting if flawed line of logic.

Soon, Sylvia did not even try to control her anger, for in her mind it was justified. She had neither deserted nor betrayed her husband; she would never even have considered it. Her only crime was wanting to have everything—children, husband, home, career.

One afternoon, that anger finally got the best of her. In a fit of rage,

Plath built a fire in the backyard on the spot where they usually burned rubbish. Then, with her mother looking on in disbelief, she ripped up the manuscript of her new novel—the sequel to *The Bell Jar*—and threw it piece by piece into the fire. Just days before, Sylvia had described the book to Aurelia at length. She told her that it focused on a narrator who, after enduring severe hardships in her youth, returns to health when she enters into a nourishing and supportive marriage. She had based the husband in the book on Ted—the reason she intended the rough draft to be his birthday present. After all that had happened, Plath could never finish the book. So there it was—her only copy, torn to shreds, disappearing in the flames.

This was not the only bonfire Sylvia built that summer. On another occasion, she burned all of the letters—upwards of a thousand—her mother had mailed her through the years. The loss of the letters especially hurt Aurelia, who watched as Sylvia burned them, since she had hoped that eventually she and Sylvia could publish a selection of their extensive correspondence. (Fortunately, Sylvia's letters to her mother were in Wellesley, or she might have destroyed those too.)

On still another occasion, Sylvia decided to burn some of Ted's belongings. After she had cleaned his "scum" from the desktop in his study (she did this by running her hand across the deck's surface and brushing the invisible material into her other, open hand), she accumulated letters, drafts of poems, waste paper—boxes of it—and carried the whole load out back. On the—now—familiar spot, she built her fire, and burned everything. Soon, as she threw handfuls of letters onto the flames, she began to dance around the bonfire. She did this for two reasons: to exorcise Ted from her system and to seek an omen in the form of a signal. While she danced, the documents burned. A steady stream of smoke curled skywards. Then, to air the fire, Sylvia stirred the flames with a rake. Ash and bits of charred paper floated up weightlessly. Once, when she had poked at the fire especially hard, she stood back to watch the ascending debris. And suddenly, as she would tell a friend later, a scrap of unburned paper drifted over to land conspicuously at her feet—an omen in the form of a signal. Sylvia picked up the paper. On it was written one word: "Dido."

Sylvia panicked. Was Ted having an affair with Dido too? Was Dido somehow involved in facilitating Ted's affair with Assia? Or was Dido merely the enemy?

On July 17, the BBC's "The World of Books" broadcast "A Comparison." On the 20th, Plath wrote "Poppies in July," her second poem since Assia's telephone call. On the 21st, she submitted "Elm," "The Rabbit Catcher," and "Event" to Alvarez. Six days later, he wrote back. "They seem to me the best things you've ever done," he stated. "By a long way. Particularly, 'The Rabbit Catcher,' which seems to me flawless . . . The last half of 'Elm' is superb." In the end, Alvarez could convince *The Observer*'s editors to buy only "Event." It would be a foreshadowing of the treatment Plath's poems would receive over the coming months. In rapid succession she produced the most remarkable poems of her career, yet magazine editors, in both England and America, would reject almost every one she submitted.

In July, it was decided that a photograph should be taken of the three generations—Aurelia, Sylvia, and Frieda and Nicholas. To do so, the four of them gathered in the yard—armed with a camera, Ted followed—where Aurelia knelt on the ground so that she could position her granddaughter in front of her. Sitting beside her mother, Sylvia held Nicholas in her lap. With her long hair pulled up into one fat braid worked across the top of her head, Sylvia had rarely looked so severe. In the photograph, she forces a smile. Her eyes squint, just enough to show her uneasiness at having to look at the photographer— her husband.

On August 4, as she had planned, Aurelia Plath left Devon. Sylvia, Ted, and the children accompanied her to the train station. "When I left . . . the four of them were together," Aurelia Plath would write, "waiting for my train to pull out of the station. The two parents were watching me stonily—Nick was the only one with a smile." On board, Aurelia positioned herself at the window to see Sylvia and her family standing on the platform. Soon the train lunged forward, picking up speed, and slowly Sylvia faded from sight.

4

In August, with her mother gone, Sylvia had to face her deteriorating marriage by herself. That same month, it became clear that the Knopf *Colossus,* in print three months now, was going to be a failure. As a result of these personal and professional disasters, Plath could not write. In all of August, she managed only "Burning the Letters," a poem narrated by a woman who, to make her attic safe, cleans all the old papers from it and burns them in the backyard. Stabbing the fire with a rake, the narrator spots a scrap of paper drifting through the air to land at her feet. She reads the disturbing message—a name—written on it. At that same instant, she hears in the distance a fox being killed by dogs—an event that, the poem implies, reflects the situation in which the narrator now finds herself.

On August 15, eleven days after Aurelia's departure, Sylvia and Ted put the best face on their shattered marriage and traveled into London to visit Olive Higgins Prouty, in England for an extended summer vacation. (The children were kept by the Kanes, a couple who had been evicted from their London flat and had temporarily moved into the Court Green guest cottage.) Prouty treated Ted and Sylvia to cocktails, supper, and Agatha Christie's *The Mousetrap.* During the evening, she was impressed by Sylvia's extravagant talk of, among other things, her and Ted's careers. Afterwards, at Prouty's expense, Sylvia and Ted spent the night at the Connaught, the same hotel in which Prouty was staying. Before coming to London, Sylvia and Ted had struck a deal. Under no condition would either even hint that their marriage was falling apart. So, when Ted and Sylvia told Mrs. Prouty good-bye the next morning, Sylvia thought she was none the wiser.

In Devon on August 21, Plath wrote a letter to Anne Sexton, who had just sent her a copy of her latest book, *All My Pretty Ones.* Declaring that the book delighted her and describing it as unique, Plath predicted—she was blessed with clairvoyance, she said—that *All My Pretty Ones* would earn Sexton a Pulitzer Prize and a National Book Award. (Five years later, Sexton did win a Pulitzer for *Live or Die.*)

Then Plath asked Sexton a most revealing question. How did it feel, she wanted to know, to be a female Poet Laureate? With *The Colossus* a failure in England and America, Plath posed the question out of at least some unacknowledged jealousy. Next, Sylvia told Sexton about Nicholas and Frieda, about tending bees and planting potatoes, and about trudging into the BBC to record broadcasts. However, she did not so much as allude to Ted, or her marriage.

"I hope you will not be too surprised or shocked when I say I am going to try to get a legal separation from Ted," Sylvia wrote to her mother on August 27, adding that, although she did not believe in divorce and would never consider filing for one, she simply could not continue to lead the "degraded and agonized life" that Ted forced her to live. Since Aurelia's departure, Ted was still seeing Assia. By late August, he spent most of the week in the city where, according to Plath, he was using up their joint savings. Soon Sylvia began to imagine, though she had no proof, that Ted maintained a secret flat in London. As it was, he came to Court Green only on weekends. If Ted preferred this other woman, he could have her, but not without paying a price— literally. One reason Plath wanted a legal separation, she told Aurelia, was to force Ted to pay the children's daily expenses. Finally, Sylvia could not control her fury. She did not want her children to have a liar and an adulterer for a father, she wrote to her mother. But they did.

Throughout August, Sylvia saw Elizabeth and David Compton, who gave her emotional support. She also continued to employ Nancy Axworthy. Additionally, the Kanes (whom Plath now described as an American playwright, who was depressive, and his pleasant Irish wife, who was manic), helped out with the children. Still, the strain of the past six months, and in particular the last seven weeks, had drained Sylvia so badly that she got the flu. One day, by accident or on purpose, she had veered the station wagon off the road into an abandoned airfield. Some people—Ted, in fact—read this as a symptom of her unstable mental state, possibly an effort to harm herself.

In September, she would go to Ireland, she decided. There she and Ted would attempt a reconciliation, should he honor his promise to try one, while the Kanes kept the children in Devon. After Ireland, Plath thought, she might close up Court Green and go to Spain for the winter. In the warm, sunny climate she could regain her health as she wrote and cared for her children. She had to make some move— that was certain. Life as she had known it at Court Green had ended.

Edge

1

Lately, Sylvia had been thinking a lot about Yeats. In early September, after she had finished some minor literary business (she wrote a letter to Judith Jones to tell her that Heinemann would be forwarding her a copy of *The Bell Jar*), she was free to go on the trip with Ted and attempt the reconciliation they had discussed. When the two of them thought about where to go, only one place seemed logical—Ireland. There they could try to communicate with Yeats's spirit, who, perhaps, would tell them what to do with their lives.

Because the Kanes had become exhausted by caring for the children during the Hugheses' mid-August trip to London, and by the stress they themselves felt over the Hugheses' marital trouble, they moved from Court Green instead of staying to baby-sit. To take their place, Sylvia hired an employment-agency nanny, whom she put in charge when she and Ted left for Ireland by train on September 11. That evening, they arrived in Dublin in time to be treated to oysters, brown bread, and Guinness by Mairé and Jack Sweeney, their Harvard friends, who were also visiting Ireland. The next day, Plath and Hughes traveled to Galway; from there, they continued fifty miles by car along the Connemara coast to Cleggan, the village in which Richard Murphy lived. In July, Plath had written Murphy to inform him that "Years Later," the epilogue from his poem "The Cleggan Disaster," had won first prize in that year's Guinness Awards at the Cheltenham Festival, for which Plath, George Hartley, and John Press had served as judges.

In her letter Plath also asked Murphy if he would take her and Ted out on the *Ave Maria,* his commercial boat, should they come to Ireland. Murphy wired Plath to say that he would be happy to; they could even stay with him. When Plath and Hughes arrived on Wednesday evening at the Old Forge, his Cleggan cottage, Murphy awaited them. Tired, the Hugheses spent the night in twin beds in Murphy's guest room, the first of what they told Murphy would be a six-night visit.

After breakfast the next morning, Murphy took Plath and Hughes out on the *Ave Maria.* On the six-mile sail to Inishbofin, Plath, as Murphy would later recall, "lean[ed] out over the prow like a triumphant figurehead, inhaling the sea air ecstatically." The next day, Murphy drove them in his minivan to Ballylee, where Yeats had lived. At Ballylee, they visited Coole Park and observed a copper-beech tree protected by a spiked fence. Sylvia talked Ted into scaling the fence to carve his initials beside Yeats's—because he "deserved to be in that company"—but Ted could not make it over the spikes. After this, they all climbed the spiral staircase in Yeats's abandoned tower. At the top, while she tossed coins down into a stream below, Plath felt overcome with joy. It was as if a powerful religious force had enveloped her. For some time, she had identified with Yeats and his work. Standing in his tower, she sensed that she had actually fallen into mystic harmony with him. Later, back on the ground, Ted and Sylvia noticed an apple tree heavy with fruit and persuaded Seamus, Murphy's fifteen-year-old helper, who had come along with them, to climb the tree and shake down apples. When he did, they gathered up some before returning to Murphy's cottage.

During their visit, Ted and Sylvia were open about the problems they were having with their marriage. According to Murphy, Ted told him that "the marriage had somehow become destructive" and that he was involved with another woman. Privately, Sylvia confided in Murphy that she wanted a legal separation, not a divorce. Himself divorced, Murphy advised against this move; it would be better for them both if they could make a clean break.

On Saturday the 15th, Murphy took the Hugheses cottage-hunting. One possible future plan for their domestic arrangements had Sylvia living with the children for six months not in Spain but in Ireland, while *Ted* traveled to Spain. They had discussed this scenario before coming to Ireland; once there, Sylvia seemed even more intrigued by the idea. To accomplish the move, Sylvia agreed in principle to rent a cottage beginning November 1 from Kitty Marriott, a friend of Murphy's. With the deal struck, the three of them—Murphy, Plath, and Hughes—whiled away the rest of Saturday. That night, they ate a huge supper prepared by Seamus's mother; for the meal, they were joined by Thomas Kinsella, an Irish poet who had just driven from Dublin. During supper, an awkward moment occurred when Plath brushed her knee against Murphy's in such a way that Murphy would later accuse her of "rubb[ing] her leg against mine under the table, provocatively." Besides Sylvia and Murphy, no one knew about the incident. Following supper, no doubt mindful of Yeats's mysticism, the company began to talk about the Ouija board, which Ted and Sylvia volunteered to demonstrate. Murphy refused to be involved, and Sylvia soon lost interest, but Ted and Kinsella stayed up for hours communicating with spirits and writing poems based on information given to them from the other side.

After his night at the Ouija board, Ted was walking along a hallway in Murphy's cottage when he saw the face of a portrait suddenly change. He read this paranormal transformation as a sign that he should leave the cottage—indeed Cleggan—at once. Three days before he and Sylvia had planned to go back to England, or so she would claim to a friend, Ted picked up and left. If he related this tale to Sylvia at Murphy's cottage, she may or may not have believed him. Certainly, Sylvia could only feel his sudden departure was an abandonment. After their semi-idyllic day at Coole, and in the middle of their reconciliation trip, Ted just disappeared. She tried to explain to Murphy where Ted had gone, although she did not repeat the story of the portrait whose face changed. Instead, she told him that Ted had decided to go alone to County Clare to visit the American painter Barrie Cooke. Nor did she relate the portrait episode to her mother in her September 23 letter. Ted had deserted her in Ireland, Sylvia declared; he said that he was going hunting with a friend and never came back. In her heart, of course, Sylvia believed that Hughes had returned to London—and

Assia. Whatever she did or did not believe (or know, for that matter) became academic. The fact was, Ted had left her.

Murphy responded curiously. Construing that Sylvia had somehow masterminded all this as a way to spend time alone with him, Murphy all but charged her with wanting to have an affair. He insisted then that she join Kinsella in driving back to Dublin. Astonished and hurt, Sylvia went with Kinsella the next morning; she remained in Dublin for two nights with Kinsella and his wife, Eleanor, whom she found unusually understanding.

On the 18th, Sylvia returned to Court Green to find a letter from Ruth Barnhouse, to whom she had written about her problems with Ted. Unflinching in her recommendation, Barnhouse demanded that Sylvia not wait for Ted to grow out of his immaturity (or, more to the point, tire of Assia) but file for divorce at once. Besides Barnhouse's letter, Sylvia also discovered a telegram from Ted. Sent from London, it said only that he might come to Court Green within the next week or so. As she read his—to her—spineless message, Sylvia became furious. It was bad enough that Ted had deserted her in Ireland. Now he could not even face her. Instead, he spent his time—and their money—in London with Assia.

When she realized that Ted did not intend to come back to Court Green, Sylvia came closer to having a breakdown than she had in years. Desperate to speak with someone, she approached Winifred Davies, who one evening in mid-September spent three hours talking to her. Several days later, Davies related the episode to Aurelia by letter. She wrote:

> Sylvia came up here in great distress the other night when Ted did not come back. . . . [I]t seems to me that Ted has never grown up. He is not mature enough to accept his responsibilities, paying bills, doing income tax, looking after his wife and children, so Sylvia has taken over all that practical side of the partnership, of necessity. . . . He wants to be free for parties, traveling, etc. . . . It seems to be that success has gone to his head. I feel awfully sorry for them all but I do not think Sylvia can go on living on a rack and it will

really be better for the children to have one happy parent rather than two arguing ones, especially as he has taken such a dislike to Nicholas.

Soon afterwards, Sylvia wrote to her mother that she had enjoyed a wonderful four days in Ireland. Then, after telling her that she planned to go back there to spend December, January, and February, she made, for the first time to Aurelia, the more startling revelation that Ted had never really been fond of Nicholas. On one occasion, Sylvia wrote, Nicholas had fallen out of his pram after Ted refused to buckle him in, although Sylvia had told him to. Amazingly, Ted did not even bother to get up to see about him. Hearing Nicholas screaming in another part of the house, Sylvia ran to find him sprawled on the floor. Some time later, Ted admitted to her that he had never wanted children, but had not been able to muster the courage to tell her. Curiously, he did seem to approve of Frieda—Sylvia believed she flattered him—and was happy to have her. Yet he now chose to live with a woman who, because she had had numerous abortions, was probably barren.

Through the rest of September, Sylvia became deeply depressed. She began to smoke cigarettes and often broke down weeping when she was by herself. To vent her rage, she wrote Murphy an angry letter; she still planned to move to Ireland temporarily, she said, but she did not wish to have anything to do with him. Actually, her anger at Murphy was nothing compared to the way she felt about Ted. Her list of complaints about him was endless. He wrote checks he never recorded in their books. He spent huge sums of cash drawn from their bank account without her knowledge. He used up her Saxton grant before she could properly renovate the cottage, her home in the future for a full-time nanny. He would probably try to retain custody of Frieda, if there was a divorce, since he favored her over Nicholas, whom he rarely ever touched. And, finally, because of Ted's history of violent behavior, Sylvia now worried that she and the children would need protection from him indefinitely. Nor was his behavior improving. Lately, through the mail, Sylvia had been receiving police summonses for traffic tickets that, according to Sylvia, Ted had gotten but refused to pay.

On September 25, Sylvia went into London to confer with a lawyer, Charles Mazillius of Harris, Chetham and Company. From Mazillius, Plath learned that in England a wife was entitled to one-third of a husband's salary, although, if he refused to pay, she would have to sue—a lengthy and expensive process. Second, since Ted had deserted her and his children, Sylvia could register their joint banking accounts in her name alone. By Sylvia's calculations, all of the seven thousand dollars they had earned the year before, of which her income from writing accounted for about one-third, was gone. Mazillius had also offered his opinion of Ted: he was worthless. Sylvia would be better off if she just got rid of him. Because no one knew where Ted was, Mazillius would have to hire someone to search for him before he could serve him with papers. Sylvia felt sure that Ted would try to avoid being found. Indeed, as of September 29, she had not heard a word from him since Ireland, except for his telegram. Back at Court Green, Sylvia wrote to Aurelia and instructed her to withdraw the one thousand dollars in her and Ted's Boston account; she should send the money to her in two five-hundred-dollar checks as "gifts," one in September and one at Christmas.

On the day after her conference with Mazillius, Plath secluded herself in her study in the morning and wrote a poem. September had been a good month for her poetry. *The New Yorker* published "Blackberrying," *The Listener* "The Surgeon at 2 a.m.," and *The Observer* "Crossing the Water." Also, Howard Moss had accepted "Elm," which he planned to run as "The Elm Speaks." So, she felt confident as she worked on her poem that morning. Entitled "For a Fatherless Son," the poem is a monologue spoken by a mother to her infant son, who soon, she tells him, will notice an "absence" emerging beside him. In the meantime, she wants him to know that she loves his "stupidity."

Three days later, Plath wrote Olive Prouty to tell her about Ted, although, judging from Prouty's comments in August at the Connaught about unfaithful men, Plath suspected that she already knew. Ted had deserted her, Sylvia told Prouty, for—naturally—another woman. At the moment, Sylvia believed Ted had become a stranger who had assumed the name of the man she married. Regarding the night at the

Connaught, Sylvia now remembered it as her final happy night with Ted; "happiness" was a word that no longer held meaning to her.

The next morning, alone in her study, having drunk cup after cup of coffee to counteract the sleeping pills she had started to take at night, Plath wrote "A Birthday Present," a rambling, energetic monologue. Several days later, at the very end of September, Ted finally appeared at Court Green, out of the blue. Sylvia had not seen him since Ireland and was enraged by his mere presence. He would have to come another time to gather his belongings, she said, and ordered him to leave immediately.

On the morning of October 1, Plath awoke around five, drank her coffee, and, alone in her study, wrote the longish poem "The Detective." The next day, the same routine resulted in "The Courage of Shutting-up." Over the ensuing week, Plath wrote the five poems— "The Bee Meeting," "The Arrival of the Bee Box," "Stings," "The Swarm," "Wintering"—which she collectively called "Bees." By writing these poems, because the subject of bees was obviously tied to memories of her father, Plath seemed to be announcing, at least to herself, a resolve to tackle once again the issue of the father, something with which she had toyed since her year of therapy in Boston. Finishing "Wintering" on the 9th, Sylvia wrote her mother, not to discuss "Bees" but to respond to Aurelia's suggestion that she move home. America was out of the question, Sylvia said. She did not want to flee from Ted or his fame. Instead, she would stay in England. Anyway, she could not be around Aurelia just now. "The horror of what you saw and what I saw you see last summer is between us," Sylvia wrote, "and I cannot face you again until I have a new life." As for the fifty dollars per month that Aurelia had offered, Sylvia could not accept it. She also really did not need it, because Ted had finally agreed to pay a yearly maintenance of one thousand pounds. That sum would at least cover the children's needs and allow her to support herself by writing.

Sylvia found out that Ted had agreed to the maintenance when he came to Court Green on the 4th to pack his clothes, books, and papers. Ted took longer to pack than Sylvia had expected; indeed, his visit turned into a nightmarish week during which, Sylvia wrote Aurelia, he nearly murdered her as he tried to force her to give him the last installment of her Saxton grant. Sylvia refused, for she now planned to use that money, combined with a one-hundred-dollar birthday check from Aunt Dotty and a three-hundred-dollar birthday check from Olive Prouty, to hire nannies. At one point during his Court Green stay, Sylvia also said Hughes made an admission: he and Assia had speculated that, in light of her past emotional problems, Sylvia might have already killed herself. If she were dead, Hughes told Plath, he could sell Court Green and take Frieda. (He did not mention Nicholas.) Ted had another reason to hope for Sylvia's suicide. David Wevill had recently tried to kill himself when Assia left him for Ted.

At last, the day arrived—the 11th—for Ted to go. That afternoon, Sylvia drove him to the train station. In a parting shot, Ted told her that he had not hated living in London—one reason they had bought a house in Devon—he had hated living *with her*. At Court Green, Sylvia was so relieved Ted was gone that she went about the house singing. The following day, writing her mother, Sylvia claimed she was thoroughly happy, more than she had been in years. Now that she knew Ted would not fight a divorce, she could get on with her life. If Ted wanted to marry Assia, which Sylvia expected he would do when both divorces were final, he would have the honor of being Assia's fourth husband. Which was just fine with her. Sylvia only wished that Ted, whom she now regarded as a bastard and a criminal, had overcome his cowardice and admitted to her years ago that he had wanted to leave her—another recent revelation. That way, she could have started dating someone else, a man who would appreciate her for who she was.

2

As if the only way she could cope with her separation from Ted was through writing, Plath began to produce poems at a pace she never had before. On October 10, she wrote "A Secret," a biting, acidic poem about the public disclosure of a secret. On the 11th, in the morning before she drove Ted to the Exeter train station, she finished "The Applicant," a poem that, after one false start, seemingly wrote itself. Replete with savage wit and irony, "The Applicant" is a surreal monologue spoken by a sort of pseudo–marriage broker to a man whom he wants to set up with a woman. Plath chose to write such a poem on the 11th, the date that, essentially, marked the end of her marriage to Ted Hughes.

On the 12th, Plath returned to a familiar subject—the father. In the eighty-line poem "Daddy," which was originally called "Daddy, Daddy, Lie Easy Now" and which shaped up quickly as she hurried through draft after draft, Plath unleashed a fury made acceptable to the reader only by the poem's singsongy cadences. Speaking directly to her dead father, the poem's narrator admits that she had considered him to be godlike (the way Sylvia had once seen Ted) and accuses him of being a German Nazi. Then the narrator, turning her logic in on itself, confesses that she loves him—her father—because "[e]very woman adores a Fascist." This is why, she says, she married whom she did—someone like her father. Now, the marriage has ended, and she's fed up. "Daddy, daddy, you bastard, I'm through," reads the last line. Ultimately, it becomes clear that what she is through with is varied and complicated—her father, her husband, perhaps even her life.

On the weekend of the 14th, Sylvia and the children visited briefly with friends in Saint Ives, Cornwall. Home at Court Green, Sylvia came down with the flu, one of the worst cases she had ever had. Lifeless and feverish, she could barely force herself to crawl from bed. Fortunately, she did not have to; she kept a steady string of nannies to help her with the children. On the morning of the 16th, still sick, Plath wrote "Medusa," a poem about a young woman who is victimized by a monster. That afternoon, she wrote her mother a letter in which she speculated that she was a "genius of a writer," that she was writing the poems that would "make my name." Then, in that same letter, Sylvia made some disconcerting revelations. To begin with, her first—secret—novel was finished and accepted. Also, she had already completed much of a second, and the idea for a third had recently come to her. Finally, Ted's parents, Sylvia gathered from a recent letter of Edith's, were going to oppose the yearly maintenance Ted had agreed to pay. Though she had once considered the Hugheses her second family and Edith a lovely woman, Sylvia now expected them to try to torture her until she did what Ted wanted her to do.

For her part, Edith wrote Aurelia that she was shattered by the goings-on at Court Green, although she expected that Aurelia knew more about the situation than she, because Aurelia had been there when the problems started. Yet Edith felt sure that Ted had arrived at his decision to leave after much anguish, since Court Green represented his and Sylvia's complete financial portfolio. Still, the world offered so much opportunity, Edith said, that she believed both Ted and Sylvia would have a prosperous future.

On the morning of the 17th, Plath completed "The Jailer," a stinging lyric about a woman who wants the man in her life "dead or away," neither of which seems feasible. The following morning, she produced "Lesbos," a long domesticity-gone-haywire monologue inspired by her recent visit with friends in Cornwall. By this day, her fever had broken, and she felt well enough to write, besides "Lesbos," four important letters: one to Peter Orr, the radio producer, to agree to record poems and an interview for the British Council; one to Olive Higgins Prouty to let her know that Ted had left her for good, that his final desertion had settled her on suing for divorce, but that, despite these setbacks, she was writing with a vengeance; one to Warren to tell him that *The Bell Jar*—a secret because it was a "pot-boiler [that] no one must read . . . !"—was about to be published; and one to her mother to relate a recent episode in which a Health Visitor arrived to treat her for the flu and blurted out, "My, Mrs. Hughes, you've lost weight!" (Since last summer, she had lost at least twenty pounds.) But Sylvia hoped to get some help soon. Upon receiving a telegram from Aurelia, Winifred Davies was now searching for a live-in au pair for Sylvia. In the end, Sylvia blamed all of her trouble on Ted and had recently decided *how* she could get even with him—by writing a novel.

As October passed, Plath continued to produce poems at an astonishing pace. On the 19th, she wrote "Stopped Dead," a poem that

Olwyn Hughes would later identify as a meditation on Ted's Uncle Walter. The 20th brought "Fever 103°," a stunning poem informed by her terrible fever, which had now returned. Then, on the 21st, she finished "Amnesiac" and "Lyonnesse," the same day on which she wrote her mother one of the harshest letters she would ever mail her. Telling her that she did not want any money from her and that she did not wish to hear about "the world needing cheerful stuff [writings]," Sylvia attacked Aurelia for sending the telegram to Winifred Davies. Her business was her own, she wrote, furious—not her mother's. In the future, Aurelia had to keep her advice to herself.

In fact, Aurelia's telegram prompted Davies to call friends until she found a young girl who was free to help Plath during days through mid-December. Twenty-two years old, a nurse, and the daughter of a middle-class family in nearby Belstone, Susan O'Neill Roe started working for Plath on October 22. Arriving in the morning around the time the children awoke, Susan remained the whole day to mind the children and clean the house. After a morning in her study, Plath prepared lunch, and they all ate together. In the afternoon, Plath napped, wrote some more, and drank tea with Susan, who left before supper. Once the children were in bed, Plath returned to her study to write for an additional hour or two.

On the 23rd, only Susan's second day there, Plath already thought of her as a member of the family. Feeling deeply relieved, Plath wrote her mother to apologize for her recent angry letter. With Susan around to watch the children, Plath felt like a new person, so she continued to write poems at a startling rate. On the 24th, she finished "Cut," a poem, dedicated to O'Neill Roe, which was based on a real event. Just days before, Sylvia had accidentally cut herself while cooking, all but slicing off the whole fatty tip of her thumb. When she completed "Cut," Plath composed "By Candlelight," a poem in which a mother cares for her infant boy late at night. After writing "The Tour" on the 25th, Plath produced two poems on her birthday, the first birthday she celebrated without Ted since she had met him. (Among the presents she received was a fifty-dollar check from her mother.) One poem she wrote that day, "Poppies in October," a sort of companion piece to her earlier "Poppies in July," captures an ominous scene of a field of poppies so astonishing that they outdo even the beautiful morning clouds.

The second poem she would write on her birthday—"Ariel"—would be quite different. In *The Tempest*, on an otherworldly island where magic and deceit are commonplace, Prospero is master to an airy creature of extraordinary power. Ariel is indentured to Prospero, because in the past Prospero freed him from the evil witch Sycorax's terrible curse, which had trapped him in a pine tree for twelve years. Though she obviously knew of the overriding connotations of the name, Plath made her Ariel a horse, who is ridden by the poem's narrator. (Plath still regularly took horseback-riding lessons at a nearby stable; on her birthday, in fact, she planned to ride her usual horse, Sam.) In "Ariel," the narrator, holding on as best she can, leans into the horse as it gallops along violently. But the ride is not just a ride; the narrator seems to be approaching—metaphorically—her own sure death. A perfect lyric, "Ariel" creates a seamless metaphor, with the action of the poem and that action's meaning overlapping identically. Finally, the ride on Ariel becomes Plath's. The ride's culmination is chilling. But whereas the rider may be headed for a particular destination— the morning sun—the poet's destination is not yet fixed.

3

On October 28, after she wrote two new poems, "Purdah" and "Nick and the Candlestick," Plath completed one she had started about a week before, "Lady Lazarus." A wild lyric that she would eventually describe as light verse, the poem is spoken by a thirty-year-old woman who each decade tries to commit suicide. Once she finished these poems on the 28th, Plath did not write poetry again for a week. Her main distraction was a trip into London that she took while Susan stayed with the children at Court Green. She arrived by train at London's Waterloo Station on the morning of the 29th to record "Berck-Plage" for George MacBeth's program, "The Poet's Corner," at the BBC beginning at ten-forty-five. She then wasted time window-shopping and running errands before, later that afternoon, she headed for A. Alvarez's flat.

"For heaven's sake, yes, I'd like nothing better than to hear your new poems," Alvarez had written in response to Plath's recent request to drop in on him. "I thought the last you sent were superb. And Ted told me, rather wryly, that your recent lot were even better. God knows you're the only woman poet I've taken seriously since Emily Dickinson. And I never knew her." Alvarez had been talking with Ted because Ted spent several nights on his sofa when he did not have a place to stay. If Ted *had* had a secret flat in London, it had not been permanent. Eventually, beginning in late October, Ted ended his apartment-hopping by settling down in the huge Montagu Square flat of Dido's mother, who had recently died. He could remain there, Dido had told him, until she cleared up her mother's estate. In a strange way, the signal from the summer's bonfire had come true. Dido *was* integrally involved in Ted's life, now that he and Sylvia had separated.

Divorced also, Alvarez lived on Fellows Road in a tiny rented studio in which, as he would write, "there was nothing to lounge on—only spidery Windsor chairs and a couple of rugs on the blood-red uncarpeted lino." Alvarez met Sylvia at the door. Welcoming her, he then made drinks. Soon, they settled down in his living room: Alvarez took a chair but Plath sat beside the coal stove on the floor. As they sipped their whiskey, the two of them chatted. When Alvarez asked, Plath admitted that she was in London (in part) to hunt for a flat for her and the children, since they were "living on their own for the time being." (From Ted of course Alvarez knew about the separation.) Eventually, Plath began to talk about her poetry, the writing of which, according to Alvarez, she "made . . . sound like demonic possession." Finally, she asked if he wanted to hear some, and Alvarez enthusiastically said yes. Pulling a sheaf of poems from her shoulder bag, she reproached Alvarez, who wanted to read them silently. These poems must be read *aloud,* she said—and began "Berck-Plage." Unable to follow the difficult poem, Alvarez asked her to reread parts of it when she was done. Finished, she waited for his response. He liked it a great deal, he said, so she read him several others, among them "The Moon and the Yew Tree" and "Elm." By the end of her reading, Alvarez concluded that she was developing something "strong and new" in her work—and told her so. Delighted, Plath agreed that the next time she came into London she would stop by his flat again and read him some more.

Later, Plath went to a PEN party held to celebrate the publication of an anthology that contained her work and that Ted had helped edit. Her attendance at the gathering served as a statement: she and Ted might be divorcing, but she was still a part of the literary scene. During this trip to London, Plath also had agreed to stay with Helder and Suzette Macedo. Earlier in October, when Suzette had telephoned Sylvia at Court Green and learned that she had separated from Ted, Suzette insisted that Sylvia come visit her and Helder. Sylvia declined, since Suzette and Assia were friends. But Suzette argued that she and Sylvia were friends too, so Sylvia eventually agreed.

Plath decided that seeing the Macedos would also allow her to inform Ted's friends that she planned to file for divorce. She did this during her first night at the Macedos'. Her present freedom overjoyed her, Sylvia told Suzette; she would not even consider taking Ted back. When Suzette tried to explain that this situation had also disturbed David and Assia (after all, David had tried to kill himself), Sylvia did not want to hear it. In the end, Suzette was concerned by Sylvia's preoccupied state, now so severe that she had apparently forgotten to change the bandage on her injured thumb for some time: the filthy bandage was surely preventing the thumb from healing properly. That night, Suzette was awakened by the sound of sobs coming from the bedroom in which Sylvia slept. Rushing in, Suzette discovered Sylvia, her face drenched in tears, sound asleep.

The next morning, Plath saw Eric White, literary director of the British Arts Council, who extended to her an invitation, which she accepted, to organize American Night for the upcoming International Poetry Festival, scheduled to take place in London at the Royal Court Theatre in July 1963. Afterwards, Plath met Peter Orr at Albion House. Following a twelve-thirty lunch at the Star Steak House, Orr and Plath returned to the studio so Plath could record her poems. The consummate professional, she read one after another of those she had written over the past month, including three—"Nick and the Candlestick," "Purdah," "Lady Lazarus"—that she had finished just before her trip to London. In all, Plath recorded a total of fifteen that day, among them "Ariel," "The Applicant," "Cut," "Fever 103°," and "Daddy." As she read these poems—written about a world where children hate parents, where parents are unsure of their own parenthood, where marriages break up—the emotion of the moment, and the strain of the subjects of the poems themselves, came through only once. When Plath reached the second and third stanzas of "Daddy," which contained the lines about the father's death, her voice weakened, quivering as she spoke the words. Then, after an almost imperceptible pause, she continued.

Plath did not shout these poems of rage. Her sharp Boston "a"s—"art," "heart," "scar"—cut through any British intonations. In a tight, controlled voice, she delivered these emotion-filled poems. She declared them in direct statements. She addressed the reader—or listener, in this case—just as she had taken on her subjects: without flinching. Finally, Plath's voice sounded as if it belonged to someone much older than thirty. Full, resonant, mature, it resembled, in tone and clarity and intonation, a voice not unlike her mother's.

When Plath finished, Orr interviewed her. Beginning innocently enough, he asked: "Sylvia, what started you writing poetry?" Plath answered: "I don't know what *started* me, I just wrote it from the time I was quite small. I guess I liked nursery rhymes, and I guess I thought I could do the same thing. I wrote my first poem, my first published poem, when I was eight and a half years old. It came out in the Boston [*Herald*], and from then on, I suppose, I've been a bit of a professional." Next Orr asked her about influences, which prompted Plath to mention Lowell—his *Life Studies* was seminal—and Sexton, "who writes about her experience as a mother . . . who has had a nervous breakdown." Later, when Orr wanted to know if her poems tended to emerge from books rather than her life, Plath said:

No, no: I would not say that at all. I think my poems immediately come out of the sensuous and emotional experiences I have, but I must say I cannot sympathize with these cries from the heart that are informed by nothing except a needle or a knife, or whatever it is. I believe that one should be able to control and manipulate experiences, even the most terrifying, like madness, being tortured, this sort of experience, and one should be able to manipulate these experiences with an informed and an intelligent mind. I think that personal experience is very important, but certainly it shouldn't be a kind of shut-box and mirror-looking, narcissistic experience. I believe it should be relevant, and relevant to the larger things, the bigger things, such as Hiroshima and Dachau and so on.

Finally, Orr asked: "But basically this thing, the writing of poetry, is something which has been a great satisfaction to you in your life, is it?" And Plath could hardly contain herself. "Oh, satisfaction! I don't think I could live without it. It's like water or bread, or something absolutely essential to me. I find myself absolutely fulfilled when I have written a poem, when I'm writing one. Having written one, then you fall away very rapidly from having been a poet to becoming a sort of poet in rest, which isn't the same thing at all. But I think the actual experience of writing a poem is a magnificent one."

4

On reflection, Plath decided that going to Ireland would be an evasion of the problems at hand. It made more sense for her to find a flat in London and move into the city right away. So, when she returned to Devon on October 30, she knew that she would be coming back to London soon. Indeed, she remained at Court Green only until November 5, long enough for her to arrange for Susan to baby-sit, to see Winifred Davies on the 3rd about her injured thumb (convinced that Dr. Webb had bungled treatment of it, she had gone to Horder while in London; it was better but healing slowly), and to write one poem on the 4th, "The Couriers." In London, where she again stayed with the Macedos, Sylvia met up with—as arranged—Ted, who went with her to look at flats.

Their first afternoon out, Sylvia and Ted found nothing. Then, one day as she was walking by herself through her old neighborhood on her way to Horder's office for him to re-examine her thumb, Sylvia noticed a "Flat for Let" sign outside a house on Fitzroy Road. Approaching the building—Number 23—she discovered that it sported one of the blue plaques that adorned many historic structures in London. Unbelievably, this one read, "William Butler Yeats 1865–1939 Irish Poet and Dramatist Lived Here." Excited by her luck, Plath asked construction workers refurbishing the house if she could walk through the two available flats. When they agreed, she proceeded inside and immediately fell in love with the top flat. Consisting of three bedrooms upstairs and a bath, kitchen, and living area down, it seemed perfect for her and the children. It even had access to a balcony garden, ideal to sit in during warm weather. Sylvia learned that Morton Smith and Sons were the flat's agents and headed straight for their offices; there, without hesitation, she made an offer. The agent with whom she talked said he would consider her bid, although he would have to verify her references. Thrilled nevertheless, Sylvia returned to Court Green. On the 7th, she wrote her mother a letter enumerating the many reasons why she desperately wanted 23 Fitzroy Road: it was close to Primrose Hill and the London Zoo, only minutes from the BBC, and literally around the corner from the friends she had made during her Chalcot Square days like Katherine Frankfort, who had already advised her about au-pair girls. "*And* [it is] in the house of a famous poet," Sylvia added, "so my work should be blessed."

The more she thought about it, the more she wanted to live in Yeats's house. Plath recalled her trip to Ireland with fondness. She could vividly remember how, as she tossed coins out of a window from the top of Yeats's tower into a stream below, she had actually sensed the presence of Yeats's spirit. Indeed, even though she had been physically ill, her soul became invigorated merely by being where Yeats had lived. She almost felt as if she could still communicate with his spirit—just as she had at his tower in Ireland. One night in Devon, while she waited for the agents to approve her references, Sylvia decided to try to receive a message from Yeats, who had, after all, been a medium. So, with Susan looking on, she flipped through her copy of Yeats's *Collected Plays* until she stopped at a particular line in *The Unicorn from the*

Stars. "Get the wine and food to give you strength and courage," the line read, "and I will get the house ready." That settled it. Obviously, fate demanded that she move into Yeats's house.

In her first days back at Court Green, Plath produced in quick succession "Getting There," a meditation on an approaching death; "The Night Dances," yet another poem spoken by a mother to her infant at night; "Gulliver," a retelling of the Gulliver story; and "Thalidomide," about a sedative popular in the late fifties and early sixties that, doctors eventually determined, caused birth defects. Then, on the 11th, she composed "Letter in November" and, three days after that, "Death & Co.," a poem she would describe as concerning "the double or schizophrenic nature of death." In the poem, Plath symbolized the two sides of death by personifying them as contrasting men, but the most haunting section is the ending. As she contemplates these two men, the narrator realizes "[s]omebody's done for."

Around the time she finished "Death & Co.," Plath gathered together all of the poems she had written over the last few weeks. Beginning with an older poem, "Morning Song," and ending with "Wintering," the last of the bees sequence, Plath arranged the poems into a manuscript (of its forty-one poems, she had written well over half in October alone) that would begin with the word "love" and end with the word "spring." In England she would dedicate the book to Frieda and Nicholas, in America to Olive Higgins Prouty—or so Plath wrote her mother. And after rejecting several titles—*Daddy, A Birthday Present, The Rival, The Rabbit Catcher,* all followed by the obligatory *and Other Poems*—Plath decided that she should name the manuscript for what she believed to be its best poem. *Ariel and Other Poems*—that would be the title of her second volume of poetry.

Though Plath admired these new poems enough to assemble them into a manuscript, editors did not share her enthusiasm. In November, after *The London Magazine* accepted "The Applicant" and "Stopped Dead," Plath met with a flood of rejections. The most notable ones came from *The New Yorker*'s Howard Moss, who out of the countless new poems she sent him—and during the fall, in numerous submissions, she mailed him almost all of *Ariel*—accepted only "Amnesiac." Towards the end of November, *The Atlantic Monthly*'s Peter Davison rejected seven poems, although he did keep six from which Weeks eventually accepted "The Arrival of the Bee Box" and "Wintering." Plath even received rejections from small literary journals. While her *Ariel* poems met with a reception as cold as the one *The Colossus* had been afforded in America, Plath came to realize that what she had to say in her poems would remain, for the most part, private. It looked as if they would never reach the wide audience of which she had dreamed. She had produced poems she knew to be far better than any she had written, and the editors of the periodicals who had accepted her work in the past simply did not care. Faced with this response, Plath saw herself as a failure.

Despite these rejections, Plath continued to write poems during the last half of November. On the 16th, she turned out "Years" and "The Fearful," the latter a dark piece about a woman who calls on the telephone but pretends to be a man and who detests even the thought of a baby because she would rather have only her man. On the 18th, Plath wrote "Mary's Song," which she dedicated to Father Michael, a priest with whom she had corresponded through the years. And, on the 26th, she composed "Winter Trees."

One weekend in November, Plath also hosted Clarissa Roche, who came to Devon with her one-month-old infant—her fourth child—from Kent, where she and Paul now lived. On the Monday after Clarissa left, heartened by seeing her old friend, Plath tried to strike up a new friendship. Writing to Stevie Smith, Plath told her that she enjoyed the recordings Smith had made for Peter Orr, that she considered herself a Smith-addict (she particularly liked *Novel on Yellow Paper*), and that she herself had a novel forthcoming. Plath then added that she hoped to move into London by New Year's; perhaps Smith might stop by for tea when she did. (Eventually, in late 1962, Stevie Smith answered Plath: she wished her luck on her novel and suggested that they meet. They never did.)

It had been well over a month since Ted had moved out of Court Green, but Sylvia remained furious. The mention of his name could sometimes throw her into a rage. On the 19th, as she wrote a letter to her mother, she fell into a vicious attack on Ted. Throughout their marriage, Sylvia had made countless sacrifices for him: she had placed his work before hers, taken part-time jobs when she did not want to, served as his typist and his agent, and deprived herself of luxuries like new clothes and a stylish haircut. And for what? So that Ted could date, as he was now, fashion models? Three days later, in a separate letter to Aurelia, Sylvia continued to express her disgust with Ted. She didn't care if he *was* a genius, he was also a bastard and a gigolo. Yes, for six years he tried, and fairly well succeeded, at being pleasant and faithful, but in the end the pressure of living a lie got to him.

Soon Sylvia became worried about her London flat. She suspected that an application placed by another person, Trevor Thomas—an artist who worked, she would learn, as the fine-arts editor at the Gordon Fraser Gallery, located near Fitzroy Road, on Fitzroy Yard—might be accepted instead of hers. In all fairness, Thomas had made his bid on the Friday *before* Plath put in one on Sunday. But Thomas had made the mistake of asking for the weekend to secure the lump sum of three months' rent—180 pounds—which the agents wanted him to pay before he could sign the lease. From the start, Sylvia had offered fifty pounds a year more than Thomas. She had also argued her case well: she and Hughes—she did *not* tell the agents that they were separated—needed the large space for themselves and their two small children. Still, by Thanksgiving, she had no definite answer. Because of this, Sylvia made a second offer: she would be willing to sign a five-year lease, pay the whole first year in advance, and secure from America a reference from her mother, "*Professor* A. S. Plath." This final ploy on Sylvia's part worked. By the end of November, the agents agreed to the deal and issued her a move-in date of December 17. Delighted, Sylvia wrote to her mother about a trip she was going to make into London to apply for a telephone and to buy straw mats and a new gas stove. She could more easily afford these purchases, she said, because of an unexpected gift—a seven-hundred-dollar check from Aunt Dotty.

During November, unknown to Plath, Knopf took actions on *The Bell Jar* which, if she *had* been aware of them, would have left her somewhat less ebullient. On the 7th, Knopf's Koshland informed Heinemann's Anderson that Knopf did not know why they had been sent *The Bell*

Jar by Victoria Lucas but that they would not be publishing the book. Afterwards, Anderson reminded Koshland that Heinemann had forwarded Knopf the novel because Sylvia Plath, its real author, was obliged to submit her next book to them, since her *Colossus* contract contained a first-option clause. On the 30th, Koshland wrote back to Anderson. At Knopf, they "were knocked galley west" to learn that Victoria Lucas was Sylvia Plath. Nevertheless, though he and others had reread the novel, they still could not "warm up" to it, "despite her obvious way with words to say nothing of the sharp eye for unusual and vivid detail." It seemed to those at Knopf, Koshland said, that Plath needed to get the novel "out of her system" so that she could move forward and deal with the book's subject matter "in a novelistic way." After all, *The Bell Jar* read "as if it were autobiographical, almost flagrantly so." Because of the nature of the novel, Koshland continued, Knopf would rather that Plath withhold the book from the American market altogether. And, naturally, Koshland wanted Anderson and Plath to know, should another American house *not* pick up *The Bell Jar*, Knopf still retained the right of first refusal on her next work. On December 10, Anderson put that wish to rest. Yes, Heinemann would attempt to place *The Bell Jar* with another American publisher—and they would do so right away.

Plath might have referred to *The Bell Jar* as a "pot-boiler" to Warren—as she also would to her mother—but the novel still represented the product of endless months of agonizing writing as well as the physical symbol of her own years of emotional upheaval. As a consequence, Plath was both upset over Knopf's decision and heartened by Heinemann's willingness to submit the book elsewhere. She learned these two pieces of news in early December, when Anderson wrote to tell her that they were looking at other American houses that might be appropriate for the novel. Plath suggested Harper and Row, Ted's publisher, where his editor was Elizabeth Lawrence.

In late November and early December, some good things did happen. The Home Services commissioned a two-thousand-word piece on her childhood landscape; two weeks later, she finished "Ocean 1212-W," an airy, impressionistic memoir whose title refers to her grandmother's Winthrop telephone number. In December, the BBC's

George MacBeth assigned her a review of an anthology of American poetry edited by Donald Hall (one in which her work did not appear) and Douglas Cleverdon asked her to record a program of her new poems. Finally, *Three Women*, translated into Norwegian, was scheduled to play on Oslo radio. Despite these successes, Plath still faced two realities. Judging from Knopf's reaction, Heinemann would have trouble placing *The Bell Jar* in America. And, judging from the response of magazine editors on both sides of the Atlantic, Plath would encounter similar trouble selling her *Ariel* poems, the BBC's support notwithstanding. Moss remained firm in his dislike for her new poetry, as did another editor, *The New Statesman*'s Karl Miller. At one point, he too rejected a huge batch of *Ariel* poems, telling Alvarez, when he ran into him on the street, that he found them "too extreme." Instead, Miller set Plath to writing reviews of historical novels. Her last, a piece on Malcolm Elwin's *Lord Byron's Wife*, appeared on December 7. Ultimately, only Alvarez seemed to be excited by her recent work, yet because of space limitations at *The Observer* he could convince his superiors to purchase nothing but short poems. Recently, they had bought "Winter Trees" and "Ariel," the latter of which the editors renamed (since they expected readers to be confused by the poem's action) "The Horse."

Perhaps because of this cool reception, Plath again returned to fiction-writing. With her *Bell Jar* sequel destroyed, she now poured all of her creative energy into her newest novel, *Doubletake.* In a November 20 letter to Olive Prouty, Plath said that the novel's title referred to the notion that a re-examination of events is often deeply revealing. In the novel, the heroine discovers that her perfect paragon of a husband is an adulterer. Plath hoped to complete *Doubletake*, which she would soon rename *Double Exposure*, by the new year. And, if it turned out to be good enough, Plath told Prouty, she wanted to dedicate the novel to her.

5

On December 3, Plath took the train to London to sign the five-year lease and pay the first year's rent for 23 Fitzroy Road. While there, she also arranged for the electricity to be turned on and the gas stove she had bought to be delivered. Back in Devon, she began closing up Court Green, which she hoped to retain through the separation—or divorce—process. Over the next week and a half, she also packed, disposed of her bees, lined up Nancy Axworthy to feed her cats, and saw friends like Winifred Davies. During the first week in December, she telephoned her mother to say that she and the children would be moving to London within a couple of days. On the 10th, as things turned out. With Susan accompanying her, Sylvia drove her loaded-down Morris from North Tawton to London; her Devon mover followed. In London, Sylvia arrived at Fitzroy Road to discover that the electricity had not been switched on and that the gas stove had not been connected. Then a comedy of errors ensued. A gust of wind blew the door to her flat shut while her keys were inside—and she and Susan were outside. Seeing Trevor Thomas, her neighbor, emerge from the building, Sylvia said excitedly, "Oh, wonderful! You have keys and can let me in. I'm moving into the flat upstairs and I've locked myself out and the babies are crying and my husband has gone off with the keys." Thomas replied by suggesting that she call the police. Instead, Sylvia hurried to the gas board to convince them to install the stove that day: it was the "gas boys," as she called them, who climbed along the back roof, pried open a window, and unlocked the door. Later, after the Devon mover unloaded her belongings into the flat by candlelight, Sylvia complained to the electric board until a man showed up and turned on the power.

During the next week, Sylvia tried to accustom herself to the new flat, to London, and to the fact that, now that she was in the city, Ted dropped in on a regular basis to see her. In those early days, she painted floors and bureaus, reintroduced herself to neighbors and area merchants, and contacted friends, especially the Frankforts and the Macedos. The latter introduced her to the Beckers, with whom she struck up an instant relationship. Gerry, a professor at Hendon Polytechnic, and Jillian, an author who would one day write *Hitler's Children*, lived around the corner from Douglas Cleverdon and his wife, Nest. Of late, Plath had been in touch with Cleverdon to tell him that she had used the excuse of free-lancing for the BBC to apply for a priority telephone, which would speed up an installation process that normally took several months. In mid-December, not long after she had received her advance copy of *The Bell Jar* from Heinemann's David Machin, the editor who had taken over her work now that James Michie had left for another publishing house, Plath submitted her new poems to Cleverdon for her reading on the BBC. None of the huge batch had been accepted by magazines, Plath wrote Cleverdon, except for "The Applicant," by *The London Magazine*, and "Ariel," by *The Observer*. Cleverdon was more than receptive, since he had been the one to suggest the program, on Ted's recommendation.

Ted knew the quality of Plath's new work as a result of his visits to Fitzroy Road. On the morning of December 12, he and Sylvia took the children to the London Zoo. Being around him only made her angry again. She wrote her mother that she was happy she had eliminated Ted from her life. But Aurelia now had her doubts. Perhaps what she had suspected all along might be true: Sylvia still held "the hope of a reconciliation with Ted," Aurelia would write later.

Alvarez thought so too. On most of her trips to London during late October and November, Sylvia had dropped by Alvarez's studio to spend part of an afternoon with him. Each visit progressed in almost the same way. After drinks, they chatted idly until Plath read Alvarez a handful of new poems. In this manner Alvarez had heard the bees sequence, "A Birthday Present," "The Applicant," "Daddy," "Lady Lazarus," "Getting There," "Fever 103°," "Letter in November," and "Ariel." Of these afternoons, Alvarez would write: "Cross-legged on the red floor, after reading her poems, she would talk about her riding [her Devon horseback-riding lessons] in her twangy, New England voice. And perhaps because I was also a member of the club, she talked, too, about suicide in much the same way: about her attempt ten years before which, I suppose, must have been very much on her mind as she corrected the proofs of [*The Bell Jar*], and about her recent incident with the car." There were other reasons why Plath sought out Alvarez. He was sympathetic to her poetry. She felt Alvarez's introduction to his recent Penguin anthology, *The New Poetry*, more or less vindicated her present work. And she knew that Ted remained in contact with Alvarez. But as Plath read him her poems on visit after visit, Alvarez saw something more. In the wake of Ted's departure, Sylvia was undergoing a severe emotional crisis. The key was "Daddy." Ted's desertion had obviously triggered in her the same feelings of isolation that had tormented her following her father's death. "I suspect that finding herself alone again now, whatever the pretense of indifference," Alvarez would write, "all the anguish she had experienced at her father's death was reactivated: despite herself, she felt abandoned, injured, enraged, and bereaved as purely and defenselessly as she had as a child twenty years before. As a result, the pain that had built up steadily inside her all that time came flooding out. There was no need to discuss motives"—which they did not—"because the poems did that for her."

The obvious, also, had not escaped Alvarez. Because she was again "single," Plath made it clear that she would be willing to become romantically involved with him. Alvarez could not, although he did not tell her why. At the moment, he was seeing a fledgling young writer, Jill Neville; he had also recently met the woman who would become his second wife.

In her early days at Fitzroy Road, Sylvia tried to order her life. By December 21, she had finished decorating the living area, painting walls white and covering the floors with rush matting. For furniture, she bought pine bookcases, straw Hong Kong chairs, a small glass-topped table, and a large container in which she could arrange flowers. The decor, pleasing as it was, lacked warmth, which more than one guest remarked. Katherine Frankfort looked into a neighborhood nursery school for Frieda, now three. But Sylvia could not find a good au-pair girl (she had been spoiled by Susan, who had now assumed a nursing job in London). Without one, she got little work done. During all of December, she wrote only three poems ("Brasilia" and "Childless

Woman," the last of the Devon poems, plus "Eavesdropper," the first poem she finished at Fitzroy Road), two radio scripts, and "Ocean 1212-W."

Also, Plath had some minor run-ins with Trevor Thomas, who had decided that she and Hughes had tricked him out of the upstairs flat, which was rightfully his and which he needed for himself and the two sons from his own failed marriage. Thomas complained to Sylvia that she did not keep the entranceway clean (as she was supposed to), that she did not purchase her own garbage can but used his, and that her perambulator blocked the building's main doorway from the street. But Plath had to endure other problems. She still had neither a telephone nor a reliable au pair. Also, the immediate stress of the past few weeks, not to mention the emotional upheaval of the last six months, had seriously strained her physical health. It seemed she had no sooner moved into Fitzroy Road than she got the flu. To make matters worse, the children developed colds.

With Christmas approaching, Sylvia became more depressed: this Christmas would be her first without Ted. During late December, presents flooded in—a one-hundred-dollar check from Olive Prouty, one for fifty dollars from Aurelia—but Sylvia realized that she and the children had no friends with whom they could celebrate the holidays. Despondent, she called several people; invitations were finally issued. On Christmas, Sylvia and the children had tea at the Frankforts'; they then ate Christmas supper with the Macedos, who gave Frieda a toy piano and Nicholas a rubber rabbit. The next day, Boxing Day, the three of them shared supper with the Frankforts as a steady snow fell in the city. Yet Sylvia remained haunted by thoughts of Ted frolicking on a carefree Spanish holiday with Assia or with one of the models he was dating.

As this sense of abandonment weighed on her, Sylvia had finally, on Christmas Eve, confronted Alvarez about a romantic involvement. Telephoning him, she asked him to come over for the evening—drinks, supper, poetry. He had already been invited to a supper party at V. S. Pritchett's, Alvarez said, but he would stop by for a drink. Later, after the wine and the poetry—she read "Death & Co.," among others—

Sylvia aggressively forced the issue of an affair. "It would have been very easy to become involved with her," remembers Alvarez. "She was in the most terrible state. Absolutely desperate. But it was the kind of situation where I realized I would have had to involve myself with her much more seriously than I wanted. In other words, it wouldn't have been easy to take our friendship any further with her without going to bed, and I didn't want to go to bed with her. It would have been trouble. So I backed off." And left. Following an awkward good-bye, Alvarez headed for his supper at Pritchett's.

Alvarez's rebuff, as Plath came to view it, was a serious blow to their friendship. "She must have felt I was stupid and insensitive," Alvarez later wrote. "Which I was. But to have been otherwise would have meant accepting responsibilities I didn't want and couldn't, in my own depression, have coped with. When I left about eight o'clock to go on to my dinner party, I knew I had let her down in some final and unforgivable way. And I knew she knew. I never again saw her alive."

Professionally, the year 1962 ended on a disturbing note for Plath. In the last week in December, Judith Jones finally wrote her a letter to explain Knopf's rejection of *The Bell Jar*. Although she knew that Heinemann had already informed Plath that Knopf "would have to let your novel go," Jones wanted to write her personally, because she felt bad about the rejection, since she admired "so much [Plath's] lovely use of language and [her] sharp eye for unusual and vivid detail." Indeed, Jones had hoped that Plath would "put [her] talents" to use on a novel so that she could become "more accessible to more readers," the poetry market being as small as it is. But Jones and others at Knopf felt that Plath neither "managed to use [her] material successfully in a novelistic way" nor "succeeded in establishing a point of view." Also, Jones did not "accept the extent of [the narrator's] illness and the suicide attempt." In short, *The Bell Jar* "never really took hold for" her. Finally, Jones wrote, she wanted Plath to know how hard it was to launch a first novel—"particularly your kind of novel"—and because everyone at Knopf who read the manuscript had such reservations about it, she could not guarantee that they could give the book "a fair shake" in terms of advertising and promotion. Nevertheless, even though she was not going to publish *The Bell Jar,* Jones wanted Plath to consider Knopf "her publishers," for they had "a great deal of faith in [her] future."

6

The Boxing Day snowstorm was nothing compared to the horrible weather that lasted throughout January. It was the worst January in London in recent memory. Snow would fall, melt, turn to sludge, and then, as the temperature dropped, the sludge froze and more snow fell on top of that. Traffic in the city virtually ground to a halt. With space heaters putting a strain on the electricity lines, the power failed regularly. Pipes froze, ruptured—and stayed out of service. The weather conspired to complicate the day's simplest tasks: cooking breakfast, shopping at the corner market, or giving the baby a bath became a major undertaking. As Londoners begged for repairmen to fix the cracked pipes and for the electric board to restore power, they succumbed to flu, pneumonia, or depression. Hospitals were over-crowded and the suicide rate rose dramatically. For Sylvia, whose body had always responded poorly to cold weather, the season was especially painful. In her flat, the radiator pipes groaned and popped but produced no heat, the children lay bundled in bed while they fought colds, and Sylvia herself wandered about sick with the flu and sinusitis. It seemed as if winter would hang on forever.

In January 1963, *The London Magazine* printed Plath's "Stopped Dead" and "The Applicant," *The Observer* "Winter Trees." Because so few of her *Ariel* poems had been accepted, Plath was greatly pleased by these publications. She also eagerly awaited the January 14 release of *The Bell Jar.* Though she had hoped that her move into London would not put a stop to her hours of frenzied writing, it had. For she had written few poems and no prose in the last half of December and did not feel the urge to write now. Fighting the cold weather and her sicknesses, Sylvia could barely get through each day. Lately, Nicholas had been awaking at six in the morning—an added strain. Immediately after New Year's Day, Sylvia had enrolled Frieda in the nearby nursery school Katherine Frankfort had found for her. It cost four dollars a week. Frieda attended weekdays from nine-thirty until twelve-thirty; some mornings she cried when Sylvia left her, some mornings she did not. Judging from the children's behavior, they were both affected by the breakup of their parents' marriage. Sylvia, who recognized this and described in letters to her mother how Frieda cried when Ted left at the end of his visits to Fitzroy Road, felt both angry with Ted and guilty over upsetting their young lives.

In the first days of January, Plath sought treatment from Dr. Horder, who, worried about the twenty pounds she had lost over the summer and the high fevers she ran in October, prescribed a tonic to help her gain weight and X-rayed her chest to rule out anything more serious than the flu. Plath had Horder look at Nick's eye, which because of a minor deformity would probably require surgery. During early January, Plath was seeing more of Ted than she had been. On January 3, they again took the children to the zoo; on the 5th, he dropped by the flat at seven in the evening for a visit. Not long afterwards, Sylvia admitted to her mother that Ted came about once a week, under the guise of seeing Frieda. At times he treated Sylvia pleasantly; other times he could be dreadful. No matter what his behavior, his presence—or so Sylvia told Aurelia—unsettled her terribly. She could hardly bear to think of him living in an elegant flat, meeting important literary and publishing figures for supper, and taking carefree vacations with his girlfriend when it had been she—*Sylvia!*—who had worked so hard to put them in a position to enjoy the better things in life. Now the marriage had ended, and the sight of Ted made her furious. Even so, as Aurelia and others noticed, Sylvia would not put a stop to his coming by.

January 9th was an unusually bad day. The power failed, and the frigid weather would not let up. She had to write a cover letter to an editor at *The London Magazine* by candlelight, her fingers frigid as she typed, because the flat had neither electricity nor heat. At this point, she and the children, all three of them down with the flu, became so ill that Horder arranged for a live-in nurse, who stayed at the flat for a week, until Sylvia could recover enough to eat boiled eggs and chicken broth. Home Help Service, a government agency, sent her a cleaning woman, a Mrs. Vigors, who straightened up the flat while Sylvia was bedridden. But above all, she needed a good au-pair girl, Sylvia wrote to her mother on the 16th, a candidate for which she would soon interview.

In that same letter, Sylvia tried to convey how unbearable the winter really was. Because of electric strikes, all the lights and heat went out sometimes for hours. When this happened, meals went uncooked and parents bundled up their children to keep them warm. From those she cared about, Sylvia simply wanted encouragement. Occasionally she just needed someone to tell her she was doing fine, Sylvia wrote to her mother, under the conditions.

Actually, people *did.* The Beckers routinely saw Sylvia and the children. Gerry dropped by Fitzroy Road to check if all was going well (it often was not). Jillian invited Sylvia to a film festival at the Everyman Cinema in Hampstead in January; later that month, Sylvia attended a party at the Beckers' to which the Cleverdons brought Richard Murphy. (The Cleverdons had warned Murphy that Plath was in a "very tense state," which seemed an understatement; at the party she did not confront him, as some had thought she might.) Other supporters appeared. At mid-month, Susan O'Neill Roe and her boyfriend, Corin Hughes-Stanton, treated Sylvia to a night at the movies. On the 19th, Patty Goodall, a niece of Mildred Norton, and her husband had tea with Sylvia. Late in the month, Olive Prouty mailed Sylvia a $250 check. Around this time, the Beckers took her out for coffee to an all-night café in Soho, where they sat talking until dawn.

Still, throughout January, Sylvia fought the flu and her depression. Continuing to take her tonic to help eat, she now needed sleeping pills at night to go to sleep. Finally, late in the month, she hired an eighteen-year-old au pair to watch the children. In January, she also wrote two nonfiction pieces that *Punch* commissioned: "America! America!," a remembrance of her school days in Winthrop and Welles-ley, and "Snow Blitz," a humorous sketch about the awful winter. But mostly she struggled to get well. Clarissa Roche visited Fitzroy Road early in February. Arriving to find Sylvia tired and sick, Clarissa cooked her a meal of pork chops and corn. "Sylvia devoured this so ravenously that I was suspicious," Roche would later write, "and, sure enough, she confessed eventually that she had not been eating. . . . In fact, I think she was ill enough to muddle the days and nights. Sylvia then went to bed for a time and slept until my husband arrived. . . ." The sleep worked wonders. "When she came down there was no apparent trace of her feeling awful. She was a past master at disguising any state." The Roches left, but not before they had arranged with Plath to go to the theatre one night in mid-February. Days later, Sylvia phoned the Roches from a coin box and they made plans. The three of them and Duncan Grant, Paul Roche's former mentor, whom Plath wanted to meet, would go to *King Lear* the week of February 11. Clarissa would arrange for the tickets.

In January, Heinemann published *The Bell Jar* under the pseudonym Victoria Lucas. Dedicated to "Elizabeth and David" ("Compton" was omitted), the book was given a modest first run—the house would one day describe the initial printing as "token"—and received mostly very positive reviews. In the month following the novel's release, about fifteen reviews appeared in a range of periodicals, from *Time and Tide* to the London *Times*. In his *New Statesman* review, Robert Taubman identified *The Bell Jar* as "the first feminine novel I've read in the Salinger mode." The *Times Literary Supplement*'s anonymous reviewer set the tone of his piece with the lead sentence—"Few writers are able to create a different world for you to live in; yet Miss Lucas in *The Bell Jar* has done just this"—before he went on to say: "Miss Lucas can certainly write and the book is convincing. It reads so much like the truth that it is hard to disassociate her from Esther Greenwood, the 'I' of the story, but she has the gift of being able to feel and yet to watch herself: she can feel the dissolution and yet relate it to the landscape of everyday life. There is a dry wit behind the poetic flashes and the zany fiascos of her relationships, and when the last part of the book begins to trail a little and details seem both ugly and irrelevant one finds oneself thinking 'but this is how it happened.' " The BBC's review, which appeared in *The Listener* on January 31, also praised the book. "I recommend *The Bell Jar* strongly," Laurence Lerner said. "There are criticisms of American society that the neurotic can make as well as anyone, perhaps better, and Miss Lucas makes them triumphantly. . . . This is a brilliant and moving book."

While *The Bell Jar* was accumulating good reviews in England, no American publisher would touch it. Ted's editor at Harper and Row, Elizabeth Lawrence, to whom Heinemann had submitted the novel after Knopf turned it down, rejected it. She did so because she believed that, following Esther's breakdown, "the story ceases to be a novel and becomes a case history." In retrospect, *The Bell Jar* seems to be a victim of its time. Society allowed a man to write about going mad—Salinger and Ken Kesey did, to name two—but when a woman approached the subject she was disparaged. In Plath's case, the editors who did not recognize the historical (if not literary) value of the book were women. Two *men* had edited *The Bell Jar* at Heinemann; two *women* turned the novel down in America.

At the very end of January, Plath began to write poetry again. On the 28th, she finished a poem she had drafted in early December, "Sheep in Fog." On that day, she also completed, beginning from scratch, three more poems. "Child" is yet another poem concerning motherhood. "Totem" is, as Plath described it, "a pile of interconnected images, like a totem pole"—a sort of collage poem. And "The Munich Mannequins" recalls Plath's visit to Munich with Gordon. After her marriage to Hughes had failed and an anticipated affair with Alvarez ended before it even started, Plath used as source material for a poem her disastrous trip with Gordon. Had her Munich trip turned out to be a reconciliation with Gordon, and not a debacle, Plath could surely not help but think, how different her life would have been. Perhaps they would have married, settled down, had a family. Perhaps she would never have married Ted Hughes.

The next day, Plath wrote the poems "Paralytic" and "Gigolo." The latter, spoken by its title character, is about a narcissistic man dressed in black. On February 1, Plath produced three poems. "Mystic" is a religious poem in which the narrator thinks about love and faith. "Kindness" centers on a character named Dame Kindness, a woman who drips with sweetness, although her intentions may not be so pleasant as they appear on the surface. The last poem Plath wrote on the 1st, "Words," deals with language, yet the poem's final sentiment—"fixed stars / Govern a life"—also indicates the narrator's resolve to accept her fate.

On February 4, Plath finished one short poem, "Contusion." The next day, she wrote "Balloons" and "Edge." The first paints a charming picture of a boy playing with balloons. Also dealing with children, "Edge" is not so quaint. A brief lyric, the poem describes a dead woman—her body is now "perfected"—who is shown with her two dead children. The disturbing reality of the poem is clear. The woman has committed suicide. "Edge" was possibly the last poem Sylvia Plath wrote.

7

Since the summer, Plath's emotional state had gradually deteriorated. Her various physical illnesses, which proved to be unrelenting, only aggravated her condition. Her behavior had become disturbing at times. One day in January, after Trevor Thomas had shouted at her from the downstairs landing that the doorbell was ringing for her and it was up to her to answer it, Sylvia stormed out of her flat. "Can't you see I'm very ill?" she yelled. "I'm a very sick woman and I've a lot to do. I don't want to see anyone."

Not long after that, on Sunday the 27th, the day *The Observer* ran Anthony Burgess's review of *The Bell Jar*, Sylvia went down to Thomas's and knocked on his door. When he answered, Thomas saw Plath crying hysterically. "I am going to die," she said through her sobs, "and who will take care of my children?" Deeply concerned, Thomas took Sylvia into his flat, sat her down, and gave her a glass of sherry. Then he asked what had happened to make her this upset. "We were so happy," Sylvia said. "It's that awful woman's fault. She stole him. We were so happy and she stole him away from me. She's an evil woman, a scarlet woman, the Jezebel. They're in Spain spending our money, my money. Oh! How I hate them!" Barely able to control herself, Sylvia picked up *The Observer* lying on a table. She flipped to Ted's poem "Full Moon for Little Frieda," which appeared in the literary section, and showed it to Thomas. Turning to Burgess's review of *The Bell Jar,* she said: "That's me, though that's not my real name. I'm Sylvia Plath." The revelation startled Thomas. He knew the byline from seeing it in magazines, but he had no idea that the "Mrs. Hughes" who lived upstairs was Sylvia Plath.

From her outburst, the source of Plath's anguish became obvious. She might have pretended not to be jealous of Assia—she had even borrowed a table from her, she told her mother—yet Sylvia *was,* now as much as ever. It did not help that Ted continued to stop by Fitzroy Road regularly. "Daddy come soon?" Frieda would ask sometimes when she woke up at night crying. In a recent letter, Sylvia explained to her mother *why* she kept seeing Ted even if she hated him. As long as he visited the children, or at least Frieda, he would make his $280 monthly maintenance payment. However, others, like Aurelia, suspected that Sylvia saw Ted because she loved him. As January progressed, Colin and Valerie St. Johnson, neighbors who lived directly across Fitzroy Road and whose boy played with Frieda and Nicholas, noticed that lately Sylvia had taken to standing at a window in her living room and looking down towards the corner at which Ted would appear when he came from the nearby tube stop. During January, the St. Johnsons on occasion spotted Ted walking down Fitzroy Road. Each time, he wore all black; usually he had a black scarf thrown dramatically around his neck. By the end of the month, the St. Johnsons realized that Sylvia was standing at the window for longer and longer periods of time. Some days, she remained there, without moving, for hours. Though each St. Johnson mentioned it to the other, neither confronted Sylvia herself. Her neighbors simply assumed that Sylvia felt so strongly about the husband from whom (they knew) she was separated that she would wait at her window indefinitely, merely to glimpse his approaching figure.

Despite her problems, Sylvia still made plans for the future. On February 4, even as she admitted in a letter to her mother to feeling "grim" because of the "finality of it all," she catalogued upcoming events:

Marcia Brown would visit in March, a BBC critics' program had offered her a $150 assignment for May, and she would travel in the summer. Also, though she did not tell her mother, John Richardson, a friend, had asked her to the Spike Milligan evening for March 3, and she had set up a lunch date with her new Heinemann editor for February 11. She did tell Aurelia, however, that Horder had arranged for her to start sessions with a woman psychiatrist supplied by the National Health. Until then, she kept in close contact with Horder; after February 4, she saw him daily. Horder knew of Plath's marital and emotional problems. As of February 1963, he had diagnosed her as being "pathologically depressed," a condition he considered much too severe to be a result of the breakup of her marriage. Instead, Horder believed the source of this depression was "a combination of things of which the broken marriage was very important." She had an upper-respiratory infection, which can cause depression. She had just set up another new house in a foreign country—no easy task. She had a past history of severe—sometimes suicidal—depression. Worst of all, she was abnormally sensitive, as many artists are.

Horder himself had suffered for years with chronic depression. So, although he attempted to arrange for Plath a full-time National Health psychiatrist, he felt confident that he could treat her depression on his own. His decision about method proved crucial, for at some point early on in the week of the 4th Horder placed Plath on antidepressants. At that time, a physician had available to him two groups from which he could choose—tricyclics, which take three weeks or longer to go into effect and which can help the patient sleep, and monoamine-oxidase inhibitors, which work much faster—usually within two weeks—but can cause dangerous side effects if a patient eats the wrong foods, especially cheese. Since Plath did not need help sleeping—she still took barbiturates—Horder concluded that she needed relief as soon as possible. He put her on the latter and warned her about which foods not to eat.

On Thursday the 7th, Sylvia appeared to be nearing her breaking point. In the afternoon, she and the au pair got into a disagreement. According to the au pair, Sylvia, in a bad mood and sick, attacked her. According to Sylvia, who told two separate stories, the au pair either quit for no reason, or was fired by Sylvia because Sylvia discovered that she had left the children alone. Whatever really happened, when the au pair asked for the money Sylvia owed her, Sylvia *did* assault her; pushing and hitting her, she demanded that she go at once. Frightened, the au pair left without being paid. Almost hysterical, Sylvia telephoned Jillian Becker to ask if she and the children could come stay with her for a few days. This would be a stopgap measure while Horder, now gravely concerned about Sylvia's condition, searched for a bed in a suitable hospital so that she could be admitted. More than receptive, Jillian demanded that Sylvia come over right away. Driving across London in the Morris, Sylvia arrived at the Beckers' Mountfort Crescent flat around teatime, whereupon Jillian discovered that Sylvia had brought nothing with her except Nicholas and Frieda—no clothes, no suitcase, no baby paraphernalia. Apparently, she had just gathered up the children and rushed out of the flat. Jillian put the three of them in an upstairs bedroom, drove Sylvia's car back over to Fitzroy Road, and collected the things Sylvia and the children would need to spend the weekend. She brought back clothes for the children, bottles for Nicholas, and, for Sylvia—at Sylvia's request—curlers, cosmetics, and a party dress. At Mountfort Crescent, Jillian bathed and dressed Nicholas and Frieda, prepared a steak supper that Sylvia enjoyed enormously, and, after Sylvia had asked her to, went with her upstairs to her bedroom. Jillian watched as Sylvia swallowed one sleeping pill after another. She then stayed with her until the pills took over and Sylvia drifted off to sleep.

About three-thirty in the morning, Sylvia awoke Jillian—and the rest of the house—crying out for help. She wanted Jillian to sit with her until five-thirty, when she could take her next antidepressant. The hardest depression to endure, Sylvia told Jillian, was the one in the early morning. Fearful for Sylvia's welfare, Jillian settled in a chair and listened to a two-hour tirade against Ted, Assia, and the entire Hughes family. Her ideal marriage, Sylvia said, had now ended. She felt abandoned, just as she had after her father's death. She also brought up a list of names that meant nothing to Jillian—Richard, Dick, Gordon. They all had loved her and wanted to marry her. She could have been happy with them. Instead, she made the mistake of marrying Ted.

Finally, Sylvia dozed off again, and Jillian, exhausted by the scene, returned to bed. The next morning, though sick with the flu, Gerry went off to work; Jillian remained to care for Nicholas and Frieda. Soon after breakfast, Jillian took a telephone call from Horder, who told her he hoped to locate a hospital bed soon. Two hospitals he had approached had no rooms available; a third, which could admit her, seemed unsuitable to Horder. As they spoke, Horder implored Jillian to encourage Sylvia to care for the children herself. Sylvia adored the children. If she realized how much they depended on her, Horder believed, she might feel more worthy.

Later in the morning, well after Jillian had hung up with Horder, Sylvia called him herself to set up an appointment. At that time, she also telephoned the au-pair girl, who, when Sylvia asked her to come back, refused to work for her again. In the afternoon, once she had rested and taken one of the four hot baths she would have that day, Sylvia drove back across town to see Horder. But when Trevor Thomas carried his milk bottles out, an hour or so after coming home from work, he discovered Sylvia sitting alone in the Morris in front of their building. Because the weather was cold and snowy, Thomas approached Sylvia to ask if she felt all right. Fine, Sylvia assured him; she was just thinking. Should he call Dr. Horder? Thomas said. (Like almost everyone in the neighborhood, he too used Horder.) "No," Sylvia answered, "I'm going away for a long holiday, a long rest." Then Thomas wanted to know where the children were; with friends, Sylvia said. Finally, Thomas returned to his flat and Sylvia drove off. At the Beckers', she stayed only long enough to eat supper before she left again. This time, she took with her the curlers, cosmetics, and party dress. On her way out to the Morris, she told the Beckers not to wait up. She had a "very important" date.

That night, Sylvia met Ted at Fitzroy Road. The two of them did not remain long, or so Hughes would say years later; Sylvia seemed in a hurry. Whether their conversation was brief, Ted ultimately left. Apparently, Sylvia then dressed and curled her hair (if she had not done so already). It is uncertain what she did next: she may have gone elsewhere, or she may simply have not felt like driving across town.

At any rate, she hired a taxi back to Mountfort Crescent, where Jillian noticed a decided change in her personality. Her actions were direct and purposeful, as if after much uncertainty some vital issue had been settled. Had she finally come to realize that Ted did not intend to come back to her? Had he told her so in their conversation? Assia had become pregnant—a pregnancy she aborted around March 1; if Sylvia learned of Assia's pregnancy that night, certainly the news would have further depressed her. Any reconciliation between Ted and Sylvia, if that was what Sylvia wanted, would have been rendered all but impossible. This, more than the resolution of any other unfinished business in her life, would have accounted for the new attitude Jillian saw. Or, as friends of Sylvia's later speculated, perhaps something more ominous occurred Friday night at Fitzroy Road. After years of repeatedly being hypnotized by Ted and acting on his posthypnotic suggestions, Sylvia was highly sensitive to any signal—conscious or unconscious—that she perceived him to be sending. Several times during the fall she had told her mother that Ted wanted her to kill herself; if she believed this, it might have propelled her on some new and purposeful path of action tonight.

The next morning, Gerry, now very ill, stayed in bed, while Jillian watched the children and Sylvia rested. In the evening, Jillian and Gerry reluctantly kept a supper date with friends. Gerry arranged for one of his students to come sit with Sylvia. With the Beckers away, Sylvia and the student listened to music, mostly Beethoven. Later, when the Beckers came back, Sylvia began her nightly routine: she took the sleeping pills, awoke in the middle of the night, and, calling out to Jillian, confided in her until she dropped back off to sleep.

On Sunday, Gerry felt well enough to go with the children to the zoo. Jillian's two children (by a previous marriage) had been staying with their father so that Sylvia and her children could sleep in their rooms. Today they joined Gerry, along with Nicholas and Frieda as well as the two Cleverdon children (Douglas and Nest lived on the same square as the Beckers), to make it a real outing. The group was back by lunch, at which Sylvia ate heartily. Then she went upstairs to her bedroom and took a long nap, the best rest she had had in days.

Late in the afternoon, when she awoke, Sylvia decided that she wanted to go home. Because her car was elsewhere, she asked Gerry to drive her and the children to Fitzroy Road. The Beckers protested. There was no reason for her to leave, they insisted. She should stay until she felt better, or until Horder could find her a bed in a suitable hospital. But she *did* feel better, Sylvia said. The sleep had made her feel like a different person. Anyway, Horder had lined up a nurse, whom she needed to meet at the flat early in the morning, and Sylvia had things to do tomorrow: wash clothes, take Frieda to nursery school, and have lunch with her Heinemann editor. Even so, the Beckers argued against her going—but to no avail. Finally, Sylvia collected the children and all the family's belongings and convinced Gerry to drive her across town.

Although Sylvia cried most of the way, Gerry could not persuade her to go back with him. After he left around seven, Sylvia fed the children and put them to bed; then Horder checked in on her. Next Sylvia must have written letters. At eleven-forty-five, she walked down and rang Thomas's bell to ask for stamps. Immediately upon answering his door, Thomas realized that, in addition to whatever she had been doing while he heard her pacing about upstairs, she had also taken some kind of medication. She looked drugged, distracted. "Would you be able to let me have some stamps, please?" Sylvia asked. Her letters were "airmail for America," and she wanted to put them in the box tonight. Certainly, Thomas answered. But before fetching the stamps, he asked why she had not gone away for her holiday. "The children were difficult and I wanted to write," Sylvia said. Thomas handed the stamps to Sylvia, who asked how much she owed him—an offer Thomas refused. "Oh! But I must pay you or I won't be right with my conscience before God, will I?" Finally, as if Sylvia's behavior had not been peculiar enough, she wanted to know what time he left for work in the morning. Around eight-thirty, Thomas answered. Why? "Oh, nothing, I just wondered, that's all." With this, Thomas shut the door. Ten minutes later, when he spotted the hallway light still burning, he opened the door to find Sylvia standing in the same place. I'm calling Horder, Thomas insisted. "Oh no, please, don't do that. I'm just having a marvelous dream, a most wonderful vision." Confused, Thomas shut the door once again and, since it was almost twelve-thirty, went to bed, although he was kept awake by the sound of Sylvia walking on her wooden floors upstairs.

At some point, Sylvia must have mailed her letters. If she slept, she did not sleep much. Thomas could hear her footsteps until he drifted off to sleep at five. It would probably have been around this hour, the time of her early-morning depression, the one that was hardest to endure, that she began the actions that ended in her death. She wrote a note—"Please call Dr. Horder," it said under his telephone number—and crept down the stairs into the main entryway to tape the note to the perambulator, just inside the building's front door. Back in her flat, she prepared a plate of bread and butter and two mugs of milk, which she carried upstairs and placed in Frieda and Nicholas's bedroom. She opened the window in the children's room; then, going into the hall, sealed the room shut behind her by stuffing towels into the crack at the sill jamb and taping up the top and two sides. The children's safety secured, Sylvia went downstairs and sealed herself in the kitchen. Again, towels under the door, tape over the cracks. Finally, in the heart of the blue hour, that part of the early morning during which she had written her best poems, Sylvia Plath opened the oven door, folded a cloth on which she could rest her cheek, turned on the gas full-tilt, and, kneeling down on the floor before the oven, rested her cheek on the folded cloth she had placed on the oven door.

At nine o'clock, Myra Norris, the nurse Plath was expecting, arrived at 23 Fitzroy Road. Because the house's front entrance was locked, Norris could not get into the building to knock on Plath's door. Also, the name of the patient, Sylvia Plath Hughes, did not appear on either doorbell, and Norris was not even sure that she was at the correct address. She rang Thomas's bell—no answer. In time, she decided to telephone her agency to verify the patient's name and address. After waiting in line at the coin box—a new frost had burst more pipes, so neighbors queued up to telephone plumbers—Norris contacted her office. Sylvia Plath Hughes, 23 Fitzroy Road—the information was correct. Returning to the building, Norris walked around back to look for a second entrance. When she did, she spotted the two children crying at their bedroom window. Deeply concerned, Norris ran around front and bumped into Charles Langridge, a builder working on the block. With his help, Norris gained access to the house. Outside the upstairs flat's door, they could both smell the unmistakable odor of gas. When Langridge broke down the door, they rushed in, forced their way into the kitchen, and found Sylvia sprawled out on the tile floor, her head still in the oven.

Hurriedly they turned off the gas and opened the windows. Then they carried Sylvia's body into the living room, and Norris began artificial respiration. Meanwhile, Langridge called the police from the coin box. When the policeman arrived, Langridge helped him rescue the children from upstairs. At some point, Langridge spotted the note taped on the perambulator and telephoned Horder. Soon Horder arrived with a friend, a doctor from America. Examining her, Horder agreed with the nurse, who had given up on the artificial respiration: Sylvia's condition was hopeless. Horder pronounced Plath dead at ten-thirty. Afterwards, an emergency team removed her body from the flat on a stretcher and transported it by ambulance to University College Hospital, on Gower Street in Saint Pancras. On her death certificate, which was registered on the 16th, Plath was described as being dead when she arrived at the hospital. Listing her occupation as "an authoress . . . wife of Edward James Hughes an author," the certificate documented her cause of death as "Carbon monoxide poisoning (domestic gas) while suffering from depression. Did kill herself." On a desk in a room at 23 Fitzroy Road, the flat in which William Butler Yeats had lived and in which Sylvia Plath had now died, lay a finished manuscript, *Ariel and Other Poems*.

Horder telephoned Jillian Becker, who was devastated by the news. Jillian, who did not have Ted's number, called Suzette Macedo, who reached Hughes at his Soho flat. Suzette arrived at Fitzroy Road to watch after the children, whom Horder had examined and found to be in good condition. Though the children survived, Trevor Thomas almost did not. Gas from the upstairs flat had seeped down into his room and knocked him out as he slept. Awaking late in the afternoon,

Thomas felt sick and confused. When he saw him, Horder diagnosed Thomas as suffering from carbon-monoxide poisoning.

On February 12, Hughes cabled not Aurelia but Aunt Dotty. The cable was simple. "Sylvia died yesterday," it stated flatly; then it documented the details of the funeral, which Ted was now planning without consulting the Plath family.

On Friday the 15th, an inquest took place at Saint Pancras County Court, a small brick building off the huge wooded Saint Pancras Gardens. Inside, in the cramped, dark courtroom, the coroner called witnesses to the box and asked them questions about the "sudden death" of Sylvia Plath Hughes. On this day the court heard testimony from Ted Hughes, who identified the body; Myra Norris and Constable John Jones, who presented evidence; Dr. Peter Sutton, who reported on the postmortem (he had concluded Plath "[d]id kill herself"); and Dr. Horder, who was criticized by the coroner for not finding Plath a hospital bed. With officialdom satisfied, only the funeral remained.

After the inquest, Ted traveled with Sylvia's body to Yorkshire, where he had decided she would be buried in his family's cemetery in Heptonstall. The next day, in the early afternoon of February 16, a brief service was held at the Hugheses' local church. Overseen by Oliver Forshaw, who knew almost nothing about Ted and Sylvia, the service was attended by a handful of people—the Beckers, Ted's parents, a local church devotee named Joan Mason, and Warren and Margaret, who had flown from America. The children did not come, but remained in London with Aunt Hilda; nor did Olwyn, ill with the flu. Shattered by the blow of her daughter's death, Aurelia did not attempt the trip over. At the conclusion of the ceremony in the church, the funeral party reconvened at the cemetery, which, like much of the moors, lay under a layer of snow. When the minister had completed the prayers, the gathering of mourners dispersed; the open grave would be filled in by the undertaker. Though a tombstone had not yet been put in place, one eventually would be. Along with her married name—Sylvia Plath Hughes—and the dates—1932–1963—Hughes would select as an inscription a line from the *Bhagavad Gita:* "Even amidst fierce flames the golden lotus can be planted."

*   *   *

Over the years, Plath's family and friends would try to understand her death. "Sylvia was doomed," Wilbury Crockett remembered. "I don't want to say she had a death wish. What I'm saying is, I was not surprised by the way her life ended. I grieved but I was not shocked." Gloria Steinem placed Plath in social context. "Sylvia Plath was an early prophet who described a societal problem by describing her own suffering, who described the problem without knowing why. And when the why finally came along, she became even more tragic." Alvarez openly acknowledged his (and others') guilt. "When I look back on her life, it fills me with shame about how badly everyone behaved towards her near the end . . . , myself included." Aurelia Plath isolated her daughter's most basic character defect. "Sylvia's tragic flaw lay in her own very weak ego strength." And Marybeth Little summed up the pathos of Plath's death. "Her death was tragic but her life was a triumph. How many of us have recovered from the (almost) perfectly natural nervous breakdown of the sensitive scholarly student? Much more important, how many of us left poems that will live? And children who live, yes, in a shadow but, yes, in the light of a light undimmed."

A Posthumous Life

1

Though Plath did not become famous during her lifetime, she would in the years following her death, as a quasi-cultish audience—the sort that rarely forms around an author, living or dead—bought almost anything written by her. Indeed, in her "second," and posthumous, life it was as if Plath had not died at all. Beginning in February 1963 and continuing over the next two decades, Plath's poetry, fiction, nonfiction, and even drama appeared regularly both in periodicals and in book form, the presentation and frequency similar to that of an author who was very much alive.

The release of this material was overseen by Ted Hughes. Since Plath was legally married to Hughes at the time of her death, and since she did not leave a will stipulating otherwise, Hughes became not only the custodian of Frieda and Nicholas (after toying with the idea of letting Aurelia raise the children, he decided to do so himself) but also, under British law, heir to her estate. The inheritance included both Plath's material property and, more important, the copyright to her entire canon of published and unpublished work. All monies made from the sale of that work went to the Estate of Sylvia Plath, which for all intents and purposes was Ted Hughes.

Sylvia Plath's posthumous life began on Sunday, February 17, 1963, when *The Observer* in London printed A. Alvarez's short but poignant homage, "A Poet's Epitaph." The single paragraph read:

Last Monday, Sylvia Plath, the American poetess and wife of Ted Hughes, died suddenly in London. She was thirty. She published her first and highly accomplished book of poems, *The Colossus*, in 1960. But it was only recently that the particular intensity of her genius found its perfect expression. For the last few months she had been writing continuously, almost as though possessed. In those last poems, she was systematically probing that narrow, violent area between the viable and the impossible, between experience which can be transmuted into poetry and that which is overwhelming. [Her final work] represents a totally new breakthrough in modern verse, and establishes her I think as the most gifted woman poet of her time. . . . The loss to literature is inestimable.

To accompany Alvarez's epitaph, *The Observer* ran a black-and-white photograph of Plath. In the shot, her face appears delicate and innocent, its tenderness enhanced by the black turtleneck she wears and by her dark hair curving inward against her ashen cheeks. Completing the tribute, the paper printed four of Plath's poems—"Contusion," "The Fearful," "Kindness," and "Edge." If these poems underscored the tragedy Alvarez tried to capture—the poems' brilliance suggested at least some justification for his praise—"Edge" and "The Fearful," whose narrators contemplate self-destruction, cast some doubt on Alvarez's terse statement that Plath had "died suddenly."

The topic of *The Observer*'s homage was no doubt discussed one week after Plath's funeral at a gathering at 23 Fitzroy Road. (Because Plath owned a long-term lease on the flat and had paid the whole first year's rent, Hughes, whom the real-estate agents believed to be living there anyway—and Assia—moved in.) To the gathering Assia invited about a dozen people, including Olwyn, Daniel and Helga Huws, friends of the Huwses', Aunt Hilda, and Luke Myers, who, hearing of Plath's suicide, had come to Ted's support. They put on some records—Olwyn remembers playing a Joan Baez album—and guests stayed until well after midnight. Years later, Trevor Thomas published a memoir of Plath in which he referred to this event as a party. He also said he heard the sound of bongo drums in the flat above him. Olwyn vehemently denied the accusations. Though they did have people over and they did talk loudly and play music, this, to Olwyn, was not a party. And, she said, there were *no* bongo drums!

Some time in March, Ted and Assia drove down to Court Green to look around, now that Ted had decided to sell the property. At Court Green, they ate lunch with Elizabeth and David Compton, who, at Ted's request, had moved in temporarily to show the house to real-estate agents and potential buyers. Following lunch, Assia asked to walk through the house (she had not been there since the fateful weekend in May 1962), and Ted, uneasy with the idea, asked Elizabeth to go with her. Reluctantly, Elizabeth agreed to. But upstairs, as she and Assia passed the door to Plath's study and she pointed out that this was the room in which Plath had worked, the strain of the moment took over and Elizabeth broke down. To which Assia said: "You really did like her, didn't you?" Upset, Elizabeth rushed back downstairs, where she told Ted that *he* could show Assia the house. He wouldn't, he and Assia eventually argued, and they headed back for London.

Elizabeth thought the ugly episode was over. Several days later, she was opening the mail one morning, and ran across a gas bill. She had been receiving utility bills for Court Green, but this bill came from London, not Devon. Examining it, she discovered that in fact the bill was for 23 Fitzroy Road and covered the period that included February 11. And when Elizabeth turned the bill over, she could not believe what she saw. On it Assia had written, "She was your friend. You pay the bill."

Others responded to Plath's death less bitterly. While rummaging through old photographs, Wilbury Crockett ran across two of Sylvia, taken during her high-school years. When he mailed them to Aurelia Plath, he enclosed a brief letter.

Dear Mrs. Plath,

Not a day goes by that does not bring the question—"Why?" I grieve more than I can say.

These pictures I thought you would like to have. Isn't the one by the fire lovely?

I hardly know how to bring you comfort as I can't find any myself.

My Best,
Wilbury Crockett

Like other Wellesley residents, Crockett had read about Plath's death in her obituary in the Wellesley *Townsman* on February 21, 1963. The newspaper revealed Plath's cause of death as "virus pneumonia." The error did not lie with the *Townsman*. At the time, the surviving family provided information for an obituary, in the same way that a subscriber did when he bought a wedding announcement or a classified ad. In this case, the family, both the Plaths and the Hugheses, had reached a decision. In deference to the children, no one would confirm the true nature of Plath's death, even though rumors about her suicide were already becoming widespread among friends, acquaintances, and the literary community.

Actually, Plath's suicide had been reported in the February 22 edition of the Saint Pancras *Chronicle*, a small weekly newspaper that covered events in Camden Town, the London neighborhood in which Plath had died. The article, "Tragic Death of Young Authoress," began: "Found with her head in the gas oven in the kitchen of their home in Fitzroy road, N.W.1, last week was 30-year-old authoress Mrs. Sylvia Plath Hughes, wife of one of Britain's best known modern poets, Ted Hughes." After detailing her final days, the article quoted from the coroner's inquest. "Mr. Hughes told the Deputy Coroner (Dr. George McEwan) that his wife had lately had mysterious temperatures and nervous troubles." The article's last sentence summed up the facts of the case, known so far. "The Deputy Coroner recorded his verdict that she died of carbon monoxide poisoning while suffering from depression, and that she killed herself."

Because the Saint Pancras *Chronicle*'s audience numbered only several thousand, few people in London read the article. No one, outside Plath's immediate family perhaps, read it in America. As a result, the March 7 Wellesley *Townsman* published a follow-up to its obituary that did not take into account any of the *Chronicle*'s revelations. Instead, " 'A Poet's Epitaph' Honors the Late Sylvia Plath Hughes" identified her cause of death as—again—"virus pneumonia."

Two additional notes commemorating Plath's death appeared. *The Spectator* in London ran a brief remembrance. The April 1963 *Smith Alumnae Quarterly* published a short citation, which included Plath's name and date of Smith graduation and a paragraph touching on the high points of her career, in an alphabetically arranged list of all recently deceased Smith graduates. The *Quarterly* did not mention the circumstances of Plath's death.

Fewer than a half-dozen obituaries of Plath appeared. As the rest of the year unfolded, though, many magazines began to publish her work. In April, her poems appeared in *The Critical Quarterly, The London Magazine,* and *The Atlantic Monthly; Punch* printed her essay "America! America!" In June, *The London Magazine* published "Berck-Plage." In August, *Poetry* (Chicago) offered three poems and a paragraph remembering Plath that stated that "[t]he death of Sylvia Plath on February 11 of this year was a shock and great sorrow to the world of poets here and in England." But on August 3, 1963, the most noteworthy tribute to Plath appeared to date, in *The New Yorker*. The editors ran a two-page spread of her poems, seven in all, and added below her byline, which appeared after the last of her seven poems, two simple dates—"1932–1963."

Two more anthologies of Plath's poems appeared in 1963, both in October. In England, *Encounter* ran ten poems and *The Review,* edited by Ian Hamilton, devoted a good portion of that month's issue to Plath and placed a photograph of her on the cover. Snapped in 1957 by Olwyn Hughes, the picture shows a peaceful-looking Plath sitting in front of a wall of books, her blondish hair hanging down onto her shoulders. The plaid-trimmed wool cardigan sweater she wears lends a girlish naïveté to her appearance. The nine poems inside, however, were anything but naïve. From "Daddy" to "Lesbos," poem after poem depicted a world shattered by warring emotions—love versus hate, rage versus happiness, insecurity versus self-determination. As a companion piece, *The Review* ran Alvarez's "Sylvia Plath," an adaptation of a talk he wrote for the BBC's "Third Programme." The piece ended with the inflammatory statement, "Poetry of this order is a murderous art."

In October, *The Observer* printed "Poppies in October," in November "The Horse" (the renamed "Ariel"). Each poem appeared alone, accompanied by Plath's byline, without any biographical information whatsoever.

*   *   *

On the front page of the June 30, 1963, *New York Times Book Review*, M. L. Rosenthal published "New Singers and Songs," a discussion of several modern and contemporary poets. To define Theodore Roethke's importance, Rosenthal cited the poetry of Sylvia Plath and Ted Hughes. "Recently, [Roethke] has received a good deal of recognition in England," he wrote, "where among others he has influenced the gifted poet Ted Hughes and his American wife, Sylvia Plath. Miss Plath's very last poems, as represented in a recent issue of the Sunday *Observer*, were morbid but brilliant. In the absolute authority of their statement they went beyond Roethke into something like the pure realization of the latter-day Emily Dickinson." A passing reference in a long essay, these three sentences foreshadowed the literally hundreds of critical essays and book-length studies that would be published on Plath's work over the coming years.

2

It was Ted Hughes who had combed through Plath's belongings in the days after her death to find the poetry and prose he knew she had been writing during the last months of her life. It was Hughes who negotiated with the editors who wanted to publish her work in periodicals in 1963 and 1964. So, not surprisingly, it was Hughes who, as early as mid-1963, began planning a posthumous collection of his late wife's poetry.

When he read through the manuscript of *Ariel* that Plath had arranged just before Christmas, Hughes decided that, because he wanted to incorporate poems she had written in the weeks immediately preceding her death, and because he wanted to excise some of the "more personally aggressive" poems from those she had written in 1962, he would delete fourteen poems, add thirteen others, and rearrange the order of the book. This done, in the summer of 1963 he submitted *Ariel* to William Heinemann, who held an option on Plath's next book because they had published *The Bell Jar*. Heinemann offered Hughes a contract for *Ariel*, but ultimately the two could not agree on terms. In time, Hughes and his own publisher, Faber and Faber, came to an agreement after Faber gave Hughes considerable concessions—a larger-than-normal advance ($750), a 15 percent royalty rate on all hardback books sold, and a 100 percent royalty on anthology and broadcast rights. By the end of 1963, negotiations were complete. Faber would bring out *Ariel* in England as soon as they could rush it into print once Hughes had finished the introduction that he planned to write.

In America, Alfred A. Knopf was interested in acquiring *Ariel*. By mid-October 1963, not long after *The New Yorker* had published its two-page spread of Plath's final poems, Knopf was ready to make an offer. But by February 1964, Knopf, hopeful yet, feared Hughes would want too much for *Ariel*. In March, Knopf received their answer: Elizabeth Anderson, of Heinemann, wrote to William Koshland, of Knopf, to inform him that Olwyn Hughes, working as agent for the Plath estate, requested the rights for *The Colossus* to revert back to the estate. Obviously, the Hugheses wanted to control the rights to Plath's late *and* early poems, since they believed both would be valuable soon. (In the end, Knopf retained rights to *The Colossus* because they still owned books—about seven hundred, selling at the rate of six copies per month; Heinemann, who had not kept an edition in print, lost control of the British rights to Faber.) As 1964 passed, Hughes and Knopf could not agree on terms. Knopf offered a standard contract for a poetry collection—a two-hundred-dollar advance and a 10 percent hardcover royalty—but Hughes insisted that Knopf meet Faber's deal. The stalemate continued on in March 1965, the month Faber released the British edition of *Ariel*—without an introduction by Hughes, who had been emotionally incapable of writing one.

Referring to the poems themselves and to the death of the poet who produced them, the blurb on the book's dust jacket stated only that these poems "were all written between the publication in 1960 of Sylvia Plath's first book, *The Colossus;* and her death in 1963." The jacket copy did not mention details of her "death," much less her suicide.

Almost as a group, *Ariel*'s early critics also refused to reveal that Plath had died a suicide. In all honesty, they seemed puzzled by something much more basic: exactly what to make of these poems that defied the rules of traditional book-reviewing.

In *The Listener*, P. N. Furbank called Plath's art "hysterical bravado"; in *The Spectator*, M. L. Rosenthal expressed concern about her "fascination with death"; and in *The New Statesman*, Francis Hope questioned "how great a talent Plath's premature death destroyed." Finally, in *The Observer*, Alvarez stated that, although *Ariel*'s poems might be "despairing, vengeful, and destructive," they are ultimately "works of great artistic purity and, despite all the nihilism, great generosity." Alvarez also made the observation (and he was one of the first to do so) that since Plath's death "a myth has been gathering around her work." This myth stemmed from her premature death, which seemed, to Alvarez, "prepared for and, in some degree, understood"—"in a way, even justified, like some final unwritten poem."

Although he credited her death with the creation of the myth, he did not reveal that the death was a suicide. This veil of secrecy, one disregarded only by the tiny Saint Pancras *Chronicle,* would finally be dropped on October 7, when George Steiner disclosed in the *Reporter* what many of the readers of his review, "Dying Is an Art," already knew: Plath had not simply "died suddenly," she had committed suicide. "The spell does not lie wholly in the poems themselves," Steiner wrote, addressing why *Ariel* had affected an audience the same way Dylan Thomas's *Deaths and Entrances* had. "The suicide of Sylvia Plath at the age of thirty in 1963, and the personality of this young woman who had come from Massachusetts to study and live in England (where she married Ted Hughes, himself a gifted poet), are vital parts of it. To those who knew her and to the greatly enlarged circle who were electrified by her last poems and sudden death, she had come to signify the specifics, honesties and risks of the poet's condition."

In November, both the daily *Times* and the *Times Literary Supplement* finally went on record concerning *Ariel*—almost eight months after the book's publication. On the 4th, in "Poems for the Goodhearted," the daily *Times* called Plath's book "important," adding,

ROUGH MAGIC · 342

"They are notable poems." Three weeks later, in "Along the Edge," the *TLS* praised *Ariel* further. It was, according to the anonymous reviewer, "one of the most marvelous volumes of poetry published for a very long time."

In the fall of 1965, Knopf was still trying to purchase *Ariel*'s American rights from Ted Hughes. But Hughes had been approached by a number of other houses. Harper and Row, his publisher, had presented him with, as he wrote to Judith Jones at Knopf, a handsome offer— the same deal he struck with Faber and Faber. When Knopf firmly refused to meet those terms, Hughes made definite arrangements with Harper and Row.

To prepare readers for the poems and to ensure a successful launch of the book, Harper and Row commissioned Robert Lowell to write an introduction. "Everything in these poems is personal, confessional, felt," Lowell declared in his 750-word piece, "but the manner of feeling is controlled hallucination, the autobiography of a fever. She burns to be on the move, a walk, a ride, a journey, the flight of the queen bee. She is driven forward by the pounding pistons of her heart." Then Lowell pushed his argument even further. "These poems are playing Russian roulette with six cartridges in the cylinder," he wrote; they are poems engaged in "a game of 'chicken,' the wheels of both cars locked and unable to swerve." And the "surprise, the shimmering, unwrapped birthday present" is what if not "death"? In charged language, Lowell elevated these poems to a whole new level of meaning, one where the line of distinction between a poet's life and her art is so blurred as to become nonexistent. Yet even Lowell did not reveal the true cause of Plath's death. This point finally became moot on June 10, 1966—the date on which *Time* magazine ran its review of *Ariel*.

One dank day in February 1963, a pretty young mother of two children was found in a London flat with her head in the oven and the gas jet wide open. The dead woman was Sylvia Plath, 30, an American poet whose marriage to Ted Hughes, a British poet, had gone on the rocks not long before. Her published verses, appearing occasionally in American magazines and gathered in a single volume,

The Colossus, had displayed accents of refinement, but had not yet achieved authority of tone.

But within a week of her death, intellectual London was hunched over copies of a strange and terrible poem she had written during her last sick slide toward suicide. "Daddy" was its title; its subject was her morbid love-hate of her father; its style was as brutal as a truncheon. What is more, "Daddy" was merely the first jet of flame from a literary dragon who in the last months of her life breathed a burning river of bile across the literary landscape.

So began *Time*'s piece on *Ariel*. It was not so much a discussion of the poems themselves as a thumbnail sketch of Plath's life and death, an overview that focused, predictably, on the darker elements, those worthy of banner headlines. In fact, throughout the article the magazine referred to Plath as "Sylvia"—an intimacy the editors heightened by illustrating the text with a sort of miniature family album featuring pictures of "Sylvia at 4, with mother," "at 21" sunbathing on the beach in a stunning white two-piece, "at 23" arm in arm with Hughes, "at 25" in a pensive mood in her study. This intimate tone was echoed ten days later, when *Newsweek* ran its review of *Ariel*, which took up two-thirds of a page and contained a photograph of Plath holding an infant Nicholas. Despite the sensational slant of these reviews, *Ariel* had achieved a rarity for a book of poetry. It had been written up in the two largest weekly news magazines in America.

Over the coming weeks, some critics, like Gene Baro writing in *The New York Times Book Review*, questioned whether *Ariel* would endure once the hoopla surrounding its release wore off. Even so, the book was reviewed in numerous publications. Largely because of this attention, by March 1967—two years after the first copy of *Ariel* was sold in a London bookstore—the collection was on its way to becoming an extraordinary success. Both *Time* and *Newsweek* reported that, in its first year of publication in England alone, the book sold more than fifteen thousand copies—probably a conservative estimate. Sales in America easily surpassed those in England. And as the years passed, the book continued to sell well. After its first twenty years in print,

Ariel would sell upwards of a half-million copies, making it one of the best-selling volumes of poetry to be published in England or America in the twentieth century.

3

In September 1963, after he had lived briefly both at 23 Fitzroy Road and in a house in Yorkshire, Ted Hughes moved back to Court Green. He simply could not force himself to sell the house he and Plath had bought together. He was joined there by Olwyn, who quit her job in Paris to become Nicholas and Frieda's "mother"—she would never have children of her own—and give Ted the freedom he needed to write.

In the summers of 1964 and 1965, Aurelia Plath came to Devon to visit her grandchildren. (In the summer after Sylvia's death, she had seen them in London.) She was planning to return to Devon in the summer of 1966 when, around the first of the year, Hughes wrote and told her not to. He said he and the children would be living in Germany while he filled a writer-in-residence position funded by the German Embassy. In reality, he did not want Aurelia to arrive in Devon and discover that Olwyn, who lived at Court Green for two years, had departed only to be replaced by Assia.

As time wore on, Aurelia was apprised of the situation. To remain on good terms with Ted, her link to her grandchildren, she "approved" tacitly by refusing to confront him. By the summer of 1967, Aurelia felt comfortable enough with the arrangement to visit the children at Court Green once again. At that time, she met Assia, who from then on assumed the lion's share of Ted's correspondence with her. When Nicholas and Frieda flew to America for the first time, in the summer of 1968, for example, Assia maintained most of the letter-writing with Aurelia concerning the children's travel plans. In June 1968, in a letter to Ted's Aunt Hilda, Aurelia attempted to come to terms with the strange predicament in which she now found herself—being forced to befriend "the other woman" in her daughter's life. "Whatever has been and is—[Assia] wanted to keep in touch with me and I feel she is trying to find something she can tell me that will give me some happiness," Aurelia Plath wrote. "I want to be absolutely open about this, for my concern is to keep the channels between Ted and me and the children open. . . . What concerns the welfare of Frieda and Nicholas concerns me as their grandparent—the children of my lost daughter will always hold priority in my heart. Anything else is simply not my business."

On January 20, 1967, Assia, who never legally divorced David Wevill, gave birth to a daughter, whom she named Alexandra Tatiana Elise (nicknamed Shura). On Shura's birth certificate, which was recorded in Saint Catherine's House in London, the surname is listed as Wevill; however, Assia wrote in the blank reserved for the identity of the child's father: "Edward James Hughes, author." So, in the summer of 1966, Assia arrived at Court Green already pregnant, and in the summer of 1967, Aurelia met not just Assia, but Shura as well. It would be the first and last time she would see them.

By March 1969, Assia and Ted had been friends and lovers for the better part of a decade. They had endured catastrophes together, although they had enjoyed good times too, most notably the birth of their daughter. Because of her background in the arts, Assia had assumed more than a passing interest in Hughes's career, which flourished in spite of setbacks in his personal life. In 1963 and 1964, Hughes published several children's books, which sold respectably. His first major collection of poems to appear after Plath's suicide, *Wodwo*—which Faber and Faber released in England on May 18, 1967, Harper and Row in America on November 22—was widely praised by critics, who believed the book reflected a deepening of his subjective voice. In the winter of that same year, Hughes's translation of Seneca's *Oedipus* opened at the Old Vic Theatre in London. Directed by Peter Brook, the play, which starred Irene Worth and John Gielgud, met with good reviews and enthusiastic audiences.

During these years, Assia attempted to break into print in her own right. In 1968, she translated Yehuda Amichai's *Poems,* a book that was published by Harper and Row in 1969. But as she tried to make her way in the literary world, she could not shake the curse of being Plath's "successor." In time, she must have realized that she would never equal Plath in professional achievement—and surely never in sheer notoriety. She might have replaced Plath in her husband's life personally, but replacing her professionally would be another matter altogether. By the third week in March 1969, the burden of living in the shadow of Plath became too much for Assia, who herself suffered deep emotional instability. On a frigid spring morning in a flat in Clapham Common in London, Assia Gutmann swallowed a handful of sleeping pills and then, groggy and disoriented, gathered up her baby, Shura, and went into the kitchen. She switched on the gas in the oven and, as she held Shura, waited for the gas to fill the room. At the time of their deaths, Assia was thirty-four, Shura just two. Years later, unsubstantiated rumors about that morning would still circulate in literary circles. It was said that Assia had carried out her desperate act on— or beside—a trunk that contained the unpublished manuscripts of Sylvia Plath.

The shock to Hughes—he had now endured three deaths in six years—was overwhelming. In April, in a letter to a literary friend in England, he referred to Assia as his wife and admitted Shura was his daughter; as for their suicide-murder, he called it a "disaster." On April 19, Aurelia wrote Hughes to tell him that, if an "emergency situation" arose and he "fe[lt] it desirable for [the children] to leave England earlier [for their summer trip to America], telephone me and I'll work out the arrangements." On May 5, Hughes responded by saying that the children would vacation in America in August—as planned. Hughes kept the news of Assia's death from both Aurelia and his mother. On May 13, following an operation on her knee in a local Yorkshire hospital, Edith Hughes died. She had recovered well enough for her doctors to discuss releasing her in a week or so, when Ted's father went against Ted's wishes and told her about Assia and Shura's death. She died within two days. Afterwards, the family buried her in Heptonstall, at a spot in the cemetery not far from Plath's grave.

In an effort to somehow cope with this spate of tragedies, Hughes moved with his children to Yorkshire. In the fall of 1969, he purchased a huge house in Heptonstall, the Manor on Lumb Lane. Placing the children in a local school, he focused on writing poetry that would be among the most brutal, violent—and original—he ever wrote. All of the poems in Yorkshire portrayed a fantastic character named Crow, a bird who assumed human qualities. Day after day, the poems came effortlessly. By the summer of 1970, the poems were appearing in magazines and literary journals—*Michigan Quarterly Review, The Critical Quarterly, The Listener, The London Magazine, The New Yorker*. On October 13, 1970, Faber and Faber brought out an English edition of *Crow: From the Life and Songs of the Crow*. Five months later, on March 3, 1971, Harper and Row published the book in America. The dedication page of each edition read the same: "In Memory of Assia and Shura."

4

On April 14, 1971, just one month after their release of *Crow,* Harper and Row finally brought out *The Bell Jar* in America. The true identity of its author had been known for years: William Heinemann had disclosed that the book was Plath's not long after her suicide, and by 1966 Faber and Faber had published a subedition in England under Sylvia Plath's name. Because it had appeared in England before Plath's death, the novel could legally be distributed in that country; the American copyright had not been sold, so no American house could print the book without acquiring the rights from Hughes. Not Hughes but Aurelia Plath had prevented *The Bell Jar* from being released in the United States. Aurelia believed that certain characters—Esther's dimwitted mother, the wealthy popular-novelist whose scholarship subsidizes Esther's education at an expensive Eastern college, the boyfriend who makes a sexual advance towards Esther by exposing himself—were grotesque caricatures of living individuals—herself, Olive Higgins Prouty, Dick Norton—who would be hurt by the book and by the publicity its release would produce. Also, Aurelia did not think that the overall achievement of *The Bell Jar* did justice to the memory of her daughter. After all, Sylvia had felt so apprehensive about the novel that she referred to it as a "pot-boiler" and demanded that her British publisher print it pseudonymously. Over the years, Aurelia made it clear that she would put up any roadblock, personal or legal, to keep the novel out of American bookstores. For his part, Hughes feared lawsuits and the possible negative reaction of an American audience to a novel that seemed to be autobiographical.

Finally, by 1970, Plath was so famous that Hughes could not resist selling *The Bell Jar*. He offered Aurelia a deal. If she would not block the novel, Hughes, who controlled the copyright, would give her the permission she needed to publish excerpts from the nearly one thousand letters Sylvia had written her. Aurelia accepted Hughes's offer. Then Hughes negotiated with Harper and Row on terms for the book's publication.

The Bell Jar met with mostly excellent reviews. Many critics agreed with Robert Scholes, who, in *The New York Times Book Review*, contended that *The Bell Jar* "is literature" and that it "is finding its audience, and will hold it." As if Scholes had predicted it, the book immediately climbed onto *The New York Times* best-seller list and remained there for twenty-four weeks—an unprecedented accomplishment for a first novel written by an author known primarily for her poetry. *The Bell Jar* became so popular that, when Bantam Books brought out an initial paperback edition in April 1972—a run of 375,000 copies—it sold out that printing, plus a second and a third, in one month. In the mid-eighties, more than a decade and a half later, the *Bell Jar* paperback edition was selling some fifty thousand copies a year.

On May 31, 1971, six weeks after Harper and Row's release of *The Bell Jar*, Faber and Faber published *Crossing the Water* in England— the first major collection of poems by Plath to come out since *Ariel*. Because the thirty-four poems in *Crossing* were selected from those Plath had written between finishing *The Colossus* in late 1959 and beginning *Ariel* in early 1962, Hughes, who took even greater editorial liberty with this book than he had with *Ariel*, called *Crossing* "transitional poems." The tag also implied, quite accurately, that, in producing these poems, Plath was trying to move from an objective to a more subjective style of writing. Fewer periodicals than expected reviewed *Crossing* because, even as the first copies of the book were being shipped, Hughes announced that a second Plath collection would be published soon. The wait was not long. On September 27, 1971, four months after the release of *Crossing*, Faber and Faber issued *Winter Trees*.

To help explain the contents of the book, just eighteen poems and the radio play *Three Women*, Hughes wrote a brief two-paragraph prefatory note. He stated that Plath had finished all of the poems in *Winter Trees* during "the last year" of her life, which made them part of the large batch of poems from which he had chosen *Ariel* "more or less arbitrarily." According to Hughes, *Three Women*, "written slightly earlier," should be viewed as "a bridge between *The Colossus* and *Ariel*," which would have placed it in the so-called transitional phase that *Crossing* represented. Hughes's introductory note raised some interesting questions. For example, if Plath *had* written *Three Women* during her transitional phase, why had that piece not been included in *Crossing*? One answer was obvious. Without *Three Women*, *Winter Trees* would have been too slim to print.

On October 1, 1971, in *The Observer*, A. Alvarez took Hughes to task. "With such a vast potential audience," Alvarez wrote in "Publish and Be Damned," a review of both *Crossing* and *Winter Trees*, "there must be an overwhelming temptation to make the stuff last, with a new volume every few years." Alvarez also probed Hughes's censorship of his late wife's work. "Offhand, I can think of two [uncollected poems], both as powerful and new as anything she wrote: 'The Fearful,' published in *The Observer* the Sunday after her death, and 'The Jailer,' which appeared in *Encounter* later the same year. If poems in the public domain have been left out, how many others, I wonder, remain in manuscript? Unless she was grossly exaggerating when she said she was writing at least a poem a day, the number must be large." Despite the controversy surrounding the release of the book, *Winter Trees* received good reviews—unusually good, considering that in his introduction Hughes essentially dismissed the poems as *Ariel* out-takes. Like *Crossing the Water, Winter Trees* chalked up impressive sales figures.

A second—and more dramatic—battle between Alvarez and Hughes erupted on November 14, 1971, when *The Observer* published the first of a scheduled two-part installment of Alvarez's memoir of Plath—a piece *The Observer* called "Sylvia Plath: The Road to Suicide"—which was to be the preface to Alvarez's forthcoming study of suicide, *The Savage God.* "As I remember it, I met Sylvia Plath and her husband Ted Hughes in London in the spring of 1960," began Alvarez. From there, he sketched in his friendship with Plath up until—or at least this was where the *Observer* excerpt ended—the "gloomy November afternoon" on which she discovered the vacant Yeats flat on Fitzroy Road, put in an application for it at the agent's office, and "walked across dark, blowy Primrose Hill to tell me the news." A tangible feeling of foreboding hung in Alvarez's prose as he described Sylvia heading across the park. This disquiet was spelled out clearly by the newspaper's advertisement for the promised conclusion: "NEXT WEEK: The last gamble."

Hughes could not bear the idea of someone deeply familiar with Plath's life revealing publicly, in one of England's most widely read periodicals, the details of her suicide. He demanded that *The Observer* cancel the second installment, and he wrote to Weidenfeld and Nicholson to insist that the section of *The Savage God* concerning Plath be eliminated. Weidenfeld and Nicholson did not cave in to Hughes's pressure; *The Observer* did. On the following Sunday, the newspaper announced, "At the request of the Hughes family, we have cut short the story of Sylvia Plath. . . . Readers may find its continuation in Mr. Alvarez's book, *The Savage God*, from which we publish further extracts this week. . . ."

The Observer also printed a statement provided by Hughes. "I would like to make it known to readers of A. Alvarez's memoir of Sylvia Plath, in last week's *Observer*, that it was written and published without my having been consulted in any way. Though at one time Mr Alvarez mentioned he was writing 'something,' and would show it to me when it was done, he did not say it was a 'memoir,' or I would have made more effort to see it and check the nature and accuracy of his facts." The newspaper included Alvarez's rejoinder as well. "I did not consult Mr Hughes because I was not writing a memoir of him. I was writing about Sylvia Plath as a person—I think, a genius—in her own right. The memoir is also of the girl as I knew her, during a period when she was mostly living on her own." What was more, Alvarez declared, Olwyn Hughes had read the memoir in an American magazine "at least by the last week in September" and suggested only three minor factual changes.

Two days later, on November 19, the *TLS* ran an angry letter from Hughes who contended that Alvarez's facts were "misremembered" and that Alvarez's "main *trouvé*"—that Plath had "gambled" with her suicide—"was, in fact, a notion of mine, which haunted me at the time, and which I aired to him, even though it went against the findings of the coroner, and against other details which I imparted to no one." On November 26, the *TLS* published Alvarez's response:

> Mr Hughes says he distorted the evidence when he spoke to me. I am, of course, not responsible for that. Mercifully, I was not relying only on information he gave me. I based my memoir on my own impression of Sylvia and on what she herself told me. . . . There is, however, one distortion I admit to: I deliberately suppressed all mention of the personal situation between Sylvia and her husband during the last months of her life. I did this both out of consideration for the feelings of the living and because I felt it was nobody else's business.

Hughes prevented the second installment of Alvarez's memoir from reaching a mass audience through *The Observer,* but the complete memoir finally *did* enjoy a huge readership, since *The Savage God* proved to be an unqualified popular success. Indeed, Hughes's references to his theory that Plath may have "gambled" with her life in her last suicide attempt, a notion not included in *The Observer*'s first installment, may have intrigued readers so much that it *increased* book sales. Finally, Alvarez's memoir of Plath reached a large audience—both in England and in America, where Random House published it—

because his portrait of her rang true. It is a document written by an author who adores his subject and who is guilt-ridden because he did not answer her final, desperate, soul-searching cry for help.

On September 29, 1971, Harper and Row published *Crossing the Water* in America. Of the thirty-four poems included in the British version, six were omitted in the American to be replaced by the five sections of "Poem for a Birthday" that had been eliminated from the Knopf *Colossus* nine years earlier. Bolstered by *The Bell Jar*'s exceptional sales, *Crossing* became an immediate commercial success. *The Saturday Review* Book Club even chose it as one of its selections—an unusual achievement for a volume of poetry.

In America, a year elapsed between the release of *Crossing* and *Winter Trees*—not four months, as in England. Once again, the American and British editions differed. This time, three poems were cut and nine added, three new ones plus the six left out of the American *Crossing*. This book too sold unusually well for a volume of poetry; it was chosen as an alternate selection for The Book-of-the-Month Club.

In the posthumous life of Sylvia Plath, the years 1971 and 1972 marked the height of her popularity. "During the past year or so," Marjorie Perloff wrote in *The Iowa Review* in the spring of 1973, "Sylvia Plath has become a true cult figure. At this writing, the Savile Book Shop in Georgetown, D.C., has a huge window display in which copies of *The Colossus, The Bell Jar, Ariel*, and *Crossing the Water* encircle a large photograph of Sylvia Plath, which rests against a copy of A. Alvarez's *The Savage God: A Study of Suicide*, that ultimate tribute to Sylvia Plath as our Extremist Poet par excellence." Not since Dylan Thomas had there been this sort of response to a poet's work following his death, or before him Hart Crane.

5

Soon after she made the deal with Hughes, Aurelia Plath approached Harper and Row with her idea for *Letters Home,* excerpts from Sylvia's letters to her. Immediately, Harper and Row offered Aurelia a contract. When Hughes had granted Aurelia permission to print Sylvia's letters, it had been with the stipulation that the estate would exercise final editorial judgment on the project. In time, Aurelia submitted the proposed manuscript to Hughes, who asked her to cut the book, strictly for editorial reasons, because he felt it was too long. Even though she had already drastically reduced the material from Sylvia's original letters, Aurelia agreed. Hughes approved the new, shorter version. But only weeks before publication, Hughes read the galleys and decided that the text revealed too many personal details about himself, his friends, and his children. Nearly all of the material that he wanted eliminated was, at most, only mildly revelatory in nature; however, Harper and Row—and Aurelia Plath—grudgingly obliged. Finally, after three years in the works, *Letters Home* appeared on December 3, 1975.

The book received a number of ambivalent reviews. A typical one was "Letters Focus Exquisite Rage of Sylvia Plath" by Erica Jong, which appeared in the Los Angeles *Times.* Jong criticized Aurelia Plath for editing the letters to a level she considered "appalling," and Hughes for pruning Sylvia's work when he was "the very man who pruned her life," but she concluded that *"Letters Home* is an immensely valuable work and I am grateful that Mrs. Plath and Ted Hughes let it be published." Many more reviews followed—and even a profile of Aurelia Plath in *People* magazine—before Faber and Faber brought out a British edition of *Letters Home* on April 20, 1976.

Around this time, the estate decided to assemble a sampling of Plath's prose. On October 17, 1977, Faber and Faber released *Johnny Panic and the Bible of Dreams,* an anthology containing short stories, pieces of journalism, and excerpts from Plath's notebooks and diaries. Later, Harper and Row published an American edition that had been expanded to include six stories and the novel fragment *Stone Boy with Dolphin*. The American reviews of *Johnny Panic* would be few—and mixed. "I have to admit at the outset that this kind of publication makes me uneasy by definition, hinting as it does of rummaging in bureau drawers that the author, had she lived, would doubtless have kept firmly locked," Margaret Atwood wrote in *The New York Times Book Review* on January 28, 1979. "What writer of sane mind would willingly give to the world her undergraduate short stories, her disgruntled jottings on the doings of unpleasant neighbors, her embarrassing attempts to write formula magazine fiction?" When the enlarged, American version, updated yet again to include two more short stories, was published in England in April 1979, no news items or reviews of the book appeared at all.

It was only a matter of time until the estate published a book-length excerpt of the journal that Plath had kept since age twelve. The job of editing the original manuscript did not appeal to Ted Hughes. Instead, the real work of carving the book into shape fell to Frances McCullough, who had edited Plath's posthumously published books at Harper and Row and now worked for The Dial Press. Consulting with Hughes, McCullough decided to limit the book to essentially the years 1950–59 and to use only about one-third of the material available to them from that period—decisions that significantly altered the content of the book. Perhaps because of the fragmentary nature of the manuscript, or perhaps because they feared that maybe—just maybe— Plath's marketability had fallen into a sharp decline since both *Letters Home* and *Johnny Panic* had posted anemic sales figures, Harper and Row did not purchase *The Journals of Sylvia Plath*. However, The Dial Press jumped at the chance to acquire the volume, which was released on March 31, 1982.

The public interest in the book was so strong that, almost immediately, the first hardback printing of thirty-five thousand copies sold out completely. Wide critical coverage spurred sales on. Within weeks of the book's release, major reviews appeared in a great variety of publications—*Newsweek, The Atlantic Monthly, The Saturday Review*, and most large city newspapers. In almost every review, one criticism surfaced—a criticism that Ted Hughes openly invited in the final paragraph of his brief foreword when he alluded to the two notebooks in which Plath had kept her diary from late 1959 until "within three days of her death." Hughes declared: "The last of these contained entries for several months, and I destroyed it because I did not want her children to have to read it (in those days I regarded forgetfulness as an essential part of survival)." And what of the second notebook? "The other disappeared," Hughes stated flatly, offering no further explanation. Revelations of this sort left Hughes—indeed, the project itself—vulnerable to harsh attack. None was harsher than Peter Davison's. "How can we content ourselves, with a book so riddled with editorial expurgations, with omissions that stud the text like angry scars, with allusions to destroyed and 'disappeared' parts of the journals?" Davison wrote in the Washington *Post* on April 18. "Does anyone imagine that Sylvia Plath herself, had she lived, would have permitted these journals to be set in type?" In fact, they never were in England—or anywhere else, for that matter. Though *The Journals of Sylvia Plath* became an unqualified financial success in America, the estate never allowed the book to be published in any other country.

Hughes had recorded the history of the notebooks much differently in an earlier, longer version of his foreword, which McCullough refused to print. Admitting that "her husband destroyed" the second notebook, Hughes postulated that "[the] earlier one disappeared more recently (and may, presumably, still turn up)." Regardless of these statements, people close to Hughes believe that both versions of his story are inaccurate. According to them, at the time of the publication of *The Journals,* the two notebooks existed intact. They still do. Hughes denies these claims.

Despite numerous calls for a "collected" Plath, pleas that started in the mid-sixties and did not stop for the next decade and a half, the estate did not seriously begin the preparation of such a volume until well into the seventies. The resulting *The Collected Poems* finally appeared in England (Faber and Faber) on September 28, 1981; in America (Harper and Row) on November 28. For the first time in the publishing history of Plath's poetry, the American and British editions were the same. *The Collected Poems* contained 224 "mature" poems (poems composed between 1956 and her death), an appendix of some fifty poems considered juvenilia (poems composed before 1956), a complete list of all poems identified as juvenilia (the total number of juvenile poems listed is 221, of which only the fifty were printed), an introduction written by Hughes, and extensive notes to many of the poems.

In the deluge of reviews following *The Collected Poems'* release, critic after critic praised Plath's achievement. Only one criticism tended to surface—more questions about Hughes's decisionmaking. On November 22, 1981, in his front-page review of *The Collected Poems* in *The New York Times Book Review,* Denis Donoghue pointed out some important transgressions involving the "haphazard" publishing history of Plath's work, the sloppy way *The Collected Poems* was assembled, and—most damning—missing poems. For instance, "Mad Girl's Love Song," Plath's famous poem first published in *Mademoiselle* in the same month as her 1953 breakdown and suicide attempt, is not mentioned in *The Collected Poems* at all.

In the end, critics focused on Plath's poetic achievement, not Hughes's shortcomings as an editor and an estate administrator. *The Collected Poems* confirmed what all of Plath's previous single volumes had only suggested: Plath was, as Alvarez had declared only a week after her death, "the most gifted woman poet of her time." On April 22, 1982, almost two full decades since her suicide, Sylvia Plath's *Collected Poems* received the highest honor the American literary community can bestow on a writer's work, the Pulitzer Prize.

6

In 1963, Betty Friedan published *The Feminine Mystique,* a revolutionary study of women in America. In part, Friedan contended that society prevented a woman from achieving a complete and fulfilled life by forcing her to function within the narrowly defined role of mother-wife-homemaker. The book gave voice to a pervasive problem; soon women were demanding a change of the status quo. In 1965, Friedan, along with a small group of concerned women, formed the National Organization for Women in Washington, D.C. Over the next few years, the women's movement grew dramatically. In July 1971, Gloria Steinem founded *Ms.* magazine, the first national publication devoted to addressing the problems of the "new" woman.

In the single decade following *The Feminine Mystique*'s release, a sociopolitical movement of staggering size emerged. It was in this climate, in April 1971, that *The Bell Jar* hit the bookshelves in the United States. Many women responded to the plight of Esther Greenwood, who is disgusted by the hypocritical society in which she lives. They also responded to the "story" of Sylvia Plath, whose destruction, they believed, could be blamed on society's patriarchal power structure. On the surface, the facts seemed to support this theory. As of the early seventies, almost everything written by or about Plath—her four books of poems, *The Bell Jar, The Savage God,* and several memoirs and biographical notes—suggested that she had suffered her last suicidal breakdown because she became disillusioned when she realized that what society had promised her and what she had gotten in her life were two different things entirely. After all, she had excelled at Smith, earned a Fulbright to Cambridge, chiseled out, with gritty determination, the beginnings of a serious literary career—all without neglecting the required goal of marrying a man and producing a family—and what had she ended up with? A husband who left her for another woman—left her, that is, in a cold flat in London with two small children and no way to make a good living.

One vicious indictment of Ted Hughes came from Robin Morgan. In the first stanza of "Arraignment," a poem included in her 1972 volume *Monster,* Morgan wrote:

> How can
> I accuse
> Ted Hughes
> of what the entire British and American
> literary and critical establishment

has been at great lengths to deny,
without ever saying it in so many words, of course:
the murder of Sylvia Plath. . . .

Then, in the rest of the poem, Morgan criticizes Hughes for making
"a mint / by becoming Plath's posthumous editor"; relates the suicide
of "Assia Gutmann Wevill," the woman Hughes never "formally" married; praises Gutmann, "a Jewish mother in the most heroic sense,"
for murdering her daughter to save her from a life with Hughes; attacks
Alvarez, Steiner, and Lowell for "aiding, abetting, rewarding / her perfectly legal executor"; and, threatens to dismember Hughes, stuff "that
weapon" in his mouth, and sew up his lips. After that, "we women
[will] blow out his brains."

Though *Monster* became a manifesto of the feminist movement, it
was never released outside the United States. Instead, pirated editions
appeared in countries like Canada, England, and Australia. On the
back of the British edition, the editors echoed the sentiments of "Arraignment." They quoted two lines from "Mushrooms" that ostensibly
reflected the hopes of the women's movement and ran Plath's "dates":
"Born 27-10-32 / Driven to Suicide: 11-2-63."

During the seventies, radical feminists conducted what they saw as
a "holy war" against Hughes. In England, Canada, and especially America, feminists harassed Hughes during his public poetry readings. A
woman would stand up in the audience and either launch into a diatribe
against him or on occasion recite "Arraignment." Hughes gave fewer
and fewer readings.

Still, Plath's devoted followers persisted. Through the years, they
traveled to Heptonstall to decorate her grave with flowers. The visitors
became so numerous that local church officials proposed putting up
signs to direct tourists to the grave—an idea eventually dropped at,
some insist, Hughes's demand. Not content with a floral tribute, eventually visitors, with a hammer and a chisel, would chip Hughes's surname from the "Sylvia Plath Hughes" engraved on her tombstone,
leaving only "Sylvia Plath." It was generally assumed that feminists,
angry still with Hughes, had committed the acts. Each time that Hughes
replaced a defaced stone with one that displayed Plath's full married

name, vandals would chisel away the "Hughes" again. In the early eighties, workers, at Hughes's request, put into place a third new tombstone.

7

In the sixties, Ted Hughes went through the violent breakup of his first marriage to a young poet, had an affair with another woman that dragged on into a complicated long-term relationship, and endured the suicides of these two women. The seventies, on the other hand, were a time of comparable tranquillity, as Hughes matured into a father, husband, and "family man." In 1970, he married Carol Orchard, a nurse, and settled down in London at 74 Fortess Road, so that Nicholas and Frieda could attend an excellent boarding school and still come home every other weekend. Nicholas outperformed Frieda, but eventually both graduated from British public (equivalent to American private) school. Frieda did not go to college; she married and (soon afterwards) divorced. Nicholas went to Oxford University, then entered graduate school in marine biology at the University of Alaska. As Nicholas advanced in the sciences, Frieda pursued the arts. In the eighties, she published two children's books.

After his children grew up, Hughes left London to return, now with Carol Orchard, to Court Green. In the seventies and early eighties, he published a number of books, among them *Selected Poems: 1957–1967* (1972), *Season Songs* (1976), *Moon-Whales and Other Moon Poems* (1976), *Gaudete* (1977), *Moortown* (1979), *New Selected Poems* (1982), and *River* (1983).

On May 19, 1984, Sir John Betjeman, who had replaced C. Day Lewis as Britain's poet laureate twelve years earlier, died of a heart condition at his holiday home in Trebetherick, Cornwall. In the wake of his death, speculation ran high concerning who would replace him as poet laureate. Officially, Queen Elizabeth II would make the announcement, although the Queen really only formalized the nomination made by the Prime Minister, whose appointment secretary drew up a list of candidates. London bookmakers began accepting wagers on which man—or woman—the Queen might select. Several seemed to be possibilities—Stephen Spender, Robert Graves, Roy Fuller, Kathleen Raine—but, finally, one man, Philip Larkin, emerged as the favorite. Hughes was considered, at best, a long-shot. His age, fifty-four, and his violent poetry worked against him.

Consequently, many observers were shocked when the Queen, upon consulting with Margaret Thatcher, appointed not Larkin but Hughes. It was rumored that Larkin had been Her Majesty's first choice, but had turned down the honor for medical reasons. (On December 2, 1985, Larkin died in a hospital in Hull, ending what newspapers called "a chronic illness.") Hughes's name was second on the Prime Minister's list, so the Queen offered the job to him. Finally, appointed to the post, Hughes joined the company of John Dryden; William Wordsworth; Ben Jonson; Alfred, Lord Tennyson. Sylvia Plath would have been the first American ever married to the poet laureate of England.

8

After several producers had approached the estate, Jerrold Brandt, Jr., and Michael Todd, Jr., purchased the film rights to *The Bell Jar* in the mid-seventies for a reported one hundred thousand dollars. They then lined up Marjorie Kellogg to write the screenplay, which Larry Peerce would direct. Best known for the critically acclaimed *Goodbye, Columbus* and the commercially successful *The Other Side of Midnight,* Peerce hired a veteran cast in the supporting roles (Julie Harris would portray Mrs. Greenwood; Anne Jackson, Dr. Nolan; Barbara Barrie, Jay Cee; and Robert Klein, the country-western disc jockey) to complement the newcomer he had chosen to play Esther, Marilyn Hassett. The film was shot in and around Manhattan during the summer of 1978.

When *The Bell Jar* was released by Avco Embassy Pictures on March 21, 1979, it met with disastrous reviews. *The New York Times'*

Janet Maslin compared Hassett's Esther to "a cheerleader whose team has just lost a big game"—certainly not the complicated young woman in the novel. Also, Maslin attacked the filmmakers for tampering with the novel's plot and characters. One major difference between the book and the movie was the way Esther tried to kill herself. Instead of hiding in a crawl space and swallowing fifty sleeping pills, as she does in the novel, in the film Esther dances drunkenly around the basement of her home, washing down a handful of pills with a bottle of liquor, until she dissolves into a heap on the floor. Maslin wrote: "This sequence, which lasts a long time and isn't affecting in the slightest, is emblematic of the movie's way of spelling things out ad nauseam and still not making them clear." Ultimately, the decision to change the novel's plot and characters would bring *The Bell Jar*'s filmmakers more than just bad reviews.

On March 19, 1982, Jane Anderson, Plath's Smith acquaintance with whom she was hospitalized at McLean, and by then a psychiatrist at Harvard Medical School, filed a six-million-dollar lawsuit against *The Bell Jar*'s filmmakers because she felt she had been defamed by the movie. When the filmmakers had developed the character Joan Gilling, whom Anderson thought Plath had based on her, they changed her from the heterosexual she had been in the novel to a lesbian. One sequence in the movie, which was not in the book, particularly bothered Anderson. Kneeling on the ground in a field, Joan kisses Esther's breasts as she tries to convince her to enter into a suicide pact "like lovers." Esther rejects Joan, who dashes off into the woods, near the mental institution where they are hospitalized, to hang herself from the low branch of a tree.

"We have no problem with the book," Anderson's lawyer, Harry L. Manion III, stated when, after almost five years of delays and postponements, the suit came to trial in Boston in January 1987. The problem that necessitated the suit arose "when Hollywood got its hands on this property." So, Anderson sued only those individuals and companies who had filmed the novel or who had distributed or broadcast the movie. One party was Ted Hughes, who, as estate executor, had sold the novel's film rights.

The trial began on January 20, 1987, before Judge Robert Keeton. Manion represented Anderson. Victor Kovner defended Hughes; Alexander H. Pratt, Jr., the media interests. Immediately, Manion put Anderson on the stand. "I never, never in any way attempted to seduce Sylvia Plath into a homosexual relationship," Anderson said, her voice controlled yet full of emotion. "I never in any way attempted to get her into a 'suicide pact like lovers.' I also never made any suicide attempts or had scars on my breasts"—details in the film, not in the novel. On the Friday night in March 1979, in Boston's Paris Theatre, where she had first watched *The Bell Jar*, Anderson testified, she suffered vivid flashbacks, a series of "colored, visual images of various components of the painful aspects" of her torturous months at McLean. However, Anderson proved most effective on her final day of testimony. When Manion asked if she "was then or ever had been" a homosexual, she responded: "I am not now a homosexual, and I have never been a homosexual." An awkward silence fell in the courtroom. No one was more moved than the jury—the four men and four women, all older, solid, middle-class citizens, who, like Anderson, would not have appreciated having anyone portray them as something they were not, particularly a homosexual.

Because the defense attorneys could sense the jury's sympathy for Anderson, they struck a compromise with her. Both sides convened at the courthouse the next morning, January 29, 1987, to announce that a settlement had been reached. Instead of the six million dollars (five million for libel and one million for intentional emotional distress), Anderson would receive $150,000 and the defendants' admission that the film had "unintentionally defamed" her. Also, all new copies of the movie and the video cassette would prominently display a disclaimer that said that "any similarity [of the film's characters] to living or actual persons is purely coincidental." To reach the settlement, Anderson dropped four defendants from the lawsuit. One was Hughes, because, according to agreement, "there was no wrongdoing on the part of Mr. Hughes [since], to the extent the plaintiff was defamed, it was by the motion picture alone, not the novel and occurred unintentionally and purely by coincidence."

*   *   *

Of all the defendants, only Ted Hughes attended the trial itself. Each morning, as the bailiff called the court into session, he stood like everyone else to acknowledge the judge and the jury as they entered the room. Then he took his place next to Kovner. No longer the brooding young man whom Plath had married, Hughes, now nearing sixty, was showing his age. His hair, peppered with gray, was thinning; lines had appeared on his rugged, angular face. His body, once tall and lean, had started to thicken. Indeed, Hughes slouched, as though exhausted, in his chair behind the defendants' table. Almost a quarter of a century had passed since Plath's suicide, during which Hughes had done everything he could to get on with his life, yet here he was—sitting in a courtroom on a frigid January morning in his late wife's hometown, there to defend her only novel. No matter what, Hughes could not escape the consequences of his life with Plath, or her death.

9

In the late fall of 1988, in the Heptonstall cemetery in which Sylvia Plath is buried, no tombstone marked her grave. Many months had passed since the third one—defaced, like the two previous stones, by vandals who chipped the word "Hughes" from her name—had been taken away. On this cold November afternoon, a sharp wind blew dead leaves from the trees surrounding the cemetery. Sunless and cloudless, an empty sky weighed down heavily against the moors' rolling landscape. To the traveler who had come here from America, the starkness of the day only made the starkness of Plath's grave seem sadder. Recently, a local resident had erected a temporary commemorative: two stout two-foot-long sticks tied into a cross with a piece of cord. On the horizontal stick, he had carefully printed, using a green marking pen, "Sylvia Plath." He had then hammered the homemade cross into the ground at the head of the grave. As the traveler stood before Plath's grave, he thought of her life and her work, which included, he believed, some of the century's most accomplished poetry. And when he began to consider why she—an artist of her caliber—should lie in a grave so embarrassingly marked, he noticed something that seemed to explain much about what had transpired before her death, and after. The plot next to Plath's is empty.

Acknowledgments

The two major Sylvia Plath archives are housed in the Lilly Library at Indiana University and in the Rare Book Room at Smith College. At Smith, I was fortunate to have the assistance of Ruth Mortimer, Sarah Black, Karen Kukil, and Barbara Blumenthal; their skill, caring, and professionalism are unmatched. At Indiana, I would like to thank Saundra Taylor, but mostly Kate Siebert-Medicus and Rebecca Cape, who tirelessly helped me as I read this enormous collection. I am also grateful to Janet Wagner at Hofstra University.

I received additional research materials from Henri Cole and Bruce Cammack at the Academy of American Poets; The Atlantic Monthly Press; the BBC's Written Archives Centre; Boston University's University Archives; Mary R. McGee at *The Christian Science Monitor* Library; Dr. Stuart W. Campbell at Clark University's University Archives; Columbia University's Rare Book and Manuscript Room; the Condé Nast Library; the Fulbright Alumni Association; Harvard University's Houghton Library; the University of Houston; Frederick Morgan at *The Hudson Review*; the Library of Congress's Motion Pictures, Broadcasting, and Recorded Sound Division; Elain D. Trehub at Mount Holyoke College's College History and Archive; the National Sound Archives in London; the New York Public Library's Berg Collection; Steven Siegal at the Ninety-second Street Y in New York City; Northwestern College's Office of the Registrar; the Princeton University Library; the Public Record Office in London; Rice University's Fondren

ACKNOWLEDGMENTS · 366

Library; Bonni Price at *Seventeen* magazine; Smith College's Sophia Smith Collection; Saint Catherine's House in London; Cathy Henderson at the Harry Ransom Humanities Research Center at the University of Texas; the University of Chicago's Joseph Regenstein Library; Anne Armour at the Jessie Ball Dupont Library at the University of the South; Anne Posega at the Olin Library at Washington University in St. Louis; the Wellesley Free Library; Ann Rote at the Wellesley Middle School; Wellesley Public Schools; Margaret Hinckley at the Winthrop Public Library; Margaret T. Peters at the Office of Town Clerk in Winthrop; UCLA Special Collections.

For interviews, letters, and other help I would like to thank A. Alvarez, Sarah Arvio, Ruth Barnhouse, Ellyn Berman, Ann Birstein, Sarah G. Bobbitt, Vance Bourjaily, Mary Lynn Broe, Linda K. Bundtzen, Lee Camp, Margaret Cantor, Marjorie Chester, Nest Cleverdon, Barbara Sugarman Cohen, Edward Cohen, Judy Ettlinger Cohen, Joan Cohn, Elizabeth Cooper, Grant Cooper, Connie Corson, Richard Corson, Wilbury Crockett, Catherine Criswell, Shirley Dallard, Gwenda David, Peter Davison, Deborah Digges, Margaret Drabble, Elaine Henderson Duble, Stewart Duncan, Ruth Fainlight, Macey Feingold, Aryeh Finklestein, Judith Flanders, Katherine Fleming, Oliver Forshaw, Betty Friedan, Max Gaebler, Amy Gardner, Ruth Freeman Geissler, Louise Giesey, Max Goldberg, Donald Hall, Michael Hamburger, Ronald Hayman, Lianne Hart, John Harnson, Malinda E. Hildeburn, Dr. John Horder, Olwyn Hughes, Sally Jenks, Diane Johnson, Nora Johnson, Judith Jones, Erica Jong, Lawrence Joseph, Dr. Stephen Josephson, Terry Karten, Eileen McLaughlin Kelly, Frances Kiernan, Cindy Klein, Martha Wood Kongshang, Jean Hanff Korelitz, Tony Lacey, the late Gordon Lameyer, Lori M. Laubich, Lynne Lawner, Laurie Levy, Lise Liepman, Polly Longsworth, Alden Macchi, David Machin, Norman Mailer, Carole Mallory, Georgette Marion, Timothy Materer, William McBrien, Philip McCurdy, Lucie McKee, Elsbeth Melville, Kory Meyerink, Jeffrey Meyers, James Michie, Robin Morgan, Ruth Mortimer, the late Howard Moss, Dona Munker, E. Lucas Myers, Audrey Nicholson, Jill Neville, Peter Orr, Kenneth Pitchford, Lawrence Pitkethly, Aurelia S. Plath, Stanley Plumly, Janet Wagner Rafferty, Sonia Raiziss, Adrienne Rich, Phyllis

Rifield, Clarissa Roche, Paul Roche, Joan Romans, M. L. Rosenthal, Mark Rudman, Neva Nelson Sachar, David Sandy, Grace Schulman, David Secker-Walker, Lorna Secker-Walker, Kate Siebert-Medicus, Karl Shapiro, Norman Shapiro, Margaret Shook, Elizabeth Compton Sigmund, Eileen Simpson, Elizabeth Skerritt, Dave Smith, Mrs. Mason Smith, Roger Smith, Ron Smith, Ted Solotaroff, Barbara Soulnier, Monroe Spears, Mary Spelman, Colin St. Johnson, Valerie St. Johnson, George Starbuck, Gloria Steinem, Marcia Brown Stern, Anne Stevenson, Libby Stone, Stephen Tabor, Renā Taylor, Trevor Thomas, Susan van Dyne, Helen Vendler, Betsy Powley Wallingford, Aileen Ward, Polly Weaver, Daniel Weissbort, John Wellington, Marybeth Little Weston, M. S. Whitlock, Richard Wilbur, Laura Woolschlager, Kenneth Wright, Bertram Wyatt-Brown.

Finally, I want to thank W. O. Chitwood, Jr., in whose class I first read Sylvia Plath.

Notes

The Blue Hour

Page 7 "*'I am a genius of a writer . . .'*": *Letters Home* (hereafter cited as *LH*) by Sylvia Plath, edited by Aurelia S. Plath (New York, Harper and Row, 1975), p. 468. **7** "*No matter what, Plath . . .*": Plath's quote—"'still, blue, almost eternal hour'"—comes from a commentary she wrote for the BBC. **8** "*'One might criticise . . .'*": "Poetic Knowledge" by Thomas Blackburn, *The New Statesman* 60, December 24, 1960, p. 1016. **9** "*'Well, it's a nice gift book.'*": *LH*, p. 399. **10** "*'I can go nowhere with the children . . .'*": *LH*, p. 469. **10** "*That night, Plath . . .*": The quotes from Plath's letter are from *LH*, p. 470.

Otto and Aurelia

12 "*On the last day . . .*": The quotes about Otto Plath are from Boston University yearbooks. **12** "*To demonstrate man's illogic . . .*": The information about the "rat" episode comes from an unpublished memoir by Max Gaebler. **13** "*At German Club picnics . . .*": The scene with Otto Plath and the student is taken from a description in a Boston University yearbook. **15** "*On April 13, 1885 . . .*": Much of the information about Otto Plath and Aurelia Schober Plath's family history was obtained from a private genealogist, whom I hired to do research for this book. **16** "*Devastated but relieved . . .*": Information in this paragraph comes from university archive files at Boston University. **19** "*Later that same day, Otto Plath . . .*": Plath and Schober's marriage license. **20** "*Finally, on Thursday, October 27, 1932 . . .*": Sylvia Plath's birth certificate. **21** "*'The foundations of this book . . .'*": *Bumblebees and Their*

Ways by Otto Plath (New York, the Macmillan Company, 1934), introduction. **22** *"For her work on the book . . ."*: From the acknowledgment page of *Bumblebees and Their Ways*. **23** *" 'By the end of my first year of marriage . . .' "*: *LH*, p. 13. **24** *"In the spring of 1936 . . . "*: Information about the Freemans comes from Aurelia Plath's introduction to *LH* and from my interview with Ruth Freeman Geissler. **27** *"Sylvia had been writing poetry . . ."*: "Thoughts" is in an unpublished manuscript of Plath's juvenilia at the Morgan Library in New York. **32** *" 'I hereby certify . . .' "*: Otto Plath's death certificate. **32** *" 'I'll never speak to God again' . . ."*: *LH*, p. 25. **32** *"Because she believed the children . . ."*: Information about Otto Plath's funeral and grave comes from the public record books at Winthrop Town Cemetery.

Wellesley

36 *" 'I marveled at the moving beacons . . .' "*: *Johnny Panic and the Bible of Dreams* (hereafter cited as *JP*) by Sylvia Plath (New York, Harper and Row, 1979), p. 269. **36** *"To Sylvia, the single most important day . . ."*: "Poem" appeared on "The Good Sport Page" in the Boston *Herald* on August 11, 1941. **37** *" 'I remember sitting by the radio . . .' "*: *JP*, p. 271. **38** *" 'My father died . . .' "*: Ibid., p. 26. **38** *"The Charles River . . ."*: Information about Wellesley comes from *Five Pounds Currency, Three Pounds of Corn: Wellesley's Centennial Story* by Elizabeth M. Hinchliffe; the catalogue was published by the Town of Wellesley in 1981. **40** *" 'Gas rationing so tight . . .' "*: Ibid., p. 86. **41** *"Appreciably smaller than 92 Johnson Avenue . . ."*: My description of 26 Elmwood Road is based on a visit I made there in April 1983. **42** *" 'I'll never forget what she and I did . . .' "*: From my interview with Betsy Powley Wallingford. **43** *"In July, while Aurelia recovered . . ."*: Plath's postcards to her mother are in the Plath archive at the Lilly Library at Indiana University. **44** *" 'They were completely transported . . .' "*: Aurelia Plath's unpublished commentary to *LH* is in the Sylvia Plath archive in the Rare Book Room at Smith College. **45** *"For her scholastic achievement . . ."*: From Plath memorabilia at Indiana. **45** *"On July 1 . . ."*: Ibid. **46** *"In February 1946 . . ."*: Information about Plath's dates with boys comes from her unpublished journals at Indiana. **47** *"In July . . ."*: Plath described her camp experiences in letters to her mother; the unpublished letters are at Indiana. **48** *"Philip had grown up . . ."*: From my interviews with Philip McCurdy. **49** *"Before the dance, Sylvia and Wayne . . ."*: From Plath's unpublished journals at Indiana. **50** *"On September 8, 1947 . . ."*: The descriptions of Wilbury Crockett and Gamaliel Bradford High School are based on my interviews with Crockett and McCurdy. **51** *"Also, 'I Thought That I Could Not Be Hurt' . . ."*: *LH*, p. 33. **53** *"On July 1, 1948 . . ."*: Plath's unpublished letters to her mother at Indiana.

53 *"In March, the month when she won . . ."*: The Plath-Woods-Edman letters are in the Rare Books and Manuscripts Room in the Butler Library at Columbia University. **54** *"Finally, near the end of the term . . ."*: Copies of *The Bradford* are at Indiana. **55** *"Sylvia would spend the summer of 1949 . . ."*: The information in the next four paragraphs is from Plath's unpublished journals at Indiana. **58** *" 'Sylvia is a superior candidate for college. . . .' "*: Plath's letters of recommendation are at Smith. **60** *"Early in the spring term . . ."*: "A Youth's Plea for World Peace" by Sylvia Plath and Perry Norton, *The Christian Science Monitor*, March 16, 1950, p. 19. **61** *"During the spring, as she worked hard . . ."*: The Thomas Mann comment comes from Plath's unpublished journals at Indiana. **61** *"Early in the semester . . ."*: Plath's letters to Hans Neupert are at Smith. **62** *" 'Warm smile . . .' "*: Plath's high-school yearbook. **62** *"Until the summer of 1950 . . ."*: The information about Lookout Farm and Ilo Pill comes from *The Journals of Sylvia Plath* (hereafter cited as *J*) by Sylvia Plath, edited by Frances McCullough (New York, The Dial Press, 1982). Additional information comes from Plath's unpublished journals at Smith. **64** *" 'And Summer Will Not Come Again,' the story . . ."*: "And Summer Will Not Come Again" by Sylvia Plath, *Seventeen*, August 1950, pp. 275–6. **65** *" 'Why it should have so captivated me . . .' "*: Edward Cohen's unpublished letters to Plath are at Indiana. **65** *"Flattered, Sylvia responded . . ."*: Information in the next four paragraphs is based on Cohen's letters and on my interviews with him. **67** *"That August . . ."*: The description of the episode with Emile is based on *J* and on unpublished journals at Smith. **68** *" 'And, then, suddenly, . . .' "*: "Rewards of a New England Summer" by Sylvia Plath, *The Christian Science Monitor*, September 12, 1950, p. 15.

Full Fathom Five

69 *"By way of Elm Street . . ."*: My description of Northampton and Smith College is based on my visits there and on my interviews with Gloria Steinem, Margaret Shook, Ruth Mortimer, Libby Stone, Barbara Soulnier, and others. **69** *" [T]he design to furnish . . .' "*: From Sophia Smith's will. **70** *" 'We were lemmings unto the sea . . .' "*: From my interview with Judy Ettlinger Cohen. **70** *" 'At Smith, you were attempting . . .' "*: From my interview with Gloria Steinem. **71** *" 'In the fifties we were girls . . .' "*: From a letter to me by Polly Longsworth. **72** *"Recently, Sylvia had accused . . ."*: Cohen's unpublished letters. **73** *"Best known for* Now, Voyager *. . ."*: Information about Prouty comes from my interviews with her daughter, Mrs. Mason Smith. **73** *"In November,* Seventeen *published Plath's . . ."*: "Ode to a Bitten Plum" by Sylvia Plath, *Seventeen*, November 1950, p. 104. **74** *"Determined to meet her social obligations . . ."*: Plath's letter to Prouty was published anonymously in *The*

Smith Alumnae Quarterly in the February 1951 issue. 74 " *'I have read your letter with great interest . . .'* ": From a letter from Prouty to Plath that I obtained from Prouty's daughter. 75 *"On that cold, beautiful December afternoon . . .":* The descriptions of Prouty and her home are based on an unpublished memoir by Plath. 76 " *'I can never do it, never . . .'* ": *LH*, p. 64. 76 " *'I must remember to look up . . . Ann . . .'* ": Cohen's unpublished letters. 78 *"At the end of the note, he said . . .":* Richard Norton's unpublished letters to Plath are at Indiana. 78 " *'Regardless of how much . . .'* ": Cohen's unpublished letters. 78 *"His chance to meet Sylvia in person . . .":* The information in the next three paragraphs comes from Cohen's unpublished letters and from my interviews with him. 79 *"Vacation did contain some pleasant experiences for Sylvia. . . .":* From my interview with Marcia Brown Stern. 80 *"After writing her one letter . . .":* Cohen's unpublished letters. 80 *"In mid-April, while Dick . . .":* From Norton's unpublished letters. 81 *"She longed for a male 'organism' . . .": J,* p. 21. 81 " *'You are good, Syl— . . .'* ": Cohen's unpublished letters. 82 " *'I do question whether . . .'* ": Ibid. 82 *"On June 18, Sylvia escaped . . .":* The description of Plath's summer in Swampscott is based on her published and unpublished journals and on my interview with Marcia Brown Stern. 84 " *'If I seem a bit harsh at times . . .'* ": Cohen's unpublished letters. 85 *"Soon after Sylvia returned to Smith . . .":* The description of the Buckley party is based on a letter in *LH,* and on my interview with Elizabeth Skerritt. 86 " *'You were your own incomparable self . . .'* ": Norton's unpublished letters. 87 " *'Sinusitis plunges me . . .'* ": *J,* p. 40. 87 " *'Doesn't it sound just . . .'* ": Cohen's unpublished letters. 88 *"The revelation disgusted her . . .":* Plath's unpublished letters to Ann Davidow are at Smith. 88 " *'Why is your face and form . . .'* ": Norton's unpublished letters. 89 *"Eddie responded with a demand . . .":* Cohen's unpublished letters. 90 " *'I really feel that a second try . . .'* ": Ibid. 90 *"The month's strangest episode . . .":* From Plath's unpublished journals at Smith. 90 " *'One night we went into Boston . . .'* ": From my interviews with Cohen. 91 *"In her journal she revealed that . . .": J,* p. 46. 93 *"Days later, Sylvia felt well enough . . .":* My description of Plath's summer at the Cantors' is based on her published and unpublished journals and on my interview with Margaret Cantor. 93 *"A longish, cleanly written story . . .":* "Sunday at the Mintons' " by Sylvia Plath is included in *JP,* pp. 295–305. 94 " *'Sylvia is an exceptionally fine girl . . .'* ": Cantor's letter is in the Plath archive at Smith. 96 " *'I was a little taken aback . . .'* ": Cohen's unpublished letters. 96 *"According to contest rules . . .":* From my interviews with Marybeth Little Weston. 97 *"After that weekend, Dick described Sylvia . . .":* Norton's unpublished letters. 97 " *'Sick with envy . . .'* ": *J,* p. 60. 97 *"On the 14th, in Marcia's off-campus bedroom . . .": J,* p. 64. 98 " *'I am driven inward . . .'* ": Ibid. 98 *"To complicate matters . . .":* Cohen's unpublished letters. 99 *"In*

several letters at the beginning of the month . . .": From Norton's unpublished letters. 100 *"Wiring her mother . . .*": From *LH*, p. 101. 100 *"When a
friend inquired . . .*": Norton's unpublished letters. 101 *"Over Christmas, bad
with . . .*": Some information in this paragraph is taken from my interview
with Cohen; the quotes are from Cohen's unpublished letters. 103 *"Besides
Mike, who was so taken . . .*": The Lotz quote is from an unpublished letter
at Indiana. 103 *"In one recent journal entry . . .*": From *J*, p. 74. 104 " *'When
Sivvy came home from the Cape . . .' *": Aurelia Plath's unpublished letter to
Richard Norton is at Indiana. 108 *"In the aftermath of World War II . . .*":
The information about New York in this paragraph comes from *New York,
New York* by Oliver E. Allen (New York, Atheneum, 1990). 108 *"Victorian,
stately, ornate . . .*": The information about the Barbizon Hotel and *Mademoiselle* comes from my interviews with Marybeth Little Weston, Neva Nelson
Sachar, Janet Wagner Rafferty, Laurie Levy, Martha Wood Kongshang, Sally
Jenks, Laura Woolschlager, and Polly Weaver. 108 " *'She was something of a
paradox . . .' *": From my interview with Jenks. 111 " *'I too was on the verge
of crying . . .' *": From my interview with Sachar. 113 " *'The morning of
the executions . . .' *": From a letter by Rafferty. 115 " *'Sylvia came in my
room . . .' *": From a letter by Rafferty. 115 *"The world had 'split open . . .' *":
J, p. 120. 116 " *'By the way, Frank O'Connor's class . . .' *": *LH*, p. 123. 116
"As she wrote an entry in her journal . . .": *J*, p. 85. 117 *"In a letter in early
July . . .*": Norton's unpublished letters. 117 " *'You saw a vision . . .' *": *J*,
p. 87. 125 " 'HAVE JUST LEARNED SYLVIA . . .' ": *LH*, p. 126.

Doom of Exiles

126 *"In late August . . .*": The unpublished letters in this paragraph are at
Indiana and Smith. 127 " *'Talking to you makes living worthwhile. . . .' *":
Gordon Lameyer allowed me to read his unpublished manuscript, *Dear Sylvia*.
The quote is from that manuscript. 128 " *'The symptoms suggest an acute . . .' *":
Donald McPherson's letter was provided to me by Prouty's daughter. 129
" *'Unfortunately the shock treatments . . .' *": Prouty's letter was provided
to me by her daughter. 130 " *'She wouldn't talk. . . .' *": From my interviews
with Ruth Barnhouse. 131 " *'Sylvia had lost touch with words . . .' *": From
my interview with Wilbury Crockett. 131 *"Sylvia had complained about 'the
long . . .' *": Prouty's letter was provided to me by her daughter. 132 " *'She
continues getting . . .' *": Paul Howard's letter to Prouty was provided to me
by Prouty's daughter. 133 " *'I usually find Sylvia wandering . . .' *": Prouty's
letter was provided to me by her daughter. 133 " *'There are things about . . .' *":
Franklin Wood's letter to Prouty was provided to me by Prouty's daughter.

134 " '*I convinced her that she had to . . .*' ": From my interviews with Barnhouse. 134 " '*The fact is they . . .*' ": Prouty's letter was provided to me by Prouty's daughter. 134 "*It was not the first time . . .*": The information in this paragraph comes from my interviews with McCurdy and from Plath's letters to McCurdy at Smith. 136 "*As for her concern about . . .*": From a letter written to me by Kenneth Wright. 137 " '*A brief expedition into . . .*' ": *A Closer Look at Ariel* (hereafter cited as *Closer Look*) by Nancy Hunter Steiner (New York, Harper's Magazine Press, 1973), p. 44. 138 " '*She talked freely about her father's death . . .*' ": Ibid., p. 45. 138 " '*When I was writing you . . .*' ": Cohen's unpublished letters. 140 " '*I suggest, flatly . . .*' ": Ibid. 141 " '*How much free-lancing will you . . .*' " : Ibid. 142 "*A philosophy major . . .*": Melvin Woody's unpublished letter to Plath is at Indiana. 143 "*When Sylvia arrived home . . .*": Some information in this paragraph is based on *Closer Look*. 146 "*Up to that point . . .*": The information in the next three paragraphs is based in part on *Closer Look*. 147 "*When Gordon returned from Virginia . . .*": The information for the rest of this paragraph is taken from my interview with Lameyer. 148 " '*The teacher can help the student . . .*' ": "The Neilson Professor" by Sylvia Plath, *The Smith Alumnae Quarterly*, Fall 1954, p. 12. 149 " '*[Kazin] told me it's my . . .*' ": "Letters from Sylvia" by Sylvia Plath, *The Smith Alumnae Quarterly*, February 1976, p. 3. 149 " '*Although I know you are not thinking . . .*' ": *Dear Sylvia*. 150 " '*Worst, what no woman . . .*' ": Richard Sassoon's unpublished letters to Plath are at Indiana. 150 "*Also, beginning in December . . .*": Plath's letters of recommendation from Mary Ellen Chase, Elizabeth Drew, Alfred Kazin, George Gibian, Ruth Barnhouse, and Estella Kelsey are at Smith. 153 " '*Do not think I am scolding . . .*' ": Sassoon's unpublished letters. 155 "*Beginning the ceremony . . .*": Marianne Moore's quotes are taken from "Judges Hear Glascock Poetry Contestants" by Mary Handy, *The Christian Science Monitor*, April 18, 1955, p. 2. 155 " '*[Moore] commends your spirit . . .*' ": The unpublished letter from the Glascock committee is at Indiana. 157 " '*[Y]ou will torture tonight! . . .*' ": Sassoon's unpublished letters. 158 "*When she wrote to Lynne Lawner . . .*": "Nine Letters to Lynne Lawner" by Sylvia Plath, *Antaeus*, Winter 1978, p. 31. 158 " '*[M]y love lies in waiting . . .*' ": Sassoon's unpublished letters. 159 " '*I think we were in a condition of mind . . .*' ": From a letter written to me by Longsworth. 160 " '*I have taken all you had to give . . .*' ": *Dear Sylvia*. 160 " '*I and the sky are both . . .*' ": Sassoon's unpublished letters. 160 " '*It's an awfully long time . . .*' ": Ibid. 161 " '*I hope to see . . .*' ": *Antaeus*, p. 32. 161 " '*At last a whiff of perfume . . .*' ": Sassoon's unpublished letters. 161 " '*I want . . . very much . . .*' ": Ibid. 161 " '*Darling, darling, thank you . . .*' " Ibid. 162 " '*I tried very hard . . .*' ": Ibid. 162 " '*I do not believe . . .*' ": Ibid. 162 "*But the high point of the week . . .*": The information about Plath's affair with Peter Davison comes from my interviews with him. 164 " '*I was far less*

impressed . . . '": "Peter Davison," *Contemporary Authors Autobiography Series* (Detroit, Gale Research Company, 1986), p. 134. **164** *"She 'spoke in such a way . . .'* ": Ibid.

Abroad

167 *"Venturing out . . ."*: Plath's quote is from *LH*, p. 185. **169** *"As they strolled between . . ."*: Plath's quotes are from *LH*, p. 191. **173** *" 'Rarely have I felt . . .' "*: "Gone, Very Gone Youth" by Jane Baltzell Kopp, *Sylvia Plath: The Woman and the Work*, edited by Edward Butscher (New York, Dodd Mead, 1977), p. 70. **174** *"Slowly Sylvia entered and 'in the heart . . .' "*: *LH*, p. 205. **176** *" 'Wanted to burst out in tears . . .' "*: *J*, p. 109. **176** *" 'And I cry so to be . . .' "*: *J*, p. 100. **178** *"By the time they reached . . ."*: The information in this paragraph comes from Plath's published and unpublished journals, from my interviews with Bertram Wyatt-Brown, and from my correspondence with Lucas Myers. **178** *"Then, as Sylvia would later write . . ."*: Plath's quotes in this paragraph come from *J*, p. 111. **179** *"Now, Sylvia began quoting . . ."*: The information in the next two paragraphs comes from Plath's published and unpublished journals. **181** *"Daniel Huws, 'just over six feet . . .' "*: "Ah, Youth . . . Ted Hughes and Sylvia Plath at Cambridge and After" by Lucas Myers, an appendix in *Bitter Fame* by Anne Stevenson (Boston, Houghton Mifflin, 1989), p. 308. **181** *". . . Daniel Weissbort, an American . . ."*: The phrase "only slightly fictionalized" comes from a letter written to me by Weissbort. **181** *"In the story, the narrator's psychiatrist . . ."*: Weissbort provided me with his unpublished story. **181** *" 'He was an inch or so taller . . .' "*: *Bitter Fame*, p. 308. **182** *" 'In a very vehement and dreadful way . . .' "*: *The Woman and the Work*, p. 72. **183** *" '[I]t hurts, Father . . .' "*: *J*, p. 123. **183** *" 'I rail and rage . . .' "*: *J*, p. 128. **184** *"Before she could go to Europe . . ."*: The information in this paragraph comes from Plath's unpublished journal and day-to-day calendar. **185** *"On April 4, Gordon arrived . . ."*: The information in the next three paragraphs comes in part from *Dear Sylvia* and my interviews with Lameyer. **187** *"And, as bookends . . ."*: Plath's quotes about Hughes come from *LH*. **188** *"She implored Aurelia . . ."*: Plath's quotes come from *LH*, p. 239. **189** *" 'Sylvia was extraordinarily modest . . .' "*: "Recollections of Sylvia Plath" by Dorothea Krook, *The Woman and the Work*, p. 54. **189** *" 'I can see you are going through . . .' "*: Prouty's unpublished letter to Plath is at Indiana. **193** *" 'Every evening at dusk the lights . . .' "*: "Sketchbook of a Spanish Summer" by Sylvia Plath, *The Christian Science Monitor*, November 15, 1956, p. 15. **194** *"Only one episode, in Sylvia's account . . ."*: The information for this paragraph comes from my interviews with a confidential source. **195** *"Over time, Sylvia learned . . ."*: The information in this paragraph comes from *Bitter Fame*, my trip to Yorkshire, and my interviews with Olwyn Hughes. 197 *"Plath's letters indicate . . .":* The information and quotes in the next three paragraphs are taken from my interviews with Kenneth Pitchford. Plath's reference to abortion appears in an unpublished portion of her journal entry for January 4, 1958. The journal is at Smith. 201 *" 'There is really no reason for me . . .' ":* Sassoon's unpublished letters. 202 *"While Plath waited for Smith's . . .":* From *J*, pp. 156–7. 203 *" 'I am more happy than if . . .' ":* LH, p. 297. 203 *" 'The only difficulty facing us . . .' ":* John Bleibtreu's unpublished letters are in the Buttenweiser Library at the Ninety-second Street Y in New York. 205 *" 'I [bike] home for lunch between . . .' ":* Antaeus, p. 33.

Fixed Stars

209 *" 'Last night I felt . . .' ":* J, pp. 175–8. 210 *"To help divert her mind . . .":* The information about the Roche-Hughes friendship comes in part from my interviews with Clarissa Roche and Paul Roche. 211 *" 'Paul and I saw Ted and Sylvia . . .' ":* "Sylvia Plath: Vignettes from England" by Clarissa Roche, *The Woman and the Work*, p. 81. 211 *" 'I have been exhausted, frustrated . . .' ":* Antaeus, p. 41. 212 *" 'If I fainted . . .' ":* J, p. 179. 212 *" '[Hughes] would be seen walking . . .' ":* From an unpublished interview conducted with Lee Camp by Ron Smith. Camp provided me with the interview. 214 *"In February, Plath's publishing . . .":* "Spinster" by Sylvia Plath, *The Smith Alumnae Quarterly*, Winter 1958, p. 71. 215 *"In one journal entry, she recorded . . .":* From Plath's unpublished journals at Smith. 215 *" 'From being the proud boast . . .' ":* *New York Jew* by Alfred Kazin (New York, Alfred A. Knopf, 1978), p. 227. 216 *". . . Plath listed in her journal . . .":* J, p. 211–12. 217 *"Whereas many publish . . .":* J, p. 200. 218 *"Then he stopped and glared . . .":* From J, p. 219. 219 *"When she approached the couple . . .":* The information in this paragraph is from Plath's published and unpublished journals. 219 *"Yet she would not 'jump out . . .' ":* J, p. 233. 219 *" 'I got hit . . .' ":* J, p. 235. 221 *"Certain phrases caught her eyes . . .":* Howard Moss's unpublished letters to Plath are at Smith. 221 *"At the end of June . . .":* From J, p. 240. 222 *" 'And perhaps even those who have . . .' ":* "Beach Plum Season on Cape Cod" by Sylvia Plath, *The Christian Science Monitor*, August 14, 1958, p. 17. 223 *" 'Two rooms, each with . . .' ":* Antaeus, p. 41. 224 *"From the first session, Barnhouse . . .":* The information in the next three paragraphs comes from Plath's published and unpublished journals and from my interviews with Barnhouse. 225 *"In mid-December, she and Ted . . .":* The information about Truman Capote comes from *Capote* by Gerald Clarke (New York, Simon and Schuster, 1988). The information about Hughes comes from Plath's published and un-

published journals. **226** " *'Isn't this an image . . .'* ": *J*, p. 279. **226** " *'It was a look that didn't . . .'* ": From a letter written to me by Lucie McKee. **227** *"The article focused on the . . ."*: "Four Young Poets" by Corinne Robins, *Mademoiselle* 48, January 1959, pp. 34–5, 85. **229** *"She would reject the 'Feminine (horror) . . .'* ": *Antaeus*, p. 45. **229** " *'Felt cheated . . .'* ": *J*, p. 299. **230** *"On the day Plath finished . . ."*: Plath's quote is from *J*, p. 301. **231** " *'I would always park illegally . . .'* ": "The Barfly Ought to Sing" by Anne Sexton, *Ariel Ascending: Writings About Sylvia Plath*, edited by Paul Alexander (New York, Harper and Row, 1985), pp. 178–9. **233** " *'I would very much like to have you . . .'* ": Emilie McLeod's unpublished letters to Plath are at The Atlantic Monthly Press. **233** " *'I was grateful as a puppy . . .'* ": *Contemporary Authors Autobiography*, p. 137. **235** " *'It is amazing . . .'* ": *LH*, p. 352. **235** *"Along the way, they stopped . . ."*: The information about Plath and Hughes's stop in Sewanee, Tennessee, comes from my interview with Monroe Spears. **235** " *'[I]t seems to me . . .'* ": Spears's unpublished letters to Plath were provided to me by the *Sewanee Review*. **235** " *'I'm sorry there has been such . . .'* ": McLeod's unpublished letters. **236** *"In early September . . ."*: The description of Yaddo comes from my interviews with Grace Schulman and Frances Kiernan. **237** " *'Despite the strength of her poetry . . .'* ": From my interview with Sonia Raiziss. **238** " *'Seeing two new poems of yours . . .'* ": James Michie's unpublished letters to Plath are at Smith. **239** " *'In its double focus . . .'* ": "Sylvia Plath and Her Journals" by Ted Hughes, *Ariel Ascending*, p. 158. **239** *"Reviewing the book . . ."*: "Poetry as Confession" by M. L. Rosenthal, *The Nation* 190, September 19, 1959, pp. 154–5. **240** *"Marilyn Monroe came to her . . ."*: *J*, p. 319. **240** " *'On the day they left . . .'* ": *LH*, p. 356.

England

243 *"To Plath, who wrote . . ."*: Plath's quote is from *Antaeus*, p. 48. **243** " *'She had this feeling of being superior . . .'* ": From my interview with Anne Stevenson. **244** " *'I like your poems . . .'* ": From Michie's unpublished letters. **244** *"She had suffered nothing but . . ."*: *Antaeus*, p. 49. **246** *"It was Otto's sister Frieda . . ."*: Plath's quote comes from *LH*, p. 352. **247** *"Because she now saw herself . . ."*: *Antaeus*, p. 50. **251** " *'Miss Plath neither asks . . .'* ": "The Poet and the Poetess" by A. Alvarez, *The Observer*, December 18, 1960, p. 21. **252** *"Sylvia and Ted's week . . ."*: The information in the next three paragraphs comes from Plath's published and unpublished letters to her mother, from *Bitter Fame*, and from my interviews with Olwyn Hughes. **253** " *'Sylvia Plath writes clever . . .'* ": "Farewell to the World" by John Wain, *The Spectator* 206, January 13, 1961, p. 50. **254** " *'This girl is a poet . . .'* ": Judith Jones's Knopf correspondence, including her letters to Plath, is in the

Harry Ransom Research Center at the University of Texas. **255** *"On the 5th, in response . . ."*: Plath's letters to Anne Sexton are in the Sexton archive at Texas. **257** " *'The language of this poetry . . .' "*: Untitled review by Roy Fuller, *The London Magazine*, March 1961, pp. 69–70. **257** " *'Miss Plath . . . is unusually . . .' "*: Untitled review by Howard Sergeant, *English* 13, Spring 1961, pp. 156–8. **259** " *'One reason . . . that we . . .' "*: Jones's unpublished letters. **259** *"On April 26, in a letter . . ."*: Plath's unpublished letter to Kazin is at the New York Public Library. **260** " 'ALFRED KNOPF will publish . . .' ": *LH*, p. 417. **261** " 'The Colossus *is a volume . . .' "*: Untitled review by A. E. Dyson, *Critical Quarterly*, Summer 1961, pp. 181–5. **264** " *'Miss Plath tends to be . . .' "*: "Innocence and Experience," *The Times Literary Supplement*, August 18, 1961, p. 550. **264** *"Next, they called . . ."*: The phrases "a young Canadian poet" and "German-Russian" are from *LH*, p. 423. **267** *"To reassure her mother . . ."*: From *LH*, p. 437. **269** *"Finally, when Sylvia . . ."*: From *LH*, p. 443. **270** *"Ted's coldness towards Nicholas . . ."*: Hughes's reaction to his son is recorded at length in unpublished letters from Plath to her mother, at Indiana. **270** " *'The poet's only hope . . .' "*: "Context" by Ted Hughes, *The London Magazine*, February 1962, pp. 44–5. **270** " *'The issues of our time . . .' "*: "Context" by Sylvia Plath, ibid., pp. 45–6. **271** " *'Poems should be criticized . . .' "*: From "The Tranquilized Fifties" by E. Lucas Myers, *Sewanee Review* 70, Spring 1962, pp. 212–20.

The Bitter Season

275 *"In early May, the Hugheses . . ."*: The information about the Sillitoes' visit to Court Green is based on my interview with Ruth Fainlight. **279** " *'This is the richest and happiest . . .' "*: *LH*, p. 455. **279** " *'Keith Douglas was born . . .' "*: "The Poetry of Keith Douglas" by Ted Hughes, "Third Programme," BBC, May 31, 1962. **279** *"Before that, Sylvia saw Alvarez . . ."*: The information in this paragraph comes from my interview with Alvarez and from "Prologue," *The Savage God* by A. Alvarez (New York, Random House, 1972). **280** " *'I'm writing again . . .' "*: *Savage God*, p. 13. **280** " *'No longer quiet and withheld . . .' "*: Ibid. **280** " *'The welcome I received . . .' "*: *LH*, p. 458. **282** " *'This was a joyous book . . .' "*: From Aurelia Plath's unpublished commentary for *LH*. **283** " *'I have everything in life . . .' "*: *LH*, p. 458. **283** " *'[T]he marriage was seriously troubled . . .' "*: Aurelia Plath's unpublished commentary to *LH*. **284** " *'Then suddenly, late one . . .' "*: "Sylvia in Devon: 1962" by Elizabeth Sigmund, *The Woman and the Work*, p. 104. **286** *"On still another occasion . . ."*: The information in this paragraph is based in part on my interviews with Clarissa Roche. Plath told Roche that the name "Dido" was written on the charred scrap of paper, not "A———," as appeared in

Roche's memoir in *The Woman and the Work*. According to Roche, Butscher changed the name from "Dido" to "A———"—without her knowledge—to make the scene more dramatic. 287 " *'They seem to me the best . . .'* ": Alvarez's unpublished letter to Plath is at Smith. 287 " *'When I left . . . the four of them . . .'* ": *LH*, p. 458. 288 *"In Devon on August 21 . . ."*: Plath's unpublished letters to Sexton. 289 " *'I hope you will not be . . .'* ": *LH*, p. 460. 289 *"If Ted preferred this other woman . . ."*: From Plath's unpublished letters at Indiana.

Edge

292 *"After breakfast the next morning . . ."*: The description of Plath and Hughes's trip to Ireland is based in part on "A Memoir of Sylvia Plath and Ted Hughes on a Visit to the West of Ireland in 1962" by Richard Murphy, an appendix to *Bitter Fame*. Additional information comes from Plath's published and unpublished letters to her mother. 292 *"On the six-mile sail . . ."*: Murphy's quote is from *Bitter Fame*, p. 349. 293 *"During supper, an awkward moment . . ."*: Ibid. p. 351. 294 " *'Sylvia came up here . . .'* ": Winifred Davies's unpublished letter to Aurelia Plath is at Indiana. 295 *"Through the rest of September . . ."*: The information in the next two paragraphs comes from Plath's unpublished letters to her mother, at Indiana. 297 " *'The horror of what you saw . . .'* ": *LH*, p. 465. 297 *"Sylvia found out that Ted . . ."*: The information in the next two paragraphs is based on Plath's unpublished letters to her mother, at Indiana. 300 *"For her part, Edith wrote Aurelia . . ."*: Edith Hughes's unpublished letter to Aurelia Plath is at Indiana. 301 *"Telling her that she did not . . ."*: From *LH*, p. 473. 303 " *'For heaven's sake, yes, I'd . . .'* ": Alvarez's unpublished letter to Plath is at Smith. 303 *"Divorced also, Alvarez . . ."*: The information in this paragraph comes from *The Savage God* and my interview with Alvarez. The quote—*"there was nothing . . ."*—is from *Savage God*, p. 14. 304 *"Later, Plath went to a PEN . . ."*: The information in this paragraph is from *Bitter Fame*. 304 *"Afterwards, Plath met Peter Orr . . ."*: My description of Plath's afternoon with Orr comes from my interview with Orr. 305 " *'Sylvia, what started you . . .'* ": The quotes from Orr and Plath are taken from *The Poet Speaks*, edited by Peter Orr (London, Routledge & Kegan Paul, 1966), pp. 167–72. 307 " *'And [it is] in the house . . .'* ": *LH*, p. 478. 309 *"Writing to Stevie Smith . . ."*: Plath's letter to Smith is published in *Me Again: Uncollected Writings of Stevie Smith*, edited by Jack Barbera and William McBrien (New York, Farrar, Straus & Giroux, 1982), p. 6. 309 *"It had been well over . . ."*: Plath's unpublished letters to her mother, at Indiana. 310 *"During November, unknown to Plath . . ."*: The Koshland-Anderson letters are part of the Plath file in the Knopf archives at Texas. 313 *"Seeing Trevor Thomas . . ."*: Plath's dialogue with Thomas comes from an

unpublished version of his memoir "Last Encounters." The piece, drastically changed, eventually appeared in *Zymergy* in the Spring 1990 issue. 314 " '*Cross-legged on the red floor* . . .' ": *Savage God*, p. 18. 315 " '*I suspect that finding herself*' ": Ibid., p. 21. 315 "*The obvious, also* . . .": From my interviews with Alvarez and with Jill Neville. 317 " '*It would have been very easy* . . .' ": From my interview with Alvarez. 317 " '*She must have felt* . . .' ": *Savage God*, p. 33. 317 "*In the last week in December* . . .": Jones's unpublished letters. 321 " '*Sylvia devoured this so* . . .' ": *The Woman and the Work*, p. 93. 321 "*In his* New Statesman *review* . . .": "Anti-Heroes" by Robert Taubman, *The New Statesman* 65, January 25, 1963, pp. 127–8. 321 " '*Few writers are able* . . .' ": "Under the Skin," *The Times Literary Supplement*, January 25, 1963, p. 53. 322 " '*I recommend* The Bell Jar . . .' ": Untitled review by Laurence Lerner, *The Listener* 69, January 31, 1963, p. 215. 324 "*As January progressed, Colin and Valerie St. Johnson* . . .": The information in the rest of this paragraph is based on my interview with the St. Johnsons. 325 "*Until then, she kept* . . .": The information in the rest of this paragraph and the following paragraph comes in part from my interview with John Horder. 327 "*But when Trevor Thomas* . . .": The unpublished version of Thomas's memoir. 327 "*That night, Sylvia met Ted* . . .": The information in this paragraph is based in part on *Bitter Fame* and on my interviews with two confidential sources. 329 "*Next Sylvia must have written* . . .": The unpublished version of Thomas's memoir. 331 "*Listing her occupation* . . .": Plath's death certificate. 331 "*Horder telephoned Jillian* . . .": As I worked on this book, I received an anonymous telephone call, on my unlisted number, from someone who told me that Plath had tried to kill her children at the same time she killed herself. When I interviewed Horder at his home in London, I asked him if he believed Plath had tried to harm her children. According to Horder, she went to great lengths to protect them from the gas. 332 "*On this day the court heard* . . .": From my interviews with Alvarez and Thomas, both present at the inquest. 332 "*After the inquest* . . .": My description of the funeral is based on my interview with Oliver Forshaw. 333 " '*Sylvia was doomed* . . .' ": From my interview with Crockett. 333 " '*Sylvia Plath was an early* . . .' ": From my interview with Steinem. 333 " '*When I look back on her life* . . .' ": Alvarez, *Savage God*. 333 " '*Sylvia's tragic flaw* . . .' ": Unpublished commentary by Aurelia Plath. 333 " '*Her death was tragic but her life* . . .' ": From a letter written to me by Little.

A Posthumous Life

335 " '*Last Monday, Sylvia Plath* . . .' ": "A Poet's Epitaph" by A. Alvarez, *The Observer*, February 17, 1963, p. 23. 335 "*The topic of* The Observer's *homage* . . .": The information in this paragraph comes from my interviews with Olwyn Hughes. 336 "*Some time in March* . . .": The information in the next two paragraphs comes from my interviews with Elizabeth Sigmund. 337 " '*Found with her head in the gas oven* . . .' ": "Tragic Death of Young Authoress," the Saint Pancras *Chronicle*, February 22, 1963, p. 5. 340 "*In America, Alfred A. Knopf* . . .": The information in this paragraph comes from the Knopf archives at Texas. 341 "*Finally, in* The Observer . . .": "Poetry in Extremis" by A. Alvarez, *The Observer*, March 14, 1965, p. 26. 341 " '*The spell does not lie* . . .' ": "Dying Is an Art" by George Steiner, *The Reporter*, October 7, 1965, pp. 51–4. 342 "*It was, according to* . . .": "Along the Edge," *The Times Literary Supplement*, November 25, 1965, p. 1071. 342 " '*Everything in these poems* . . .' ": "Foreword" by Robert Lowell, *Ariel* by Sylvia Plath (New York, Harper and Row, 1966), pp. vii–ix. 342 " '*One dank day in February 1963* . . .' ": "The Bloodjet Is Poetry," *Time* 87, June 10, 1966, pp. 118–20. 344 " '*Whatever has been and is* . . .' ": Aurelia Plath's unpublished letter to Ted's Aunt Hilda is at Indiana. 346 "*In April, in a letter to a literary* . . .": Hughes's unpublished letter is at the New York Public Library. 349 " '*With such a vast potential audience* . . .' ": From "Publish and Be Damned" by A. Alvarez, *The Observer*, October 3, 1971, p. 36. 350 " '*As I remember it* . . .' ": *Savage God*, p. 3. 350 " '*I would like to make it known* . . .' ": Letter by Ted Hughes, *The Observer*, November 21, 1971, p. 10. 351 " '*I did not consult Mr Hughes* . . .' ": Letter by A. Alvarez, ibid. 351 "*Two days later, on November 19* . . .": Letter by Ted Hughes, *The Times Literary Supplement*, November 19, 1971, p. 1448. 351 " '*Mr Hughes says* . . .' ": Letter by A. Alvarez, *The Times Literary Supplement*, November 26, 1971, p. 1478. 353 "*Jong criticized Aurelia Plath* . . .": "Letters Focus Exquisite Rage of Sylvia Plath" by Erica Jong, *The Los Angeles Times Book Review*, November 23, 1975, pp. 1, 10. 354 " '*I have to admit at the outset* . . .' ": "Poet's Prose" by Margaret Atwood, *The New York Times Book Review*, January 28, 1979, p. 10. 355 " '*The last of these* . . .' ": "Foreword" by Ted Hughes, *J*, p. xiii. 355 " '*How can we content ourselves* . . .' ": "Sylvia Plath: Consumed by the Anxieties of Ambition" by Peter Davison, *The Washington Post Book World*, April 18, 1982, pp. 3, 11. 355 "*Admitting that 'her husband* . . .' ": *Ariel Ascending*, p. 152. 361 " '*This sequence, which lasts* . . .' ": A review by Janet Maslin, *The New York Times*, September 6, 1987, p. 15d.

Index